THE

CATECHETICAL LECTURES

OF

S. CYRIL,

ARCHBISHOP OF JERUSALEM.

THE CATECHETICAL LECTURES

OF

S. CYRIL,

ARCHBISHOP OF JERUSALEM,

Translated,

WITH NOTES AND INDICES.

FOURTH EDITION

WIPF & STOCK · Eugene, Oregon

Wipf and Stock Publishers
199 W 8th Ave, Suite 3
Eugene, OR 97401

The Catechetical Lectures of S. Cyril, Archbishop of Jerusalem,
Translated, with Notes and Indices, Fourth Edition
By Cyril of Jerusalem and Newman, John Henry
Softcover ISBN-13: 978-1-6667-3172-9
Hardcover ISBN-13: 978-1-6667-2448-6
eBook ISBN-13: 978-1-6667-2449-3
Publication date 6/23/2021
Previously published by James Parker & Co., 1872

This edition is a scanned facsimile of
the original edition published in 1872

PREFACE.

S. CYRIL, the author of the Catechetical Lectures which follow, was born in an age ill adapted for the comfort or satisfaction of persons distinguished by his peculiar character of mind, and in consequence did not receive that justice from contemporaries which the Church Catholic has since rendered to his memory. The Churches of Palestine, apparently his native country, were the first to give reception to Arius on his expulsion from Alexandria, and without adopting his heresy, affected to mediate and hold the balance between him and his accusers. They were followed in this line of conduct by the provinces of Syria and Asia Minor, till the whole of the East, as far as it was Grecian, became more or less a large party, enduring to be headed by men who went the whole length of Arianism, from a fear of being considered Alexandrians or Athanasians, and a notion, for one reason or other, that it was thus pursuing a moderate course, and avoiding extremes. What were the motives which led to this perverted view of its duty to Catholic truth, then so seriously endangered, and what the palliations in the case of individuals, need not be minutely considered here. Suffice it to say, that between the Churches of Asia and the metropolis of Egypt there had been distinctions, not to say differences and jealousies of long standing; to which was added this great and real difficulty, that a Council held at Antioch about sixty years before had condemned the very term, Homoüsion, which was the symbol received at Nicæa, and maintained by the Alexandrians. The latter were in close agreement with the

Latin Church, especially with Rome; and thus two great confederacies, as they may be called, were matured at this distressing era, which outlived the controversy forming them, the Roman, including the West and Egypt, and the Asiatic, extending from Constantinople to Jerusalem. Of the Roman party, viewed at and after the Arian period, were Alexander, Athanasius, Eustathius, Marcellus, Julius, Ambrose, and Jerome; of the Asiatic, Eusebius of Cæsarea, Cyril, Meletius, Eusebius of Samosata, Basil of Cæsarea (the Great), Basil of Ancyra, Eustathius of Sebaste, and Flavian. Of the latter, some were Semi-arian; of the former, one at least was Sabellian; while the majority of both were, to say the least, strictly orthodox; some of the latter indeed acquiescing with more or less of cordiality in the expediency of adopting the important Symbol of the Nicene Council, but others, it need scarcely be said, on both sides, being pillars of the Church in their day, as they have been her lights since. Such was the general position of the Church; and it is only confessing that the early Bishops and Divines were men "of like passions with" ourselves, to add, that some of them sometimes misunderstood or were prejudiced against others, and have left on record reports, for the truth of which they trusted perhaps too much to their antecedent persuasions, or the representations of their own friends. When Arianism ceased to be supported by the civil power, the controversy between East and West died; and peace was easily effected. And the terms of effecting it were these:—the reception of the Homoüsion by the Asiatics, and on that reception their recognition, in spite of their past scruples, by the Alexandrians and Latins. In this sketch the main outlines of S. Cyril's history will be found to be contained; he seems to have been afraid of the term Homousion [a], to have been disinclined both to the friends of Athanasius and to the Arians [b], to have allowed the tyranny of the latter, to have shared in the general reconciliation, and at length both in life and death to have received honours from the

[a] v. Bened. note iv. 7. xvi. 23.   [b] Lect. iv 8. xi. 12, 16, 17. xv. 9.

PREFACE. iii

Church, which, in spite of whatever objections may be made to them, appear, on a closer examination of his history, not to be undeserved.

CYRIL is said to have been the son of Christian parents, but the date and place of his birth is unknown. He was born in the first years of the fourth century, and at least was brought up in Jerusalem. He was ordained Deacon probably by Macarius, and Priest by Maximus, the Bishops of Jerusalem; the latter of whom he succeeded A.D 349, or 350. Shortly before this, (A.D. 347, or 348,) during his Priesthood, he had delivered the Catechetical Lectures which have come down to us. With his Episcopate commence the historical difficulties under which his memory labours. It can scarcely be doubted that one of his consecrators was Acacius of Cæsarea[c], the leader of Arianism in the East, who had just before (A.D. 347) been deposed by the Council of Sardica; yet, as the after history shows, Cyril was no friend of the Arians or of Acacius[d]. He was canonically consecrated by the Bishops of his province, and as Acacius was still in possession of the principal see, he was compelled to a recognition which he might have wished to dispense with. He seems to have been a lover of peace; the Council of Sardica was at first as little acknowledged by his own party as by the Arians; and Acacius, being even beyond other Arians skilful and subtle in argument, and admitting the special formula[e] of Cyril on the doctrine in controversy, probably succeeded in disguising his heresy from him.

A more painful account, however, of his consecration is given by S. Jerome[f], supported in the main by other writers, which can only be explained by supposing that Father to be misled by the information or involved in the prejudices of Cyril's enemies. He relates, that upon Maximus's death, the

[c] v. Diss Bened. p. xviii sq
[d] Theod. ii. 26
[e] The κατὰ πάντα ὅμοιον vid. Lecture iv. 7 xi. 4. 9 18
[f] Jer. Chron. Socr. ii. 38. Sozom. iv 20.

Arians seized upon the Church of Jerusalem, and promised Cyril the see on condition of his renouncing the ordination he had received from Maximus, and submitting to re-ordination from their hands; that he assented, served in the Church as a mere Deacon, and was then raised by Acacius to the Episcopate, when he persecuted Heraclius, whom Maximus had consecrated as his successor. This account, incredible in itself, is contradicted, on the one hand, by the second General Council, which in its Synodal letter plainly states that he had been "canonically ordained" Bishop, and on the other by his own writings, which as plainly show, that in doctrine he was in no respect an Arian or an Arianizer.

If he suffers in memory from the Latin party as if Arian, he suffered not less in his life from the Arians as being orthodox. Seven or eight years after his consecration, he had a dispute with Acacius about the rights of their respective Churches [g]. Acacius in consequence accused him to the Emperor Constantius of holding with the orthodox; to which it was added that he had during a scarcity sold some offerings made by Constantine to his Church, to supply the wants of the poor. Cyril in consequence was deposed, and retired to Tarsus [h]; where, in spite of the efforts of Acacius, he was hospitably received, and employed by Silvanus the Semi-arian Bishop of the place. We find him at the same time in friendship with Eustathius of Sebaste and Basil of Ancyra, both Semi-arians [i]. His own writings, however, as has already been intimated, are most exactly orthodox, though he does not in the Catechetical Lectures, use the word Homoüsion; and in associating with these men he went little farther than S. Hilary [k], during his banishment in Asia Minor, who calls Basil and Eustathius "most holy men," than S. Athanasius, who acknowledges as "brethren" those who but scrupled at the *word* Homoüsion [l],

[g] Socrat. ii. 40 Sozom iv 25. Theod ii. 27
[h] Theodor. ii. 26
[i] Sozom iv. 25 Philostorg iv. 12.
[k] Hilar de Synod 77, 88 &c v. fragm II. 4 (Ed Ben. Cyr. p. lx. D)
[l] Athan. de Synod. 41

or than S. Basil of Cæsarea, who till a late period of his life was an intimate friend of Eustathius.

In A.D. 359, two years after his deposition, he successfully appealed against Acacius to the Council of Seleucia[m], one of the two branches of the great Council of East and West, which was convened under the patronage of Constantius to settle the troubles of the Christian world. But the next year, Acacius contriving to bring the matter before a Council at Constantinople, where the Emperor was staying, Cyril with his friends was a second time deposed, and banished from Palestine[n].

On Constantius's death all the banished bishops were restored[o], and Cyril, who was at that time with Meletius of Antioch, returned to Jerusalem, A.D. 362. He was there at the time of Julian's attempt to rebuild the Temple[p], and from the Prophecies boldly foretold its failure.

He was once more driven from his see, during the reign of the Arian Valens[q], (A.D. 367,) and he remained dispossessed till A.D. 378.

About the time of the death of Valens, the last of the Arian princes, he was restored, but under what circumstances is unknown. The Arians fell once for all with their imperial protectors; and soon after, that union of Christian Churches took place, which would never have been interrupted, had not a few bold and subtle-minded men contrived to delude them into the belief of mutual differences. S. Athanasius, the great peace-maker of the Church, was gone to his rest; and S. Basil also, who had mourned over evils which he had no means of remedying. Gregory of Nyssa, the brother of the latter, Gregory of Nazianzum, Meletius of Antioch, remained; and were present together with Cyril in the second General Council[r], which formally restored the latter to his see, and in

---

[m] v. Dissert 1. Ed. Bened p lvi F.
[n] Sozom. iv. 25. Philostorg. iv. 12
[o] Sozom v. 5
[p] Socrat. iii. 20. Ruffin. i. 37.
[q] Sozom. iv 30 Jerom. Catal. Script. Eccles 112.
[r] Socrat. v. 8 Sozom. vii. 7. v. Dissert. Bened. p lxxxii.

its letter to the Western Bishops speaks of him as "the most reverend and religious Cyril, long since canonically appointed by the Bishops of the province, and in many ways and places a withstander of the Arians[s]." He died about the year 386. Except one or two short compositions and fragments, nothing remains of his writings but his Catechetical Lectures.

No ecclesiastical writer could be selected more suitable to illustrate the main principle on which the present "Library of the Fathers" has been undertaken, than S. Cyril of Jerusalem. His Catechetical Lectures were delivered, as we have seen, when he was a young man; and he belonged, till many years after their delivery, to a party or school of theology, distinct, to say the least, from that to which the most illustrious divines of his day belonged; a school, never dominant in the Church, and expiring with his age. It is not then on the score of especial personal authority that his Lectures are now presented to the English reader; and if the simple object of this Publication were to introduce the latter to the wise and good of former times, S. Cyril would have no claims to a place in it beyond many who have lived since.

In saying this, it is far indeed from being asserted, that the personal claims of the Fathers of the Church on our deference are inconsiderable; for it happens, not unnaturally, that the works which have been preserved, were worth preserving, or rather that their writers would have been extraordinary men in any age, and speak with the weight of great experience, ability, and sanctity. To those who believe that moral truth is not gained by the mere exercise of the intellect, but is granted to moral attainments, and that God speaks to inquirers after truth by the mouth of those who possess these, the writings of S. Basil or S. Augustine must always have an authority independent of their date or their agreement; nor is it possible for serious persons to read them, without feeling the authority which they possess as individuals. This, how-

[s] Theod. Hist. v. 9.

ever, whatever it be, is not the main subject to which the present Translations propose to direct attention. The works to be translated have been viewed simply and plainly in the light of witnesses to an historical fact, viz. the religion which the Apostles transmitted to the early Churches, a fact to be ascertained as other past facts, by testimony, requiring the same kind of evidence, moral not demonstrative, open to the same difficulties of proof, and to be determined by the same practical judgment. It seems hardly conceivable that a fact so public and so great as the religion of the first Christians should be incapable of ascertainment, at least in its outlines, that it should have so passed away like a dream, that the most opposite opinions may at this day be maintained about it without possibility of contradiction. If it was soon corrupted or extinguished, then it is obvious to inquire after the history of such corruption or extinction; such a revolution every where, without historical record, being as unaccountable as the disappearance of the original religion for which it is brought to account. At first sight there is, to say the least, a considerable antecedent improbability in the notion, that, whereas we know the tenets and the history of the Stoic or the Academic philosophy, yet we do not know the main tenets, nor yet the fundamental principles, nor even the spirit and temper of Apostolic Christianity.

Under a sense of this improbability, in other words with an expectation that historical research would supply what they sought, our Divines at and since the Reformation have betaken themselves to the extant documents of the early Church, in order to determine thereby what the system of Primitive Christianity was; and so to elicit from Scripture more completely and accurately that revealed truth, which, though revealed there, is not on its surface, but needs to be *deduced* and *developed* from it. They went to the Fathers for information concerning matters, on which the Fathers at first sight certainly do promise to give information, just as inquirers into any other branch of knowledge might study those authors who have treated of it; and, whether or not they found what they sought, it surely was reasonable so to seek it, and cannot be condemned except by the *event*,—that is, by showing that their expectation, however reasonable antecedently, is mistaken in fact, that after the search into history, no evidence is forthcoming concerning the tenets, nor yet the principles, nor even the temper which the Apostles inculcated.

A like expectation has actuated the present Publication; it has been conceived probable, to say the least, that the study of the writings of the Fathers will enable us to determine morally, to make up our minds for practical purposes, what the *doctrines* of the Apostles were, for instance whether or not they believed in our Lord's Divinity, or the general necessity of Baptism for salvation;—or if not the doctrines, still what were their *principles*, as whether or not or how far they allowed of using secular means for advancing Christian truth, or whether or not they sanctioned the monarchical principle, or again the centralizing principle, or again the principle of perpetuity in Church matters, or whether they considered that Scripture should be interpreted in the mere letter, or what is called spiritually;—or at least what was their *temper*, for instance, whether or not it was what is now called in reproach superstitious, or whether or not exclusive, or whether or not opposed to display and excitement. On some or other of these points there are surely grounds for expecting *information* from the Fathers, sufficient for our practice, and therefore having claims upon it.

Recourse then being had to the writings of the Fathers, in order to obtain information as to this historical fact, viz. the doctrines, the principles, and the religious temper of Apostolical Christianity, so far we have little to do with the personal endowments of the Fathers, except as these bear on the question of their fidelity. Their being men of strictest lives and most surpassing holiness, would not prove that they knew what it was the Apostles taught; and, were they but ordinary men, this need not incapacitate them from being faithful witnesses and serviceable informants, if they were in a position to be such. We should have only to take into account, and weigh against each other, their qualifications and disqualifications, for being evidence to a fact; we should have to balance honesty against prejudice, education against party influence, early attachments against reason, and so on. Thus we should treat them, taken one by one; but even this sort of personal scrutiny will be practically superseded, when we consult them, not separately, but as our Reformed Church ever has done, together; and demand their *unanimous* testimony to any point of doctrine or discipline, before we make any serious use of them: for it stands to reason, that, where they agree, the peculiarities of their respective nations, education, history, and period, instead of suggesting an indefinite suspicion against the subject-matter of their testimony, does but increase the evidence of its truth. Their testimony becomes the concurrence of many independent witnesses in behalf of the same facts; and, if it is to be slighted or disparaged, one does not see what knowledge of the past remains to us, or what matter for the historian. Viewing S. Cyril, for instance, as one of a body who bears a concordant evidence to the historical fact, that the Apostles taught that Christ is God[t], or that Baptism is the remedy of original sin[u], or that celibacy is not imperative on the clergy[x], whether he was Asiatic or African, of the Roman or the Oriental party, as little matters, as when we consider him as one of a company bearing witness to the historical fact, that the Apostles and their associates wrote the New Testament. Indeed, as the matter stands, there is something very remarkable and even startling to the reader of S. Cyril, to find in a divine of his school such a perfect agreement, for instance as regards the doctrine of the Trinity, with those Fathers who in his age were more famous as champions of it. Here is a writer, separated by

[t] iv. 7, &c.   [x] xii. 25.
[u] Introd. 16. ii 5. iii.4. 11. xii. 15.

whatever cause from what, speaking historically, may be called the Athanasian School, suspicious of its adherents, and suspected by them; yet he, when he comes to explain himself[y], expresses precisely the same doctrine as that of Athanasius or Gregory, while he merely abstains from the particular theological term in which the latter Fathers agreeably to the Nicene Council conveyed it. Can we have a clearer proof that the difference of opinion between them was not one of ecclesiastical and traditionary doctrine, but of practical judgment? that the Fathers at Nicæa wisely considered that, under the circumstances, the word in question was the only symbol which would secure the Church against the insidious heresy which was assailing it, while S. Cyril[z], with Eusebius of Cæsarea, Meletius, and others, shrunk from it, at least for a while, as if an addition to the Creed, or a word already taken into the service of an opposite heresy[a], and likely to introduce into the Church heretical notions? Their judgment, which was erroneous, was their own; their faith was not theirs only, but shared with them by the whole Christian world.

At the same time it must be granted, that this view of the Fathers as witnesses to Apostolic truth not individually but collectively, clear and unanswerable as it is, considered as a view, is open to some great practical inconveniences, when acted on in such an undertaking as that in which the present Editors are engaged. For since, by the supposition, no one of the Fathers is necessarily right in all his doctrine, taken by himself, but may be erroneous in secondary points, each taken by himself is in danger, by his own peculiarities, on the one hand of throwing discredit on all together, on the other of perplexing those who by means of the Fathers are inquiring after Catholic truth. And whereas in any publication of this nature, they cannot appear all at once, but first one and then

[y] iv. 7 vi. 1. x. and xi. xii. 1 de Synod 12 (ed. Bened Cyr. In B)
[z] v Hilar. Contr. Const. 3 12. Athan [a] vid. Bull. Defens. F. N ii 1.

another, and at all events cannot be read altogether, it follows that, during their gradual perusal, unavoidable prejudice will often attach to the Fathers, and to the Catholic Faith, and to those who are enforcing the latter by means of the former. And thus Editors of the Fathers are pretty much in the condition of Architects, who lie under the disadvantage, from which Painters and Sculptors are exempt, of having their work exposed to public criticism through every stage of its execution, and being expected to provide symmetry and congruity in its parts independent of the whole.

Such are the circumstances in which we find ourselves, open to remark for every opinion, every sentence, every phrase, of every Father, before its meaning, relevancy, importance, or bearings are ascertained; before it is known whether it will be, as it were, obliterated by others, or completed, or explained, or modified, or unanimously witnessed. And since the evil is in the nature of the case itself, we can do no more than have patience, and recommend patience to others, and with the racer in the Tragedy look forward steadily and hopefully to the *event*,—*ΤΩι ΤΕΛΕΙ* πίστιν φέρων,—when, as we trust, all that is inharmonious and anomalous in the details, will at length be practically smoothed. Meanwhile, as regards the condition of the reader himself, we consider that we shall sufficiently provide for his perplexity by reminding him of his duty to take his own Church for the present as his guide, and her decisions as a key and final arbiter, as regards the particular statements of the separate Fathers, which he may meet with; being fully confident, that her judgment which he begins by taking as a touchstone of each, will in the event be found to be really formed, as it ought to be, on a view of the testimony of all.

In expressing, however, these thoughts, it is obvious to anticipate an objection of another sort which is likely to be urged against our undertaking, to the effect that all these dangers and warnings are gratuitous, Scripture itself containing sufficient information concerning the doctrines, principles, and mind of the Apostles, without having recourse to the difficult and, as has been above confessed, the anxious task, whether ultimately successful or not, of collecting the object of our inquiry from the writings of the Fathers. This is not the place to treat of an objection, to which much attention has been drawn for several years past; yet thus much may be observed in passing :—If the sufficiency of Scripture for teaching as well as proving the Christian faith be maintained as a theological truth, the grounds in reason must be demanded, grounds such as are independent of that inquiry into history which it is brought forward to prohibit. If it is urged as a truth obvious in matter of fact, and practically certain, then its maintainers have to account for the actual disagreement among readers of Scripture as to *what* the faith, principles, and temper of the Apostles were. And if it be urged on the authority of the sixth Article of our Church, then they must be asked, why if this Article contained a reason against deferring to Antiquity, the Convocation of 1571, which imposed it, at the same time, as is well known, ordered all preachers to teach *according to the* Catholic Fathers, and why our most eminent Divines, beginning with the writers of the Homilies themselves, have ever pursued that very method.

Nothing can be more certain than that Scripture contains all necessary doctrine; yet nothing, it is presumed, can be more certain either, than that, practically speaking, it needs an interpreter; nothing more certain than that our Church and her Divines assign the witness of the early ages of Christianity concerning Apostolic doctrine, as that interpreter.

Without, however, entering into a question which our Church seems to have determined for us, a few words shall be devoted to the explanation of a verbal difficulty by which it is often perplexed. An objection is made, which, when analyzed, resolves itself into the following form.

"Either Antiquity does or does not teach something over and above Scripture: if it does, it adds to the inspired word;—if it does not, it is useless.—Does it then or does it not *add* to Scripture?" And, as if showing that the question is a perplexed one, of various writers who advocate the use of Antiquity, one may be found to speak of the writings of the Fathers as enabling us to ascertain and revive truths which have fallen into desuetude, while another may strenuously maintain, that they impart the knowledge of no new truths over and above what Scripture sets before us. Now, not to touch upon other points suggested by this question, it may be asked by way of explanation, whether the exposition of the true sense of any legal document, any statute or deed, which has been contested, is an addition to it or not? It is in point of *words* certainly; for if the words were the same, it would be no explanation; but it is no addition to the sense, for it professes to be neither more nor less than the very sense, which is expressed in one set of words in the original document, in another in the comment. In like manner, when our Saviour says, "I and My Father are One," and Antiquity interprets "One" to mean "one in substance," this *is* an addition to the *wording*, but no addition to the sense. Of many possible means of interpreting a word, it cuts away all but one, or if it recognizes others, it reduces them to harmony and subordination to that one. Unless the Evangelist wished his readers to be allowed to put any conceivable sense upon the word, the power of doing so is no privilege; rather it is a privilege to know that very meaning, which to the exclusion of all others is the true meaning. Catholic Tradition professes to do for Scripture just which is desirable, whether it is possible or not, to relieve us from the chance of taking one or other of the many senses which are wrong or insufficient, instead of the one sense which is true and complete.

But again, every diligent reader of the Bible has a certain

idea in his own mind of *what* its teaching is, an idea which he cannot say is gained from this or that particular passage, but which he has gained from it as a whole, and which if he attempted to prove argumentatively, he might perplex himself or fall into inconsistencies, because he has never trained his mind in such logical processes; yet nevertheless he has in matter of fact a *view* of Scripture doctrine, and that gained from Scripture, and which, if he states it, he does not necessarily state in words of Scripture, and which, whether after all correct or not, is not incorrect merely because he does not express it in Scripture words, or because he cannot tell whence he got it, or logically refer it to, or prove it from, particular passages. One man is a Calvinist, another an Arminian, another a Latitudinarian; not logically merely, but from the impression gained from Scripture. Is the Latitudinarian necessarily adding to Scripture because he maintains the *proposition*, "religious opinions matter not, so that a man is sincere," a proposition not *in terminis* in Scripture? Surely he is unscriptural, not because he uses words not in Scripture, but because he thereby expresses ideas which are not expressed in Scripture. In answer then to the question, whether the Catholic system is an addition to Scripture, we reply, in one sense it is, in another it is not. It is not, inasmuch as it is not an addition to the range of independent *ideas* which Almighty God intended should be expressed and conveyed on the whole by the inspired text: it is an addition, inasmuch as it is in addition to their *arrangement*, and to the *words* containing them,—inasmuch as it stands as a conclusion contrasted with its premises, inasmuch as it does that which every reader of the Scriptures does for himself, express and convey the ideas more explicitly and determinately than he finds them, and inasmuch as there may be difficulty in duly referring every part of the explicit doctrine to the various parts of Scripture which contain it.

PREFACE. xv

Nothing here is intended beyond setting right an ambiguity of speech which both perplexes persons, and leads them to think that they differ from others, from whom they do not differ. No member of the English Church ever thought that the Church's creed was an *addition* to Scripture in any other sense than that in which an individual's own impression concerning the sense of Scripture is an addition to it; or ever referred to a supposed deposit of faith distinct from Scripture existing in the writings of the Fathers, in any other sense than in that in which asking a friend's opinion about the sense of Scripture, might be called imputing to him unscriptural opinions. The question of words then may easily be cleared up, though it often becomes a difficulty; the *real* subject in dispute, which is not here to be discussed, being this, *how* this one true sense of Scripture is to be learned, whether by philological criticism upon definite texts,—or by a promised superintendence of the Holy Ghost teaching the mind the true doctrines from Scripture, (whether by a general impression upon the mind, or by leading it, text by text piecemeal into doctrine by doctrine;) —or, on the other hand, by a blessing of the Spirit upon studying it in the right way, that is, in the way actually provided, in other words, according to the Church's interpretations. In all cases the text of Scripture and an exposition of it are supposed; in the one the exposition comes first and is brought to Scripture, in the other it is brought out after examination into Scripture; but you cannot help assigning some exposition or other, if you value the Bible at all. Those alone will be content to ascribe no sense to Scripture, who think it matters not whether it has any sense or not. As to the case of a difference eventually occurring in any instance of importance, between what an individual considers to be the sense of Scripture and that which he finds Antiquity to put upon it, the previous question must be asked, whether such difference is likely to arise. It will not arise in the case of the majority, nor again in the case of serious, sensible, and humble minds;

and where men are not such, it will be but one out of many difficulties. A person however, thus circumstanced, whether from his own fault or not, *is* in a difficulty; difficulties are often our lot, and we must bear them, as we think God would have us. We can cut the knot by throwing off the authority of the Fathers; and we can remain under the burden of the difficulty by allowing that authority; but, however we act, we have no licence to please our taste or humour, but we act under a responsibility.

Two main respects have been mentioned, in which the concordant testimony of the Fathers may be considered to throw light upon the sense of Scripture: on these a few words are now necessary with a special reference to S. Cyril,—first as regards the *doctrine* of Scripture, next as regards the *interpretation of texts*. Now it will be found that they are more concordant as to the doctrines themselves contained in Scripture, than as to the passages in which these are contained and their respective force; and, again, that they are more concordant in their view of the principles upon which Scripture is to be interpreted, than in their application of these principles, and their view of the sense in consequence to be assigned to particular texts. This was to be expected, as may easily be made appear.

There seems to have been no Catholic exposition of Scripture, no traditionary comment upon its continuous text. The subject-matter of Catholic tradition, as preserved in the writings of the Fathers, is, not Scripture *interpretation* or *proof*, but certain *doctrines*, professing to be those of the Gospel: and since among these we find this, "that Scripture contains all the Gospel doctrines," we infer, that, according to the mind of the Fathers, those very doctrines which they declare to be the Christian faith are contained in and are to be proved from Scripture. But *where* they occur in Scripture cannot be ascertained from the Fathers, except so far as the accidental course of controversy has brought out their joint witness concerning certain great passages, on which they do seem to have had traditionary information. The Arian and other heresies obliged them to appeal to Scripture in behalf of a certain cardinal doctrine which they held by uninterrupted tradition; and thus have been the means of pointing out to us particular texts in which are contained the great truths which were assailed. But while we are thus furnished with a portion of the Scripture proof of Catholic doctrine, guaranteed to us by the unanimous consent of the Church, it is natural also, under the circumstances above mentioned, that many of the discussions which occurred should contain appeals to Scripture of a less cogent character, and evidencing the exercise of mere private judgment upon the text in default of Catholic Tradition. The early Church had read Scripture not for argument but for edification; it is not wonderful that though holding the truth, and seeing it in the inspired text, and often seeing there what we fail to see, she should nevertheless be as little able to distribute exactly each portion of the truth to each of its places in the text, and to analyze the grounds of those impressions which the whole conveyed, as religious persons in the private walks of life may be now-a-days. Accordingly her divines, one by one, while they witness to the truth itself most sufficiently, as speaking from Tradition, yet often prove it insufficiently, as relying necessarily on private judgment.

For instance, the text, *He that hath seen Me, hath seen the Father*, is taken by S. Cyril, agreeably with other early writers, as a proof that Christ is in all things like (ὅμοιος ἐν πᾶσιν) to the Father; (Lect. xi. 18.) and the text, *Except a man be born of water and of the Spirit*, as a proof of the necessity of Baptism. (Lect. iii. 4.) But though there are many of equal cogency, there are many also, about which there may be fairly difference of opinion, as when he interprets, *Surely God is in thee* (Isa. 45, 14) of the Indwelling of the Father in the Son. (Lect. xi. 16.)

c

And, while it is not at all surprising even though the Fathers should occasionally adduce texts as proofs of certain doctrines which are not so, neither is it strange that they should overlook proofs which did exist, and which we are able to discern. For they were in the light of a recent Tradition; we are in the twilight of a distant age; and our minds, like eyes accustomed to the twilight, may discern much in the dark parts of Scripture, which were hid from them by their very privilege.

Such imperfections, however, in the Scripture proofs adduced by the Fathers, whether in excess or defect, do not interfere at all with their maintenance of the great principles that there is a Faith, and that it is in Scripture. As far as S. Cyril is concerned, the following passages witness both truths clearly. "This Seal," he says, speaking of the Creed, "have thou ever in mind; which now by way of summary has been touched on in its heads, and, if the Lord grant, shall hereafter be set forth according to our power with Scripture proofs. For concerning the divine and sacred mysteries of the Faith, we ought not to deliver even the most casual remark without the Holy Scriptures; nor be drawn aside by mere probabilities, and the artifices of argument. Do not then believe me because I tell you these things, unless thou receive from the Holy Scriptures the proof of what is set forth; for this salvation, which is of our faith, is not by ingenious reasonings, but by proof from the Holy Scriptures." (Lect. iv. 17.)

Again: "Take thou and hold that faith only as a learner and in profession, which is by the Church delivered to thee, and is established from all Scripture. For since all cannot read the Scripture, but some as being unlearned, others by business, are hindered from the knowledge of them, in order that the soul may not perish for lack of instruction, in the Articles which are few we comprehend the whole doctrine of the faith ... Commit to memory the Faith, merely listening to the words, and expect at the fitting season the proof of each of its parts from the Divine Scriptures. For the Articles of the Faith were not composed at the good pleasure of man; but the most important points chosen from all Scripture, make up the one teaching of the Faith. And as the mustard seed in a little grain contains many branches, thus also this Faith, in a few words, has enfolded in its bosom the whole knowledge of godliness contained both in the Old and New Testaments." (Lect. v. 12.) The doctrine, expressed in these and other passages of S. Cyril, is implied and assumed in a most striking way in a number of others[b].

So much on the Scripture proof of doctrine as contained in the Fathers; as to the doctrinal sense of Scripture, the second point to be spoken of, what has been already observed is quite consistent, not to say connected with the remark to be made concerning it, viz. that the Fathers are far more concordant in assigning principles of Scripture interpretation, than in the interpretation of particular passages. Indeed the very view they took of the Bible led to variety, apparent discordance, and private conjecture in interpreting it. They considered it to be a sort of storehouse of sacred treasures[c], contained under the letter in endless profusion, piled, as it were, one on another, with order indeed and by rule, but still often so deeply lodged within the text, that from ordinary eyes they were almost hidden[d]. Hence it was considered as a duty and privilege proposed to the Christian, to find out the "wondrous things of God's law," and no meaning was so remote from the literal text as to be proved thereby to be foreign to it in the Divine intention. While then, according to their disposition or school of theology, they were led, more or less, to attempt to search into the deep mysteries of Scripture for themselves[e], they felt little difficulty in multiplicity of interpretations, little fear of inconsistency. And while such a prin-

[b] v. 12 xii 5 xiii. 8, 9. xiv 2. xvi 1, 2 24
[c] xi 12.
[d] xii 16 xiii 14 ix 13
[e] iii 16 vi 28, 29. xii 19

ciple as has been described necessarily led them to diversity in their interpretations, that diversity does but increase our evidence of the fact of their one and all holding that principle; and thus, while their value as commentators varies with their personal qualifications, their adherence to that principle comes to us as a Catholic tradition.

Instances of individual, local, or transitory opinion, that is, of what would at present, rightly or wrongly, be called fancifulness and caprice, are frequent in S. Cyril's Lectures, and scarcely need specifying. Such, for example, is his interpreting, "Look unto the rock whence ye are hewn," of the Holy Sepulchre, (Lect. xiii. 35.) or " At evening time it shall be light," of the circumstances of the Crucifixion; (Lect. xiii. 24.) and much more his considering, "Thou hast wrought salvation in the *midst of the earth*," (Lect. xiii. 28.) to allude to Golgotha, and " the fountain sealed," to Christ in the sepulchre after the sealing of the stone. (Lect. xiv. 5.)

These interpretations, whether his own or not, and whether true or not, do not profess to be traditional, and are but witnesses, to the great principle from which they proceed, of the everliving intelligence, deep and varied meaning, and inexhaustible fulness of Holy Scripture. This indeed he himself declares in one place in words which may be suitably extracted. After giving two conjectures concerning the doctrinal meaning of the Blood and Water, which came from our Lord's side, viz. that it typifies the Jews' imprecation of His blood upon them and Pilate's washing his hands of it, or again the condemnation of the Jews and the baptismal pardon of Christians, he adds, " *For nothing happened without a meaning,* (οὐδὲν εἰκῆ γέγονεν.) Our fathers who have written comments, have given another reason of this matter. For since in the Gospel the power of salutary Baptism is two-fold, that bestowed by means of water on the Illuminated, and that to holy Martyrs in persecutions through their own blood, there came out of that salutary side blood and water," &c. (Lect. xiii. 21.)

PREFACE. xxi

When then it is inquired, what information is given us by the Fathers, concerning Scripture or Catholic doctrine, we reply, that they rather declare doctrine and say that it is in Scripture, than prove it by Scripture, at once concordantly and in detail; and again, that they rather tell us how we must set about interpreting Scripture, than authoritatively interpret it for us. It is presumed that this is on the whole correct; true as it also is, that on a number of the most important points of doctrine they have preserved to us, with an unanimity which is an evidence of its Apostolic origin, the very texts in which they are contained. Still after all the Fathers are rather led to dwell on Scripture by itself, and on the doctrinal system by itself, as two distinct, parallel, and substantive sources of divine information, than to blend and almost identify the two, as a variety of circumstances has occasioned or obliged us to do at this day.

It would at first sight seem unnecessary to add to what has been said, any remark on mistakes or apparent mistakes committed by S. Cyril in matters of fact; but as this is often a ground of misconception, the subject shall be briefly noticed. For instance, as to his statement concerning the discovery of the True Cross [f], he is to be treated as any other historical witness under the same circumstances, and the weight of his evidence, whatever it is, is to be balanced against the improbability of the fact recorded, whether antecedent, or arising from the silence concerning it of Eusebius and Constantine. Again, we may well allow that he was not a natural historian, without hurting his theological character. It is true that he believed in the existence of the Phœnix [g], and argued from the analogy afforded by it in favour of the Resurrection. That is, he was philosophical on false grounds. And in like manner persons have proved, as they thought, the Noachical deluge from stones found on the top of hills, or have attributed it to the action

[f] Lect. iv. 10, x 19. xiii. 4.   [g] xviii 8.

of a comet, or have believed or doubted the existence of the sea-serpent or the dodo, and never have been reckoned worse or better divines for either success or failure in such conjectures. It as little follows that a theologian must be an ornithologist, as that an ornithologist or comparative anatomist must be a theologian; and as no one in this day would reckon ignorance of divinity as a bar to eminence and authority in scientific researches, so it betrays a poverty of argument to reproach S. Cyril, or Eusebius, or S. Clement before them, with not being proficients in a branch of knowledge which has been a peculiar study of modern times. They did not profess to be natural historians; let it be enough for this age to cultivate physical science itself, without molesting the Fathers with its new standards of intellectual superiority. Let it be enough for it to despise the province of theology, without seeking to remodel it. The Fathers did not profess the science on which it prides itself; nothing but inspiration could secure them from shewing ignorance concerning it; and no one pretends that S. Cyril or S. Clement were inspired.

It is only necessary to add with respect to the present Translation, that for almost the whole of it the Editors are indebted to Mr. CHURCH, Fellow of Oriel College. It has been made from the Benedictine Text compared with the Oxford Edition of Milles, the Benedictine Sections in the separate Lectures being marked by numbers at the beginning of the paragraphs, and the Oxford sections on the margin. The few notes which are introduced are almost confined to the elucidation of matter of fact, and have been kept clear as far as possible from the expression of opinions; in drawing them up, much use has been made of the valuable information contained in the Oxford and Benedictine Editions. Such words of S. Cyril as have a theological, controversial, or critical importance, are usually placed in the margin opposite their place in the Translation. The quotations from Scripture are given in the words of our received version, wherever the Greek of Cyril admitted of it; when otherwise, it has been signified in the margin.

J. H. N.

Oxford,
The Feast of St. Matthew, 1838.

Notice concerning the Churches in which the Lectures were delivered

---

It has already been observed, that St. Cyril delivered the following Lectures in the year 347 or 348. He delivered them without book, in the Churches raised over the spot made sacred by our Lord's death, burial, and resurrection; those addressed to the Catechumens, excepting the Introductory Lecture, in the evening, that being the usual time for religious meetings during Lent; and those on the Mysteries, at noon.

It may be interesting to the reader to be put in possession of Eusebius's description of the Basilica and Church, which Constantine erected, in which the Lectures were delivered. The circumstance of its being contemporaneous history will be considered perhaps to compensate for the turgidness of the style. In his panegyric upon Constantine, he briefly noticed the buildings in question thus:

"As regards Palestine, in the midst of the royal home of the Hebrews, at the very place of the Saving Witness[a], he employed himself in ornamenting richly and with munificent earnestness a vast House of prayer and Holy Temple to the Saving Sign; and paid honour to the Great Saviour's tomb of eternal memory, His very trophy raised over death, with decorations not to be described." c. 9.

And more at length in his life of the same Emperor. "He considered it his duty to constitute that most blessed spot in Jerusalem, of the Saving Resurrection, an object of admiration and reverence to all. Accordingly he gave orders to construct there a House of Prayer, not projecting it apart from God, but moved in spirit by the Saviour Himself. For in former

[a] Vid. Cyril, Lect. xiv. 6

days irreligious men, or rather the whole race of evil spirits by means of them, had made it a point to consign over that divine monument of immortality to darkness and oblivion.... Not sparing their labour in the work, and bringing earth from other places, they conceal the whole place; and then raising it up high and paving it with stones, they bury the divine treasure somewhere beneath under this vast mound. Then as though nothing more was to be done, above that ground, they contrive a sepulchre, dreadful indeed for souls; by building a dark shrine of dead idols to the unchaste spirit called Venus. And there they offered impure sacrifices upon profane and guilty altars...... No one ever, governor, or general, or emperor himself, was found equal for the overthrow of this daring deed, but one, the favoured of the All Sovereign God. Influenced then by a Divine Spirit, he bore not that the place aforenamed should be hidden under that unholy mass, by the counsels of enemies forgotten and unknown; he yielded not to the wickedness of the perpetrators of the deed; so, invoking God his Helper, he bids purify the place, deeming it fitting that what had been the most polluted by our enemies, should receive the noblest work of good through him. And upon the word the structures of falsehood began to fall upon the ground from their height above; and images, evil spirits, and the whole edifice of error fell into pieces and were demolished. Nor did the Emperor's zeal rest here; but he orders to carry off and cast away, far away from the spot, the materials, wood and stone. Deeds followed upon word; yet even at this point was he not satisfied. Again, divinely moved, he commanded to dig deep and carry out the soil itself, together with the mound, far away, as having been polluted by the mire of devilish sacrifices. This too was instantly done; on which another foundation instead of the first came to light, one in the depth of the earth, and the awful and all-holy Witness of the Saving Resurrection came to light beyond all hope; and then that cave, a holy of holies, began to image forth the scene of the revival of the

Saviour. Thus after its setting in darkness, it again came forth to the light; and to those who came to see, it afforded a manifest view of the history of the things done there, witnessing by facts more vocally than any voice the Saviour's resurrection. All this being done, immediately the Emperor by pious edicts and unsparing contributions, commands to build about the Saving Cave, a House of prayer, worthy of God, with rich and royal magnificence, having long proposed this, and contemplated the future with special eagerness;—sending to the Governors of the Eastern provinces, by unsparing and loving contributions to accomplish an extraordinary, great, and rich work; and to the then Bishop of Jerusalem, [Macarius,] the following letter, &c . . . .

"First of all, he set about the decorations of the Sacred Cave itself, that divine monument, by which an Angel dazzling with light once told good tidings of the regeneration manifested to all through the Saviour. This then first as the beginning of the whole, the Emperor's devotion enriched with choice pillars and much embellishment, beautifying it with ornaments of every sort.

"Next he passed over an ample space opened to the sky; which was paved with shining stone, and surrounded on three sides with long porticos.

"But on the fourth side which was opposite the Cave, and looked eastward, was added the Royal Temple, [the Basilica,] an extraordinary work, rising to an immense height, and spread out in exceeding length and width. The inner walls were covered with marble slabs of various colours, and the outside face of the walls, shining with polished stones closely fitted together, was a specimen of supernatural beauty not inferior to the look of marble. The roof without was protected with lead, as a defence against the weather; and the roof within was composed of carved fretwork, and by means of compartments stretched its vast expanse over the whole Basilica, and was covered throughout with resplendent gold, so as to make the whole Temple dazzling as with a blaze of light.

"On each side ran a portico with two ranges along the length of the temple, both above and under ground; and of this too the roof was enriched with gold. The outside ranges consisted of enormous columns; and the inside of quadrangular buttresses highly ornamented. Three handsome doors on the East let in the multitude who would enter.

" At the opposite end, was the perfection of the whole work, a hemisphere[b], at the top of the Basilica; girt with twelve pillars according to the number of the Apostles of the Saviour, with capitals ornamented with large silver cups, which the Emperor himself gave as a most beautiful offering to his God.

" Hence, as one goes forward to the entrances lying before the Temple, he interposed an open court; and on each side, first a hall, then porticos, and then hall-doors. Next, reaching into the broad marketplace, was placed the vestibule of the whole tastefully fashioned, affording to those who were passing outside a striking view of the wonders within.

" This Temple then the Emperor raised as a conspicuous Witness of the Saving Resurrection, beautifying it with rich and royal materials. And he embellished it with innumerable gifts of undescribable splendour, with gold, silver, precious stones of every kind; of which the exquisite workmanship in particular, whether in size, number, or variety, does not admit of being recounted here." (iii. 25—40.)

A ground-plan of the Church and Basilica is subjoined :—

---

[b] i. e. the Apsis where the Altar was

xxviii

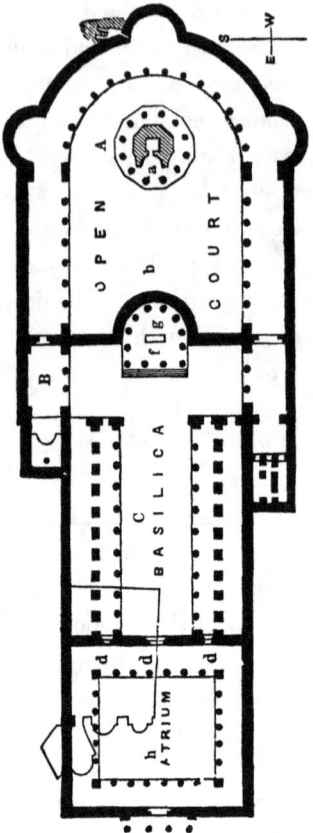

A. The Anastasis, that is, the Church upon the site of the Holy Sepulchre, where S. Cyril delivered his last five Lectures. (Lect. xviii. 33.)

The Holy Sepulchre was within a stone's cast of the top of Golgotha, on the southern side of the hill. It originally consisted of two caves, (Lect xiv. 9.) an inner and an outer, of which the latter was destroyed by Constantine. The former, which he left, and, as it would appear, (vid. above note a on Lect. xiv. 9.) cut off from the main body of the rock, is shaped round outside like a horseshoe with the circular part towards the West, and is entered by the East. Inside it remains apparently in its ancient form of a trapezium, the roof can be touched with the hand, and on the North in an opening in the face of the rock, where our Lord's body seems to have been placed. The stone which had been placed at the mouth of the cave lay in S Cyril's time near the Sepulchre whether within or without. (Lect. xiii. 39) The Church built over the Holy Sepulchre was circular.

B. Golgotha or Calvary, the place of our Lord's Crucifixion.

The whole mount, including the site of the sacred buildings, was sometimes called Golgotha. (Vid Lect iv 10. 14. xvi 4) Sometimes only its top where the Crucifixion actually took place, which was to the North of the Basilica of the Holy Cross. (Lect xiii. 4) It was without the walls of the ancient city, to the North of Mount Sion, and about a mile and a half to the West of the Mount of Olives; and in S. Cyril's time it was a wild desolate spot, some traces remaining of the garden in which the Sepulchre was situated (Lect. xiv. 5.)

C. The Basilica of Constantine, or Church of the Holy Cross, (Euseb. Laud. C. 9) called also the Martyrium or Testimony, as being built close upon and in memory of our Lord's Passion; where S. Cyril delivered his first eighteen Lectures.

The Basilica of the Holy Cross, lay to the West of the Holy Sepulchre, being connected with it by a court open above, paved with choice marble, and bounded on all but the West side with a portico. It lay higher than the court, from which it seems to have been entered by steps, and there were three doors at the entrance, through which the Holy Sepulchre and the summit of Golgotha were seen. Porticos ran along the North and South, and the Altar was at the West end.

a. The Holy Sepulchre, with the entrance on the East.

b. The open Court connecting the Anastasis or Church of the Holy Sepulchre, with the Basilica of the Holy Cross.

d. Entrances.

e. Ambo, where was the place of reading Scripture and preaching.

f. Altar.

g. Bishop's throne.

h. Spring of water for the Baptistery.

CATECHETICAL LECTURES

OF

S. CYRIL.

LECTURES ADDRESSED TO CANDIDATES FOR BAPTISM DURING LENT, IN THE BASILICA OF THE HOLY CROSS.

INTRODUCTORY LECTURE.

Page 1

[Delivered in full Church, and therefore perhaps on a Sunday.]

LECTURE I.

Page 10

ON THE PURPOSE OF MIND NECESSARY FOR BAPTISM.

Isaiah i 16—19.

Wash you, make you clean; put away the evil of your doings from before Mine eyes, cease to do evil; learn to do well; seek judgment, relieve the oppressed, judge the fatherless, plead for the widow. Come now, and let us reason together, saith the Lord · though your sins be as scarlet, they shall be as white as snow, though they be red like crimson, they shall be as wool. If ye be willing and obedient, ye shall eat the good of the land.

[Probably in the first week.]

LECTURE II

Page 14

ON THE POWER OF REPENTANCE FOR THE REMISSION OF SIN.

Ezekiel xviii 20—23.

The righteousness of the righteous shall be upon him, and the wickedness of the wicked shall be upon him But if the wicked will turn from all his sins that he hath committed, and keep all

My statutes, and do that which is lawful and right, he shall surely live, he shall not die. All his transgressions that he hath committed, they shall not be mentioned unto him; in his righteousness that he hath done he shall live. Have I any pleasure at all that the wicked should die? saith the Lord God: and not that he should return from his ways, and live?

[Probably in the first week.]

LECTURE III

Page 25

ON HOLY BAPTISM.

Romans vi. 3, 4.

Know ye not, that so many of us as were baptized into Jesus Christ, were baptized into His death? Therefore we are buried with Him by Baptism into death, that like as Christ was raised up from the dead by the glory of the Father, even so we also should walk in newness of life.

[Probably in the first week]

LECTURE IV.

Page 34

ON THE TEN POINTS OF FAITH.

Colossians ii. 8.

Beware lest any man spoil you through philosophy and vain deceit, after the tradition of men, after the rudiments of the world, and not after Christ.

[Probably in the first week]

LECTURE V

Page 52

ON FAITH.

Hebrews xi. 1, 2.

Now faith is the substance of things hoped for, the evidence of things not seen: for by it the elders obtained a good report.

CONTENTS

LECTURE VI
Page 60

ON THE UNITY OF GOD.

Isaiah xlv 16, 17.

They shall go to confusion together that are partakers of idols; but Israel shall be saved in the Lord with an everlasting salvation, ye shall not be ashamed nor confounded world without end.

LECTURE VII
Page 79

ON GOD, THE FATHER.

Eph iii 14, 15.

For this cause I bow my knees unto the Father of our Lord Jesus Christ, of whom the whole family of heaven and earth is named.

[Next day to the sixth]

LECTURE VIII
Page 86

ON THE SOVEREIGNTY OF GOD.

Jer. xxxii 18, 19.

The Great, the Mighty God; the Lord of Hosts is His Name, great in counsel, and mighty in work.

[Next day to the seventh]

LECTURE IX.
Page 90

ON GOD, THE CREATOR OF ALL THINGS.

Job xxxviii. 2, 3.

Who is this that darkeneth counsel by words without knowledge? Gird up now thy loins like a man; for I will demand of thee, and answer thou Me.

CONTENTS.

LECTURE X
Page 98.

ON THE ONE LORD, JESUS CHRIST.

1 Corinthians viii. 5, 6.

For though there be that are called gods, whether in heaven or in earth, (as there be gods many and lords many,) but to us there is One God the Father, of whom are all things, and we in Him; and one Lord Jesus Christ, by whom are all things, and we by Him.

LECTURE XI
Page 110

ON THE SON OF GOD, AS ONLY-BEGOTTEN, BEFORE ALL AGES, AND THE CREATOR OF ALL THINGS.

Hebrews i. 1, 2.

God, who at sundry times and in divers manners spake in times past unto the Fathers by the Prophets, hath in these last days spoken unto us by His Son.

[Next day to the tenth.]

LECTURE XII
Page 123

ON THE INCARNATION OF THE SON OF GOD.

Isaiah vii. 10—14.

Moreover the Lord spake again unto Ahaz, saying, Ask thee a sign of the Lord thy God; ask it either in the depth, or in the height above. And Ahaz said, I will not ask, neither will I tempt the Lord. And he said, Hear ye now, O House of David; is it a small thing for you to weary men, but will ye weary my God also? Therefore the Lord Himself shall give you a sign; Behold, a Virgin shall conceive, and bear a Son, and shall call His Name Immanuel.

[Next day to the eleventh.]

CONTENTS.

LECTURE XIII
Page 142

ON THE CRUCIFIXION AND BURIAL OF CHRIST.

Isaiah liii 1, 7.

Who hath believed our report? and to whom is the arm of the Lord revealed? .... He is brought as a lamb to the slaughter, and as a sheep before her shearers is dumb, so He openeth not His mouth.

[Some days before the fourteenth.]

LECTURE XIV
Page 165

ON THE RESURRECTION, ASCENSION, AND EXALTATION OF CHRIST.

1 Corinthians xv. 1—4.

Moreover, brethren, I declare unto you the Gospel which I preached unto you, which also ye have received, and wherein ye stand, by which also ye are saved, if ye keep in memory what I preached unto you, unless ye have believed in vain. For I delivered unto you first of all that which I also received, how that Christ died for our sins according to the Scriptures; and that He was buried, and that He rose again the third day according to the Scriptures.

[On a Monday in the beginning of the month Xanthicus (April), shortly after the Equinox.]

LECTURE XV.
Page 183

ON THE SECOND ADVENT, THE LAST JUDGMENT, AND THE PERPETUITY OF CHRIST'S KINGDOM.

Dan. vii. 9—14.

I beheld till the thrones were cast down, and the Ancient of days did sit, &c. ... The judgment was set, and the books were opened, &c. ... I saw in the night visions, and behold one like the Son of Man came with the clouds of heaven, and came to the

Ancient of days, and they brought Him near before Him. And there was given Him dominion, &c. . . . His dominion is an everlasting dominion, which shall not pass away, &c.

LECTURE XVI
Page 203

ON THE ONE HOLY GHOST, THE COMFORTER, WHICH SPAKE IN THE PROPHETS.

1 Cor. xii. 1, 4.

Now concerning spiritual gifts, brethren, I would not have you ignorant. . . . Now there are diversities of gifts, but the same Spirit.

[A few days before Easter]

LECTURE XVII
Page 220

ON THE HOLY GHOST.

1 Cor. xii. 8.

For to one is given by the Spirit the word of wisdom; to another the word of knowledge by the same Spirit, &c.

[A few days before Easter]

LECTURE XVIII
Page 240

ON THE RESURRECITON OF THE FLESH, THE CATHOLIC CHURCH, AND THE LIFE EVERLASTING.

Ezekiel xxxvii. 1.

The hand of the Lord was upon me, and carried me out in the Spirit of the Lord, and set me down in the midst of the valley which was full of bones

[On Easter Eve.]

CONTENTS.

LECTURES ADDRESSED TO THE BAPTIZED IN EASTER WEEK IN THE CHURCH OF THE HOLY SEPULCHRE

LECTURE XIX
(ON THE MYSTERIES I)
Page 258

ON THE RITES BEFORE BAPTISM.

1 Pet v. 8—14.

Be sober, be vigilant; because your adversary the devil, as a roaring lion, walketh about, seeking whom he may devour, &c.

[On Monday in Easter Week]

LECTURE XX
(ON THE MYSTERIES II)
Page 263

ON THE RITE OF BAPTISM.

Rom. vi 3—14.

Know ye not, that so many of us as were baptized into Jesus Christ were baptized into His death? &c. . . . for ye are not under the Law, but under grace.

[On Tuesday in Easter Week]

LECTURE XXI
(ON THE MYSTERIES. III)
Page 267

ON THE HOLY CHRISM.

1 John ii. 20—28.

But ye have an unction from the Holy One, &c. . . . . that, when He shall appear, we may have confidence, and not be ashamed before Him at His coming

[On Wednesday in Easter Week.]

CONTENTS.

LECTURE XXII.
(ON THE MYSTERIES. IV.)
Page 270.
ON THE BODY AND BLOOD OF CHRIST.

1 Cor. xi. 23.

I have received of the Lord that which also I delivered unto you, That the Lord Jesus, the same night in which He was betrayed, took bread, &c.

[On Thursday in Easter Week.]

LECTURE XXIII.
(ON THE MYSTERIES. V.)
Page 273
ON THE COMMUNION SERVICE.

1 Pet. ii. 1.

Wherefore laying aside all malice, and all guile, and hypocrisies, and envies, and evil speakings, &c.

[On Friday in Easter Week.]

CREED OF THE CHURCH OF JERUSALEM.

[Collected from St. Cyril's Lectures.]

WE believe in One God, the Father Almighty, Maker of heaven and earth, and of all things, visible and invisible:

And in One Lord Jesus Christ, the Only-begotten Son of God; begotten of the Father Very God, before all worlds; by whom all things were made; who came in the flesh, and was made man of the Virgin and the Holy Ghost; He was crucified and buried; He rose again the third day; and ascended into heaven, and sat on the right hand of the Father; and He cometh in glory to judge the quick and the dead; whose kingdom shall have no end:

And in One Holy Ghost, the Comforter, who spake in the Prophets: and in one Baptism of repentance for the remission of sins: and in one Holy Catholic Church: and in the Resurrection of the dead · and in the Life everlasting.

CATECHETICAL LECTURES

OF

S. CYRIL,

ARCHBISHOP OF JERUSALEM.

ADDRESSED TO

CANDIDATES FOR BAPTISM.

INTRODUCTORY LECTURE.

1. ALREADY is there on you the savour of blessedness, O ye (1.) who are soon to be enlightened: already are you gathering $_{φωτιζό-}$ spiritual flowers, to weave heavenly crowns withal: already $_{μενοι}$ hath the fragrance of the Holy Ghost refreshed you: already are you at the entrance-hall of the King's house: may you be brought into it by the King! For now the blossoms of the trees have budded; may but the fruit likewise be perfected! Thus far, your names have been given in, and the roll-call made for service; there are the torches of the bridal train, and the longings after heavenly citizenship, and a good purpose, and a hope attendant; for he cannot lie who hath said, *To them that love God, all things work together for good.* Rom. 8, God is indeed lavish in His benefits: yet He looks for each $^{28}_{προαίρε-}$ man's honest resolve: so the Apostle subjoins, *To those who* σιν. *are called according to their purpose.* Honesty of purpose makes thee *called*: for though the body be here, yet if the mind be away, it avails nothing.

2. Even Simon Magus once came to the Laver of Baptism, Acts 8, he was baptized, but not enlightened[a]. His body he dipped 13. in water, but admitted not the Spirit to illuminate his heart.

---

[a] S. Austin considers Simon Magus to be born again, but to a greater condemnation Vid in Ps. 103. i. 9.

His body went down and came up; but his soul was not buried together with Christ, nor with Him raised. I mention such instances of falls, that thou mayest not fail; *for these things happened to them for ensamples, and they are written for the admonition* of those, who up to this day are ever coming. Let no one of you be found tempting grace · let no *root of bitterness spring up, and trouble you:* let not any of you enter, saying, Come, let us see what the faithful do: I will go in and see, that I may learn what is done. Expectest thou to see, and not to be seen: and thinkest thou to busy thee with what is doing, and God not be busy with thine heart the while?

3. A certain man in the Gospels busily pried into the marriage feast: he took an unbecoming garment, came in, sat down, and ate; for the bridegroom permitted thus far: whereas, when he saw the white robes of all, he ought himself likewise to have taken such another; yet he shared like meats with them, being unlike them in fashion and in purpose. But the bridegroom, though bountiful, was not undiscerning; and, as he went round to each of the guests and viewed them, (not that he was careful how they feasted, but how they behaved,) seeing a stranger, not having a wedding-garment on, he said to him, *Friend, how camest thou in hither?* With what stained raiments? with what a conscience? What, though the porter stopped thee not, because of the bountifulness of the entertainer? what, though thou wert ignorant in what fashion thou shouldest enter into the banquet? yet thou camest in, thou didst see the glistering fashion of the guests. Shouldest thou not have learned at least from what thou sawest? Shouldest thou not have made a seasonable retreat, that thou mightest have a seasonable return? but now hast thou turned in unseasonably, that unseasonably thou mightest be thrust out. So he commands his servants, Bind his feet, which have daringly intruded,—bind his hands, which were not skilled to robe him in the bright garment; and cast him into the outer darkness; for he is unworthy of the wedding torches. Thou hast seen how he fared then; take heed to thyself.

4. For we, the ministers of Christ, have admitted every man, and holding as it were the place of door-keepers, have left the door unfastened. Thou hast been free then to enter with a

soul bemired with sins, and a defiled purpose. Entered thou hast: thou hast passed, thou hast been enrolled. Seest thou these venerable arrangements of the Church? Viewest thou her order and discipline, the reading of the Scriptures, the κανονικῶν presence of the religious, the course of teaching? Let then παρουσίαν. the place affect thee, let the sight sober thee. Depart in good time now, and enter to-morrow in better. If avarice has been the fashion of thy soul, put on another, and then come in: put off what thou hadst, cloke it not over . put off, I pray thee, fornication and uncleanness, and put on the most bright robe of soberness. This charge I give thee, before Jesus the spouse of souls come in, and see their fashion. Thou art allowed a distant day; thou hast a penitence of forty [b]; thou hast full time to put off, and to wash thee, to put on, and to enter in. But if thou abide in thy evil purpose, he who speaks is blameless, but thou must not look for grace: for though the water shall receive thee, the Spirit will not accept thee. Whoso is conscious of a wound, let him take the salve: whoso has fallen, let him rise: let there be no Simon among you, no hypocrisy, no idle curiosity about the matter.

5. Perhaps thou comest on another ground. A man may (4.) be wishing to pay court to a woman, and on that account come hither: and the same applies to women likewise: again, a slave often wishes thus to please his master, or one friend another. I avail myself of this angler's bait, and receive thee, as one who has come indeed with an unsound purpose, but art to be saved by a good hope. Thou knewest not perchance whither thou wast coming, nor what net was taking thee. Thou art within the Church's nets, submit to be taken; flee not, for Jesus would secure thee, not to make thee die, but by death to make thee live. For thou must die and rise again; thou hast heard the Apostle saying, *Dead indeed to* Rom 6, *sin, but alive unto righteousness.* Die then to thy sins, and 11 1 Pet. 2, live to righteousness: yea, from this day forth, live. 24.

6. Look, I beseech thee, how great dignity Jesus presents to thee. Thou wert called a Catechumen, which means, hearing with the ears, hearing hope, and not perceiving;

---

[b] In some Churches this period was of thirty days; in other twenty, in the Churches of Italy it seems to have been more than forty.

hearing mysteries, yet not understanding: hearing Scriptures, yet not knowing their depth. Thou no longer hearest with the ears, but thou hearest within; for the indwelling Spirit henceforth fashions thy mind into a house of God. When thou shalt hear what is written concerning mysteries, then thou shalt understand, what hitherto thou knewest not. And think not it is a trifle thou receivest. Thou, a wretched man, receivest the Name of God; for hear the words of Paul, *God is faithful;* and another Scripture, *God is faithful and just.* This the Psalmist foreseeing, since men were to receive the Name ascribed to God, said in the person of God, *I have said, ye are Gods, and are all the children of the Most High.* But beware lest with the name of believer thou have the purpose of an unbeliever. Thou hast entered into the struggle; labour therefore in the race, for season thou hast none other such. If thou hadst thy wedding day before thee, wouldest thou not make light of aught besides, and be full of preparations for the feast? And wilt thou not then, when on the eve of consecrating thy soul to a heavenly spouse, let go carnal things that thou mayest take hold of spiritual?

7. The bath of Baptism we may not receive twice or thrice; else, it might be said, Though I fail once, I shall go right next time: whereas if thou failest once, there is no setting things right, for there is *One Lord, and One Faith, and One Baptism:* none but heretics are re-baptized, since their former baptism was not baptism [c].

(5.) 8. For God seeks nothing else from us, save a good purpose. Say not, How are my sins blotted out? I tell thee, from willing, from believing; what is shorter than this? But if thy lips declare thy willing, but thy heart is silent, He knows the heart who judgeth thee. Cease then henceforth from every wicked thing: refrain thy tongue from light words, thine eye from sin, thy mind from roving after useless matters.

9. Let thy feet hasten to the Catechisings, receive with earnestness the Exorcisms; for whether thou art breathed

---

[c] The Marcionites allowed of Baptism three times. Epiph. Hær. xlii. 3. Valentinus twice Hieron in Eph. iv. 5. What Cyril says about heretical baptism should be observed. The Roman Church considered it invalid only when (the officiator being ordained) the words or water was not duly used. S Cyprian, and the African Church of his day, considered it invalid in all cases, so did the Churches of Asia Minor at the same date S. Dionysius of Alexandria is claimed on both sides

upon, or exorcised, the Ordinance is to thee salvation. It is as though thou hadst gold unwrought or alloyed, blended with various substances, with brass, and tin, and iron, and lead: we seek to have the gold pure, but it cannot be cleansed from foreign substances without fire. Even so, without Exorcisms, the soul cannot be cleansed; and they are divine, collected from the divine Scriptures. Thy face is veiled[d], that thy mind may be henceforth at leisure; lest a roving eye cause a roving heart. But though thine eyes be veiled, thine ears are not hindered receiving what is saving. For as the goldsmith, conveying the blast upon the fire through delicate instruments, and as it were breathing on the gold which is hid in the hollow of the forge, stimulates the flame it acts upon, and so obtains what he is seeking; so also, exorcisers, infusing fear by the Holy Ghost, and setting the soul on fire in the crucible of the body, make the evil spirit flee, who is our enemy, and salvation and the hope of eternal life abide; and henceforth the soul, cleansed from its sins, hath salvation. Let us then, brethren, abide in hope, surrendering ourselves (6.) and hoping; so may the God of all, seeing our purpose, cleanse us from sins, and impart to us good hopes of our estate, and grant us saving penitence! He who calls, is God, and thou art the person called.

10. Abide thou in the Catechisings: though our discourse be long, let not thy mind be wearied out. For thou art receiving thine armour against the antagonist power; against heresies, against Jews, and Samaritans, and Gentiles. Thou hast many enemies; take to thee many darts; thou hast many to hurl them at. And thou hast need to learn how to hurl them at the Greek; how to do battle against heretic, against Jew and Samaritan. The armour indeed is ready, and most ready is the sword of the Spirit; but thou also must stretch forth thy hands with good resolve, that thou mayest war the Lord's warfare, mayest overcome the powers that oppose thee, mayest escape defeat from every heretical attempt.

11. This charge also I give thee. Study the things that are spoken, and keep them for ever. Think not that they are the ordinary Homilies, which are excellent indeed, and trustworthy, but if neglected to-day, may be attended to

[d] For this custom, vid. Bingham, Antiq x. 2 § 12. Basnag. Annal. vol. ii. Dissert xii 15.

6 *Christian doctrine to be withheld from Catechumens.*

INTROD. LECT — to-morrow. On the contrary, the teaching concerning the laver of regeneration, delivered in course, how shall it be made up, if to-day it be neglected? Consider it to be the planting season; unless we dig, and that deeply, how shall that afterwards be planted rightly, which has once been planted ill? Or consider Catechising to be a kind of building: unless we dig deep, and lay the foundation,—unless by successive fastenings in the masonry, we bind the frame-work of the house together, that no opening be detected, nor the work be left unsound, nought avails all our former labour. But stone must succeed stone in course, and corner must follow corner, and, inequalities being smoothed away, the masonry must rise regular. In like manner we are bringing to thee the stones, as it were, of knowledge; thou must hear concerning the Living God; concerning Judgment; concerning Christ; concerning the Resurrection; and many things are made to follow one the other, which though now dropped one by one, at length are presented in harmonious connexion. But if thou wilt not connect them into one whole, and remember what is first, and what is second, the builder indeed buildeth, but the building will be unstable.

(7.) 12. Now when the Catechising has taken place, should a Catechumen ask, what the teachers have said, tell nothing to a stranger; for we deliver to thee a mystery, even the hope of the life to come: keep the mystery for Him who pays thee. Let no man say to thee, What harm, if I also know it? So the sick ask for wine; but if it be unseasonably given them, it occasions delirium, and two evils follow; the sick man dies, and the physician gets an ill name. Thus is it with the Catechumen also if he should hear from the Believer: the Catechumen is made delirious, for not understanding what he has heard, he finds fault with it, and scoffs at it, and the Believer bears the blame of a betrayer. But now thou art standing on the frontiers; see thou let out nothing; not that the things spoken do not deserve telling, but the ear that hears does not deserve receiving. Thou thyself wast once a Catechumen, and then I told thee not what was coming. When thou hast by practice reached the height of what is taught thee, then wilt thou understand that the Catechumens are unworthy to hear them.

13. Ye who have been enrolled, are become the sons and

daughters of one Mother. When ye have entered in before (8.)
the hour of exorcising, let one of you speak what may promote godliness: and if any of your number be not present, seek for him. If thou wert called to a banquet, wouldest thou not wait for thy fellow-guest? If thou hadst a brother, wouldest thou not seek thy brother's good? Henceforth meddle not unprofitably with external matters; what the city hath done, or the town, or Prince, or Bishop, or Presbyter. Look upward, thy present hour hath need of that. *Be still,* σχολά-*and know that I am God* If thou seest the Believers minis- σατε, 1 e. *be disen-* tering without care, yet they enjoy security, they know what *gaged.* they have received, they are in possession of grace. But Ps 46, 10. thou art just now in the turn of the scale, to be received or not: thou must not copy those who are free from care, but cherish fear.

14. And when the Exorcism is made, until the rest who are exorcised be come, let the men stay with the men, and the women with the women. Here I would allude to Noah's ark; in which were Noah and his sons, and his wife and their wives; and though the ark was one, and the door was shut, yet had things been arranged suitably. And though the Church be shut, and all of you within it, yet let there be a distinction, of men with men and women with women. Let not the ground of your salvation becomes a means of destruction. Even though there be good ground for your sitting near each other, yet let passions be away. Then, let the men when sitting have a useful book; and let one read, and another listen · and if there be no book, let the one pray, and another speak something useful; and let the party of young women be so ordered, that they may either be singing or reading, but without noise, so that their lips may speak, but others may not hear. *For,* says the Apostle, *I suffer* 1 Cor. *not a woman to speak in the Church* . and let the married 14, 34. woman do the same; let her pray, moving her lips, her voice not sounding: that Samuel may come, and thy barren Vid. soul may bear *the salvation of God who hears prayer;* for 1 Sam. 1, this is the meaning of the word Samuel. 13. 17.

15. I will behold each man's earnestness; each woman's (9.) reverence. Let your mind be refined as by fire unto reverence, let your soul be forged as metal. Let the stubbornness

of unbelief feel the anvil, let the superfluous scales drop off as of iron, and what is pure remain: let the rust be rubbed off, and the true metal be left. May God at length show you that night, that darkness which shows like day [e], concerning which it is said, *The darkness shall not be darkened from thee, and the night shall be light as the day.* At that time to each man and woman among you may the gate of paradise be opened; may you then enjoy the fragrant waters, which contain Christ; may you then receive Christ's name, and the efficacious power of divine things! Even now, I beseech you, lift up the eye of your understanding; imagine the angelic choirs, and God the Lord of all sitting, and His Only-Begotten Son sitting with Him on His right-hand, and the Spirit with them present, and thrones and dominions doing service, and each man and woman among you receiving salvation. Even now let your ears ring with the sound: long for that glorious sound, which after your salvation, the angels shall chant over you, *Blessed are they whose iniquities have been forgiven, and whose sins have been covered;* when, like stars of the Church, you shall enter in it, bright in the outward man and radiant in your souls.

σωζόμενον. vid. Acts 2, 47. translated in our version, *such as should be saved.* (10.)

16. Great indeed is the Baptism which is offered you. It is a ransom to captives; the remission of offences; the death of sin; the regeneration of the soul; the garment of light; the holy seal indissoluble; the chariot to heaven; the luxury of paradise; a procuring of the kingdom; the gift of adoption. But a serpent by the wayside is watching the passengers; beware lest he bite thee with unbelief; he sees so many receiving salvation, and seeks to devour some of them. Thou art going to the Father of Spirits, but thou art going past that serpent; how then must thou pass him?

Eph. 6, 15.

Have *thy feet shod with the preparation of the gospel of peace;* that even if he bite, he may not hurt thee. Have faith indwelling, strong hope, a sandal of power, wherewith to pass the enemy, and enter the presence of thy Lord. Prepare thine own heart to receive doctrine, to have fellowship in holy mysteries. Pray more often, that God may

---

[e] On Easter Eve lights were kept burning in the Church all through the night. Vid. Nyssen Orat 1 in Resur. pp 867, 8. Euseb. vit. Const. iv. 22. Naz. Orat. 42. p. 676.

make thee worthy of the heavenly and immortal mysteries. Let neither day be without its work, nor night, but when sleep fails thine eyes, at once abandon thy thoughts to prayer. And shouldest thou find any shameful, any base imagination rising, reflect upon God's judgment, to remind thee of salvation; give up thy mind to sacred studies, that it may forget wicked things. If thou find any one saying to thee, And art thou going to the water, to be baptized in it? what, hath not the city baths of late? Be sure that it is the dragon of the sea, who is plotting this against thee; give no heed to the lips of him who speaketh, but to God who worketh. Guard thine own soul, that thou mayest escape the snare, that abiding in hope, thou mayest become the heir of everlasting salvation.

17. We indeed, as men, charge and teach these things; (11.) for you, see you make not our building *hay and stubble,* 1 Cor. 3, *and chaff;* that we may not *suffer loss, our work being* 12. 15. *burnt;* but make our work, *gold and silver and precious stones.* It is for me to speak, but thine to second me, and God's part to perfect. Let us nerve our minds; let us brace up our souls; let us prepare our hearts; the race is for our soul, our hope about eternal things. God is able, who knows your hearts, and perceives who is sincere, and who is a hypocrite, both to preserve the sincere and to give faith to the hypocrite; nay even to the unbeliever, if he give Him but his heart. And may He *blot out the handwriting that* Col. 2, 14. *is against you,* and grant you forgiveness of your former trespasses; may He plant you in the Church, and enlist you for Himself, putting on you the armour of righteousness! And may He fill you with the heavenly things of the New Testament, and give you the indelible seal of the σφραγίδα Holy Spirit, throughout all ages, in Christ Jesus our Lord, ἀνεξάλει- πτον. to whom be glory for ever and ever! Amen.

To the Reader.

These Catechetical Lectures thou mayest put into the hands of candidates for Baptism and of baptized believers, but by no means of Catechumens, nor of any others who are not Christians; as thou shalt answer to the Lord. And if thou takest a copy of them, write this in the beginning, as in the sight of the Lord.

LECTURE I.

ON THE PURPOSE OF MIND NECESSARY FOR BAPTISM.

ISAIAH i. 16—19.

Wash you, make you clean; put away the evil of your doings from before Mine eyes; cease to do evil; learn to do well; seek judgment, relieve the oppressed, judge the fatherless, plead for the widow. Come now, and let us reason together, saith the Lord: though your sins be as scarlet, they shall be as white as snow; though they be red like crimson, they shall be as wool. If ye be willing and obedient, ye shall eat the good of the land.

LECT. I.

Ezek. 18, 31.

Luke 15, 7.

Mat. 11, 28.

Prov. 5, 22.

Ps. 32, 1.

1. DISCIPLES of the New Testament, and communicants in the mysteries of Christ, as yet indeed by calling only, but ere long by grace, *make you a new heart, and a new spirit,* that there may be gladness among the inhabitants of heaven; for *if over one sinner that repenteth there is joy,* according to the Gospel, how much more shall the salvation of so many souls move the inhabitants of heaven to gladness? Ye have betaken yourselves to a good, a most glorious path; run with awe the race of godliness. Here is present, all-prepared to redeem you, the Only-begotten Son of God, and says, *Come unto Me, all ye that labour and are heavy laden, and I will refresh you.* You that have on you the harsh clothing of offences, who are *holden with the cords of your own sins,* listen to the Prophet's voice, saying, *Wash you, make you clean; put away the evil of your doings from before Mine eyes;* that the company of Angels may chant over you, *Blessed are they whose iniquities have been forgiven, and whose sins have been covered.* Ye who have just lighted the torches of faith, preserve them in your hands unquenched: that He, who once, on this most holy Calvary, opened Paradise to the robber on account of his faith, may grant to you to sing the bridal hymn.

2. Whoever here is a slave of sin, let him promptly prepare (2.) himself through faith, for the new birth into freedom and adoption: let him put off the miserable bondage of his sins, let him take on him the blessed bondage of the Lord, that so he may be counted worthy to inherit the kingdom of Heaven. *Put off the old man, which is corrupt according to* Eph. 4, *the deceitful lusts*, by means of the Confession; that *you* 22 24. Col. 3, *may put on the new man, which is renewed after the know-* 10. *ledge of Him that created him.* Get you *the earnest of the* 2 Cor. *Holy Spirit*, through faith, that you may be able to be 1, 22. received *into the everlasting habitations.* Come for the Luke 16, mystical Seal, that you may be well-known to the Master: be 9. ye numbered with the holy and spiritual flock of Christ, so τὴν μυ- στικὴν shall ye be set apart on His right hand, and inherit the life σφραγῖδα. which is prepared for you. For they who are yet encompassed with the rough covering of their sins, have their lot on His left hand, because they come not to the grace of God, which is given through Christ at the new birth of the Holy Bath; a new birth not of bodies, but the spiritual new birth of the soul. For our bodies are born by means of parents who are seen, but our souls are born again by means of faith; *for the Spirit bloweth where It listeth.* And then it is given John 3, 8. thee to hear, if thou be worthy, *Well done, thou good and* Mat. 25, *faithful servant*, when thy conscience is found clean from 21. hypocrisy.

3. For if there be any one here who thinks to tempt grace, (3.) he deceives himself, and knows not its power. Keep thy soul free from hypocrisy, O man, by reason of Him *who searcheth hearts and reins*. for as those who make a levy for war inquire into the ages and the make of their recruits, so also doth the Lord, enlisting souls, examine into their purpose of mind. If any has a secret hypocrisy, He rejects that man as unfit for the true service: but if He find a man worthy, to him He gives grace readily. He gives not holy things to dogs; but when He discerns the good conscience, there He gives that Seal of salvation, that wondrous Seal, which devils tremble at, and Angels recognize: that the one may be scared away and flee, and the others may attend on it, as kindred to themselves. From those then who receive this spiritual or saving Seal, is required a disposition of mind kindred to it: for as a

12   *Baptism transplants into an invisible state.*

LECT. I.   writing-reed or a dart has need of one to use it, so does grace require believing minds.

(4.)   4. Such thou art receiving, no perishable instrument, but a spiritual. Henceforth thou art planted in the paradise which the mind sees. Thou receivest a new name, which before thou hadst not: before thou wast a Catechumen, now thou wilt be a Believer. Henceforth thou art transplanted among the invisible olive-trees, being grafted from the wild into the fruitful, from sins into righteousness, from pollution into purity. Thou hast communion in the Holy Vine: if then thou abide in the vine, thou shalt increase as a fruitful branch; if thou abide not, thou shalt be utterly consumed by the fire. Let us then bear fruit, as is worthy; God forbid that in us should be fulfilled what was done to the barren fig-tree, or that Jesus coming should even now curse us for our barrenness. Rather, may all be able to say, *I am like a green olive-tree in the house of God; my trust is in the tender mercy of God for ever and ever,* an olive-tree not meeting the senses, but the mind, and full of light; as then it is His part to plant and to water, so it is thine to bear fruit: it is God's to grant grace, thine to receive and preserve. Despise not the gift, because it is given freely, but when thou hast received it, devoutly treasure it.

τὸν νοη- τὸν παρά- δεισον.

Ps. 52, 10.

(5.)   5. The present is the season of Confession: confess therefore what thou hast done, whether in word, or in deed; whether in the day, or in the night; confess *in a time accepted, and in the day of salvation* receive the heavenly treasure. Devote thy time to the Exorcisms; be constant at the Catechisings, and store up in memory the matter of them, for they are spoken, not to the ears only, but that faith may stamp them on the mind; wipe out from thee every care of earth; thou art running for thy soul. Thou art utterly abandoning the things of the world; what thou art abandoning is little, what the Lord is giving is great. Forsake things present, have faith in things to come. Hast thou run so many circles of the year, fruitlessly devoted to the world, and wilt thou not for forty days, devote thyself to prayer, for thy soul's sake? *Be still, and know that I am God,* saith the Scripture. Give over talking many idle words, neither backbite, nor lend a willing ear to backbiters, rather be prompt to

2 Cor. 6, 2.

σχολά- ζετε, *be disengaged* Ps. 46, 1.

prayer. Show by ascetic exercises that thine heart is nerved. Cleanse thy vessel, that thou mayest receive the gift more abundant: for remission of sins is given equally to all: but the communication of the Holy Ghost is bestowed according to each man's faith. If thou hast laboured little, thou shalt receive little: but if thou has wrought much, ample is the hire: thou runnest for thyself: see to thine own interest.

6. If thou hast aught against any man, forgive it: thou comest here to receive forgiveness of offences; thou art bound in turn to pardon the offender; else with what face wilt thou say to the Lord, *Forgive me my many offences,* while thou thyself hast not remitted even the small offence of thy fellow-servant? Attend diligently at Church: not only now, when thy attendance is required by the Ministers, but also after thou hast received the gift: for if before it was good to do it, surely it must be good after the bestowal. If before thou wast grafted in, it was a safe course to be watered and tended, it is much more right after the planting. Wrestle for thine own soul, especially in days like these; nourish thy soul with sacred readings. For the Lord hath prepared for thee a spiritual table; therefore do thou also say, after the Psalmist, *The Lord is my shepherd, therefore can I lack nothing; He shall feed me in a green pasture, and lead me forth beside the waters of comfort; He shall convert my soul;* that Angels may share your joy, and Christ Himself the great High Priest, accepting your holy resolve and offering you one and all to the Father, may say, *Behold I, and the children whom God hath given Me.* May God Himself keep you all, well-pleasing in His sight. To whom be glory and power everlasting. Amen.

(6.)

Mat. 18, 23—35 εἰς τὰς συνάξεις.

Ps 23, 1—3.

Heb. 2, 13.

LECTURE II.

ON THE POWER OF REPENTANCE FOR THE REMISSION OF SIN.

Ezekiel xviii. 20—23.

The righteousness of the righteous shall be upon him, and the wickedness of the wicked shall be upon him. But if the wicked will turn from all his sins that he hath committed, and keep all My statutes, and do that which is lawful and right, he shall surely live, he shall not die. All his transgressions that he hath committed, they shall not be mentioned unto him · in his righteousness that he hath done he shall live. Have I any pleasure at all that the wicked should die? saith the Lord God: and not that he should return from his ways, and live?

LECT. II.

αυτεξού-σιον. προαιρέ-σεως.

Jer. 2, 21.

Eccles. 7, 29.

Eph. 2, 10.

1. SIN is a fearful thing, and unrighteousness is the sorest ailment of the soul, secretly sapping its sinews, and exposing it to eternal fire; a self-chosen evil, the offspring of a man's set purpose of mind. For that of our own purpose we sin, the Prophet says plainly in one place. *I planted thee a noble vine, wholly a right seed: how then art thou turned into the degenerate plant of a strange vine unto Me?* The planting is good, the fruit evil: and that evil is from our purpose of mind. The planter is blameless, but the vine shall be burnt with fire: for it was planted for good, yet hath of its own purpose borne fruit to evil. *For God*, according to the Preacher, *hath made man upright; but they have sought out many inventions.* And the Apostle says, *We are His workmanship, created unto good works.* The Creator then, being good, created for good works: but the creature, of its own set purpose, turned to wickedness. Sin, then, is a fearful evil, as was said, but not an incurable one; fearful to him who clings to it, but quite admitting of a cure when a man through penitence puts it off. For suppose a man holding fire in his

hand: while he holds the live coal, he is certainly on fire; but were he to put it away, he would also rid himself of that which was burning him. And if any think that while sinning, he is not on fire, to him saith the Scripture, *Can a man take* Prov. 6, *fire in his bosom, and his clothes not be burned?* For sin 27. burns the sinews of the soul.

2. But some one will say, What can sin be? Is it a living (2.) thing—an angel—an evil spirit? What is this which works in us? It is no foe from without, O man, wrestling against thee: but a shoot of evil taking its increase from thyself. *Let thine eyes look right on,* and lust does not exist; keep Prov. 4, thine own and take not another's, and a stop is put to 25. robbery; remember the Judgment, and neither fornication, nor adultery, nor murder, nor any unrighteousness shall prevail in thee. But when thou forgettest God, forthwith thou beginnest to devise wickedness, and to accomplish unrighteousness.

3. However, nature is not the sole cause of this evil; there is another, who miserably prompts to it, the devil. He prompts all, yet he prevails only over those who listen to him. Therefore saith the Preacher, *If a spirit of the powerful rise up* Eccles. *against thee, leave not thy place.* Shut thy door, and keep 10, 4. him far from thee, and he shall not hurt thee. But if thou indulgently admit the thought of lust, through thine imaginations, it will strike its roots into thee, and enthral thy mind, and drag thee down into a pit of evils. But perhaps thou sayest, I am a Believer; lust does not gain the ascendant over me, even though my mind dwells on the objects of it: knowest thou not that even a rock is cleft at length by a root which for a long while adheres to it? Admit not the seed, for it will break in pieces thy faith: root out the mischief, ere it blossom, lest by being idle at the beginning, thou have the trouble of axes and fire afterwards. When thine eyes first ail, attend to them in time, lest after thou art blinded thou begin to seek the physician.

4. The devil then is the chief author of sin, and the parent (3.) of evils; and this hath the Lord said, not I: *The devil sinneth* 1 John *from the beginning;* before him sinned no one. But he sinned, 3, 8. not as having received by necessity of nature the principle of sin; (else the blame of sin returns to Him who thus framed

him;) but having been framed good, he became a devil from his own purpose of mind, and received his name from his conduct. For being an Archangel, he was called devil, or slanderer, from his slandering; and from a good servant of God, he became Satan fitly so named; for Satan means an Adversary. These doctrines are not mine, but the inspired prophet Ezekiel's. For he, taking up a lamentation against him, says, *Thou sealest up the sun, full of wisdom, and perfect in beauty: thou hast been in Eden, the garden of God;* and soon after, *Thou wast perfect in thy ways, from the day that thou wast created, till iniquity was found in thee.* Very rightly hath he said, *was found in thee;* for it was not brought in from without, but thou thyself didst beget evil. And the reason he assigns afterwards: *thine heart was lifted up, because of thy beauty; I will cast thee as profane out of the mountain of God, I will cast thee to the ground.* Parallel to this, is what the Lord says in the Gospel, *I beheld Satan as lightning fallen from heaven.* Thou seest the harmony of the Old Testament with the New. He, on his falling, drew many away with him. He puts lusts into those who listen to him: from him is adultery, fornication, and all evil: through him our forefather Adam was cast out, and exchanged a paradise of wonderful and spontaneous fruits, for this earth with its thorns and thistles.

(4.)   5. What then? some one will say. We have been seduced and are lost; is there no chance of salvation? We have fallen; cannot we rise? We have been blinded; cannot we recover our sight? We have been crippled; cannot our feet become straight again? In a word, we are dead; is there no resurrection? Shall not He, O Man, who woke Lazarus, a corpse of four days, which stank, shall not He much more easily raise up thee, a living man? He who shed His precious blood for us, the same shall rescue us from sin. Let us not give sentence against ourselves, brethren; let us not abandon our case as hopeless: not to believe there is hope in penitence, is dreadful indeed. For he who is without expectation of salvation, spares not to increase the evil; but he who hopes for a cure, is easily induced to spare himself. Thus the robber who expects no mercy runs into recklessness; but if he hopes for pardon, often betakes himself to repentance. Nay does the serpent strip himself of old age, and shall not we cast the slough of wickedness? Does thorny ground by good tillage become fruitful, and is salvation to us irrecoverable? Nature then admits of salvation; all that is wanting is the purpose of mind

6. God is loving to man, and that not a little. For say (5.) not, "I have committed whoredom and adultery: fearful things have been done by me, nor once only but often; will He forgive, will He forget?" Hear what the Psalmist says; *O how plentiful is Thy goodness, O Lord.* Thy accumulated sins surpass not the multitude of the mercies of God; thy wounds baffle not the skill of the chief Physician. Only give thyself to Him in faith: tell the Physician thine ailment; say thou also as David did; *I said, I will confess my sins unto the Lord:* and what he says next shall also be fulfilled in thee; *And so Thou forgavest the wickedness of my sin.* [Ps. 31, 20.] [Ps 32, 5.]

7. Wouldest thou see the loving-kindness of God, O thou that art lately come to the Catechising? wouldest thou see the loving-kindness of God, and the abundance of His long-suffering? Hear thou concerning Adam. Adam disobeyed, the first whom God created; might He not at once have visited him with death? But see what the Lord does, in His great love towards man: though He casts him out of Paradise, his sin making him unfit to continue there, yet He places him *opposite to Paradise,* that seeing what he had forfeited, and what a downfall he had suffered, he thenceforth might be saved by repentance. Cain, the first born man, became a fratricide, a deviser of evils, the cause of murders, and the first who envied; yet when he had slain his brother, to what is he doomed? *a fugitive and a vagabond shalt thou be in the earth.* How great the sin, how light the doom! [κατέναν- τι τοῦ παραδεί- σου Gen 3, 24 Septuag. vers.] [Gen. 4, 12.]

8. This then in very deed is loving-kindness in God, yet it is small compared with what follows: for consider, I pray, the history of Noe. The giants sinned, and lawlessness was there lavishly poured out upon the earth; and in consequence the deluge was ordained to come upon it. In his five hundredth year God puts forth the threat, and in his six hundredth He brought the deluge on the earth. Seest thou

c

the breadth of God's loving-kindness, extending over the space of a hundred years? what He did then after the hundred years, could He not have done at once? but on purpose did He extend it, to give room for repentance. Seest thou the goodness of God? And had those men repented, they would not have come short of His loving-kindness.

(6.) 9. Let us proceed to others, who have been saved by repentance. Perchance some among the women will say, "I have committed whoredom and adultery, I have defiled my body with excesses; is there salvation?" Cast thine eyes, O woman, to Rahab, and do thou also expect salvation; for if she who openly and publicly committed whoredom was saved through repentance, shall not she, who has committed one such act before the gift of grace, be saved through penitence and by fastings? For enquire how she was saved: this only said she, *The Lord your God, He is God in heaven above, and in earth beneath.* Your God, for she dared not call Him her own, on account of her unchastity. And if thou wouldest receive a written witness that she was saved, thou hast it recorded in the Psalms, *I will think upon Rahab and Babylon with them that know me* [a]. Oh the great loving-mercy of God, which makes mention even of harlots in the Scriptures: and not simply *I will think upon Rahab and Babylon*, but with this added, *with them that know me*. On men therefore, and likewise on women, is salvation, viz. that which is secured to us through repentance.

10. And though the people sin as one body, it does not surpass God's loving-kindness. The people made a calf, yet did not God give over His loving-kindness. Men denied God, but God denied not Himself. *These are thy gods, O Israel*, they said; yet again, as was His wont, *The God of Israel became their Saviour.* And not only did the people sin, but Aaron too the high-priest. For it is Moses who says, *And upon Aaron came the wrath of the Lord; and I entreated,*

---

[a] In the Psalm referred to, Rahab stands for Egypt. Vid Ps 89, 10 Isai. 51, 9 S. Jerome, in Ps 87, 4 considers Rahab a type of the Gentile Church called out of Jericho, the world Egypt in the Psalm is a type of the same. Penitent Rahab then may as naturally stand for a type of penitent Egypt, as the abandoned woman in the Revelations for impenitent Babylon And as what is said of Hagar in Gen. 21, 10. is meant of Jerusalem, so Rahab may really be named in this Psalm, yet Egypt meant as its scope, and beyond that the Gentile Church.

Instance of the Israelites and Aaron in making the golden calf. 19

he says, *for him,* and God forgave him. What then? Did Moses, entreating for a high-priest who had sinned, prevail with the Lord, and does not Jesus, the Only-begotten, when He entreats for us, prevail with God? And did He admit Aaron, in spite of his fall, to the high-priesthood, and will He obstruct thy entrance to salvation who art come from the Gentiles? Repent, O man, henceforth thyself, and the gift shall not be withheld thee. Present thy conduct unrebukable before Him henceforward: for God is in very truth loving to man, nor can the whole race of man worthily tell out His loving-kindness. No, not if all the tongues of men were to come together, could they even thus unfold some part of His loving-kindness. For we declare some part of what is written concerning His loving-kindness to men: but we know not how much He forgave to Angels: for them also did He forgive [b], since One only is sinless, Jesus, who purgeth our sins;—but of these enough.

11. If thou wilt, I will set before thee additional precedents (7.) respecting our state. Let us come to the blessed David, and take him for an example of repentance. He fell, that highly gifted man. Walking in the evening-tide on the house-top

---

[b] Very little having been authoritatively delivered to the Apostles on the subject of the Angels, what was believed or surmised in the early Church seems to have been gathered from various sources, trustworthy and not, and of the latter especially Platonism The proof that the sources in question were not apostolic, is the discordance or uncertainty of the opinions themselves The Fathers indeed bear witness concordantly to the truth, that God alone is singly and absolutely perfect and above all judgment, using it as an argument for the divinity of the Son and the Holy Ghost, that they too are sinless or beyond judgment. (vid Clem Pædag. 1 2. Origen in Cant. Hom. 3. fin Theodor in Num 9 Ambros de Sp S iii. 18. n. 132, &c. Hieron in Pelag 3 p 203 col 1 Athan.Orat.in Arian ii 6 Ambros in Fid v 11. n 140, 141. Cyril Alex Thesaur. 21. They built this doctrine on such passages of Scripture as Job 4, 18 Rev 2 and 3 (which they considered to imply the truth of the literal sense in the truth of the figurative, which was primarily and directly intended.) Col. 1, 20. Eph. 3, 10. Acts 17, 31 &c. Some of the Fathers considered, that, besides the devil and his angels, who were beyond grace, there were orders of angels still on their trial, or who were, or had been, responsible for more or less of sin, or in danger of sin, and within the reach of mercy, or who on their trial had sinned more or less, and been forgiven, as Cyril seems here to hold (vid. Nyss. vol ii p 644 Hieron. in Eph. 4, 16 Ambrosiast in Eph 3, 10. Origen. Tom 13, 28 in Luc Hom. 35 Ignat ad Smyrn. 6. Nazianz. Carm p 169.) Such, for instance, (as they considered,) were the tutelary angels of countries, places, or persons. Origen in Num. Hom. 20 3. Hieron. in Mich 6. 1. And such "the Sons of God," who were seduced in the interval between the creation and the flood. (Justin. Apol. ii. 5 Athenag Apol. 24. Iren. iv. 16. Clem Strom v. p. 550 Tertul. de Idolatr. 9 Origen. in Cels. Ambros de Noe, iv 8 9 Nazianz. Carm p. 64) Origen, and even Gregory Nyssen, are accused of admitting the restoration of the author of evil Vid. Diss. Bened. in Cyril, iii. 5.

after his sleep, he looked unguardedly, and was moved by human passion. His sin was completed; but in it perished not that nobleness of mind which confesses a transgression. Nathan the prophet came, swiftly, to detect and to heal his wound. *The Lord is wroth,* he says, *and thou hast sinned.* So spoke the subject to him who had the kingdom; yet the king, though in purple clad, did not take it ill, as regarding not the speaker, but. Him that sent him. He was not blinded by the military circle which stood about him; for his mind discerned the Lord's angelical host, and as seeing the Invisible, he submitted to the anguish, replying to his visitor, or rather through him to Him who sent him, *I have sinned against the Lord.* Thou seest how a king could be humble-minded, how he could make confession. Had it been brought home to him by any one? Were many privy to the matter? The matter was done quickly, and forthwith the Prophet came an accuser, and the sinner acknowledges the crime. And according to the frankness of his confession was the speed of his cure, for the prophet Nathan who had threatened him, says straightway, *And the Lord hath put away thy sin.* Thou seest how very quick was the relenting of the God of loving-kindness. Yet he says, *Thou hast given great occasion to the enemies of the Lord to blaspheme.* For though on account of thy righteousness thou hadst many foes, yet thy self-command was thy protection; but now that thou hast let go thy best weapon, thy foes, who were standing ready, are risen up against thee. The Prophet then thus comforted him.

12. But holy David, for all he heard it said, *The Lord hath put away thy sin,* shrunk not from penitence, king though he was: but put on sackcloth for purple, and for his gilded throne sat down, a king, in ashes on the ground; not only sat but fed on ashes, (as he saith himself, *I have eaten ashes as it were bread,*) and wasted with tears his lustful eye. *Every night,* he says, *wash I my bed and water my couch with my tears.* When his lords urged him to eat bread, he would not: for seven whole days he prolonged his fast. If a king thus made confession, oughtest not thou a private man to make confession? And after Absalom's rebellion, though he had many roads for escaping, he chose to flee by the Mount of Olives, all but invoking mentally the Redeemer who

should thence ascend to heaven. And when Shimei cursed 2 Sam. him bitterly, he said, *Let him alone;* for he knew that he 16, 10 who forgiveth, shall be forgiven. 11

13. Thou seest how excellent it is to confess; thou seest (8.) that to the penitent there is salvation. Solomon also fell; but what saith he? *Afterwards I repented*^c. Though Ahab, Prov. king of Samaria, was a most abandoned idolater, a monster, 24, 32. the murderer of prophets, a stranger to godliness, the coveter vers. of other men's fields and vineyards, yet when the prophet Elias came to him after he had slain Naboth through Jezebel, and only threatened him, he rent his clothes and put on sackcloth; and what says the merciful God to Elias? *Seest thou* 1 Kings *how Ahab humbleth himself before Me?* as if, almost, He would 21, 29. persuade the fiery temper of the prophet to condescend to the penitent: for *I will not bring,* He saith, *the evil in his days.* Thus, though Ahab on his pardon was not about to leave his evil courses, the God of pardon pardoned him;—not as ignorant of the future, but bestowing on the penitence of the moment its corresponding pardon: for a just judge suitably answers each case as it arises.

14. Again, as Jeroboam stood sacrificing to idols on the (9.) altar, his hand withered, when he bade seize the Prophet who denounced him. On this experience of his power, he says, *Entreat the face of the Lord thy God;* and for this 1 Kings word his hand was restored. If the Prophet healed Jero- 13, 6. boam, has not Christ healing power to deliver thee from thy sins? Manasses, again, was most extravagant in his crimes, who sawed asunder Esaias, and was polluted with idolatries of every kind, and filled Jerusalem with innocent blood: yet, when he was led captive to Babylon, he converted his afflictions into a healing course of penitence: for Scripture says, that Manasses *humbled himself greatly before the God of his* 2 Chron. *fathers, and prayed to Him; and He was entreated of him,* 33, 12. *and heard his supplications, and brought him again into his* 13. *kingdom.* If he who sawed a Prophet in sunder, was saved through penitence, mayest not thou be saved, who hast not done ought so great.

^c The following Fathers agree with Cyril in considering that Solomon repented, Hilar in Ps. 52. n 12. Ambros. Apol. David. 3. n. 13. Hieron. Ep. 85 init. vid also in Eccles. 1, 12 The opposite opinion is held by others, e. g apparently by Aug. in Ps. 126. n. 2. Basil. Ep. 42 n. 2.

15. Beware lest thou rashly mistrust its power; wouldest thou know how great force it hath? wouldest thou know this strong weapon of salvation, and learn what strength Confession hath? An hundred and eighty-five thousand enemies did Hezekias turn to flight through Confession. Yet great as this really is, it is but trifling compared with what is still to be told. Through repentance, the same king recalled a Divine decree which had already gone forth. For when he was sick, Esaias said to him, *Set thy house in order; for thou shalt die, and not live.* What was there to expect more? what remaining hope of life, when the Prophet said, *For thou shalt die?* Yet Ezekias did not stop from penitence; for remembering what was written, *For turning away and sighing thou shalt be saved,* he turned away to the wall, and lifting his thoughts from his bed heavenwards, (for no thickness of walls hinder prayers devoutly offered up,) he said, " Lord, remember me: for it is sufficient for my cure that Thou remember me. Thou art not controlled by times, but Thou Thyself givest law to life; for not on our nativity, and on stars in conjunction, depends our life, as some idly talk; but of life and its duration Thou Thyself art the Lawgiver, according to Thy will." And thus he, who through the Prophet's sentence despaired of life, received an addition of fifteen years, the sun, in sign of it, tracing his course back. Now the sun turned back for Ezekias; for Christ, it was eclipsed; not retracing his steps, but suffering eclipse, and thereby shewing the difference of the two, Ezekias and Jesus. Ezekias prevailed to the cancelling of a sentence of God; and will not Jesus vouchsafe His free gift, the forgiveness of sins? Turn away, and bewail thyself, shut to thy door, and pray Him to forgive thee, and remove from around thee the burning fires; for Confession[d] has strength to quench even fire; has strength to tame even lions.

---

[d] The ecclesiastical word ἐξομολόγησις, here translated Confession, means properly a declaration in God's presence of the facts of religion of whatever kind, with relation to God or man; and is thus contrasted with Prayer, which contemplates objects not realized as yet Praise, thanksgiving, profession of our faith, are parts of it, as well as confession of sin Psalms, Hymns, Creeds, are Confessions 'Εξομολογεῖσθε and Contitemini, are the words used respectively in the Septuagint and Vulgate versions of the Psalms, for "Praise," and "Give thanks to the Lord." Hence S Cyril here calls the Song of the Three Children, and the meditations of Daniel in the lions' den, Confessions; whereas, grant-

16. But if thou disbelieve, consider what befel Hananiah and the rest. What fountains did they open? How many waterpots had quenched a flame, which rose to forty-nine cubits? But wherever the flame exceeded ever so little, there faith gushed out like a river, and there they uttered a spell against their sufferings, saying, *Just art Thou, O Lord, over all things which Thou hast done towards us*[e] : *for we have sinned, and broke Thy commandments.* And penitence destroyed the flames. If thou disbelieve that it can quench the fire of hell, learn it from the history of Hananiah. But some quick hearer will say, "Them God rescued justly; because they would not commit idolatry, God gave them this power." Since this has been suggested, I will proceed to one more example of penitence.

<small>(11.) Shadrach, Meshach, and Abednego. Dan 1, 6. 7. Song of Three Children, 4. &c.</small>

17. What thinkest thou of Nebuchadonosor? Hast thou not heard from the Scriptures that he was bloodthirsty, savage, having a lion's mind? hast thou not heard how he disinterred the bones of the kings? how he led the people into captivity? how he blinded the eyes of the reigning prince, first giving him to see the slaughter of his children? Hast thou not heard that he broke to pieces the cherubim, not the invisible—no, suppose it not, O man—but the carved cherubim; and that mercy-seat, from which God used to speak audibly? Nebuchadonosor trampled down the veil of holiness: he carried off the censer to a temple of idols; he seized on all the offerings; and burned down the Temple to its foundations? What multiplied punishments did he deserve for slaying kings, setting fire to holy things, leading captive the chosen people, and placing the sacred vessels within idol temples? Was he not worthy of ten thousand deaths?

18. Such was the greatness of his evil deeds; now turn to the loving-kindness of God. He was turned into a wild beast; he abode in the wilderness, he was scourged that he might be saved. He had claws like a lion, for he made the saints his prey; he had a lion's mane, for he was *a ramping and a roaring lion.* He ate grass as an ox; for he was as cattle not knowing Him who had given him the kingdom.

<small>Dan. 4. Ps. 22, 13.</small>

<small>ing they were confessions of "the sin of their people," (Song, 5—10. Dan. 9, 20) still they were much more.
[e] i.e. *Towards Thy people Israel.*</small>

His body was bathed with the dew, because he had already seen the fire quenched by dew, and believed not. And what happened? After these things, he saith, *I Nebuchadnezzar lifted up mine eyes unto heaven, and I blessed the Most High, and I praised and honoured Him that liveth for ever.* When, therefore, he perceived the Most High, and offered up sounds of thanksgiving to God, and came to feel grief for what he had done, and learnt his own weakness, then God restored to him the honour of the kingdom.

Lect. II
Song 27.
Dan. 4, 32.

(12.) 19. What then? Hath He given Nebuchadonosor, after such acts, pardon and the kingdom, on his confession, and shall He not give to thee on repenting the forgiveness of sins, and the kingdom of heaven, if thy life be in accordance? The Lord is loving to men, and swift to pardon, slow to vengeance; let no one then despair of his own salvation. Peter, the chiefest and first of the Apostles, before a little maid thrice denied the Lord; but when remorse touched him he wept bitterly; and to weep shews a heartfelt penitence. Wherefore, not only received he forgiveness for the denial, but was spared his Apostolic dignity.

20. Having then, brethren, many ensamples of men who have sinned, and repented, and been saved, do ye also heartily make your confession to the Lord: that ye may both receive the pardon of your past sins, and be counted worthy of the heavenly gift, and inherit the heavenly kingdom with all the Saints in Christ Jesus; to whom is the glory for ever and ever. Amen.

LECTURE III.

ON HOLY BAPTISM.

ROMANS vi. 3, 4.

Know ye not, that so many of us as were baptized into Jesus Christ, were baptized into His death ? Therefore we are buried with Him by Baptism into death, that like as Christ was raised up from the dead by the glory of the Father, even so we also should walk in newness of life.

Let the heavens rejoice, and let the earth be glad, for those who are to be sprinkled with hyssop; to be cleansed with the invisible hyssop, by His power, who at His passion received the hyssop and the reed. Let the Heavenly Powers rejoice, and let the souls now to be joined to their Invisible Spouse, get ready. For there is *the voice of one crying in the wilderness, Make ready the way of the Lord.* For this is no light matter, no ordinary and chance union according to the flesh: but the All-searching Spirit's election that is of faith. For the world's espousals and arrangements are not always made with judgment; but wealth or beauty forthwith attracts the bridegroom; here it is not beauty of person, but the soul's clear conscience, not the condemned mammon, but the soul rich in seriousness. [Ps 96, 11.] [Is 40, 3.] [1 Cor 11, 10.]

2. Yield then, O ye children of righteousness, to John's persuasion, exhorting you, and saying, *Make straight the way of the Lord.* Remove all blocks and stumbling-stones, that ye may hold straight on unto life eternal. Make ready the chambers of the soul, purifying them through faith unfeigned, for the reception of the Holy Ghost. Begin to wash your robes through penitence, that when summoned to the bride-chamber ye may be found clean. For the Bridegroom invites indeed all without conditions, because His grace is lavish, and the voice of His loud-sounding Heralds brings [John 1, 23.]

26 *The Water of Baptism has in it a power of cleansing the soul.*

LECT. III.
Matt. 22, 12.
Matt. 25, 21.
Cant. 1, 4.
Is. 61, 10 Sept
Eph 5, 27.

together all; but ever afterwards He is separating between those who have come in to the figurative marriage-feast. O may none of those now enrolled hear those words, *Friend, how camest thou in hither, not having a wedding-garment?* But may you all hear it said, *Well done, good and faithful servant; thou hast been faithful over a few things; I will make thee ruler over many things; enter thou into the joy of thy Lord.* Hitherto thou hast stood without the gate; may you all be able to say, *The King hath brought me into His chambers. My soul shall be joyful in my God, for He hath clothed me with the garments of salvation, He hath covered me with the robe of righteousness, as a bridegroom decketh himself with ornaments, and as a bride adorneth herself with her jewels:* so that all your souls may be found *not having spot, or wrinkle, or any such thing.* I say not, before you have received the gift; (if so, why should you be now called to the remission of sins?) but so that, on its being given, your conscience being found blameless, may keep pace with it.

(2.)   3. This is in truth a serious matter, brethren, and you must approach it solemnly. You are, each of you, on the point of being presented to God, before innumerable hosts of Angels: the Holy Ghost is on the point of setting a seal on your souls · ye are coming for enlistment under the Great King. Make ready therefore; prepare, not by wearing robes of shining whiteness, but arraying the soul with the devoutness of a clear conscience. Regard the Sacred Laver not as simple water; regard rather the spiritual grace given with the water. For as the sacrifices at the altars, being by nature without meaning, by invocation of the idols become polluted, so contrariwise, plain water, after the invocation of the Holy Ghost, and of Christ, and of the Father, gains a sanctifying power.

4. For whereas man's nature is twofold, soul and body, twofold also is his cleansing; the spiritual for the spiritual, the material for his body. The water cleanses his body, the

Heb. 10, 22.

Spirit seals his soul: that being by the Spirit *sprinkled in heart, and washed in body with pure water, we may draw near to God.* Now then that thou art to descend into the waters, consider not the bare element; look for its saving power by the operation of the Holy Ghost; for without the two thou canst not be made perfect. This is not my word, but the Lord Jesus Christ's, who has the power to do it; He saith, *Except a man be born again,* and he enlarges, *of water* Joh. 3, 3. *and of the Spirit, he cannot enter into the kingdom of God.* Neither he who is baptized with water, without the privilege of the Spirit, hath the gift entire; nor be he ever so virtuous in his deeds, shall he enter into the kingdom of heaven, except with the seal vouchsafed through water. A bold word, but it is not mine; Jesus hath uttered it; and here is the proof of it from Holy Scripture. Cornelius was a just man; Acts 10. he was honoured with visions of Angels; he had raised his prayers and alms in the sight of God, as a goodly monument in the heavens. Peter came, and the Spirit was poured on them that believed, and they spake with other tongues, and prophesied. Yet after the gift of the Spirit, the Scripture saith, that Peter commanded them to be baptized in the name of Jesus Christ: that the soul having been regenerated through their faith, the body also, by means of the water, might share the gift [a].

5. And if any one is anxious to know, why the gift is given through water and not through some other element, let him take up Holy Scripture, and he shall learn. For water is a noble thing, and, of the world's four visible elements, the most beautiful. Heaven is the abode of Angels, and the heavens are of the waters: earth is the place of men, and the earth is of the waters: and before all the six days fashioning of creation, the Spirit of God moved on the face of the waters. Gen 1, 2. Water was the beginning of the world: the Jordan was the beginning of the Gospel preaching. Rescue from Pharaoh came to Israel through the sea: rescue from sins to the world through *the Laver of water of the word* of God. Where Eph. 5, 26. there is a covenant with any, there also is water: after the flood, a covenant was made with Noe: a covenant with Israel from Mount Sina; but *with water, and scarlet wool, and* Heb. 9, *hyssop.* Elias is received up, but not without water: for first 19. he crosses Jordan, then horses carry him to heaven. The highpriest first bathes, and then burns incense: for Aaron first,

---

[a] S Cyril considers that Cornelius and his friends were regenerated, as the Apostles were, apart from Baptism, as August. Serm. 269 n 2. and Chrysost. in Act. Apost. Hom. 25. seem to do.

bathed, and then was made high-priest; for how might he intercede for the rest, who had not yet been cleansed by water? Moreover the Laver, set apart within the Tabernacle, was an emblem of Baptism.

(3.) 6. Baptism is the end of the Old Testament, and the beginning of the New. For John who began it, than whom was not one greater among those born of women, was the end of the Prophets; for *all the Law and the Prophets were until John.* Moreover, he was the first-fruits of the Gospel-state, for it is said, *The beginning of the Gospel of Jesus Christ, &c.* and then, *John was in the desert baptizing.* You may instance indeed Elias the Tishbite, who was taken to heaven, yet is not greater than John. Enoch was translated, yet he is not greater than John. Moses was the greatest law-giver, and the Prophets are all wonderful men, yet not greater than John. I do not venture to compare prophet with prophet: but their Master and ours, the Lord Jesus hath declared; *Among those that are born of women, there hath not risen a greater than John.* Not "among those born of virgins," but *born of women.* The comparison is between the chief servant, and his fellow-servants: for the Son's pre-eminence and grace over the household is beyond all comparison. Seest thou how great a man God hath chosen to be the first minister of this grace? a man possession-less and solitary, yet not a misanthrope; eating locusts, and pluming his soul for heaven; feasting on honey, and speaking what is sweeter and more wholesome; clad in camel's hair, and shewing in himself what an ascetic's life should be: who also while yet borne in his mother's womb, was sanctified by the Holy Ghost. Jeremiah was sanctified, but he prophesied not in the womb: only John, while yet unborn, leaped for joy: and though he saw not with the eyes of the flesh, knew his Master by the Spirit: for since great was the grace of Baptism, great must needs be its minister.

(4.) 7. He began to baptize in Jordan, and *all Jerusalem went out to him*, enjoying the first-fruits of Baptism: for the prerogative in all good things was in Jerusalem. But, men of Jerusalem, observe how they that went out were baptized of him; *confessing their sins*, saith he. First they shewed their wounds, then he applied the remedies, and gave to them that believed, redemption from eternal fire [b]. And if thou wouldest be persuaded of this, that the Baptism of John is redemption from the peril of fire, hear thou him saying, *Ye generation of vipers, who hath warned you to flee from the wrath to come?* Be thou then no longer a viper, he saith, but as thou hast been one of the brood, put off thy former sinful self. And as the snake is wont to delve into some corner to cast away his age, and rubbing off his old slough, is henceforth young in body; so thou too, saith he, force thee through the narrow and strait gate: and roughly handling thee with fasting, strip thee of thy ruin; put off the old man with his deeds, and say in the words of the Canticles, *I have put off my coat, how shall I put it on?* Matt. 3, 7.
Prov. 16, 26. Sept.
Cant. 5, 3.

But perhaps there is some one among you, a hypocrite, a man-pleaser, professing religion, but not believing from his heart: having the hypocrisy of Simon Magus, approaching not to partake of grace, but busily to pry into what is given. Let this one also hear from John, *And now also the axe is laid unto the root of the trees, therefore every tree which bringeth not forth good fruit, is hewn down, and cast into the fire.* The Judge cannot be worked upon; so put away hypocrisy. Matt. 3, 10.
ἀδυσώ-πητος.

8. What then oughtest thou to do? and what are the fruits of repentance? *He that hath two coats, let him impart to him that hath none.* Trustworthy was the teacher, as being the first to do what he taught; he had no shame in speaking, whose tongue was not checked by conscience. *And he that hath meat, let him do likewise.* Wouldest thou enjoy the grace of the Holy Ghost, yet countest the poor unworthy of earthly meats? Seekest thou great things, yet givest not of small?—Though thou be a publican, though a fornicator, yet hope for salvation; *The publicans and the harlots go into the kingdom of God before you:* and Paul witnesseth the same, saying, *Neither fornicators, nor idolaters, nor any of this sort, shall inherit the kingdom of God; and such were some of you; but ye are washed, but ye are sanctified.* He saith not, *such are some of you,* but *such were some of you.* (5.)
Luke 3, 11.
Matt. 21, 31
1 Cor. 6, 9. 10.

---

[b] That S John's Baptism conveyed remission of sins, seems to be the opinion also of Nyss. in Laud Bas p 914. Aug. de Bapt v. 11. Christian Baptism having the further gift of the Holy Ghost.

LECT. III. Sin in the state of ignorance is pardoned, but depravity which continues is condemned.

(6.) 9. Thou hast, as the glory of Baptism, the Son of God Himself, the Only-begotten. For why should I henceforth speak of man? John was great, but what is he to the Lord? Loud was that voice, but what is it to the Word? Most glorious was the herald, but what to the King? Glorious was he who baptized with water, but what to Him who baptizeth with the Holy Ghost and with fire? With the Holy Ghost and with fire the Saviour baptized the Apostles, when Acts 2, 2 *suddenly there came a sound from heaven as of a rushing mighty wind, and it filled all the house where they were sitting; and there appeared unto them cloven tongues as of fire, and it sate upon each of them, and they were all filled with the Holy Ghost.*

(7.) 10. Unless a man receive Baptism, he hath not salvation; except Martyrs alone, who even without the water, receive the kingdom. For the Saviour who redeemed the world through the Cross, when His side was pierced, gave forth blood and water: that in times of peace men should be baptized with water, in times of persecution with their own blood. For the Saviour was minded to call martyrdom, Baptism, saying, *Can ye drink of the cup which I drink of, and be baptized with the baptism that I am baptized with?* Martyrs too make confession, *being made a spectacle to the world, and to Angels, and to men:* and thou shalt make confession shortly: but it is not yet time for thee to hear concerning these matters.

Mark 10, 38.

1 Cor. 4, 9.

(8.) 11. Jesus sanctified Baptism, being Himself baptized. Since the Son of God was baptized, what religious man can despise Baptism? He, however, was baptized, not to receive forgiveness of sins, for He was sinless: but being sinless, to grant divine grace and dignity to the baptized. Since the children are *partakers of flesh and blood, He also Himself likewise shared the same,* that we, partaking of His bodily presence, might partake also of His divine grace; and so again Jesus was baptized, that through this also, we by the participation, might with salvation receive dignity. The Dragon was in the waters, according to Job, he *who receiveth Jordan in his mouth:* whereas then He was to crush the *heads of the Dragon,* He descended, and in the waters

Heb. 2, 14. τῆς ἐν- σάρκου παρου- σίας κι- νωνοί.

Job 40, 18 Sept. 23 Engl. vers.

Baptism a necessary introduction to preaching the Gospel. 31

bound the mighty one, that we might receive power to *tread* Ps. 74, *upon serpents and scorpions*. It was no common monster, 14 but a terrible one. *No ship of fishers could bear one scale of* Job 40, *his tail: before him ran destruction,* wasting those that en- 26 Sept countered him. Life then encountered him, that henceforth the mouth of death might be closed, that we the saved might all say, *O death, where is thy sting? O grave, where is thy* 1 Cor *victory?* By Baptism, the sting of death is destroyed. 15, 55.

12. Thou descendest into the water bearing sins, but the (9.) invocation of grace having sealed thy soul, allows not that ἡ τῆς thou shouldest henceforth be swallowed up by the fearful χάριτος ἐπίκλη- Dragon. Dead in sins thou wentest down, quickened in σις. Vid. righteousness thou comest up: *for if thou wert planted* above n. 3. *together in the likeness of the Saviour's death, thou shalt* Rom 6, *be counted worthy of His resurrection also.* For as Jesus 2. 5 took on Him the world's sins, and died, that having been the death of sin, He might raise thee up in righteousness, so thou also, by descending into the water, and in some sense being in the waters buried, as He was in the rock, are raised again, to walk in newness of life.

13. Afterwards, when thou hast been counted worthy of the gift, He gives to thee the faculty to wrestle against the powers that are against thee [c]. For like as after His Baptism, He was tempted forty days, not because He could not overcome even before this, but because He would do all things regularly and in order, so thou also, though before Baptism afraid to wrestle with thine adversaries, yet when thou shalt have received the grace, being henceforth confident in *the armour of righteousness,* do battle, and, if thou wilt, preach 2 Cor. 8, the Gospel. 7.

14. Jesus Christ was the Son of God, yet before Baptism (10.) He preached not. If the Master Himself entered upon His time in regular order, ought we the servants to venture out of order? Jesus began to preach from the time that the Holy Ghost descended upon Him in a bodily shape, like a dove: not that Jesus might see Him as if for the first time; (for He knew Him even before He came in a bodily shape;) but that John who baptized Him, might behold Him. *For,* as he says, John 1, *I knew Him not: but He who sent me to baptize with water,* 33

[c] i.e in Confirmation. Cat xvii. n. 36, 37. Vid. Cat. xxi. n. 4

LECT. III. the same said unto me, Upon whom thou shalt see the Spirit descending, and remaining upon Him, the same is He. And if thou hast seriousness unfeigned, the Holy Ghost is coming down on thee likewise, and upon thee, the Father's voice shall sound from on high, not, "He is my son," but, "He hath now become My son." For "is" belongs to Him alone; since *In the beginning was the Word, and the Word was with God, and the Word was God.* To Him belongs that word, "Is;" since at all times He is the Son of God; but to thee belongs, "Is now become;" since thou hast not the Sonship by nature, but receivest it by adoption : He is Son eternally; thou receivest this grace by advancement.

John 1, 1.

(11.) 15. Therefore, make ready the vessel of thy soul, that thou mayest become a Son of God, *an Heir of God, and Joint-heir with Christ;* if thou preparest thyself, that thou mayest also receive; if thou by faith drawest near, that thou mayest be made a faithful man; if thou of thine own set purpose put away the old man. For every thing that thou hast committed shall be forgiven thee, even fornication, or adultery, or any other sort of licentiousness. What is greater than crucifying Christ? Yet even of this is Baptism a purification. For thus spake Peter to the three thousand who came to him; and they the crucifiers of the Lord, when they asked and said, *Men and brethren, what shall we do?* for great is our wound; thou hast turned our thoughts, O Peter, to our fall, in saying, Ye have killed the Prince of life. What salve is there for so great a wound? What cleansing for so great pollution? What salvation for so great a death? to them, I say, Peter saith, *Repent, and be baptized each of you in the name of Jesus Christ our Lord for the remission of sins, and ye shall receive the gift of the Holy Ghost.* O unspeakable loving-kindness of God! they look not for salvation, and they are vouchsafed the Holy Ghost. Behold the power of Baptism! If any of you hath by blasphemous words crucified Christ; if any of you hath through ignorance denied Him before men; if any of you, through wicked works, hath led to the doctrine's being evil spoken of, let him be of good hope in repenting, for the same grace is also present now.

Rom. 8, 17.

Acts 2, 37. &c.

(12.)

Zeph 3, 14. 15. Sept. Is 4, 4.

16. *Be of good courage, Jerusalem, the Lord will take away all thine iniquities. The Lord shall wash away the*

filth of His sons and daughters, by the Spirit of judgment and by the Spirit of burning: He shall sprinkle clean water upon you, and ye shall be cleansed from all your sin. Ezek. 36, 25. Angels in their choirs shall surround you, and shall say, *Who is this that cometh up in white apparel, leaning on her near of kin?* Cant. 8, 5. Sept. For the soul that was before a servant, hath now professed her Master to be her kindred, and He, favourably allowing her sincere purpose, will cry out in response, *Behold, thou art fair, my love, behold, thou art fair; thy teeth are as flocks of shorn sheep,* Cant. 4, 1. 2. because of her true hearted confession; and farther, *All of them bearing twins,* because of the twofold gift, that, I mean, perfected by water and the Spirit[d], or that announced in the Old and the New Testaments. And may all of you, having finished the course of fasting, remembering what hath been said, bearing fruit in good works, standing blameless before the Invisible Bridegroom, obtain the remission of sins at God's hand: to Whom be glory with the Son and the Holy Ghost, for ever. Amen.

[d] The Fathers sometimes speak as if Baptism was primarily the Sacrament of remission of sins, and *upon* that came the gift of the Spirit, which notwithstanding was but begun in Baptism and completed in Confirmation Vid Tertullian de Bapt. 7 8 supr 1 5 fin. Hence, as in the text, Baptism may be said to be made up of *two* gifts, Water which is Christ's blood, and the Spirit. There is no real difference between this and the ordinary way of speaking on the subject;—Water, which *conveys* both gifts, is considered as a *type* of one especially,—*conveys* both remission of sins through Christ's blood and the grace of the Spirit, but is the *type* of one, *viz* the blood of Christ, as the Oil in Confirmation is of the other. And again, remission of sins is a complete gift given at once, sanctification an increasing one.

LECTURE IV.

ON THE TEN POINTS OF FAITH [a].

COLOSSIANS ii. 8.

Beware lest any man spoil you through philosophy and vain deceit, after the tradition of men, after the rudiments of the world, and not after Christ.

LECT. IV

2 Cor 11, 14

1. WICKEDNESS imitates goodness: and the tares strive to be taken for wheat, being like it in appearance, but detected in their taste by the discerning. Even the devil *transformeth himself into an angel of light:* not that he may reascend to where he was; for being in heart like an anvil, incapable of all impression, he has now and for ever an impenitent will; but that he may environ in the darkness of blindness, and amid the pestilence of unbelief, those who are living an Angel's life. Many wolves are ranging about *in sheep's clothing,* in the clothing, I say, of sheep, but with claws and fangs too. Enveloped in the skin of a gentle animal, and by their appearance deceiving the guileless, they shed on them from their jaws the deadly poison of impiety. Need have we then of Divine grace, and of an abstinent spirit, and of seeing eyes: lest eating tares as wheat, we out of ignorance come to harm; lest taking the wolf for a sheep, we be made his prey; lest imagining the Devil, the Destroyer, to be an Angel of mercy, we be devoured; *for he goeth about like a roaring lion, seeking whom he may devour,* according to the Scriptures. For this cause the Church admonisheth; for this cause are the present classes; for this, the reading of lessons.

Matt. 7, 15.

1 Pet. 5, 8.

---

[a] This title is taken from Theodoret. The number is variously made out. Some MSS say eleven for ten. An enumeration is here made somewhat different both from that in Milles' and in the Benedictine Edd.

2. For the course of godliness is made up of these two; (2.) pious doctrines, and good works: neither are the doctrines without good works acceptable to God; nor are works allowable works done apart from pious doctrines. For what boots it, to know excellently the doctrines concerning God, and to commit vile fornication? or what again avails it to possess an excellent self-command, and to blaspheme impiously? An exceeding great gain then is learning in doctrines; and we have need of sobriety of mind, since many are they who would *spoil you through philosophy and vain deceit.* And the Greeks by their smooth tongues draw Col. 2, 8. you aside, *for honey distils from the lips of a strange woman:* Prov. 5, but they of the circumcision by means of the Holy Scrip- 3. tures, which they miserably wrest from their meaning, deceive those who come to them, versed in them from childhood to age, and growing old in ignorance. And the sons of the Heretics, *by good words and fair speeches deceive the hearts of* Rom 16, 18 *the simple,* disguising with the name of Christ, as with honey, the envenomed darts of their irreligious doctrines: concerning all of whom together, the Lord saith, *Beware lest any deceive you.* This gives occasion to the teaching of the Mat 24, Faith, and expositions upon it. 4.

3. But before making this tradition of the Faith, it seems to me fitting, to make at this time a short summary of necessary doctrines: lest the multitude of things to be spoken, and the lengthening out of the sacred season of Lent, be too much for the memories of the more simple among you: and that having now strewn some seeds in a general way, we may retain the same things, when provided in a larger crop afterwards. And let those here who are more practised in these things, *and have their senses now exercised to dis-* Heb 5, *cern both good and evil,* bear with things rather fitted for 14 children, and to a course (as it were) of milk: so that while they who stand in need of Catechising receive benefit, they Heb 5, who have knowledge, may now freshen the remembrance of 13. what they knew before.

I. Of God.

4. Lay then in your souls as a sure foundation the doctrine (3.) concerning God: That God is only one, unbegotten, unorigi-

God is One and Self-dependent.

LECT. IV.

nated, unchangeable, unalterable: neither by another begotten, nor having another to succeed Him in His being: who neither began in time to be, nor shall ever have an end. And that He is also good and just: so that, if ever thou hear a heretic saying, that the Just God is one and the Good God another, being put on thy guard, thou mayest at once detect the poisoned dart of heresy. For some have dared impiously to divide the One God in their teaching [b]. Again, some have said that the Artificer and Lord of the soul was one, and of the body another [c], a doctrine at once absurd and blasphemous. For how should man become the one servant of two masters, when the Lord saith in the Gospel, *No man can serve two masters?* There is then One Only God, the Maker both of souls and bodies: there is One the Artificer of heaven and earth, the Maker both of Angels and Archangels,—the Artificer of many things, but the Father of One only before the worlds, even of His One Only-begotten Son our Lord Jesus Christ, *by whom He made all things, visible and invisible.*

ἐν εὐαγγελίοις Mat. 6, 24.

Joh 1, 3. Col 1, 16.

5 He, the Father of our Lord Jesus Christ, is not confined to any place [d]; nor is He less than the heavens: but *the heavens are the work of His fingers*, and the *whole earth is holden in the hollow of His hand.* He is in and around all things. Think not that the sun is brighter than He, or is equal to Him: for He who formed the sun in the beginning, must needs be without comparison far greater and brighter. He foresees the future: He is mightier than all things: He knows all things, and does what He wills; not subjected to antecedents or consequents, or to nativities, or chance, or fate; in all things perfect, and possessing in Himself the absolute form of every excellence; neither waning, nor increasing, but in mode and circumstances ever the same; who hath prepared chastisement for the sinners, and a crown for the righteous.

Ps 8, 3. Is 40, 12.

(4.) 6. Seeing then that many have in divers ways gone astray from the One God,—some having deified the sun, and so forsooth, when he went down, abiding during the night-season

---

[b] This was the doctrine of Marcion, Iren III 25 § 2 3 and the Manichees.
[c] These were the Manichees Epiph Hær. i. 26
[d] As the Manichees held Theodor. Hær. lxvi. 8

godless,—others the moon, so as in the day-time to have no god,—others, the other parts of the world,—some, again, having deified the arts,—others, meats,—others, pleasures,—while some, mad after women, have set up on high the image of a naked woman, and calling it Venus, have bowed down to their own lusts, under the visible emblem,—and others, dazzled by the brightness of gold, have deified that, and other portions of matter,—seeing, I say, that these things are so, and that if one first stablish in his soul the doctrine of the One God, from whom are all things, and believe in it, he gets rid at once of all the multiplied evils of idolatry, and heretical error, do thou first settle firmly this doctrine of godliness in thy soul, by means of faith.

II. Of Christ.

7. Believe also in the Son of God, One and Only, our Lord Jesus Christ · God of God begotten: Life of Life begotten: Light of Light begotten · like in all things ᵉ to Him that begat Him: who began not His existence in time, but was before all ages eternally and incomprehensibly begotten of the Father: who is God's Wisdom and Power, and Righteousness personally subsisting; who before all ages is set down at the right hand of the Father. Not that He received the throne on God's right hand, as some have thought, by reason of His patient suffering merely, being after His passion crowned as it were by God; but all the time He hath been in being, which is from an everlasting generation, He hath the Kingly prerogative, sitting together with the Father, being God, and Wisdom, and Power, as hath been shown; together with the Father reigning, and by reason of the Father being the Artificer of all things; wanting nothing to the dignity of Godhead, and knowing His Father, even as He is known by His Father,—and, to speak briefly, remember what is written in the Gospel, *None knoweth the Son, but the Father; neither knoweth any the Father, save the Son.* (5.) ἐν εὐαγγελίοις Mat. 11, 27.

8. And neither do thou separate the Son from the Father, nor by confusing them together believe that the Son is the

---

ᵉ Τὸν ὅμοιον κατὰ πάντα This was one of the symbols of the Semiarians, as opposed to the ὁμοούσιον of orthodoxy, and the ἀνόμοιον of Arianism.

LECT. IV.

προφορικός.
ἀνυποστάτοις.
λογικῶν ποιητής.

Father[f]. But believe that of One God is One Only-begotten Son, who was before all ages, God the Word: the Word, not uttered externally, and dispersed abroad in the air, nor like to words impersonal[g], but the Word, the Son, the Maker of all who have the Word, the Word who hears the Father and Himself speak. And of these things we will speak more at large in due season, if God permit: for we do not forget our purpose, that at present we are but introducing the Faith after the manner of a summary.

III. Of His Incarnation.
His Birth of the Virgin.

(6.)

ὁμοιοπαθῆ.

δοκήσει.

διὰ σωλῆνος.

9. And believe that He, the Only-begotten Son of God, for our sins came down from heaven to the earth, having taken a manhood of like feelings with us, and being born of the Holy Virgin and the Holy Ghost, not in appearance or imagination[h], but in truth: nor did He pass through the Virgin as through a channel[1]; but truly took flesh of her, and of her was truly nourished with milk, and truly ate as we do, and truly drank as we do: for if the Incarnation was a phantom, salvation likewise is a phantom. Christ was twofold, Man in what was seen, God in what was not seen: eating truly as Man like us, (for He had like feelings of the flesh with us,) but feeding with five loaves the five thousand as God: dying as Man truly, but as God raising him who had been four days dead: sleeping in the ship truly as Man, and walking on the waters as God.

His Cross.

(7.)

10. He was crucified for our sins truly: shouldest thou be disposed to deny it, the very place which all can see refutes thee, even this blessed Golgotha[k], in which, on account of

---

[f] Συναλοιφὴν ἐργασάμενος υἱοπατορίαν πιστεύσῃς These were Noetus, Sabellius, &c. Vid Theodor Hær in. 3. Athan Orat iv. 2

[g] The followers of Paul of Samosata, and of Marcellus of Ancyra Euseb Eccles Theol. ii 11 15 Concil. Sirmiens A.D 357 (Hard vol 1 p 703)

[h] The heretics here alluded to, were, from their tenet, called Docetæ.

[1] This was the doctrine of the Valentinians. Vid Iren Hær. 1. 1. § 13

[k] The spot where our Lord was crucified and buried had been hidden by an artificial mound, and desecrated by a statue of Venus Constantine cleared the ground, and his mother Helena built a church there. Euseb. Vit. Const. iii. 25, 26.

Him who was crucified on it, we are now assembled: and further, the whole world is filled with the portions of the wood of the Cross[1]. But He was crucified, not for sins of His, but that we might be freed from our own sins. And though He was despised of men and beaten as a man, yet He was acknowledged by the creature as God; for the sun, beholding his Lord outraged, hid his light in trembling, not enduring the sight.

His Burial.

11. He was laid truly as man in a tomb of rock, but the (8.) rocks burst asunder through fear because of Him. He descended to the regions beneath the earth, that from thence also He might redeem the just[m]. For wouldest thou, I pray, that the living should enjoy His grace, and that, being most of them unholy; and that those who from Adam had been imprisoned long while, should not now obtain deliverance? The prophet Esaias heralded with a loud voice so many things concerning Him: and wouldest thou not that the King should descend and rescue His herald? David was there, and Samuel, and all the Prophets, and John himself, who said by his messenger, *Art thou He that should come, or do we look for another?* Wouldest thou not that He should descend and rescue such as these? Mat. 11, 3.

His Resurrection.

12. But He who descended to the regions beneath the (9.) earth, again ascended thence, and Jesus who was buried, rose again truly on the third day. And should the Jews ever harass you, meet them quickly by asking thus: Did Jonas after three days come forth from the whale, and hath not Christ then after three days risen from the earth? Was the dead man raised who touched the bones of Eliseus, and shall

---

[1] Vid. also Catech x 19 xiii 4. Helena is said to have discovered the true Cross on the occasion mentioned in the last note. The account is contained in Socr. Hist.i 17 Soz Hist ii 1 Theodor i. 18. Ambros. in Ob Theod. 45 &c Chrysost in Joan 8. 5. 1. besides Rufinus and Paulinus. Eusebius is altogether silent on the subject, and Constantine, in his Epistle written to Macarius, Bishop of Jerusalem, on the subject of the discovery of the Holy Sepulchre Euseb Vit. iii 30

[m] Vid. Euseb. Dem. Evang. x. p. 501. Hieronym. in Eccles. ix. 10. &c.

LECT. IV. not the Maker of men much more easily be raised by the power of the Father? He rose then truly; and being risen, He was again seen by His disciples. And the Twelve disciples were witnesses of His resurrection; not witnessing with flattering words, but striving for the truth of the resurrection even to tortures and deaths. Further *at the mouth of two or three witnesses shall every word be established,* according to the Scriptures; but twelve bear witness to Christ's resurrection, and disbelievest thou yet concerning the resurrection?

Deut. 19, 15.

His Ascension.

(10.) 13. And Jesus having finished His race of patience, and having redeemed men from their sins, ascended again into the heavens, a cloud receiving Him: and Angels stood by as He went up, and Apostles gazed. But if any doubt what he hears, let him believe the power of what he now sees. All kings when they die, have their power extinguished with their life: but Christ after being crucified, is worshipped by the whole world. We proclaim the Crucified, and the devils tremble; yet many others have in course of time been crucified, but when has the invocation of any one of these scared away the devils?

14. Let us not then be ashamed of the Cross of Christ; but though another hide it, do thou openly seal it on thy brow[n]: that the devils beholding that princely Sign, may flee far away trembling. But make thou this Sign, when thou eatest and drinkest, sittest or liest down, risest up, speakest, walkest: in a word, on every occasion; for He who was here crucified, is above in the heavens. For if, when crucified and buried, He had remained in the tomb, then we had had shame: but now He who was crucified on this Golgotha, hath from the Mount of Olives on the East ascended into heaven: for having hence descended into hell, and come back again to us, from us did He ascend again into heaven, His Father addressing Him and saying, *Sit Thou on My right hand, until I make Thine enemies Thy footstool.*

Ps. 110, 1.

[n] Vid Tertull de Cor. 3 Cyprian. de Laps. p. 181. Hier. Ep. 1. ad Heliodor. Aug. de Cat rud 34 (20)

IV. OF THE FUTURE JUDGMENT.

15. This Jesus Christ who hath ascended, cometh again (11.) from heaven, not from earth. And I say, not from earth, because many Antichrists are now to come from earth; for, as thou hast seen, many have already begun to say, *I am* Mat 24, *Christ*: and besides there is to come *the Abomination of* 5. 15. *Desolation*, usurping the name of Christ. But do thou look for the true Christ, the Son of God, the Only-begotten, who is henceforth to come not from the earth, but from heaven, appearing to all more bright than any lightning or other brilliance, with Angels for His guards, that He may judge quick and dead, and reign with a kingdom, heavenly, eternal, and without end. Be sure to settle your belief in this point also, since there are many who say that Christ's kingdom has an end°.

V. OF THE HOLY GHOST.

16. Believe also on the Holy Ghost, and hold concerning (12.) Him the same opinion which has been delivered to thee to hold concerning the Father and the Son · and not according to those who teach blasphemous things of Him ᴾ. But do thou learn that this Holy Ghost is One, indivisible, of manifold power; working many things, yet Himself without parts; who knoweth mysteries, *who searcheth all things, even the* 1 Cor. 2, *deep things of God;* who descended on our Lord Jesus 10. Christ in the form of a dove; who wrought in the Law and the Prophets. who, even now, at the season of Baptism sealeth thy soul; of whose holiness every intellectual nature hath also need; against whom if a man dare to blaspheme, he hath no forgiveness, *either in this world, or in that which* Mat 12, *is to come;* who with the Father and the Son is exalted ³². with the glory of the Godhead; of whom Thrones also, and Dominions, Principalities and Powers, stand in need. For there is One God, the Father of Christ; and One Lord Jesus Christ, of the Only God the Only-begotten Son: and One Holy Ghost, who halloweth and deifieth all, who spake in τὸ θεο-the Law and the Prophets, both in the Old and New ποιόν, Testaments.

° Viz. the followers of Marcellus of Ancyra.   ᴾ E. g the Montanists, Arians, and Macedonians.

42 *Nothing not taught and proved out of Scripture is of the Faith.*

LECT.
IV.

17. This seal have thou ever on thy mind; which now by way of summary has been touched on in its heads, and if the Lord grant, shall hereafter be set forth according to our power, with Scripture-proofs. For concerning the divine and sacred Mysteries of the Faith, we ought not to deliver even the most casual remark without the Holy Scriptures: nor be drawn aside by mere probabilities and the artifices of argument. Do not then believe me because I tell thee these things, unless thou receive from the Holy Scriptures the proof of what is set forth: for this salvation, which is of our faith, is not by ingenious reasonings, but by proof from the Holy Scriptures.

VI. OF THE SOUL.

(13.)

18. After knowing this venerable and glorious and most holy Faith, next thou hast to know thyself: know that thou art a twofold man consisting of soul and body, and that, as was said a little before, the same God is the Artificer both of the soul and of the body. And know thou hast a soul possessed of freedom^q, the fairest work of God, made after the image of Him who formed it: immortal because of God who has made it immortal: a living thing, reasonable, undecaying, because of Him who hath bestowed these gifts: having power to do what it willeth. For it is not according to thy nativity that thou sinnest, nor is thy fornication according to thy fortune, nor, as some idly talk, do the conjunctions of the stars force thee to live in lasciviousness. Why, to avoid confession of thy wretchedness, dost thou blame the guiltless stars? Henceforth have nothing to do with astrologers: for of these saith the divine Scripture, *Let now the astrologers stand up and save thee, &c. Behold they shall be as stubble: the fire shall burn them: they shall not deliver themselves from the power of the flame.*

αὐτεξού-
σιον

Is. 47,
13 14.

19. And learn this also: that before the soul be come into the world, it hath in nothing sinned: but that having come into the world sinless^r, we now of our own choice sin.

---

q When Cyril and other writers speak so pointedly about the freedom of the will, it is by way of protest against the Manichees and others who were fatalists.

r It was both a Pythagorean and an heretical doctrine, that the soul had sinned in some pre-existent state. Clem. Strom III. Iren. Hær. 1. 25.

Listen not, I pray thee, to any one perversely expounding the Scripture, *If then I do that which I would not*, and the rest: but remember Him who says, *If ye be willing and obedient, ye shall eat the good of the land; but if ye refuse and rebel, ye shall be devoured with the sword*, and the rest: and again, *As ye have yielded your members servants of uncleanness, and of iniquity unto iniquity; even so now yield your members servants to righteousness unto holiness.* Remember also the Scripture which says, *And as they did not like to retain God in their knowledge*, and, *That which may be known of God is manifest in them:* and, *Their eyes have they closed.* Remember too how God says against them, *Yet I had planted thee a noble vine, wholly a right seed; how then art thou turned into the degenerate plant of a strange vine unto Me?* Rom. 7, 16 Is. 1, 19. 20. Rom 6, 19. Rom 1, 28. Rom. 1, 19. Mat. 13, 15. Jer. 2, 21.

20. The soul is immortal; and all souls are alike, both of men and women; only there is a difference of person[s]. There is not one order of souls[t] which by nature sin, and another order of souls which by nature act righteously, but both act from choice, the essence of the soul being one in kind and alike in all. (14.) τὰ γὰρ μέλη τοῦ σώματος διακέ- κρινται μόνον.

Now I know that I am speaking at length, and that the time is far advanced: but what is preferable to salvation? Dost thou not care, though with trouble, to take provision for the way against the heretics? wilt thou not be told the turns of the road, lest out of ignorance thou fall down a precipice? If thy teachers think it no small gain for thee to learn these things, shouldest not thou, the learner, receive gladly the multitude of the things told thee?

21. The soul has freedom: and though the devil can tempt, he is not free to force it against deliberate choice. He suggests to thee the thought of fornication; if thou wilt, thou hast admitted it; if thou wilt not, thou hast not. For if thou wert a fornicator by necessity, then wherefore did God prepare hell? If thou did justly by nature and not by choice, wherefore hath God prepared crowns of glory ineffable? The sheep is meek, yet it hath never been crowned for its meek-

---

[s] The doctrine of Apelles is here aimed at. Vid. Tertull de Anim. 36.

[t] Some of the Gnostic sects seem referred to. Vid. Iren 1. 24.

VII. OF THE BODY.

(15.) 22. Thou hast been taught, beloved, for the present, concerning the Soul: now receive, as far as may be, the doctrine concerning the Body. Endure not any of those who say, that the body belongs not to God[u]: for they who hold this, and that the soul dwells in it as in a vessel which belongeth not to itself, readily abuse it to fornication. But for what have they condemned this wonderful body? in comeliness what lack has it? And what is there of its fashioning not wrought with art? Ought they not to have considered how bright the eyes are; and how the ears placed obliquely receive sounds without hindrance; and how the sense of smell is discriminating in scents, and eagerly discerns incense; and how the tongue is the minister of two things, the faculty of tasting, and the power of speech? And how the lungs, placed out of sight, are unceasingly occupied in respiring air? Who gave the heart its unremitted beating? Who divided so many veins and arteries? Who skilfully interwove the bones with the muscles? Who while assigning a part of our food for our substance, separated the rest in a seemly manner; and hath hidden our uncomely members in a more comely disposition? Who, when mankind was like to have failed, rendered it by a simple fellowship perpetual?

(16.) 23. Say not, I pray, that the body is the cause of sin. For if the body be the cause of sin, how is it that a corpse is without sin? Put a sword in the right hand of one just dead, and there is no murder committed; let beauty of every sort pass before the young just dead, yet is no impure desire excited. Why? Because it is not the body which sins of itself, but the soul by means of the body. The body is the instrument, and as it were the garment and robe of the soul; if then it be abandoned by the soul to fornication, it becomes unclean; but if it dwell with a holy soul, it becomes the temple of the Holy Ghost. It is not I who say this, but Paul the Apostle hath said, *Know ye not that your bodies are the temple of the Holy Ghost, which is in you?* Be tender

1 Cor. 6, 19.

---

[u] This was the doctrine of Gnostics and Manichees.

then of thy body, as being the temple of the Holy Ghost; sully not thy flesh with fornication; defile not this thy fairest robe; but if thou hast defiled it, cleanse it now through penitence; while the time allows, wash it.

24. And as to the doctrine of chastity, above all, let the order of Solitaries and of Virgins attend to it, who are establishing in the world an Angelic life; and then, the rest of the Church's people also. Great is the crown laid up for you, brethren; for a poor indulgence barter not a high dignity. Listen to the Apostle, saying, *Lest there be any fornicator, or profane person as Esau, who for one morsel of meat sold his birthright.* Having been enrolled in the Angelical books for thy purpose of chastity, beware lest thou be blotted out again for thy deed of fornication. Heb. 12, 16.

25. Nor again on the other hand, while observing chastity, be thou puffed up against those who choose the humbler path of wedlock. *For marriage is honourable, and the bed undefiled,* as saith the Apostle. Thou too who keepest thy purity, wert thou not born of married persons? Do not, because thou hast a possession of gold, set at nought the silver. But let those also who are married be of good cheer, who use marriage lawfully; who subject their marriage to laws, not making it wanton by unbounded licence; who observe seasons of abstinence, *that they may give themselves unto prayer;* who with pure garments bring their bodies also pure to the assemblies of the Church; who have entered into the state of matrimony, not for indulgence, but that they may have a home. Heb. 13, 4.
1 Cor. 7, 5.
διὰ τὸ τεκνογονεῖν.

26. And let not those who have been but once married, set at nought them who have involved themselves in a second marriage[x]. Continence is indeed a noble thing and an admirable; yet we should make allowance for a second marriage, that the weak may not commit fornication. *It is good for them if they abide even as I,* saith the Apostle; *but if they cannot contain, let them marry; it is better to marry than to burn.* But every thing else, be it put away far from 1 Cor. 7, 8. 9.

---

[x] The Montanists condemned second marriages; vid Tertull de Monogam 8, de Exhort Cast. 9 and the Novatians, Epiph. Hær lix. 3 Second marriages were an impediment to holy orders. They are spoken of by the Fathers as at best a concession, e g Iren. Hær. iii. 17. Chrysost in Mat. Hom. 32. fin.

you, fornication, adultery, and every form of incontinence; and let the body be kept for the Lord, that the Lord also may look upon the body. And let the body be nourished with meats, that it may live, and serve without hindrance; but not that it may be given up to indulgence.

Meats.

(17.) 27. And concerning food, let these be your doctrines; since many stumble concerning meats also. For some indifferently draw near to things sacrificed to idols; and others, while they are austere, condemn them who eat: and thus in different ways the soul of some is defiled in the matter of meats, while they are ignorant of the profitable reasons, for eating or abstaining. For we fast, abstaining from wine and flesh, not because we abhor them as abominations, but because we look for the reward; that scorning things sensible, we may enjoy the spiritual and invisible table, and *that sowing now in tears, we may reap in joy* in the world to come. Despise not however those who eat, and partake because of their bodies' weakness; nor blame those *who use a little wine, for their stomach's sake, and their often infirmities;* nor condemn them as sinners. Nor abhor thou flesh as being an unchristian thing; for the Apostle knew some such when he spake of those, *forbidding to marry, and commanding to abstain from meats, which God hath created to be received with thanksgiving of them which believe*[y]. In abstaining then from them, abstain not from them as abominable, otherwise thou hast no reward; but look down on them though good, for the sake of those nobler spiritual things which are set before thee.

28. For thy soul's sake, at no time eat ought of the things offered to idols. For concerning these meats, not I only, but the Apostles also before now, and James, the Bishop of this Church, have taken thought; and the Apostles and Elders write to all the Gentiles a Catholic Epistle, bidding them

---

[y] The various sects of Gnostics, and the Manichees, considered certain meats and drinks, as flesh and wine, to be polluting. Vid Iren Hær. 1 28. Clem Pæd. ii. 2. p. 186 Epiph Hær xlvi 2. xlvii. 1. &c &c. August. Hær. 46 vid. Canon. Apost 43 "If any Bishop, &c abstain from marriage, flesh, and wine, not for discipline (δι' ἄσκησιν) but as abhorring them, forgetting that they are all very good, &c. and speaking blasphemy against the creation, let him amend or be deposed," &c.

abstain, chiefly from things sacrificed to idols, and then from blood also and things strangled. For many men being of a savage nature, and living like dogs, both lap up blood, copying the way of the most savage wild beasts; and also eat greedily without scruple things strangled[z]. But do thou, the servant of Christ, when eating, observe to eat with reverence. Thus much concerning meats.

Apparel.

29. Be thou clad with plain apparel, not for vain orna- (18.) ment's sake, but for a necessary covering; nor to make a display, but that thou mayest be warm in winter, and mayest hide thine uncomeliness. Beware lest, under colour of hiding thine uncomeliness, by thy extravagant robes thou fall into uncomeliness of another sort.

VIII. OF THE RESURRECTION.

30. Be tender, I beseech thee, of this body; and know (19.) that thou shalt arise from the dead, to be judged with this body. But if any thought of unbelief steal upon thee, as though the thing were impossible, consider from thine own case the things which appear not. For tell me; think where thou wert thyself, an hundred or more years ago? From what an element, from what a very small and mean substance, hast thou come to so great stature, and to such dignity of comeliness. Cannot then He who brought into being that which was not, raise up again that which has been and has decayed? He who year by year raises up the corn which we sow, when it is dead, shall He find difficulty in raising us up, for whose sakes He was raised Himself? Thou seest how the trees have stood now for so many months fruitless and leafless; but when the winter is passed, they revive in all their parts as it were from the dead. Shall not we then much rather, yea and much more easily, live again? The rod of Moses was by the counsel of God changed into the dissimilar nature of a serpent: and shall not man who has fallen into death be again restored to himself?

---

[z] The prohibition of idol-sacrifices, blood, and things strangled, was long in force in the East, but in the West, as regards blood and things strangled, it had become almost obsolete by S Austin's age Contr Faust xxxii. 13.

48 *The Canon of Scripture to be received from the Church.*

LECT IV
Is. 26, 19. Sept
Dan 12, 2. Sept.

31. Heed not them who say that this body is not raised: for it is raised: and Esaias testifieth this, saying, *The dead shall arise, and they in the tombs shall be raised.* So Daniel, *Many of them that sleep in the dust of the earth shall arise; some to everlasting life, and some to everlasting shame.* But though the resurrection is common to all men, it is not alike to all; for we all indeed receive everlasting bodies, but not all the same bodies. For the just receive them, that through eternity they may join the Choirs of Angels; but the sinners, that they may undergo for everlasting the torment of their sins.

IX. OF THE HOLY LAVER.

32. Wherefore, the Lord of His lovingkindness has been beforehand with us, giving us the repentance of the Laver, that having cast away the chief, yea rather the whole burden of our sins, and having received the seal of the Holy Ghost, we may become heirs of life eternal. But seeing that we have before spoken sufficiently of the Laver of Baptism, let us go on to what remains of our preparatory teaching.

X. OF THE DIVINE SCRIPTURES.

(20.)

Gal. 3, 23. 24.

Mat. 5, 17.

ἀποκρύ-φων.

33. These things are taught us by the inspired Scriptures, both of the Old and of the New Testament. For the God of both Testaments is one, by whom Christ who appeared in the New Testament, was foretold in the Old; who through the Law and the Prophets brought us as a Schoolmaster to Christ. *For before faith came, we were kept under the Law: and, The Law was our Schoolmaster to bring us unto Christ.* And if ever thou hear any of the heretics blaspheming the Law or the Prophets, utter against them the saving voice, saying, *Jesus came not to destroy the Law, but to fulfil.* Learn, also, diligently, and from the Church, which are the books of the Old Testament, and which of the New: and read not, I pray, any of the uncertain books [a]. For why shouldest thou, who knowest not those which are acknowledged by all, take needless trouble about those which are

---

[a] Or *apocryphal*, a word which did not convey any reproach in the early Church, but merely signified that the book so named was not in the canon Vid Pearson, Vind Ignat 1 4 The name of ἀναγινωσκόμενοι or Ecclesiastical is given by some writers to certain works which were held in reverence, and so read in Churches, but not inspired. Vid Milles in loc p 65

questioned? Read the Holy Scriptures, these two and twenty books of the Old Testament, which were interpreted by the seventy-two interpreters.

34. For[b] after the death of Alexander the king of the (21.) Macedonians, and the division of his kingdom into four principalities, into Babylonia, and Macedonia, and Asia, and Egypt, one of the kings of Egypt, Ptolemy Philadelphus, a king very fond of learning, when he was collecting the books which were in every place, heard from Demetrius of Phalerum, who was over the library, concerning the Divine Scriptures of the Law and the Prophets, and judging it far better to abstain from getting the books by force from unwilling persons, but rather to conciliate their possessors by presents and friendship, knowing moreover, that what is forced from men, being given against their choice, is oftentimes tampered with, whereas that which is given of free choice is presented with all sincerity,—he sent exceeding many gifts to Eleazar the priest at that time, for the temple at Jerusalem, and caused to be sent to him six men out of each of the twelve tribes of Israel, for the work of interpretation. Then, to prove whether the books were divine or no, and to prevent them who had been sent from combining together among themselves, he assigned to each of the interpreters his several dwelling, in the place called Pharos, which adjoins Alexandria, and bade each translate all the Scriptures. And when they had accomplished the work in seventy-two days, he brought together the translations of all, which they had made in different cells

[b] This account is also found in Euseb Præp. Evang. viii. 1—5. Philon. vit Mos ii. 658. Joseph. Antiq xii. 2. Justin. Apol. 1. § 31. p. 62 Iren. Hist. iii 25. Clem. Strom. p 342. These, to which may be added Hilary, Austin, and Philastrius, are in addition to Aristeas, who is the original authority Epiphanius makes the same general statement with some further particulars in detail. This concordant testimony of the Fathers does not prove the *fact* alleged, which seems to have come from the Jews, yet may prove the *doctrine* implied and involved in it, that there is something, more than ordinary, of the Divine Hand in the Translation in question,—a doctrine which is confirmed by the deference and reliance which the inspired writers of the New Testament evince towards it. e g Acts xiii 34. xv 17. We may believe this doctrine, and yet with entire consistency reject the particular story which symbolizes, and got currency by, the primitive belief in it. Prideaux (Connect part ii. b 1.) comes to the following conclusions — that the book which goes under the name of Aristeas, nay of Aristobulus, is a forgery of some Hellenistic Jew, with a view to add honour to the Septuagint version; and that in reality that version was gradually made in successive ages, first as far as the Law, then the Prophets, &c. It should be observed, that S Jerome rejects the history of the separate cells with great contempt. Præf. ad Pentat.

without approaching one another; and he found them agreeing not in sense only, but in words. For the matter was not one of witty invention, or a contrivance of man's cunning devices; but the interpretation of the Divine Scriptures, spoken by the Holy Ghost, was, of the Holy Ghost accomplished.

(22.) 35. Read the two and twenty books of these Scriptures: ἀπόκρυ- and have nothing to do with the uncertain books. Those only φα. study earnestly, which we read confidently even in Church. Far wiser than thou, and more devout, were the Apostles, and προστά- the ancient Bishops, the rulers of the Church, who have ται. vid. Justin. handed down these: thou, therefore, who art a child of the Apol. Church, trench not on their sanctions. And of the old Testa-1 65. ment, as hath been said, study the two and twenty books; and these, if thou art diligent, strive to remember by name, as I repeat them. Of the Law, are the first five books of Moses; Genesis, Exodus, Leviticus, Numbers, Deuteronomy: then Joshua the son of Nun: and the book of Judges and of Ruth, which is numbered the seventh. Of the remaining Historical books, the first and second books of Kings are among the Hebrews one book, and so the third and fourth books; and likewise the first and second books of Chronicles make one book; and the first and second books of Esdras are one; and the twelfth is the book of Esther: these are the Historical books. The books which are written in verses are five; Job, and the book of Psalms, and Proverbs, and Ecclesiastes, and the Song of Songs, which is the seventeenth book. After these come the five Prophetic books: the one book of the Twelve Prophets; the book of Esaias; the book of Jeremias, which with Baruch, the Lamentations, and the Epistle makes one book; then Ezekiel; and the book of Daniel is the twenty-second book of the Old Testament.

36. Of the New Testament, there are only the four Gospels: ψευδεπί- the rest are forged and mischievous. The Manichæans also γραφα wrote a Gospel according to Thomas, which, made acceptable with the fragrance of the evangelic name, corrupts the souls of the simpler sort. And receive also the Acts of the Twelve Apostles; and in addition to these, the seven Catholic Epistles, of James and Peter and John and Jude: and the final seal of all, and the last work of the disciples, the fourteen Epistles

of Paul[c]. But all the rest, let them be put aside, into the second rank; and what is not read in the churches, that read not by thyself, according as thou hast heard. Thus far of these things.

37. Fly also from every devilish work, and listen not to (23.) that apostate Serpent, who has of his own choice changed himself from a good nature; who can persuade those who are willing, but can force no one. And give heed neither to observations of the stars, nor to auguries, nor to omens, nor to the fabulous divinations of the Greeks. And sorcery, and the craft of charms, and their most wicked practices for calling up the dead, receive not even to listen to them. Stand aloof from every sort of intemperance, being neither a glutton, nor a lover of pleasure; raised above all covetousness, and the taking of usury. Nor throw thyself into the assemblies of the heathen spectacles: nor ever use amulets in thy sicknesses: and put away from thee also the pollution of tavern-haunting. And fall not into Judaism, nor into the sect of the Samaritans: for henceforth hath Jesus Christ ransomed thee. Abstain from all observance of Sabbaths, and from calling any indifferent meat "common or unclean." Especially abhor all the assemblies of wicked heretics: and in every way make thine own soul safe, by fastings, by prayers, by alms, by reading of the divine oracles: that living in soberness and godly doctrine for the rest of thy time in the flesh, thou mayest enjoy the one salvation of the Laver of Regeneration, and having been thus listed in the heavenly hosts by God and the Father, thou mayest also be counted worthy of the heavenly crown, in Christ Jesus our Lord, to Whom be glory for ever and ever. Amen.

[c] S Cyril keeps silence about the Apocalypse, after the usage of the early Greek Church (vid. Tillemont, S John, note 9) as the Latins with respect to the Epistle to the Hebrews.

LECTURE V.

ON FAITH [a].

HEBREWS xi. 1, 2.

Now faith is the substance of things hoped for, the evidence of things not seen: for by it the elders obtained a good report.

LECT. V.

1 Cor. 1, 9.

Vid Introd. Lect. n. 6.

Prov. 20, 6.

1 Cor 4, 3.

Ps. 7, 9
Ps 94.

1. How great the dignity is which the Lord bestows on you, in transferring you from the order of Catechumens to that of the Faithful, Paul the Apostle sets before you, saying, *God is Faithful, by whom ye were called to the fellowship of His Son Jesus Christ*. For as God is called Faithful, thou likewise receivest this title, receiving in it a great dignity. For as God is called Good, Just, Almighty, the Artificer of the Universe, so also He is called Faithful; think then to how great a dignity thou art rising, being on the eve of sharing a title of God.

2. Now then it is only required, that a man be found among you faithful in his conscience: for *a faithful man, who can find?* Not that thou shouldest show thy conscience to me; for thou art not *to be judged of man's judgment*; but that thou manifest to God a guileless faith, *who trieth the reins and the hearts*, and *knoweth the thoughts of men*. A faithful man is something great, and wealthier than

---

[a] S. Cyril treats in this and five following Lectures of the following articles in succession, which make up the Creed of Jerusalem "I believe," (Lecture 5) in one God (6) The Father (7) Almighty (8) Maker of heaven and earth, and of all things visible and invisible (9), And in One Lord Jesus Christ (10) the Only-begotten Son of God, begotten of the Father before all worlds, Very God by whom all things were made (11) Who was incarnate and made man (12) crucified and buried (13) and rose from the dead the third day and ascended into the heavens, and sat down at the right hand of the Father (14) and is coming to judge quick and dead (15), And in the Holy Ghost, the Paraclete, Who spake by the Prophets (16. 17) and in One Holy Catholic Church, and resurrection of the flesh, and in life everlasting (18) Milles in loc also Ed Benedict p 84.

any wealthy. *For to the faithful man belongs the whole* Prov. 17, *world of riches,* in that he thinks lightly of them, and tramples 6. Sept. them under foot. For those who in appearance are wealthy, and possess much, yet are poor in soul: for in proportion as they amass, do they pine from longing for what is still wanting. But the faithful man, most wondrously, in poverty is rich; for knowing that we need only to have *raiment and food,* 1 Tim. and being content with these, he has put riches under foot, 6, 8.

3. Nor is it only among us, who bear the title of Christ, (2.) that the dignity of faith is great: for likewise all that is accomplished in the world, even by those who are aliens from the Church, is accomplished by faith. By faith, marriage laws knit together persons unknown one to another: and one who is strange to us, through the faith placed in marriage compacts, becomes a sharer in strange persons and strange possessions. By faith is husbandry also upheld: for he who does not believe he shall receive a harvest, endures not its toils. By faith, sea-faring men, putting their trust in a very slender plank, exchange that most solid element the earth, for the unsteady motion of the waves; yielding themselves to uncertain hopes, and carrying with them as something surer than any anchor, their faith. By faith then most affairs of men hold together: and this not among us only, but likewise among those who are without, as hath been said; for though they receive not the Scriptures, but bring forward doctrines of their own, yet these also do they receive by faith.

4. To that faith which is true, the lesson which was read to-day likewise calls you, setting before you, how you also must please God; *for,* He saith, *without faith it is impossible* Heb. 11, *to please Him.* For when will a man set himself to serve 6. God, unless he believes that He is a rewarder? When will a young woman choose a virgin life, or a young man be sober minded, unless they believe that chastity has a crown unfading? Faith is the eye which enlightens the whole conscience, and creates in it understanding; for the Prophet saith, *And if ye believe not, neither shall ye understand.* Is. 7, 9. Faith stops the mouths of lions, according to Daniel; for the Sept. Scripture saith concerning him, that *Daniel was taken up* Dan. 6, *out of the den, and no manner of hurt was found upon him,* 23. *because he believed in his God.* Is there aught more fearful

than the devil? But even against him we have no other weapon than faith, an impalpable buckler against an unseen foe. For he discharges manifold darts, and shoots in the darkness those who are not watching; but, since the foe is unseen, we have, as a stout defence, faith, according to the saying of the Apostle, *Above all, taking the shield of faith, wherewith ye shall be able to quench all the fiery darts of the wicked.* For when, as oft-times happens, a fiery dart of desire of base indulgence is hurled by the devil, faith, shadowing forth the judgment, cools the soul, and quenches it.

(3.)   5. Now we have many things to say concerning faith, and the whole day would not suffice us discoursing of it: for the present be we content with Abraham alone, one of the examples of the Old Testament, seeing that we also are become his sons through faith. He was justified not only by works, but by faith also: and though he did many things well, yet was he never called the friend of God, except when he believed; moreover every deed of his was perfected by faith. By faith he left his parents: by faith he abandoned country, dwelling-place, and home. As then he was justified, so be thou also justified. Further, his body was dead: for he was an old man, and his wife Sarah was old also, and no hope of children was left him. God promises offspring to the old man: and Abraham, *not being weak in faith, nor considering his own body now dead;* thinking not of his body's infirmity, but of the power of Him who promised, and *judging Him faithful who had promised,* in a wondrous manner gained a child from bodies *as good as dead.* And when after he had gained a son, he was ordered to offer him, although he had heard that, *In Isaac shall thy seed be called,* he offered his only-begotten son to God, believing that God was able even to raise him from the dead. So having bound his son, and laid him upon the wood, in intent he offered him, but by the goodness of God, who gave him a lamb instead of his child, he received his son alive. Wherefore, he being faithful, was sealed unto righteousness, and received circumcision, *the seal of the righteousness which he had yet being uncircumcised;* having received the promise that *he should be the father of many nations.*

6. How then is Abraham the father of many nations? Of

the Jews he is confessedly, by the succession according to the flesh. But if we give heed to that which is according to the flesh, we shall be forced to say that the oracle is false: for according to the flesh he is no longer the father of us all; but a faith, of which he is the type, makes us all sons of Abraham. How and after what sort? It is incredible among men, that one should arise from the dead; it is incredible also, that of the aged, in their bodies dead, a child should be born; yet when Christ is preached, as having been crucified on the tree, dead and risen again, we believe it. By likeness then of faith we come to the sonship of Abraham: and then, upon our faith, like him, we receive the spiritual seal: being circumcised by the Holy Ghost through the Sacred Laver, not in the uncircumcision of the body but of the heart, as Jeremias saith, *Circumcise yourselves to the Lord, and take away the uncircumcision of your heart;* and as the Apostle saith, *by the circumcision of Christ, buried with Him in baptism;* and the rest. Jerem. 4, 4.
Col. 2, 11 12.

7. This faith if we keep, we shall be clear of condemnation, and shall be adorned with virtues of every kind. For so great power hath faith, that it even gives buoyancy to men walking on the sea. Peter was a man like unto us, formed of flesh and blood, and living upon like food: but believing Jesus, when He said, *Come,* he walked on the waters, having his faith for a support on the waters, surer than any foundation; and his heavy body was kept afloat by the buoyancy of his faith. But though as long as he believed, he had a sure footing on the water; yet as soon as he doubted, he began to sink: for as his faith gradually relaxed, his body also was carried along with it. And beholding his evil case, Jesus, the Corrector of the evils of our souls, said to him, *O thou of little faith, wherefore didst thou doubt?* and again, nerved by Him who took hold of his right hand, from the moment he believed again, being led by the hand of the Lord, he regained the same power of walking on the waters. For thus the Gospel hath indirectly recorded, in the words, *when they went up into the ship.* For it says not that Peter by swimming went up into the ship; but it gives us to understand, that as far as he had gone to Jesus, such a distance did he retrace, going up again into the ship. (4.)
Mat. 14, 29.
Mat. 14, 32.

8. Yea, so much power hath faith, that not only the person believing is saved, but one man has been saved by others believing. The palsied man at Capernaum was not faithful; but they who bore him, and let him down through the tiles, believed; for the soul of the sick man shared in the sickness of his body. Think not that I accuse him groundlessly; for the Gospel itself hath said, *Jesus beholding,* not his faith, but *their faith, saith to the sick of the palsy, Arise.* The bearers believed, and the sick of the palsy enjoyed the blessing of the cure.

9. Wouldest thou see yet more certainly, that some have been saved by others' faith? Lazarus died: one day passed, and a second and a third: his sinews were decayed and corruption was now preying on his body. How could a man four days dead believe, and call to the deliverer on his own behalf? But what was wanting in the dead, was supplied by his true sisters. For when the Lord came, his sister fell at His feet: and when to His question, *Where have ye laid him?* she answered, *Lord, by this time he stinketh, for he hath been dead four days,* He saith, *If thou wilt believe, thou shalt see the glory of God.* As if saying, "Fill thou up what is wanting, for the faith of this dead;" and so availed the sisters' faith, that it recalled the dead from the gates of hell. Have men then, believing one for the other, availed for a resurrection from the dead, and shalt not thou, if thou believe sincerely concerning thyself, much rather be profited? Nay, though thou be faithless, or have but little faith, yet is the Lord merciful; He will condescend to thee when thou repentest: only do thou also say to Him with a honest heart, *Lord, I believe, help Thou mine unbelief.* And if thou thinkest that thou art indeed faithful, but hast not yet attained the perfection of faith, thou hast need to say with the Apostles, *Lord, increase our faith:* for part thou hast of thine own self, but the much greater part thou receivest of Him.

10. For Faith, though in name one, is distinguished into two kinds. For there is one sort of faith, which is of doctrines, implying the acquiescence [b] of the mind concerning

---

[b] That faith is an *assent* of the mind to the truth, or a submission or acquiescence of the mind to a divine message, is maintained by Clement Alex Strom. lib ii. p 362. Basil in Psalm. cxv. p. 371, 2.

some certain thing: and this faith profits the soul, as the Lord saith, *He that heareth My words, and believeth in Him that sent Me, hath everlasting life, and shall not come into condemnation;* and again, *He that believeth on the Son is not condemned: but is passed from death into life.* O the great loving-kindness of God! The righteous were many years in pleasing Him; but what they obtained, by their pleasing Him well for many years, this is now bestowed on thee by Jesus in one hour. For if thou shalt believe that Jesus Christ is Lord, and that God hath raised Him from the dead, thou shalt be saved and translated into Paradise, by Him who brought the robber into Paradise. And do not disbelieve the possibility of this; for He who in this holy Golgotha saved the robber in one hour, the same will also save thee when thou shalt believe. [John 5, 24.] [John 3, 18.] [John 5, 24.]

11. But there is a second sort of faith, bestowed as a gift by Christ in the way of grace. *For to one is given by the Spirit the word of wisdom, to another the word of knowledge by the same Spirit: to another faith by the same Spirit, to another gifts of healing.* Now this faith which is given of grace by the Spirit, is not only a faith in doctrine; but it also worketh things beyond man's power. For he who hath this faith shall say to this mountain, *Remove hence to yonder place, and it shall remove.* For when any one shall say this by faith, believing that it shall come to pass, and shall not waver in his heart, then he receiveth the grace. And it is of this faith that it is said, *If ye have faith as a grain of mustard seed.* For like as a grain of mustard seed is small in bulk, but fiery in operation,—and though sown in a narrow space, has a circuit of mighty branches, and being grown up is able even to shelter the fowls; thus faith too accomplishes in the soul, in the briefest moment, the greatest things. Illuminated by faith the soul hath visions of God, yea, and, as far as it may, beholds God: and ranges along the bounds of the universe, and before the end of this world, already gazes upon the judgment, and the giving of rewards that is promised. Cherish then the faith in Him, which is of thyself; that thou mayest also receive from Him that faith which works things above man's power. [1 Cor. 12, 8 9.] [Mat. 17, 20.] [Mark 11, 23.] [Mat. 17, 20.]

(7.)

12. But take thou and hold that faith only as a learner and

58   *The Creed founded on Scripture.*

LECT. V.

in profession, which is by the Church delivered to thee, and is established from all Scripture. For since all cannot read the Scriptures, but some as being unlearned, others by business, are hindered from the knowledge of them; in order that the soul may not perish for lack of instruction, in the Articles which are few we comprehend the whole doctrine of the Faith. This I wish you to remember even in the very phrase, and to rehearse it with all diligence among yourselves, not writing it on paper, but by memory graving it on your heart as on a monument: being watchful, during your exercise, lest haply some of the Catechumens overhear the things delivered to you. This I wish you to keep all through your life as a provision for the way, and besides this to receive no other ever: whether we ourselves should change and contradict what we now teach; or some opposing Angel, transformed into an Angel of light, should aim at leading you astray. *For though we, or an Angel from heaven, preach any other Gospel unto you than that ye have received, let him be accursed.* And for the present, commit to memory the Faith, merely listening to the words; and expect at the fitting season the proof of each of its parts from the Divine Scriptures. For the Articles of the Faith were not composed at the good pleasure of men: but the most important points chosen from all Scriptures, make up the one teaching of the Faith. And, as the mustard seed in a little grain contains many branches, thus also this Faith, in a few words, hath enfolded in its bosom the whole knowledge of godliness contained both in the Old and New Testaments. Behold, therefore, brethren, and *hold the traditions* which ye now receive, and *write them on the table of your hearts*^c.

2 Cor. 11. 14.
Gal. 1, 8. 9.

(8.)
2 Thess. 2, 15
Prov 7, 3.

13. This keep with godly fear, lest haply any of you being puffed up, be spoiled by the enemy; lest some heretic pervert any of the things delivered unto you. For Faith is like casting down money on the table: and this we have now done; but God requires of you an account of the deposit. *I charge thee before God,* saith the Apostle, *who quickeneth all things, and before Jesus Christ, who before Pontius Pilate witnessed a good confession, that ye keep* this Faith delivered

1 Tim. 5, 21 and 6, 13 14.

^c The Nicene Creed follows here in some MSS

unto thee *without spot, until the appearing of our Lord Jesus Christ.* The treasure of life hath now been committed to thee, and the Master will seek His deposit at His appearing, *which in His own times He shall show, Who is the blessed and only Potentate, the King of kings, and Lord of lords; Who only hath immortality, dwelling in the light which no man can approach unto; Whom no man hath seen, nor can see: to Whom be honour and glory* for ever and ever. Amen.

1 Tim 6, 15 16.

LECTURE VI.

ON THE UNITY OF GOD[a].

Isaiah xlv. 16, 17.

They shall go to confusion together that are partakers of idols; but Israel shall be saved in the Lord with an everlasting salvation, ye shall not be ashamed nor confounded world without end.

Lect. VI.
2 Cor. 1, 3.

1. BLESSED be God and the Father of our Lord Jesus Christ; and blessed also be His only-begotten Son. For in the idea of God, let the idea of Father be included; that glory may be ascribed indivisibly to Father and Son with the Holy Ghost. For there is not one glory to Father, and another to Son, but one and the same with the Holy Ghost. Since the Son is the Only-begotten of the Father, and when the Father receives, the Son shares the glory; for the Son's glory is from His Father's honour: and again, when the Son is glorified, the Father of that infinitely good Gift is honoured mightily.

2. Now, though the motions of the intellect are most rapid, yet the tongue requires words, and the medium of discussion drawn out at full length. For the eye takes in at once a great company of stars; but if one wishes to tell of each in particular, which is the morning star, and which the evening, and so of each single star, there is need of many words. In like manner, the mind in the shortest moment of time compasses earth and sea, and all the bounds of the world; but that which is thought of in an instant, takes many words to express. Yet forcible as is the instance I have given, still it is after all weak and inadequate. For we speak, not what we ought concerning God, (for to Him only is this known,) but what man's nature can, and our weakness is equal to. For we explain not what God is; but we honestly confess that

---

[a] Περὶ Θεοῦ μοναρχίας, i. e. that God is the sole principle of all things, of existence, power, authority, &c.

we have no exact knowledge of Him; for on the subject of God, it is great knowledge to confess our want of knowledge[b]. *Magnify, then, the Lord with me, and let us all exalt His name together.* All of us jointly; for one is unequal to it; yea rather, though all of us united, we should not even then do it adequately; not only not you who are present, but not even if all the nurslings of all the universal Church, present and to come, should meet together, could they, worthily, sing the praises of the Shepherd. Ps. 34, 3.

3. Abraham was great and honourable,—but great in comparison of men; but when he drew nigh to God, then honestly avowing the truth, he saith, *I am earth and ashes.* He said not, "Earth" only, and then was silent, lest he should call himself by the name of that mighty element: but he added, "and ashes;" that he might represent his mouldering and frail nature. "Is there, saith he, any thing smaller or lighter than ashes?" Take, he saith, the comparison of ashes with a house, of a house with a city, of a city with a province, of a province with the Roman empire, of the Roman empire with all the earth, and all its bounds; then compare all the earth with the embosoming heaven, the earth, which holds such proportion to the heaven, as the centre of the wheel to all its circumference, (for such is the proportion between earth and heaven;)—think then that this first heaven which we see, is smaller than the second, and the second than the third, (for thus far hath Scripture named them, not that they are so many only, but so many only was it expedient for us to know,)—and when thou hast in thought surveyed all the heavens, yet not even shall the heavens be able to praise God according to what He is, no, not though they should resound with a voice louder than thunder. But if the spheres of heaven, being so many, cannot worthily sing God's praise, how shall earth and ashes, that least and smallest of things existing, succeed in sending up a worthy song to God, or worthily to speak of God, *that sitteth upon the circle of the earth, and the inhabitants thereof are as grasshoppers.* (2.) Gen. 18, 27. Is. 40, 22.

4. If any take in hand to speak concerning God, first let him declare the bounds of the earth. Thou dwellest on the (3.)

---

[b] Vid Hooker, Eccles. Pol i 2 §. 2. "Dangerous it were for the feeble brain of man," &c.

earth, and knowest not the limit of the earth which is thy dwelling; how then wilt thou be able worthily to think of its Creator? Thou beholdest the stars, but their Maker thou beholdest not: count the stars, which are seen, and then set forth Him who is not seen; *Who telleth the number of the stars, and calleth them all by their names!* The pouring rains, which lately came down on us, well nigh destroyed us: number the drops which fell in this city only: nay, on thine own house in one hour, if thou canst; but thou canst not. Know thou thine own weakness; and thence know the power of God; for *by Him are numbered the drops of rain,* which have been poured down on the whole earth, not only now, but ever. The sun is the workmanship of God, great indeed, yet but a spot in comparison of the whole of heaven; first gaze steadfastly on the sun, and then curiously scan his Lord. *Seek not that which is deeper than thou, and that which is stronger than thou search not out; but what is appointed thee, that consider.*

(4.) 5. But some one will say, If the Divine Nature is incomprehensible, why then dost thou discourse concerning these things? Shall I then, since I cannot drink up all the river, not take in due measure even what is expedient for me? Because I cannot sustain with these eyes of mine the whole sun, shall I not behold even as much of him as suffices for my wants? or, when I have entered into a great park, because I cannot eat all the fruits, wouldest thou have me depart actually hungry? I praise and glorify Him who hath made us: for it is a Divine call which says, *Let every thing that hath breath praise the Lord.* I am attempting now to glorify the Lord, not to declare Him; knowing indeed right well that I must fall short of worthily glorifying Him, but deeming it a work of godliness even to attempt it at all. For the Lord Jesus encourages my infirmity, saying, *No one hath seen God at any time.*

6. What then, some one will say, means the text, *The Angels of the little ones always behold the face of My Father which is in heaven?* Yes, but the Angels behold, not according to what God is, but as they are able. For it is Jesus Himself who saith, *Not that any hath seen the Father, save He which is of God: He hath seen the Father.* The Angels

then behold as they can bear, and the Archangels as they are able; and Thrones and Dominions, though more fully than these, yet less than God's excellency. But only the Holy Ghost, together with the Son, can behold Him worthily: for the Spirit *searcheth all things, and knoweth even the deep* 1 Cor. *things of God.* For as the Only-begotten Son, together with 2, 10. the Holy Ghost, fully knoweth the Father, (*for neither* Mat. 11, *knoweth any one the Father,* saith He, *save the Son, and he* 27. *to whomsoever the Son will reveal Him,*) so while He beholdeth fully, He, with and through the Holy Ghost, revealeth God, according as each can bear: since the Only-begotten Son together with the Holy Ghost is a partaker of the Father's Godhead. He, who without passion was begotten ὁ γεννη- *before the world began,* knoweth Him who begat; and He who θεὶς ἀπα-θῶς. begat knoweth Him who was begotten. When even Angels 2 Tim. 1, then are ignorant, (for to each according to his own capacity 9. doth the Only-begotten reveal Him through and with the Holy Ghost, as we have said,) let none of men be ashamed to own his ignorance. I am now speaking, as all do in place: but how we speak, we cannot tell: how then can I declare Him who hath given us the gift of speech? I who have a soul, yet cannot tell its lineaments; how then shall I be equal to describe its Giver?

7. It suffices us for devotion, to know that we have a (5.) God; a God who is One, a God who is, is always; always like unto Himself; and has no Father, none mightier than Himself, no successor to dispossess Him of His kingdom: manifold in name, all-powerful, in substance uniform. For μονοειδῆ though He is called Good, and Just, and Almighty, and τὴν ὑπό-στασιν. Sabaoth[c], He is not therefore distinct and various; but being Himself one and the same, He dispenses the countless operations of the Godhead, not abounding here and deficient there, but being in all things like unto Himself. Not great in loving-kindness only, and little in wisdom, but with wisdom and loving-kindness in equal measure; not seeing here, and not seeing there; but being all eye, and all ear, and all mind; not as we, perceiving here, and ignorant there; for

---

[c] This is sometimes taken in antiquity absolutely as a name of God, considered as Lord of Angels. Vid. Prudentius, Apoth v 837. Est impossibile spectare profunda Sabaoth, i. e. Dei. Ed. Bened

this is blasphemy, and unworthy of the Divine substance. He foreknows events; He is Holy, and Almighty, and kinder, greater, and wiser than all; and is unspeakable as to His beginning, and form, and nature. *Ye have neither heard His voice at any time, nor seen His shape*, says holy Scripture; and therefore Moses says to the Israelites, *Take ye therefore good heed unto yourselves; for ye saw no manner of similitude:* for if His outward appearance is utterly incapable of delineation, much less is His substance unimaginable.

8. Many and by many have been the delineations, but all have failed. Some men have thought that God is fire; others that He is like a man, but winged, because of a true text, ill understood, *Hide me under the shadow of Thy wings.* They forget that our Lord Jesus Christ, the Only-begotten, said likewise concerning Himself to Jerusalem, *How often would I have gathered thy children together, even as a hen gathereth her chickens under her wings, and ye would not!* For His guardian power being taken as wings, these men, not understanding, and grovelling among human things, conceived of the Unsearchable in a human way. And others have dared to say, that He has seven eyes, because it is written, *The seven eyes of the Lord which run to and fro through the whole earth.* For if He has but seven eyes round about Him, here and there, then His sight too is here and there, and not all-perfect: which is blasphemy. God is to be accounted perfect in all things, according to the Saviour's saying, *Your Father which is in heaven is perfect:* perfect in sight, perfect in power, perfect in greatness, perfect in foreknowledge, perfect in goodness, perfect in righteousness, perfect in loving-kindness. Not limited by place, but the Maker of all place: who is in all, and is circumscribed by none. *Heaven is His throne*, but He who is seated on it reaches far above it: *Earth is His footstool*, but His power extends to the realms beneath the earth.

9. One there is, all-present, all-seeing, all-understanding, creating all through Christ: for *all things were made by Him, and without Him was not a thing made;* a fount of all good, a fount immense and inexhaustible, a river of blessings, Light eternal beaming inexhaustibly, Power irresistible, condescending to our infirmities: whose very Name

is too awful to hear. *Wilt thou find the footstep of the Lord,* saith Job, *or hast thou attained unto the least things which the Almighty hath made?* If the least of His works cannot be comprehended, shall He be comprehended who made all things? *Eye hath not seen, nor ear heard, neither have entered into the heart of man, the things which God hath prepared for them that love Him.* If those things which God hath prepared are to our minds incomprehensible, can we in thought comprehend Him their preparer? *O the depth of the riches both of the wisdom and knowledge of God! how unsearchable are His judgments, and His ways past finding out!* says the Apostle: if His judgments and ways are unattainable, shall He Himself be attained? [Job 11, 7. Sept.] [1 Cor. 2, 9.] [Rom. 11, 33.]

10. Though God is so great, yea, and greater—(for though the whole of me became tongue, it could not speak adequately, rather, not even all Angels joined together would suffice,) though I say, the Great and Good God is such, yet did man grave a stone, and dare to say to it, *Thou art my God !* O great blindness, from such greatness descending to such abjectness! The tree which God has planted, and the rain increased, and which then is burnt to ashes, this forsooth is named God; but the true God is made light of. The wickedness of idolatry wrought lavishly; and cat, dog, wolf, were worshipped instead of God. The lion who devours man was worshipped for God who tenderly loves him; serpent and dragon, counterparts of him who cast us out of Paradise, were worshipped; He who planted Paradise, was thought lightly of. Nay, I feel shame while I say it, even onions have been before now worshipped. Wine was given, *to make glad the heart of man;* and Bacchus was worshipped in the place of God: God made corn by saying, *Let the earth bring forth grass, the herb yielding seed after its kind,* that bread might *strengthen man's heart;* whence then was Ceres worshipped? fire even to this day is struck out from stones by collision; whence then Vulcan, the maker of fire? (7.) [Is. 44, 17.] [Ps 104, 15.] [Gen. 1, 11 Ps 104, 15.]

11. Whence the Greek false doctrine of many gods? God is incorporeal; whence then the adulteries, which are charged upon their so-called gods? I will be silent of the changes of Jupiter into a swan. I am ashamed to speak of his transformations into a bull; as if lowings were worthy of a god.

The god of the Greeks is convicted of adultery, yet are they not ashamed: but if he is an adulterer, let him not be called god. They tell too of deaths among their gods, and expulsions, and blastings by thunder; seest thou how high they were and now how fallen? Surely it was not for nought that the Son of God came down from heaven, when it was to heal so great a wound; it was not for nought the Son came, that the Father might be acknowledged. Thou hast learned, what moved the Only-begotten to come down from the throne on God's right hand. The Father was despised; it behoved the Son to set right this departure; for it behoved Him by whom all things were made, to bring all things near unto the Lord of all. The wound had to be cured; for what was worse than such a sickness, the worshipping a stone for God?

Of Heresies.

(8.) 12. And not only among the Gentiles hath the Devil waged this contest; but many falsely called Christians, wrongfully designated by the sweet name of Christ, have been impious enough to dare separate God from His own works. I mean the tribe of heretics, men of evil name and utter ungodliness, in pretence lovers of Christ, but altogether His enemies: for he who blasphemes Christ's Father, is an enemy of the Son. These men[b] have dared to say that there are two godheads, one good, and one evil. Exceeding blindness! If a Godhead then, must it not be altogether good? but if not good, why called Godhead? For goodness belongs to God. For since there belongeth to God lovingkindness, beneficence, omnipotence, let them do one of two things; let them call Him God in operation as well as in name; or if they mean to deprive Him of His operative power, let them not give Him the bare name.

13. Heretics have dared to say, that there are two Gods, a source of good, and a source of evil, and that both these are unoriginate. If both are unoriginate, certainly they must be equal also, and both mighty; how then doth the light destroy the darkness? Again, are they ever together, or are they separate? Together they cannot be, *for what fellowship hath light with darkness,* saith the Apostle; but if they are far

οἱ παῖδες τῶν αἱρετικῶν.

2 Cor. 6, 14.

[b] i e. The Manichees

one from another, doubtless each has his own place, and if so, doubtless we are in the realms of one God: doubtless also we worship one God. Thus the argument holds for the worship of one God, even granting their absurd doctrine. Next let us examine what they say of the good God. Is He powerful, or powerless? If powerful, how came evil, against His will? and how does the evil substance introduce itself, without His consent? If He knows, but cannot hinder, they impute to Him want of power; but unfaithfulness, if He is able, yet hinders it not. And consider their inconsistency; at one time they say, that as to the world's creation the evil God has nothing in common with the good God: at another time, only the fourth part. And they say that the good God is the Father of Christ; yet they call the sun, Christ. If then the world, according to them, was made by the evil God, and the sun is in the world; how is the Son of the good God an unwilling minister in the works of the evil God? It is to touch mire even to say these things; but I say them, lest any here present from not knowing better fall into heretical mire themselves. I know that I am polluting my own mouth, and your ears: but it is expedient; fitter much that you should hear these monstrous things charged against third persons, than out of ignorance fall into them. that thou shouldest know the mire and hate it, than know it not and fall into it. Heretical impiety is a way with many branches; when a man once strays from the one direct road, he often gets into precipitous ground.

14. And of all heresy Simon Magus was the originator,— (9.) Simon who in the Acts of the Apostles, expected to purchase with money the unpurchaseable gift of the Spirit, and who heard these words, *Thou hast neither part nor lot in this matter*, and the rest;—of whom it is written, *They went out from us, but they were not of us; for if they had been of us, they would no doubt have continued with us.* Having come to Rome, after he had been cast out by the Apostles, and gaining over a profligate woman called Helena, he commenced by daring with blasphemous lips to say, that he had appeared as the Father on Mount Sinai; that afterward among the Jews, he had shown himself as Christ, not in the flesh, but in appearance: and after this as the Holy Ghost, of whom Christ had

Acts 8, 18—21.
1 John 2, 19.

δόκησει

LECT. VI.

promised, that He should be sent as the Comforter. And he so deceived the Roman state, that Claudius set up a statue of him, writing under it in the Roman tongue, SIMONI DEO SANCTO: which being interpreted is, "To Simon the Holy God [c]."

προστά-ται. vid. above Lect. IV § 35.

15. The error spreading, that goodly pair, Peter and Paul, the rulers of the Church, being present, set matters right again; and on Simon the supposed God attempting a display, they straightway laid him dead. Simon, that is, promised that he should be raised aloft towards heaven, and accordingly was borne through the air on a chariot of Dæmons; on which the servants of God falling on their knees, gave an instance of that agreement, of which Jesus said, *If two of you shall agree as touching any thing that they shall ask, it shall be done for them*: and reaching the sorcerer with this unanimity of their prayer, they precipitated him to the earth. For is this strange, though it be strange? for it was Peter, he who bears with him the keys of heaven: is it astonishing? for it was Paul, he who was caught up *into the third Heaven, and into paradise, and who heard unspeakable words, which it is not lawful for a man to utter.* It was these, I say, who precipitated from air to earth the supposed God, on his journey to the place under the earth. He then was the first serpent of evil: but though one head had been cut off, the root of evil turned out many-headed.

Mat. 18, 19.

Mat. 16, 19.
2 Cor. 12, 2. 4.

(10.)

16. Cerinthus wasted the Church, and Menander, and Carpocrates: and the Ebionites, and Marcion, a very mouthpiece of ungodliness; for one who teaches different Gods, one good, the other just, contradicts the Son, who says, *Righteous Father*. Again, one who says that the Father is different from the Maker of the world, is at variance with the Son who says, *If then God so clothe the grass, which is to-day in the field, and to-morrow is cast into the oven*; and *Who maketh His sun to rise on the evil and on the good, and sendeth rain on the just and on the unjust*. This Marcion, then, came

John 17, 25.

Luke 12, 28.
Mat. 5, 45.

[c] This account originates in Justin Martyr, who says he saw the statue in the island of the Tiber. A doubt, however, is cast on it, from a stone having been dug up in this very island in the Pontificate of Gregory XIII, A D 1585, with this inscription, Semoni Sango Deo Sacrum. Sex Pompeius &c. Sangus or Sancus was a Sabine God vid. Lact. 1 15 Aust de Civ D. xviii 19. That Simon was struck dead at Rome by St. Peter is confirmed by the cautious Eusebius, but the details of the occurrence are not certain.

next, the originator of another error; for being refuted by the text from the Old Testament which are cited in the New, he who had already effaced the idea of God, was the first to venture also on cutting out those very testimonies to the word of faith preached in the Gospel; and to consent to weaken the Church's faith, as though there had been no heralds of it.

17. Next came Basilides, of evil fame, plausible in his (11.) bearing, and a preacher of profligacy. Valentinus aided the wretched cause, with his announcement of thirty Gods. The Greeks tell of few: but this man, in name though not in truth a Christian, carried on their fiction to a whole thirty[d]. And he says that Bythus, the Abyss, begat Silence; (for it became him who is the abyss of wickedness, to begin his doctrine from the Abyss;) and that of Silence he begat the Word.— This Bythus is worse than the Jupiter of the Greeks, who was married to his sister: for Silence was said to be the child of Bythus. What a monstrous doctrine to be cloaked under the pretence of Christianity! but wait awhile, and thou shalt hate the impious creed. He says that of him were begotten eight Æons, or Ages: and of them, ten more: and of them, other twelve, male and female. And what is the proof of all this? their arguments are as absurd as their creed; how dost thou demonstrate the thirty Æons? because, says he, it is written, that Jesus was baptized, being thirty years old: Luke 3, granting the fact, what a demonstration is this? He broke 23. five loaves among five thousand; are there therefore five Gods? or because He had twelve disciples, must there be twelve?

18. Even this however is little compared with the impious things which follow: he says, that the last of the Gods is both male and female; (thus he dares to speak,) and that this is Wisdom: what blasphemy! for Christ is *the Wisdom of God*, 1 Cor. His only-begotten Son · and yet his doctrine degraded the 1, 2[b] Wisdom of God to a female nature, and a thirtieth principle, and the last creation. And he says, that Wisdom attempted to behold the first God; but that, not bearing his brightness, she fell from heaven, and forfeited the thirtieth place; that

---

[d] Licet Gentiles duodecim Deos appellent, isti [Valentiniani] triginti et duos Æonas colant quos appellant Deos. Ambros Ep xl. 16 ap Ed Bened.

then as she groaned, her groans begat the devil: and while she wept her downfall, she gave being to the sea. What blasphemy! as if the devil could be born from Wisdom, and evil from understanding, or from light, darkness? And he says, that the devil begat others, some of whom framed the world; and that the Christ came down, to make men revolt from the Maker of the World.

19. Now listen, whom they say that Christ Jesus is: that thou mayest hate them still more. They teach then, that when Wisdom was cast out, in order that the number of the thirty might not be incomplete, the nine and twenty Æons each contributed some little element, and formed the Christ: and him again, as they say, both male and female. Can there be aught more blasphemous, aught more miserable than this? I go through their heresy, to make you hate them more. Flee then such blasphemy, nor *bid such an one God speed*, lest thou *have fellowship with the unfruitful works of darkness*. And be not curious about them, nor seek to converse with them.

<small>2 John 11.
Eph 5, 11.</small>

(12.) 20. Thou must hate all heretics, but especially him who even in name is a Maniac; who arose lately under the Emperor Probus: (for the error is just seventy years standing,) and there are to this day men who have seen him with their own eyes. But hate him not for this, that he is of recent date; but because of his impious doctrines, hate thou this worker of evil, this reservoir of all pollution, who hath taken on him the filth of every heresy. For being ambitious of distinction among the bad, he took the doctrines of all, and having framed one heresy filled with blasphemies, and with all wickedness, he devastates the Church, (or rather those without it,) like a lion ranging about, and devouring. Heed not thou their fair speeches, nor their supposed humility: for they are serpents, the offspring of vipers. Judas too said, Hail Master, and betrayed Him: heed not that they kiss, but guard against their venom.

21. Lest I seem to bring these charges without grounds, I will go out of the way to say who this Manes is, and to a certain point what he teaches; as to giving a full account of his foul teaching, no time would be long enough. It will serve as an aid in season, to lay up in thy memory what I

have said on other occasions and shall repeat now, with the view of informing the ignorant and reminding the informed. Manes did not rise from the Christian body; God forbid! nor like Simon was he cast out of the Church, neither he, nor those who taught before him, for he is a pilferer and appropriator of other men's sins;—but how, and after what manner, ye must hear.

22. There was in Egypt a certain Scythianus, a Saracen [e] (13.) by race, without any thing in common either with Judaism, or with Christianity. This man who dwelt at Alexandria, as an Aristotelian, composed four books: one called the Gospel, yet not an account of the acts of Christ, though bearing this title; and another called the Book of Chapters; and a third called the Book of Mysteries; and a fourth, which they now use, called the Treasure. This man had a disciple, Terebinthus by name; as for Scythianus himself he passed into Judæa, and while he was engaged in infecting that country, the Lord took him off by a sickness, and stopped the plague.

23. Terebinthus, his disciple in wicked error, was heir of his gold, his books, and his heresy: he made his appearance in Palestine; but on being recognized and condemned in Judæa, he resolved to pass into Persia; and to prevent a second recognition from his name, he changed it to Buddas. But there he found opponents, the ministers of Mithras: and being subjected to a series of defeats in discussion and controversy, at last hard pressed, he betakes himself to a certain widow. Then having gone up to the top of the house, and invoked the Dæmons of the air, whom the Manichæans to this day invoke upon their detestable ceremony of the fig[f], he was stricken of God, fell headlong from the house, and gave up the ghost: and thus the second monster was cut off.

24. The books, however, the records of impiety, remained; and these and the property the widow inherited. And whereas she had neither kinsman, nor any one else, she determined out of the money to purchase a boy, named Cubricus: and having adopted him, she brought him up as a son in the

---

[e] The Saracens are first mentioned by Dionysius of Alexandria, apud   Euseb. Hist. vi. 42
[f] Vid infra, § 33

LECT. VI.

learning of the Persians, and thus sharpened an evil weapon against mankind. So Cubricus, her wicked servant, grew up in the midst of philosophers; and on her death, inherited the books and the money. Then, lest the name of slavery should be a reproach to him, he called himself instead of Cubricus, Manes, which in the Persian language means, discourse: for since a disputant seemed to be a character of weight, he so surnamed himself, as though he were a most excellent discourser. But though he put himself to pains to gain repute according to the Persian language, yet by the Divine dispensation he was made still an unwilling witness against himself; so as to honour himself in Persia, at the expense of proclaiming himself a maniac among the Greeks.

(14)
Mark 3, 29.

25. And he dared to say that he was the Paraclete[g]; though it be written, *But he who shall blaspheme against the Holy Ghost, hath no forgiveness.* He then blasphemed, saying that he was the Holy Ghost; let him that hath fellowship with them, take heed with whom he is ranking himself.

Prov 30, 21. 22.

The servant shook the world, since *for three things the earth is disquieted, and the fourth it cannot bear, when a servant reigneth.* And having come into public, he now began to promise things superhuman. The son of the king of the Persians was sick, and a great crowd of physicians was in attendance. Manes promised to restore him by prayer, as though he were a devout man. The physicians departed, and the child's life with them,—this detected the man's impiety; our philosopher came into bonds, being cast into prison, not for reproving the king for truth's sake, not for overthrowing the idols, but for promising to save, and lying; yea rather, to say truth, for committing murder. For a patient who might have been cured by medical treatment, he in sending away the physicians, murdered by want of that treatment.

26. But in this enumeration of his multiplied offences, remember first his blasphemy; secondly, his slavery; (not that slavery is a shame to a man, but that for a man who is a slave to feign himself free, is an offence;) thirdly, the falsehood of his promise; fourthly, the murder of the child;

---

[g] That Manes or Manichæus professed himself to be the promised Paraclete or Spirit of Christ, is confirmed by Eusebius, Hist. vii 31 Theodoret. Hær 1 26 and Austin contr Faust xxxii. 16. 17.

fifthly, the shame of the prison. And there was not only the shame of the prison, but also the flight from the prison; yea, he who said that he was the Paraclete, and the champion of Truth, fled. He was not a successor of Jesus, who readily came to the cross; he was the reverse, a runaway. Then the king of Persia ordered the keepers of the prison to be led off to capital punishment. Manes was through his presumption the cause of the child's death: so too was he the cause of the keeper's death through his flight. Is he then who has a share in murder, fit to be worshipped? Ought he not to have followed Jesus, and said, *If ye seek me, let these go their way*? ought he not to have said like Jonas, *Take me, and cast me into the sea; for my sake is this great tempest*? John 18, 8. Jonah 1, 12

27. He flies from prison, and comes to Mesopotamia; but (15.) there the Bishop Archelaus meets him as a weapon of righteousness, who argued with him before philosophers as judges, bringing together a Gentile audience, lest if Christians judged, the judges might be considered partial. And he says to Manes, "Tell us what thou preachest." He, *whose mouth was an holy sepulchre*, began his defence with blasphemies against the Maker of all things. "The God of the Old Testament is the inventor of evil; for he saith of himself, *I am a consuming fire*" But Archelaus skilfully met the blasphemous argument; "If the God of the Old Testament, he said, according to thy words, calls Himself fire, whose Son is He who saith, *I am come to send fire on the earth*! If thou find fault with Him who saith, *The Lord killeth and maketh alive*, wherefore honourest thou Peter, who though he raised Tabitha, yet slew Sapphira? If again thou findest fault with Him as preparing fire, wherefore not with Him who says, *Depart from me into everlasting fire*? If with Him who says, *I am the God that maketh peace and create evil*; explain how Jesus saith, *I am not come to send peace, but a sword*? Since both speak the same language, one of two things must follow: either both are right, because they agree in these words: or if Jesus is unreprovable in so speaking, why reproachest thou Him who in the Old Testament says the same?" Ps 5, 9. Deut. 4, 24. Luke 12, 49 1 Sam. 2, 6 Mat 25, 41. Is 45, 7. Mat 10, 34 ἀμφότεροι καλοί.

28 Then says Manes to him: "And what sort of God is he who blinds men? For it is Paul who says, *In whom the* (16) 2 Cor 4, 4

God of this world hath blinded the minds of them that believe not, that the light of the Gospel might not shine into them." But Archelaus retorted well, "Read what comes just before, *But if our Gospel be hid, it is hid in them that are lost.* Seest thou, it is in the lost that it is hid? For we must not give what is holy to the dogs. Again, is it only the God of the Old Testament who hath blinded the minds of the unbelievers? And hath not Jesus Himself said, *For this cause speak I unto them in parables, that seeing they may not see?* Was it because He hated them, that He would not that they should see? or was it because of this unworthiness, since they had *closed their eyes?* For where there is self-chosen depravity, there is also the withholding of grace: *for to him that hath shall be given, but from him that hath not shall be taken even that which he seemeth to have."*

29. Or we may say, as some explain, and not despicably, If He hath indeed blinded the minds of the unbelievers, He hath blinded them for good purpose, that they may look up to what is good; for He hath not said, "He hath blinded the soul," but, *the thoughts of the unbelievers.* For what He says is something of this kind; "Blind the profligate thoughts of the profligate man, and he is saved: blind the rapacious and plundering spirit of the robber, and he is saved." If thou wilt not so take it, there is yet another exposition of it. The sun too blinds those who are dull of sight; and men with weak eyes are blinded, the light distressing them; not that the sun is of a blinding nature, but because their eyes themselves do not see. And he hath not said, "He hath blinded their thoughts," that they might not hear the Gospel, but, *that the light of the glory of the Gospel of our Lord Jesus Christ should not shine unto them.* For to hear the Gospel is allowed to all: but the glory of the Gospel is set apart for them who are truly Christ's. Therefore our Lord spake in parables to them who were not able to hear; but to His disciples He expounded them privately: for the brightness of glory is for the Illuminated, but blindness for the unbelievers. These mysteries which the Church now speaks to thee who art removed from among the Catechumens, it is not the custom to speak to Gentiles: for to a Gentile we speak not the mysteries concerning the Father and the Son, and the Holy

Spirit, nor before Catechumens do we discourse plainly about mysteries; but many things many times we speak in a covert manner, that the faithful who know may understand, and that those who know not may receive no hurt.

30. With such words and many more was the serpent overcome; thus did Archelaus wrestle with Manes, and threw him. Again he, who had fled from prison, flies from this (17.) place also: and, having escaped his adversary, he comes to a very mean village; like the serpent in Paradise who left Adam, and came to Eve. But the good shepherd Archelaus taking thought for the sheep, when he heard of his flight, straightway with all speed hastened in search of the wolf. Manes seeing his adversary unexpectedly, rushed away and fled; and fled for the last time. For the guards of the king $ἐπὶ τοῦ$ of Persia, being on the search, arrest the runaway, and inflict $Ἀρχελάου$. on him the sentence which he was on the point of receiving at the from the see of Archelaus. That Manes, who is now worshipped the palace. by his disciples, is seized, and led to the king; the king cast in his teeth his falsehood and flight; derided his slavish condition; avenged the murder of his son; condemned him also for the murder of the jailors. He orders Manes to be flayed after the Persian fashion; and the rest of his body was thrown as food for wild beasts: but his skin, that receptacle of a most foul mind, was hung up like a sack before the gates. He who called himself the Paraclete, and professed to know things to come, knew not his own flight and seizure [h].

31. This man had three disciples, Thomas, and Baddas, (18) and Hermas. Let no one read the gospel according to Thomas, for it is the work, not of one of the Twelve Apostles, but of one of the three evil followers of Manes. Let no one join himself to the soul-wasting Manichees,—who affect $τοῖς$ the harshness of fasting with chaff and water, who gorge $ἀχύρων$ $ὕδασι$. themselves with the daintiest of meats, while they speak against the Creator, who teach, that he who plucks up a herb, is changed into it [1]. For if he who crops a herb, or any vegetable, is changed into it, into how many will husbandmen and the tribe of gardeners be changed? Into how

---

[h] The foregoing account of the history of Manes and his predecessors, is confirmed in substance by Socrates, Hist. i. 22. Epiphanius, Hær. 66. and Archelaus, Act Disput.

[1] Vid the account of the Manichæan heresy appended to the Translation of S Austin's Confessions

76   *Doctrine and rites of Manicheism.*

LECT. VI. many doth the gardener put his sickle, as we see;—into which then of these is he transformed? Ridiculous doctrines truly, and fraught with their own condemnation and shame! A shepherd both sacrifices a sheep and slays a wolf; into which is he changed? Many men have both netted fishes and limed birds; into which are they changed?

32. Let the Manichees, children of sloth, answer; who themselves work not, and eat up the labours of those who do; who receive with smiling countenances those who bring them meats, and return them curses instead of blessings. For when some simple person brings them any thing, the Manichee says, "Stand forth a little, and I will bless thee:" then having received the bread into his hand, (as some of them who have repented have confessed,) he says to the bread, "I did not make thee;" and he utters curses against the Highest, and curses him that made the bread, and thus eats what is made. If thou hatest food, why didst thou look with a smiling face on him who brought it? If thou art grateful to him who brought it, why utterest thou blasphemy against God who made and fashioned it? And again he says, "I did not sow thee; may the sower of thee be sown! I did not reap thee with a sickle; may the reaper of thee be reaped! I baked thee not with fire; may the baker of thee be baked!" A fair return this for kindness.

(19.) 33. These are great offences, yet but small in comparison of what remains behind. I do not venture to describe their Baptism[k] before men and women. I do not venture to say what they dispense to their wretched congregations[l]. It is truly a pollution of our lips to speak on the subject. Are Greeks more loathsome? are Samaritans more abandoned? are Jews more blasphemous? are open profligates more unclean? The Manichee at the very altar, as he thinks right, places his offering[m]; and dost thou, O man, accept teaching

---

[k] The Manichees of later times seem to have rejected Baptism, using oil for water, or considering Baptism a spiritual washing. Ed Bened

[l] The original runs Οὐ τολμῶ εἰπεῖν, τίνι ἐμβάπτοντες τὴν ἰσχάδα, διδόασι τοῖς ἀθλίοις διὰ συσσήμων δὲ μόνον δηλούσθω ἄνδρες γὰρ τὰ ἐν τοῖς ἐνυπνιασμοῖς ἐνθυμείσθωσιν, καὶ γυναῖκες τὰ ἐν ἀφέδροις Μιαίνομεν ἀληθῶς τὸ στόμα κ τ λ.

[m] Ὁ μὲν γὰρ πορνεύσας, πρὸς μίαν ὥραν δ' ἐπιθυμίαν τελεῖ τὴν πρᾶξιν· καταγινώσκων δὲ τῆς πράξεως ὡς μιανθεὶς οἶδε λουτροῦ ἐπιδεόμενος, καὶ γινώσκει τῆς πράξεως τὸ μυσαρόν. Ὁ δὲ Μανιχαῖος θυσιαστηρίου μέσον, οὗ νομίζει, τίθησι ταῦτα, καὶ μιαίνει καὶ τὸ στόμα καὶ τὴν γλῶτταν παρὰ τοιούτου στόματος, ἄνθρωπε κ τ λ

at such a mouth? dost thou meet him and greet him at all with a kiss; and not rather, without reference to his other blasphemy, flee from this defiled teacher, from a man worse than dissolute, more loathsome than any haunt of profligacy?

34. These things the Church tells of and teaches thee, and touches mire, that thou be not bemired: she tells of wounds, that thou be not wounded. Suffice it thee to know the fact; attempt not to learn by experience.—God thunders, and we all tremble; but they blaspheme. God lightens, and we all bow down to earth; but they have blasphemous tongues concerning the heavens,—which are written in their books, and which we have read, disbelieving those who affirmed them· yes, for your salvation, we have closely inquired into their deadly doctrines [n].

35. But may the Lord deliver us from such error: and may (20.) you be vouchsafed enmity against the serpent; that as they watch the heel, so you in turn may trample on their head. Remember the text, *What agreement* is there between our matters and theirs? what hath *light* to do *with darkness*? 2 Cor. 6, 14. What the majesty of the Church with the abomination of the Manichees? Here is order, here is discipline, here majesty, ἐπιστή- here chastity: here even a wanton glance is condemnation. μὴ vid. supr In- Here is marriage with seriousness, and perseverance in conti- trod nence, and the angelical rank of a virgin life, feasting with Lect. § 4. thanksgiving, and towards the Maker of the world an affec- βρωμά- tionate heart Here the Father of Christ is worshipped; here is τῶν με- τοχή. taught fear and trembling towards Him who sends us rain, 1 Tim. and praise ascribed to Him who thunders and lightens. 4, 3.

36. Fold thou with the sheep: flee the wolves; depart not from the Church. Nay, abhor those who at any time have come into suspicion of such things; and unless in the course of time thou ascertain their repentance, be not hasty to trust thyself with them. The truth is now delivered to thee, how

---

[n] Κἀκεῖνοι περὶ οὐρανῶν τὰς δυσφή- μους ἔχουσι γλώσσας Ἰησοῦς λέγει περὶ τοῦ πατρὸς αὐτοῦ, Ὅστις τὸν ἥλιον αὐτοῦ ἀνατέλλει ἐπὶ δικαίους καὶ ἀδίκους, καὶ βρέχει ἐπὶ πονηροὺς καὶ ἀγαθούς. κἀκεῖνοι λέγουσιν, ὅτι οἱ ὑετοὶ ἐξ ἐρωτι- κῆς μανίας γίνονται, καὶ τολμῶσι λέγειν, ὅτι ἐστί τις παρθένος ἐν οὐρανῷ εὐειδὴς μετὰ νεανίσκου εὐειδοῦς, καὶ κατὰ τὴν τῶν καμηλῶν ἢ λύκων καιρὸν, τοὺς τῆς αἰσχρᾶς ἐπιθυμίας καιροὺς ἔχειν, καὶ κατὰ τὴν τοῦ χειμῶνος καιρὸν, μανιωδῶς αὐτὸν ἐπιτρέχειν τῇ παρθένῳ, καὶ τὴν μὲν φεύγειν φασὶ, τὸν δὲ ἐπιτρέχειν, εἶτα ἐπιτρέχοντα ἱδροῦν, ἀπὸ δὲ τῶν ἱδρώτων αὐτοῦ εἶναι τὸν ὑετόν. Ταῦτα γέγραπται ἐν τοῖς τῶν Μανιχαίων βίβλοις ταῦτα ἡμεῖς ἀνέγνωμεν κ.τ.λ.

LECT. VI.

τῆς μοναρχίας.
Vid. 1 Thess 5, 21. 22.

God only is the First Principle of all things; distinguish one pasturage of doctrine from another. Be thou a good banker°, *holding fast what is good, abstaining from all appearance of evil.* But if thou thyself wert even one of them, now that thou hast discovered thine error, abhor it. It will prove a way of salvation, to vomit it up; to hate it from thy heart; to shun them too, not with thy lips only, but with thy soul also; to bow down to the Father of Christ, the God of the Law and the Prophets; to acknowledge the Good and the Just, to be One and the same God. May He keep all of you, guarding you from fall and offence, stablished in the Faith, in Christ Jesus our Lord, to Whom be glory for ever and ever. Amen.

° Γίνου δόκιμος τραπεζίτης. These words, which are frequently quoted in antiquity, are sometimes ascribed to our Lord, sometimes to S. Paul. Vid Constit. Apost. ii. 36. Clementin. Hom. ii, 51. iii. 50 &c Dionys. Alex. ap. Euseb Hist. vii, 7 Origen in Joan viii. 20. &c. Ussher, Valesius, &c. consider it taken from the Gospel according to the Hebrews.

LECTURE VII.

ON GOD, THE FATHER.

EPH. iii. 14, 15.

For this cause I bow my knees unto the Father of our Lord Jesus Christ, of whom the whole family of heaven and earth is named.

1. OF God as the One Principle of all things I said enough yesterday; enough, I mean, not in respect to the subject, (for mortal nature cannot reach this,) but in the measure of our weakness; and I trod the bye paths which have been variously struck out by profane heretics: now, shaking from us their foul and soul-destroying doctrine, and remembering it not to our hurt, but for their detestation, let us revert to ourselves, and receive the salutary articles of the true Faith, joining to the dignity of God's sole sovereignty, the attribute of Father, and believing in One God the Father. It is not enough to believe in one God: we must receive with reverence this also, that He is the Father of the Only-begotten, our Lord Jesus Christ. περὶ τῆς μονοπ-χίας, Unity of God.

2. For thus our view of religion will rise above the Jewish. (2.) For the Jews receive indeed the doctrine of the One God; (though they have often denied this too by committing idolatry;) but they deny that He is also the Father of our Lord Jesus Christ, differing from their own Prophets, who say in Holy Scripture, *The Lord hath said unto Me, Thou art My Son, this day have I begotten Thee.* Even to this day they rage and gather against the Lord and against His Christ, thinking that the Father may be made their friend, apart from devotion towards the Son; knowing not that no man cometh to the Father, but by the Son, who saith, *I am the door, and I am the way.* He then who declines the Way which leads to the Father, and denies the Door, how shall he be vouchsafed entrance to God? They contradict too the words of the eighty-eighth[a] Psalm: *He shall cry unto Me, Thou art My Father, My God, and the rock of My salvation*; Ps. 2, 7. Ps. 2, 1. 2. John 14, 6. John 10, 9. John 14, 6. Ps. 89, 26. 27

---

[a] i. e Psalm 89. In the Greek and Latin Versions, as need scarcely be said, the Psalms are numbered differently from the English.

LECT. VII.

Ps 89, 29
Ps 89, 36. 37.
Ps. 110, 3 Sept.
Ps 72, 5. Sept

τοῖς πᾶ- σι τὸ γεννᾷν χαριζό- μενον.

(3.)

ὑποστά- σεως

also, *I will make Him My first-born, higher than the kings of the earth*. If they contend that these things are spoken to David, or Solomon, or some of their successors, they have to show how the throne of him whom they consider to be the object of the prophecy, is as *the days of heaven*, and as the *sun before God*, and as *the moon stablished in heaven*: and how is it they feel no awe about the text, *From the womb, before the star of dawn I begat thee*: and again, *He shall endure with the sun, and before the moon, from generation to generation*? To apply these things to a man, argues a mind utterly and entirely insensible.

3. But let the Jews, since they so will, be troubled with their accustomed sickness, and disbelieve these and such like Scriptures; but let us embrace the godly doctrine of the Faith, worshipping one God, the Father of Christ. For it were profane indeed, when He has given unto all the prerogative of parents, to deny to Him the like. And let us believe in One God the Father, that even before proceeding to treat of Christ, our previous discourse concerning the Father, may lay deeply in your hearts, not retard, faith in the Only-begotten.

4. For the name of the Father, in its very utterance implies the Son: as in like manner to name the Son, is at once to imply the Father also. For if He is a Father, plainly the Father of a Son; and if a Son, plainly the Son of a Father. Therefore, lest when we say, We believe, "in one God, the Father Almighty, Maker of Heaven and Earth; and of all things visible and invisible," and then add, "and in One Lord Jesus Christ," it should be irreverently thought, that the Only-begotten is second in rank to heaven and earth, therefore before naming them, we named God, the Father; that as soon as we think of the Father, we may also think of the Son, for between the Son and the Father no being whatever comes.

5. God then, though He is in an improper sense the Father of many things, yet by nature and in truth is Father of One only, the Only-begotten Son our Lord, Jesus Christ: not becoming so in course of time, but being from everlasting the Father of the Only-begotten; not first without Son, and then becoming a Father, by a change of purpose; but before all substance, and all intelligence, before times and all ages, hath God the prerogative of Father; and more honoured

in this than in all the rest. A father, not by passion, not by union, not in ignorance, not by effluence, not by diminution, not by alteration[b]: for *every perfect gift is from above, and cometh down from the Father of lights, with whom is no variableness, neither shadow of turning.* He is a perfect Father of a perfect Son: who has delivered every thing to Him who is begotten; (for *all things*, He saith, *are delivered to Me of My Father:*) and is honoured of the Only-begotten; *For I honour My Father,* saith the Son: and again, *Even as I have kept My Father's commandments, and abide in His love.* Therefore we say like the Apostle; *Blessed be God, even the Father of our Lord Jesus Christ, the Father of mercies and God of all consolation;* and *we bow our knees unto the Father, of whom the whole family in heaven and earth is named,* glorifying Him with the Only-begotten: for he who denieth the Father, denieth the Son also: and again, He who confesseth the Son, hath also the Father; knowing that *Jesus Christ is Lord to the glory of God the Father*.

πάθει, ἐκ συμπλοκῆς, ἀπορρεύσας. Jam. 1, 17. Matt. 11, 27. John 8, 49. John 15, 10. 2 Cor. 1, 3 Eph. 3, 14 15. τοῦ Κ. ἡμῶν 'Ι. Χρ of our Lord J. C. added in rec. text.

6. We worship then the Father of Christ, the Maker of Heaven and Earth, the God of Abraham, Isaac, and Jacob; to whose honour the former temple also, over against us, was built in this place; without toleration of the Heretics, who sever the Old from the New Testament, and in submission to Christ, who says of the temple, *Wist ye not that I must be in My Father's place?* and again, *Take these things hence; and make not My Father's house an house of merchandise:* which are plain avowals that the former temple in Jerusalem is His own Father's house. But if any one is so unbelieving as to require yet more proofs of the Father of Christ being the Maker of the World; let him attend to these words of his, in addition; *Are not two sparrows sold for a farthing? and one of them shall not fall to the ground without My Father which is in heaven.* And, *Behold the fowls of the*

1 John 2, 22. 23. Phil. 2, 11. Luke 2, 49 John 2. 16. Mat 10, 29 ἄνευ τοῦ πατρὸς μου τοῦ ἐν οὐρα

---

[b] These ideas were introduced by the heretics of the Gnostic and Manichæan schools, and imputed by the Arians to the Catholic doctrine, and especially to the word ὁμοούσιον. Accordingly, explanations were given on the subject at the Council of Nicæa; as e g. Constantine's, which is thus reported in Eusebius's letter to his Church; αὐτὸς ἡρμήνευσε λέγων, ὅτι μὴ κατὰ τὰ τῶν σωμάτων πάθη λέγοι τὸ ὁμοούσιον, οὔτ' οὖν κατὰ διαίρεσιν, οὔτε κατά τινα ἀποτομὴν ἐκ τοῦ πατρὸς ὑποστῆναι μήτε ὑμᾶς, γὰρ δύνασθαι τὴν ἄυλον καὶ νοερὰν καὶ ἀσώματον φύσιν, σωματικόν τι πάθος ὑφίστασθαι· κ τ λ. Socr Hist. i. 8. νοις. In rec text without your Father.

air: for they sow not, neither gather into barns, and your heavenly Father feedeth them. And, *My Father worketh hitherto, and I work.*

7. But in case any one, whether from simplicity, or perverse ingenuity, suppose Christ to be but equal in honour to righteous men, from His saying, *I ascend to My Father, and your Father:* it is well first to lay down, that though the Name of Father is one, its meaning is manifold. As understanding this, He said without hesitation, *I go to My Father, and your Father:* not saying, To our Father; but making a distinction, and using at first in its proper meaning, *to My Father,* which was by nature, and then adding, *and your Father,* which was by adoption. For though we have been allowed to say without qualification in our prayers, "Our Father, which art in Heaven," this is a privilege from God's loving-kindness. For we do not call Him Father, because we were by nature begotten of the "Father which is in Heaven:" but having been translated from bondage to adoption, by the Father's grace, through the Son and the Holy Ghost, we are by ineffable loving-kindness allowed thus to speak.

8. And if any wishes to learn, how we call God, Father, let him hear Moses, the most excellent of elementary teachers; *Is not He thy Father,* he says, *that hath bought thee? Hath He not made thee, and established thee?* And Esaias the prophet; *But now, O Lord, Thou art our Father: we are the clay, and we all are the work of Thy hand.* In the plainest way has the Prophetic gift shewn, that not by nature, but of God's grace, and by adoption, we call Him Father.

9. Let Paul too explain to thee still more certainly, that in Holy Scriptures, it is not by any means the father according to the flesh only, who is called father; for he says, *For though ye have ten thousand instructors in Christ, yet have ye not many fathers; for, in Christ Jesus have I begotten you through the Gospel.* For not by begetting them according to the flesh, but in teaching and begetting them again according to the Spirit, was Paul the Father of the Corinthians. Again, consider Job's words, *I was a father to the poor.* For he named himself a father, not as having begotten them all, but as taking care of them. And the Only-begotten Son of God

Himself, when at His crucifixion, His flesh was nailed to the tree, seeing Mary His mother according to the flesh, and John His dearest disciple, says to him, *Behold thy mother;* and to her, *Behold thy son:* teaching her the parental affection due to him, and indirectly explaining that which is said in Luke, *and His father and His mother marvelled at Him:* words which heretical schools catch at, as if He were begotten of a man and a woman. For like as Mary was called the mother of John, from her parental affection to him, not from having given him birth: so was Joseph called the father of Christ, not as being really so, (for *he knew her not,* says the Gospel, *till she had brought forth her first-born Son,*) but on account of his care in nurturing Him.

_{John 19, 26. 27.}

_{Luke 2, 33.}

_{Ἰωσήφ, Joseph, received text; but Griesbach reads as Cyril.}

_{Matt. 1, 25.}

10. Thus much then, in the way of a digression, to put you in remembrance. However, I will add yet another text in proof that God is called the father of men, but in an improper sense. Considering Isaiah says to God, *Thou art our Father, though Abraham be ignorant of us;* and *Sara travailed not with us,* is it necessary to pursue the enquiry? And when the Psalmist says, *They shall be troubled from His countenance, the Father of the fatherless, and Judge of the widows,* is it not evident at once to all, that when God is called the Father of orphans who have lately lost their own fathers, He is thus named, not as having begotten them of Himself, but as tending and shielding them? Of men, then, He is, in an improper sense, the Father, as has been said: but only of Christ the Father by nature and not by adoption: moreover, of men in time, but of Christ before all time, as Christ Himself says, *And now, O Father, glorify Thou Me with Thine own self, with the glory which I had with Thee before the world was.*

_{Is. 63, 16. vid. Is. 51, 2.}

_{Ps. 67, 6. Sept. (68, 5.)}

_{John 17, 5.}

11. We believe then in One God the Father, the Unsearchable, and the Ineffable: *whom none of men hath seen, but the Only-begotten hath declared Him:* for *He which is of God, He hath seen the Father:* whose countenance the Angels continually behold, yet behold, according to the measure of their respective orders; but the undimmed vision of the Father is reserved in its purity for the Son with the Holy Ghost.

_{(5.) John 1, 18 John 6, 46 Mat. 18, 10.}

12. At this point, recollecting what I have been just saying

concerning God being called the Father of men, I am greatly amazed at men's insensibility. For while God has with unspeakable loving-kindness deigned to be called their Father, —He in heaven, they upon earth; He the Maker of Eternity, they the production of time; He who *holdeth the earth in the hollow of His hand*, they upon the earth *as grasshoppers*, —yet man, having forsaken his heavenly Father, *has said to a stock, Thou art my father; and to a stone, Thou hast brought me forth;* and methinks, for this cause the Psalmist says to human nature, *Forget also thine own people, and thy father's house*, whom thou hast chosen for thy father, whom thou hast coveted, to thy destruction.

Is. 40, 12
Ver 22

Jer. 2, 27.

Ps. 45, 10.

13. And not only stocks and stones, but even Satan himself, some have ere now chosen for their father, even the destroyer of souls: these men the Lord thus reproves, *Ye do the deeds of your father;* that is, of the devil, who is the father of men, not by nature, but by deceit; for like as Paul for his godly teaching was called the father of the Corinthians, thus also the devil is called the father of those who of their own choice consent with him. For they are not to be tolerated who pervert the text, *By this we know the children of God, and the children of the devil*, as if by a law of nature some among men were to be saved, and some to perish: whereas neither do we come to such holy sonship of necessity, but of choice; nor was it by nature that the traitor Judas was the son of the devil and of perdition; else he would never at all have cast out devils in the name of Christ, for *Satan casteth not out Satan;* nor on the other hand would Paul have turned from persecuting to preaching the Gospel; but the adoption is at our choice, as saith John, *But as many as received Him, to them gave He power to become the sons of God, even to them that believe in His name.* For not before faith, but from faith, we of our own choice have been counted worthy to become the sons of God.

John 8, 41.

1 Cor. 4, 15.

Ps 50, 18.

1 John 3, 10
ἐκ τούτου γινώσκομεν, but in the rec text, ἐν τούτῳ φανερά ἐστι, *in this are manifest* αὐτεξούσιος.
John 1, 12.

14. Knowing this then, let us walk spiritually, that we may be counted worthy of God's adoption: for *as many as are led by the Spirit of God, they are the sons of God.* For it avails us nought to possess the name of Christians, unless the works follow; lest to us also the words apply, *If ye were Abraham's children, ye would do the works of Abraham.*

(6.)
Rom. 8, 14.

John 8, 39.

Duty of honouring and obeying our earthly parents.

For *if we call on the Father, who without respect of person* [1 Pet. 1, 17.] *judgeth according to every man's work, let us pass the time of our sojourning here in fear; not loving the world, neither the things that are in the world; for if any man love the world, the love of the Father is not in him.* [1 John 2, 15.] Therefore, my beloved children, let us offer glory to *our Father which is in heaven*, through our works: that they *may see our good works, and glorify our Father which is in heaven; casting all our care upon Him; for our Father knoweth what things we have need of.* [Mat. 5, 16] [1 Pet. 5, 7. Mat. 6, 8.]

15. And while we honour our Heavenly Father, let us also (7.) honour *the fathers of our flesh*: since the Lord hath evidently so appointed in the Law and the Prophets, saying, *Honour thy father and thy mother, that it may be well with thee, and thy days may be long in the land which the Lord thy God giveth thee.* [Heb. 12, 9. Exod. 20, 12.] This command claims especial attention from those here present, who actually have fathers and mothers. *Children, obey your parents in all things, for this is well pleasing to the Lord.* For the Lord said not, *He who loveth father or mother is not worthy of Me*, lest thou shouldest from ignorance understand badly a good word, but added, *more than Me.* [Col 3, 20. Mat. 10, 37.] For when our fathers upon earth have views at variance with those of our Father which is in *heaven*, then we must obey this word: when, however, not hindered by them in respect of godliness, but from want of affectionate feeling, and forgetfulness of their benefits to us, we despise them, then that oracle will have place, which saith, *He that curseth father or mother, let him die the death.* [Exod 21, 17. Mat. 15, 4.]

16. The first virtuous observance in a Christian is, to honour his parents, to requite their trouble, and with all his might to provide for their comfort: (for though we should repay them ever so much, yet we never can be what they have been to us.) so that they enjoying comfort of our providing, may establish us in blessings, which Jacob the supplanter knew the value of, when he appropriated them: and that our Heavenly Father approving our virtuous course, may count us worthy to shine with the just as the sun, in the kingdom of our Father: to whom be glory, with the Only-begotten our Saviour Jesus Christ, with the Holy and life-giving Spirit, now and ever, to all eternity. Amen. [ἀντιγεν-νῆσαι τούτους οὐδέποτε δυνησό-μεθα, τὴν ἀγα-θὴν προ-αίρεσιν] [Mat 13, 43.]

LECTURE VIII.

ON THE SOVEREIGNTY OF GOD [a].

JER. xxxii. 18, 19.

The Great, the Mighty God; the Lord of Hosts is His Name, great in counsel, and mighty in work.

LECT. VIII.

1. By belief " in one God," we utterly eradicate the misbelief in many gods, using it as a weapon against the Greeks, and every opposing power of heretics: and by adding " in One God the Father," we oppose those of the circumcision, who deny the Only-begotten Son of God. For, as I said yesterday, even before we speak plainly concerning our Lord Jesus Christ, yet by our speaking of God the Father, we have already implied that He is the Father of a Son; that as we understand that God is, so we may understand that He has a Son. Now we add to this, that He is also " Almighty;" and that, because of Greeks and Jews together, and all heretics.

2. For some of the Greeks have said that God is the soul of the world. Others again, that His power reaches only to heaven, but not to the earth as well. And some, going into Ps. 36, 5. the same error, and perverting the text which says, *And Thy faithfulness unto the clouds,* have dared to bound God's providence by the limits of the clouds and the heaven, and to despoil God of the things on earth; forgetting that Psalm Ps. 139, which saith, *If I ascend into heaven, Thou art there; if I go* 8. *down to hell, Thou art there.* For if nothing is higher than heaven, and if hell is deeper than earth, He who is master of the lower regions, must reach the earth also.

---

[a] Εἰς τὸ, Παντοκράτορα, *Omnipotentem,* or *Almighty,* according to the Latin and English versions of the Creed.

3. And heretics again, as was said before, acknowledge not One Almighty God. For He is Almighty, whose might is over all things, who has power over all things. But they who say that there is one God, the Lord of the soul, and another the Lord of the body, make neither of them perfect, because each lacks what the other has. For how is he Almighty, who has power over the soul, but not over the body? or how is he Almighty, who being the Lord of bodies, has no power over spirits? But the Lord confutes these men, saying on the contrary, *Rather fear ye Him which is able to destroy both body and soul in hell:* for unless the Father of our Lord Jesus Christ had power over both, how should He subject both to punishment? for how shall He be able to take what is another's, and cast it into hell, *except He first bind the strong man, and spoil his goods?* [Mat. 10, 28.] [Mat. 12, 29.]

4. But according to Holy Scripture, and the doctrines of truth, there is but one God, who has dominion over all things by His power, and suffers many things of His will. For He has dominion even over the idolaters, but He suffers them of His forbearance; and over even the heretics who deny Him, but He suffers them of His patience; over the devil too, but He suffers with him, of His patience, not from want of power, as if foiled. *He is the commencement of the Lord's creation, being made to be mocked,* not by Himself, (that were unsuitable,) but by the Angels whom He has made: and He has permitted him to live, for two objects; that his defeat might increase his infamy, and that men might be crowned. All-wise providence of God! by which a wicked purpose is converted into a means of salvation for the faithful. For as He took the unbrotherly purpose of Joseph's brethren as the groundwork of His own scheme, and after suffering them to sell their brother, from hatred, took occasion thereby to give him the kingdom whom He would; so He suffers the devil to wrestle with us, that they who conquer him may be crowned, and that upon the victory, he may have worse shame, as conquered by the weaker, and men greater glory, as conquering one who was once Archangel. (2.) [Job 40, 14 Sept. 40, 19. English Vers.]

5. Nothing then is excepted from the range of God's power, for Scripture says of Him, *For all things serve Thee.* One and all serve Him; yet in this number His One Only [Ps. 119, 91.]

LECT. VIII.

Son, and His One Holy Ghost, are not included; all things which are His servants, rather serve their Lord through the One Son and in the Holy Ghost. God therefore has dominion over all things, and endures of His long-suffering even murderers, robbers, and fornicators; having appointed a set day for recompensing every one, that they may incur heavier sentence, if after a longer respite they have still impenitent hearts. Earthly rulers are kings of men, yet not so without power from above. And this Nebuchadnezzar knew by proof, when he said, *His dominion is an everlasting dominion, and His kingdom is from generation to generation.*

John 19, 11.

Dan. 4, 34.

(3.) 6. Riches, gold and silver, are not, as some think, the devil's property; for *the whole world of riches is the faithful man's, but the unbelieving hath no peace:* and nothing is more removed from faith than the devil. Also God saith plainly by the Prophet, *The silver is Mine and the gold is Mine; and his, to whomsoever I will give it.* Do thou but use it well, and there will be nothing to condemn in silver; but when thou usest a good thing ill, then, not choosing to blame thy management of it, thou impiously blamest its Maker. A man may even be justified by means of opulence. *I was an hungred, and ye gave Me meat;* that is, from being opulent; *I was naked, and ye clothed Me;* that is, by being opulent; nay, wouldest thou be told that riches may become a door of the kingdom of heaven? *Sell,* He says, *that thou hast, and give to the poor, and thou shalt have treasure in heaven.*

Prov. 17, 6. Sept. but not according to the Alexandrian MS.
Hag. 2, 8.
Luke 4, 6.
Mat. 25, 35.

Mat. 19, 21.

7. Now I have made these remarks because of those heretics, who lay possessions, and riches, and the body under a curse: for I wish thee neither to be a slave to riches, nor yet to treat as enemies what is given thee of God to use. Never then say, that riches are the devil's: for though he say, *All these things will I give Thee, for they are delivered unto me,* yet one may even deny the assumption; for we must not believe the lying spirit. Perhaps however, compelled by the power of His presence, he spake the truth; for he said not, "All these things will I give Thee, because they are mine," but "because they have been delivered unto me." For he grasped not at the lordship of them, but he professed to have them in a certain sense committed to him, and to dispense

Mat. 4, 9 Luke 4, 6.

them. However, this point concerning his speaking truth or not, deserves consideration of expositors at a fit time[b].

8. There is then one God the Father, the Almighty, whom the tribe of heretics have dared to blaspheme; yea, they have dared to blaspheme the Lord of Sabaoth, who sitteth above the Cherubim; they have dared to blaspheme the sovereign Lord; they have dared to blaspheme Him who rested on the Prophets, the Almighty God. But thou, worship One, the Almighty God, the Father of our Lord Jesus Christ. Fly from the error of many Gods; fly from all heresy, and say with Job, *I will call upon the Almighty Lord, who doeth great things and unsearchable, glorious things and marvellous, without number;* and *For all these things, is honour from the Almighty,* to whom be glory for ever and ever.

παῖδες.

Job 5, 8.
9. Sept.

Job 37,
21 Sept.
vid. Ms.
Alexan.

[b] The Fathers speak as if the Devil were originally the head of that order of Angels to whom the administration of this world was committed. On sinning, he made use of what power was left to him over it against his Maker, seducing man into idolatry, &c. Vid. Nyssen Orat. Catech. 6. Basil, Hom. 9. §. 10. Damasc. de fid. Orth. ii. 4. Ed. Bened.

LECTURE IX.

ON GOD, THE CREATOR OF ALL THINGS.

JOB xxxviii. 2, 3.

Who is this that darkeneth counsel by words without knowledge? Gird up now thy loins like a man: for I will demand of thee, and answer thou Me.

1. WITH the eyes of the flesh it is impossible to behold God; for the incorporeal cannot be subject to fleshly sight, and the Only-begotten Son of God Himself hath testified, saying, *No man hath seen God at any time.* Should however any one, from a passage in Ezekiel, understand, that Ezekiel saw Him, let him inquire what that Scripture says; He saw *the likeness of the glory of the Lord*, not the Lord Himself; nay, the likeness of His glory, not the glory itself, as it is in truth; and beholding only the likeness of the glory, he fell to the earth with fear. But if the sight of the likeness of the glory, and not of the glory itself, wrought fear and distress in the prophets, any one who should attempt to behold God Himself, would to a certainty lose his life, according to the text, *There shall no man see Me and live.* Wherefore, of His exceeding loving-kindness, God has spread out the heaven to be the veil of His proper Godhead, lest we perish: this is not my word, but the prophet's, *If thou shouldest open the heavens, trembling would take hold of the mountains from thee, and they would melt away.* And what wonder if Ezekiel, seeing the similitude of the glory, fell down? since Daniel, when Gabriel the servant of the Lord appeared, straightway shuddered and fell on his face, and, prophet as he was, dared not answer him, until the Angel turned himself into the likeness of a son of man. For if the sight of Gabriel wrought trembling in the prophets,

had God Himself appeared according as He is, would they not all have perished?

2. The Divine Nature then with the eyes of the flesh we cannot see, but from the Divine works we may obtain some idea of His power; according to the saying of Solomon, *For by the greatness and beauty of the creatures, proportionably the Maker of them is seen.* For he says not that from the creatures, the Maker is seen, but hath added, proportionably;" for so much the greater does God appear to each, as the man hath attained a large survey of the creatures; and when by that large survey his soul is raised aloft, he gains a more excellent conception of God. (2.)

Wisd. 13, 5.

3. Wouldest thou know that the nature of God is incomprehensible? The Three Children, singing praises to God in the fiery furnace, say, *Blessed art Thou that beholdest the depths, and sittest upon the Cherubim.* Tell me the nature of the Cherubim, and then look upon Him *who sitteth upon them.* And yet Ezekiel the prophet has made a description of them, as far as could be; saying, that every one had four faces, the face of a man, and of a lion, and of an eagle, and of a calf; and that every one had six wings, and eyes on every side, and under each a wheel with four parts; yet though the prophet has so described, we are not yet able, even if we read it, to comprehend it. But if we cannot comprehend the throne which the prophet has declared, how shall we be able to comprehend Him who sits upon it, the Invisible and Ineffable God? Curiously to scan the nature of God is impossible; but we are able to offer glory to Him from His works that are seen.

Song 3 Children, 32.

Vid. Ezek. 1, 6; 10, 1. &c.

4. These things I say to you because of what comes next in the Creed, and because we say, "We believe in One God, the Father Almighty, Maker of heaven and earth, and of all things both Visible and Invisible;" that we may remember that the same is both the Father of our Lord Jesus Christ, and the Maker of heaven and earth, and thus secure ourselves against the bye paths of ungodly heretics, who have dared to speak evil of the All-wise Artificer of all this world, and who, though they see with the eyes of the flesh, are blinded in the eyes of their mind.

5. For what fault have they to find in this, the greatest of

the works of God? Truly they ought to have been struck dumb, when they viewed the vaultings of the heavens, and worshipped Him who has reared the sky as an arch, who out of the fluid waters has made the immoveable substance of the heavens. For God said, *Let there be a firmament in the midst of the waters.* God spake once, and it stood fast, and does not fall. The sky is water, and those orbs in it, sun, moon, and stars are of fire; and how run those fiery bodies in the water? But if any one is perplexed, from fire and water being of such opposite natures, let him remember the fire which in Egypt in the time of Moses flamed in the hail. Let him also behold the all-wise workmanship of God; for since there would be need of water, for tilling the earth, He made the heaven above of water, that when the region of the earth should require watering by means of showers, the heaven from its own nature might be ready for this purpose.

6. What? is there not much to wonder at in the sun, which being small to look on, contains in it an intensity of power, appearing from the east, and shooting his light even to the west. The Psalmist describes his rising at dawn, when he says, *Which is as a bridegroom coming out of his chamber.* This is a description of his pleasant and comely array on first appearing to men; for when he rides at high noon we are wont to flee from his blaze; but at his rising he is welcome to all, as a bridegroom to look on. Behold also how he proceeds; (or rather not he, but one who has by his bidding determined his course;) how in summer time aloft in the heavens, he finishes off longer days, giving men due time for their works; while in winter he straitens his course, lest the day's cold last too long, and that the nights lengthening, may conduce both to the rest of men, and to the fruitfulness of the earth's productions. And see likewise in what order the days correspond to each other, in summer increasing, in winter diminishing, but in spring and autumn affording one another an uniform length; and the nights again in like manner. And as the Psalmist saith concerning them, *Day unto day uttereth speech, and night unto night sheweth knowledge.* For to the heretics, who have no ears, they almost shout aloud, and by their order say, that there is no

other God save their Maker and the appointer of their bounds, Him who laid out the universe.

7. No one must tolerate such as say, that the Maker of light is different from the Maker of darkness; for let a man remember Isaiah's words, *I the Lord form the light and create darkness.* Why, O man, art thou offended with these? Why so annoyed at the time of rest given thee? The servant would not have gained it from his masters, but for the darkness bringing a necessary respite. And often, after toiling in the day, how are we refreshed by nights; and he who was yesterday amid labours, starts in the morning vigorous from a night's rest? And what more conduces to religious wisdom than the night, when oftentimes we bring before us the things of God, and read and contemplate the Divine Oracles? when too is our mind more alive for Psalmody and Prayer than at night? When does a recollection oftener come over us of our sins than at night? Let us not then be perverse enough to entertain the notion, that another besides God is the Maker of darkness; for experience shews that darkness is good and most useful. (4.) Is. 45, 7.

8. Those persons ought to have felt astonishment and admiration, not only at the sun and moon, but also at the well-ordered choirs of the stars, their unimpeded courses, their respective risings in due season; and how some are the signs of summer, others of winter, and how some mark the time of sowing, others introduce the season of sailing. And man sitting in his ship, and sailing on the boundless waves, looks at the stars and steers his vessel. Well says Scripture concerning these bodies, *Let them be for signs, and for seasons, and for days, and for years*; not for star-gazings, and vain tales of nativities. Observe, too, how considerately He imparts the daylight by a gradual growth; for the sun does not rise upon us, while we gaze, all at once, but a little light runs up before him, that by previous trial our eye-ball may bear his stronger ray: and again, how He has cheered the darkness of night by the gleam of moonlight. Gen 1, 14.

9. *Who is the father of the rain· and who hath given birth to the drops of dew?* Who hath condensed the air into clouds, and bid them carry the fluid mass of showers, at one time *bringing from the north golden clouds*, at another, (5) Job 38, 28. Sept. Job 37, 22. Sept.

giving these a uniform appearance, and then again curling them up into festoons and other figures manifold? *Who can number the clouds in wisdom?* of which Job saith, *He knoweth the balancings of the clouds, and hath bent down the heaven to the earth;* and, *He who numbereth the clouds in wisdom;* and, *The cloud is not rent under them.* For though measures of water ever so many weigh upon the clouds, yet they are not rent; but with all order come down upon the earth. Who *brings the winds out of His treasuries?* Who, as just now said, *hath given birth to the drops of dew? Out of whose womb cometh forth the ice,* watery in its substance, but like stone in properties. And at one time the water becomes *snow like wool,* at another it ministers to Him *who scatters the hoar-frost like ashes;* at another it is changed into a strong substance, since He fashions the water as He will. Its nature is uniform, its properties manifold. Water, in the vines is wine, *which maketh glad the heart of man;* and in the olives oil, *to make his face to shine;* and is further transformed into bread, *which strengtheneth man's heart,* and into all kinds of fruits.

10. For such wonders was the great Artificer to be blasphemed? or rather to be worshipped? And after all I have not yet spoken of that part of His wisdom which is not seen. Contemplate the spring, and the flowers of all kinds, in all their likeness still diverse from one another: the deep crimson of the rose, and the exceeding whiteness of the lily. They come of one and the same rain, one and the same earth; who has distinguished, who has formed them? Now do consider this attentively:—the substance of the tree is one,—part is for shelter, part for this or that kind of fruit; and the Artificer is One. The vine is one, and part of it is for fuel, part for shoots, and part for leaves, and part for tendrils, part for clusters. Again, how wondrously thick are the knots which run round the reeds, as the Artificer hath made them! Out of the one earth come creeping things, and wild beasts, and cattle, and trees, and food, and gold, and silver, and brass, and iron, and stone. Water was but one nature; yet of it comes the life of things that swim, and of birds; and as the one swim in the waters, so also the birds fly in the air.

11. And *this great and wide sea, in it are things creeping* (6.) *innumerable.* Who can tell the beauty of the fishes that are therein? Who can describe the greatness of the whales; and the nature of its amphibious animals? how they live both on dry land and in the waters? Who can tell the depth and breadth of the sea, or the force of its enormous waves? Yet it stays within its boundaries, because of Him who said, *Hitherto shalt thou come and no further; and here shall thy proud waves be stayed.* And to shew the decree imposed on it, when it runs up on the land, it leaves a plain line on the sands by its waves; declaring, as it were, to those who see it, that it has not passed its appointed bounds. [Ps. 104, 25. τὴν ὑπό-στασιν. Job 38, 11.]

12. Who can understand the nature of the fowls of the air? how some have with them a voice of melody; and others have their wings enriched with all manner of painting; and others soaring on high, stay motionless in the midst of the sky, as the hawk. For by the Divine command *the hawk, having spread out her wings, stays motionless, looking down towards the south.* Who of men can behold the eagle? But if thou canst not read the mystery of birds when soaring on high, how wouldest thou read the Maker of all things? [Job 39, 26. Sept.]

13. Who among men knows even the names of all wild beasts? or who can accurately classify their natures? But if we know not even their bare names, how shall we comprehend their Maker? The command of God was but one, which said, *Let the earth bring forth wild beasts and cattle and creeping things after their kinds;* and distinct natures sprung from one voice at one command,—the gentle sheep, and the carnivorous lion,—also the various instincts of irrational creatures, as representations of the various characters of men. The fox is an emblem of men's craftiness, and the snake of a friend's envenomed treachery, and the neighing horse of wanton young men, and that busy ant, to arouse the sluggish and the dull; for when a man passes his youth idly, then he is instructed by the irrational creatures, being reproved by that Scripture which saith, *Go to the ant, thou sluggard, consider her ways and be wise;* for when thou beholdest her in due season treasuring up food for herself, do thou copy her, and treasure up for thyself the fruits of good works for the world to come. And again, *Go to the bee, and learn how industrious* [Gen. 1. 25. Sept. μιμήσεις προαιρέ-σεων. Jer. 5, 8. Prov. 6, 6. Prov. 6, 8. Sept.]

LECT. IX.

Ps 119, 103. *and the honeycomb,* omitted in Hebrew text. (7.)

she is; how hovering about all kinds of flowers, she culls the honey for thy use, that thou also ranging over Holy Scripture mayest lay hold on thy salvation, and being satisfied with it mayest say, *How sweet are thy words unto my taste, yea sweeter than honey and the honeycomb to my mouth.*

14. Is not the Artificer then rather worthy to be glorified? For what if thou know not the nature of every thing? are the things therefore, which He has made, without their use? For canst thou know the efficacy of all herbs? or canst thou learn all the advantage which comes of every animal? Even from poisonous adders have come antidotes for the preservation of men. But thou wilt say to me, "The snake is terrible," fear thou the Lord, and it shall not be able to hurt thee; "The scorpion stings," fear thou the Lord, and it shall not sting thee; "The lion is blood-thirsty," fear thou the Lord, and he shall lie down beside thee, as by Daniel. And, truly, there is whereat to wonder, in the power even of the creatures; how some, as the scorpion, have their weapon in a sting, while the power of others is in their teeth, and others again get the better by means of hoofs, and the basilisk's might is his gaze. Thus from this varied workmanship, think of the Artificer's power.

15. But these things perchance thou art not acquainted with; thou hast nothing in common with the creatures which are without thee. Now then enter into thyself, and consider the Artificer of thine own nature. What is there to find fault with in the framing of thy body? Master thine own self, and there shall nothing evil proceed from any of thy members. At the first, Adam in paradise was without clothing, as was

μέλη οὐ διὰ τὰ μέλη ὁ τῶν μελῶν ποιητής.

Eve, but it was not because of aught that he was, that he was cast out; nought that we are then is the cause of sin, but they who abuse what they are: but the Maker is wise. Who hath prepared the recesses of the womb for childbearing? Who hath given life to the lifeless thing within it?

Job 10, 11.

Who hath *fenced us with sinews and bones, and clothed us with skin and flesh,* and soon as the babe is born, brings forth fountains of milk out of the breasts? And how doth the babe grow to be a child, and the child to be a youth, and then to be a man; and is again changed into an old man, no one the while discerning exactly each day's change? How also does part of our food become blood, while another part is separated for the draught, and another is changed into flesh? Who is it who gives its never ceasing motion to the heart? Who hath wisely guarded the tenderness of the eyes with the fence of the eyelids? for concerning the complicated and wonderful contrivance of the eyes scarcely do the ample rolls of physicians sufficiently inform us. Who also hath sent each breath we draw, through the whole body? Thou seest, O man, the Artificer; thou seest the wise Contriver.

16. These things has my discourse dwelt on now, passing over many, yea innumerable, other matters, and especially things incorporeal and invisible, that on the one hand thou mayest abhor those who blaspheme that good and wise Artificer; and that on the other, from what has been spoken and read, and from what thou canst thyself find out or think of, thou mayest *proportionably see the Creator by the greatness and beauty of the creations*: and that bending the knee with godly reverence to the Maker of all things, things of sense and things of mind, visible and invisible, thou mayest with an honest and holy tongue, and with unwearied lips and heart, sing praises to God, saying, *O Lord, how manifold are Thy works ! in wisdom hast Thou made them all*: for to Thee belongeth honour and glory and greatness, both now and for ever and ever. Amen.

(8.)

Wis. 13, 5.

Ps 104, 24.

LECTURE X.

ON THE ONE LORD, JESUS CHRIST.

1 CORINTHIANS viii. 5, 6.

For though there be that are called gods, whether in heaven or in earth, (as there be gods many and lords many.) but to us there is One God the Father, of whom are all things, and we in Him; and one Lord Jesus Christ, by whom are all things, and we by Him.

<small>LECT. X</small>

<small>1 John 2, 23</small>
<small>John 10, 9, 14, 6</small>
<small>Mat. 11, 27.</small>

1. THEY who have been taught to believe in One God, the Father Almighty, ought also to believe in His Only-begotten Son; for *whosoever denieth the Son, the same hath not the Father.* Jesus says, *I am the Door; no one cometh unto the Father, but by Me.* For if thou deny the Door, the knowledge concerning the Father is closed from thee. *No man knoweth the Father, save the Son, and he to whomsoever the Son will reveal Him;* for if thou deny Him who reveals, thou remainest in ignorance. There is a sentence in the Gospels to this effect, *He who believeth not on the Son shall not see life, but the wrath of God abideth upon him:* for the Father is wroth, when the Only-begotten Son is set at nought. It is a great matter to a king, if even one of his soldiers be but dishonoured; and when it is one of his more honourable guards or friends, then his anger becomes yet greater; but if any offer outrage to the king's only-begotten son himself, who shall soothe the father, when wroth concerning his only-begotten son?

<small>John 3, 36.</small>

2. If then a man wishes to be religious towards God, let him worship the Son; since otherwise the Father accepts not his service. The Father spake with a loud voice from heaven, saying, *This is My beloved Son, in whom I am well-pleased,*

<small>Mat. 3, 17</small>

the Father was well-pleased with the Son; unless thou also be well-pleased in Him, thou hast not life. Be not inveigled by the Jews, who craftily say, There is only One God; but together with the knowledge that God is one, know also that God has an Only-begotten Son. I am not the first to say this; for the Psalmist in the person of the Son saith, *The* Ps 2, 7. *Lord hath said unto Me, Thou art My Son.* Heed not therefore what the Jews say, but what the Prophets say. Wonderest thou that they who have stoned and slain the Prophets, set at nought their words?

3. Believe thou on One Lord Jesus Christ, the Only-be- (2.) gotten Son of God. We say One Lord Jesus Christ, to signify that God's Son is Only-begotten; we say, One, lest thou shouldest suppose another. We say, One, lest thou shouldest profanely disperse the many Names of power among many sons. For He is called a Door; but take not the name literally for a thing of wood, but a spiritual, a living Door, discriminating λογικήν. those who enter in. He is called the Way; that is, not one John 14, trodden by men's feet, but one which guides us to the Father 6 in heaven. He is called a Sheep; not an irrational one, but Acts 8, the one, which through its precious blood, cleanses the world 32 from its sins; and when led before the shearer knew when Isa 53, to be silent This Sheep, again, is called the Shepherd, who 7. says, *I am the good Shepherd;* a Sheep by reason of His John 10, manhood, a Shepherd on account of the loving-kindness of 11 His Godhead. And dost thou wish to know whether there are spiritual sheep? the Saviour says to the Apostles, *Behold,* λογικά. *I send you as sheep in the midst of wolves.* Again He is Mat 10, called a Lion; not a devourer of men, but as if showing by Rev. 5, 5 the title His princely and stedfast and resolute nature. Also ὑποστά- He is called a Lion, in opposition to the lion who is our σεως adversary, who roars and devours those who have been 1 Pet 5, deceived. For the Saviour came, not as having laid aside 8. the gentleness of His own nature, but as the mighty *Lion of the tribe of Judah,* to save them who believe, and to trample Ps 118, upon the adversary. He is called a Stone; not a lifeless one, 22 quarried by men's hands, but the *chief corner-stone,* on whom 16 *whosoever believeth shall not be ashamed.* 1 Pet 2, 4—6.

4. He is called Christ, the Anointed; not anointed by human hands, but having eternally from the Father an unction

100   *Manifold offices of the Only-begotten Son.*

LECT X.

Ps 88, 5.

ἰάσεως

to be High-priest over man. He is called Dead; yet not as having His abode among the dead, as all they have who are in Hades, but being alone *free among the dead*. He is called the Son of Man; not as being born of the earth, as all we are, but as coming upon the clouds to judge the quick and dead. He is called Lord, not improperly as some men are, but as having a Lordship, natural and eternal. Fitly is He called Jesus, deriving His name from His salutary medicine. He is called a Son; not advanced by adoption, but having been naturally begotten. And many are the titles of our Saviour; lest therefore His manifold appellations should make thee think that there are many sons, and because of the errors of the heretics, who say that Christ is One, and Jesus another, and the Door another, and so on, the faith secures thee beforehand, and says well, "In One Lord Jesus Christ;" for though the titles be many, their subject is one.

(3.)

1 Cor. 9, 22

νεύματι πατρός.

θελήματι π-τρ s.

5. Now the Saviour shows Himself under various forms to each, for his profit. For to those who stand in need of rejoicing, He becomes a Vine; to those who want to enter in, He is a Door; to those who need to offer prayers, He stands a mediating High-Priest. Again, to those who have sins, He becomes a Sheep, that He may be sacrificed for them; He becomes *all things to all*, remaining in His own nature what He is. For, continuing to hold the true unchangeable prerogative of Sonship, as some skilful physician or considerate teacher, He adapts Himself to our weaknesses; though Very Lord, and not receiving the Lordship by advancement[a], but having that dignity by nature; not like us, improperly called Lord, but being so in verity; since by the Father's decree, He is Lord of His own works. For whereas our lordship is over men of like rights and like passions, nay, often our elders, and often a young master over aged servants, our Lord Jesus Christ's Lordship is not so; but He is first Maker, then Lord; first He made all things by the will of the Father, then, He is Lord over the things which He has made[b].

[a] ἐκ προκοπῆς. This was the doctrine of the Samosatenes, Athan de Syn 26 § 4 and of the Arians, Alex apud Theod Hist i. 4

[b] It was a point of controversy in the early Church, (though of course not necessarily more than a verbal one,) whether God, and Christ, could be called

6. Christ the Lord is He who was born in the city of David. And wouldest thou know whether Christ is the Lord with the Father, even before His incarnation ᶜ? That thou mayest receive the doctrine, not only by faith but by proof, from the Old Testament, go to the first book, Genesis, God saith, *Let us make man,* not "in My image," but, *in Our image.* And after Adam was made, the sacred writer says, *And the Lord created man; in the image of God created He him.* For he does not confine the prerogative of Godhead to the Father alone, but includes the Son; to show that man is not the work of God only, but also of our Lord Jesus Christ, who is Himself also Very God. He, the Lord, who works when the Father works, wrought with Him in the case of Sodom also, according to the text, *And the Lord rained upon Sodom and upon Gomorrah brimstone and fire from the Lord out of heaven.* He, the Lord, afterwards appeared to Moses, as far as that was possible; for the Lord is merciful, ever accommodating Himself to our infirmities.

[Luke 2, 11. (4.)]
[Gen 1, 26]
[Gen 1, 27. Sept.]
[Gen. 19, 24.]

7. But, in order to be sure that this is He who appeared unto Moses, hear Paul's testimony, who says, *They drank of that spiritual rock which followed them, and that rock was Christ* ᵈ. And again: *By faith Moses forsook Egypt.* And shortly after he says, *Esteeming the reproach of Christ greater riches than the treasures in Egypt.* This Moses says to Him, *Show me Thyself.* You see that the Prophets too saw the

[1 Cor. 10, 4.]
[Heb. 11, 27. Ib. v 26.]
[Exod 33, 18. Sept]

Lord, Omnipotent, &c *before* creation. To avoid the difficulty, Origen is said to have held that God created all things from eternity, vid Bull, Def F n. 13 § 9 and Origen de Princip i 2 § 10 On the other hand, Tertullian contr Hermog. 3, considering the attributes in question to belong, not to the Divine Nature, but Office, denies that God was Almighty from eternity, while the Greeks affirmed this, vid Cyril Alex. in Joan. xvii 8 p. 963 Athan Orat. ii. 12—14, as understanding by the term the inherent but latent attribute of doing what He had not as yet done, τὸ ἐξουσιαστικόν, vid Method περὶ τῶν γεννητῶν, ap. Phot Cod. 235. p 933, 940

ᶜ Almost all the early heretics, except the Arians and Manichees, denied our Lord's personal existence before His incarnation.

ᵈ S. Chrysostom (in loc), Theodoret (Quæst in Josh 4) and S Athanasius (de Incarn Christ 17), agree with Cyril in understanding this text to mean, that Christ, *as God,*—S Basil (de Sp Sanct 14), and Tertullian (de Baptism 9 in Marcion iii. 5) that Christ *as already incarnate* in His mercies vouchsafed to faith,—watched over the Israelites in all their wanderings, and was typically a rock, *i. e.* as being like the rock in the desert Tertullian (de Patient 5), and S Jerome (in loco) adopt the Jewish tradition, that the stream flowing from the rock followed them all through their wanderings. Photius (vid Justinian in loc) understands "followed" to mean "indulged," "gratified," "provided for," them, as if, when they drank of the rock, they drank of His virtue who condescended to consult and answer to their wants.

Christ, that is, as far as each was able. *Show me Thyself,*
<small>Lect. X
Exod. 33, 13
20 Sept.
πρόσω-
πον.</small> *that I may see Thee with understanding.* And He answers,
There shall no man see My face, and live. Wherefore, since
no man living could see the face of the Godhead, He took
on Him the face of human nature, that we though seeing it,
might live. Yet when He wished to show even that with a
<small>Mat 17, 2</small> little majesty, when *His face did shine as the sun,* the disciples fell to the ground affrighted: if then His bodily
countenance, shining, not in the fulness of Him who wrought
but in the measure of those who followed Him, yet terrified
them, and was too much for them, how could any man gaze
on the Majesty of the Godhead? 'Thou desirest a great thing,
O Moses,' saith the Lord; 'and I allow thine unappeasable
<small>Exod 33, 17.</small> desire;' *And I will do this thing also that thou hast spoken,*
but according as thou art able; *Behold, I will put thee in a*
<small>ver 22</small> *cleft of the rock,* for being little, thou shalt lodge in a little
space.

8. Now here keep a watch on what I shall say, on account
of the Jews. For my object is to show that the Lord Jesus
<small>Exod 33, 19. Sept</small> Christ was with the Father. The Lord then says to Moses, *I will
pass before thee with My glory, and will proclaim the Name
of the Lord before thee.* Being Himself the Lord, what
Lord doth He proclaim? Thus thou seest, how He hath
covertly taught the godly doctrine of the Father and the Son.
And again in what follows, it is written in the very letter,
<small>Exod. 34, 5 &c Sept</small> *And the Lord descended in the cloud, and stood by him there,
and proclaimed the name of the Lord; and the Lord passed
before him, and proclaimed, The Lord, the Lord merciful and
gracious, long-suffering, abundant in mercy and true; keeping
righteousness and showing mercy unto thousands, taking away
iniquities, and transgressions, and sins.* And then in what
follows, Moses, having bowed his head, and worshipped
before the Lord who proclaimed the Father, says, *Do Thou,*
<small>ver 8 9.</small> *O Lord, go with us.*

<small>(5)
Ps 110, 1.</small> 9. This is the first proof; now receive a second plain one.
The Lord said unto my Lord, Sit Thou on My right hand.
The Lord says this to the Lord; not to a servant, but to the
Lord of all, and His own Son, to whom He hath put all
<small>1 Cor 15, 27. 28</small> things in subjection. *For when He saith, All things are put
under Him, it is manifest that He is excepted which did put*

all things under Him: and afterwards, *that God may be all in all.* The Only-begotten Son is Lord of all things, and yet the obedient Son of the Father, who instead of seizing on the Lordship[e], by nature received it of the Father's own will; for neither did the Son grasp at it, nor the Father reluctantly communicate it. He it is who says, *All things are delivered unto Me of My Father;* "delivered unto Me, yet not as though I had them not before[f]; and I keep them well, not withdrawing them from the Giver." $^{υἱὸς\ εὐ\text{-}}_{πειθής.}$ $^{παρ'\ αὐ\text{-}}_{τοπροαι\text{-}}$ $^{ρέτου\ λα\text{-}}_{βὼν\ φυσι\text{-}}$ $κῶς.$ Mat. 11, 27.

10. The Son of God then is the Lord,—the Lord, who was born in Bethlehem of Judæa, according to the Angel who spoke to the shepherds, *I bring you good tidings of great joy;* Luke 2, *for unto you is born this day, in the city of David, a Saviour, which is Christ the Lord.* Of whom in another place an Apostle says, *The word which God sent unto the children of* Acts 10, *Israel, preaching peace by Jesus Christ: He is Lord of all.* But when he says, *of all,* except nothing from His Lordship; whether they be Angels, or Archangels, or principalities, or powers, or any created thing named by the Apostles, all things are under the Lordship of the Son. He is Lord of Angels, according to what thou hast in the Gospels. *Then* Mat 4, *the devil departed from Him, and Angels came and ministered* 11. *unto Him;* for Scripture says not, that they succoured Him, but that they ministered to Him, which is the part of servants. When He was about to be born of a Virgin, Gabriel did Him service, having it committed to him as his peculiar privilege. When He was about to go into Egypt, that He might overthrow the gods of Egypt made with hands[g], again an *Angel appeareth to Joseph in a dream.* Mat. 2, After He had been crucified, and had risen again, the Angel 13. brought the good tidings, and as a trusty servant, said to the woman, *Go, tell His disciples that He is risen, and goeth* Mat. 28, *before you into Galilee; behold, I have told you.* As if he [7]

---

[e] Οὐχ ἁρπάσας τὸ κυριεύειν, *thought it not robbery,* ἁρπαγμὸν, Phil 2, 6

[f] The Arians argued that *communication* of power implied a time when it was not communicated, whereas the Catholic doctrine is, that the word describes a *state* which was without beginning. vid Athan Orat. 1. 14. 26 27. and Petav. de Trin. v. 9.

[g] Vid. Isa 19, 1. "Behold the Lord rideth upon a swift cloud and shall come into Egypt, and the idols of Egypt shall be moved at His presence," &c, which is considered to be fulfilled, when our Lord was taken there in His infancy, by Eusebius, also Dem vii. 20. Athan. Incain. V. 36, &c.

had said, "I have not disobeyed my command, I protest that I have told you; that if ye neglect, the blame may not rest upon me, but upon the persons neglecting." This then is the One Lord Jesus Christ, of whom now the text speaks also, *For though there be that are called gods, whether in heaven or in earth,—Yet to us there is One God the Father, of whom are all things, and we in Him; and One Lord Jesus Christ, by whom are all things, and we by Him.*

(6.) 11. And He has two names, Jesus Christ; Jesus, because He saves,—Christ, because of His priesthood. And knowing this, the inspired Prophet Moses conferred these two titles on two most special men: changing the name of his own successor in the government, Auses, to Jesus; and surnaming his own brother Aaron, Christ, that by two special men, he might represent at once the High-priesthood and the kingdom of Him who was to come, the One Jesus Christ. For Christ is a High-priest like Aaron: since *Christ glorified not Himself to be made an High-priest; but He that said unto Him, Thou art My Son, this day have I begotten Thee.* And Jesus the son of Nave was a type of Him in many things. When he began his government of the people, he began at Jordan; whence Christ also, after baptism, began His Gospel. The son of Nave appoints the Twelve, who were to divide the inheritance; and Jesus sends forth the Twelve Apostles, the heralds of truth, into all the world. The typical Jesus saved Rahab the harlot, who believed; and the true says, *Behold, the publicans and the harlots go into the kingdom of heaven before you.* With only a shout the walls of Jericho fell down before the type; and because of Jesus' word, *There shall not be left here one stone upon another,* the Jewish temple opposite us is in ruins; not indeed on the ground of the denunciation, but of the sin of the transgressors.

12. There is One Lord Jesus Christ, that wondrous Name, glanced at beforehand by the Prophets. For Esaias the Prophet says, *Behold the Saviour is come nigh thee, having His reward;* 'Jesus' among the Hebrews signifying Saviour. For the Prophetic gift, foreseeing the traitorous and bloody spirit of the Jews, veiled His name, lest from knowing it for certain, they might plot against Him leisurely. Moreover, He was called Jesus, not of men, but distinctly by the Angel,

not coming on his own authority, but as sent by the power of
God; who said to Joseph, *Fear not to take unto thee Mary
thy wife; for that which is conceived in her is of the Holy
Ghost. And she shall bring forth a Son, and thou shalt call
His name Jesus*: and he straightway adds the reason of this
name, *for He shall save His people from their sins*. Consider how could He have a *people*, who was not yet born,
unless He was in being, before He was born. And this the
Prophet says in His person, *From the bowels of My Mother
hath He made mention of My Name*, because the Angel foretold that He should be called Jesus. And again, concerning
the conspiracy of Herod, He says, *In the shadow of His hand
hath He hid Me.* Mat 1, 20.
περὶ τοῦ γεννηθῆναι ἦν.
vid Nicene Creed.
Socr. Hist 1 8.
Is 49, 1. 2.

13. Jesus then means among the Hebrews, "a Saviour,"
but in the Greek tongue, "a Healer:" seeing that He is
Physician of souls and bodies, and curer of spirits; curing
the blind in body, and leading minds into light; healing the
lame in limb, and guiding the steps of sinners to repentance;
saying to the sick of the palsy, *Sin no more*, and, *Take up thy
bed, and walk;* for since for the soul's sin the body was
palsied, He first gave a cure to the soul, that He might
extend it to the body. If any therefore is suffering in soul
from sins, he has a Physician; and if there be any here of
little faith, let him say to Him, *Help Thou mine unbelief.*
And if any be encompassed with bodily ailments, let him not
mistrust, but let him approach: (for such also does He cure,)
and let him know that Jesus is the Christ. ὁ ἰώμενος.
τυφλῶν
αἰσθητῶν
χωλῶν
φαινομένων
John 5, 14 8.
Mark 9, 24.

14. For that He is Jesus, the Jews allow, but not that He
is Christ; wherefore the Apostle says, *Who is a liar, but he
that denieth that Jesus is the Christ?* But Christ is an
High-priest, having *an unchangeable priesthood:* neither
having begun His High-priesthood at any date[h], nor delivering it to a successor; as thou heardest me say when on the
Lord's day we discoursed in church on the words, *After the
order of Melchisedek*. He has not received His High-priesthood from a carnal line, nor was He anointed with oil duly
compounded, but by the Father before the worlds; and being 1 John 2, 22 (7.)
Heb. 7, 24.
ἐπὶ τῆς συνάξεως
vid Ex 30, 22-25.

---

[h] This is a peculiar opinion of Cyril's among Catholics It had been held by Philo, (vid de Somn p 597 ed Franc 1691.) and, with a view of dishonouring our Lord, by the Arians. Epiph Hær.69. § 37 Eusebius also holds it. Demonstr. v 3 Nestorius accused the Catholics of holding it Cyril contr Nestor iii. p 64.

<small>LECT X.</small>
<small>Heb 7, 21 πρὸς αὐτὸν, unto Him added in rec text Heb. 6, 18.</small>

so much more excellent than the others, in that He is a Priest with an oath. *For they are priests without an oath; but He with an oath by Him that said, The Lord sware, and will not repent.* It was indeed an assurance enough, that the Father should but will it: but now it is twofold, for with the will the oath follows;—*That by two immutable things, in which it was impossible for God to lie, we might have strong consolation,* for our faith, who receive Jesus Christ the Son of God.

15. He, the Christ, when He came, was denied by the Jews, and confessed by devils; yet He was not unknown to our forefather David, who says, *I have ordained a lamp for my Christ,* which lamp some have interpreted to be the brightness of Prophecy, others the flesh which He took of the Virgin, according to the Apostle's words, *We have this treasure in earthen vessels.* Of Him the Prophet was not ignorant, when he said, *And who declareth unto men His Christ.* Moses also knew Him, and Esaias knew Him, and Jeremias knew Him; there was none of the Prophets who knew Him not. Him even the devils recognized; for *He rebuked them,* and the sacred writer proceeds, *because they knew that He was Christ.* The Chief-priests knew Him not, and the devils confessed Him; the Chief-priests knew Him not, and a woman of Samaria proclaimed Him, saying, *Come, see a man which told me all things that ever I did; is not this the Christ?*

<small>Ps. 132, 17
v. 2 Pet. 1, 19.
2 Cor. 4, 7
Amos 4, 13 Sept.
Luke 4, 41.
John 4, 29.</small>

<small>Heb. 9, 11.</small>

16. This is Jesus Christ, *who is come, an High-priest of good things to come;* who out of the munificence of His Godhead has imparted to us His own title. For kings among men have a royal style, which they keep to themselves; but Jesus Christ being the Son of God, has counted us worthy to be called "Christians." But some one will say, The name of "Christian" is new, and before this not in use; and new things are often objected to, on the score of novelty. The prophet has anticipated the objection, when he says, *But them which serve Me, He shall call by a new name, which shall be blessed upon the earth.* Let us inquire of the Jews: Do ye serve the Lord, or no? Show then your new name; for your name was "Jews" and "Israelites" in the time of Moses and the other prophets, and after the return from

<small>(8.)</small>

<small>Is 65, 15 16. Sept.</small>

Babylon, and up to the present time; where then is your new name? But we, since we serve the Lord, have, as might be expected, the new name; new indeed, but *that new name which shall be blessed upon the earth.* This name has got hold of the world; for Jews cover only a certain spot, but Christians reach the bounds of the world; for we preach the Name of the Only-begotten Son of God.

17. But perhaps thou wouldest know whether the Apostles received and proclaimed the Name of Christ, or rather had Christ in themselves? Paul says to his hearers, *Seek ye a proof of Christ speaking in me?* Paul preaches Christ, saying, *For we preach not ourselves, but Christ Jesus the Lord, and ourselves your servants for Jesus' sake.* Now who is this? It is the former persecutor. O mighty wonder! He who first persecuted, himself preaches Christ. But wherefore? was he bribed? There was no one to bribe him this way. Had he a sight of Him when on earth, and was awestruck thereby? He had already been taken up into Heaven. He came out to persecute; and after three days the persecutor is a preacher in Damascus. By what power? Others call friends to be witnesses for friends; but the witness I present to thee is this former enemy; and waverest thou yet? The testimony of Peter and John, though weighty, was open to suspicion, because they were His friends; but when His former foe afterwards dies for Christ's sake, what room is there for doubting the truth? 2 Cor. 12, 3. 2 Cor. 4, 5.

18. Here I am led to express a suitable admiration of this appointment of the Holy Spirit; how He has confined the Epistles of the rest to a small number, but to Paul, the former persecutor, has granted fourteen. It was not because Peter or John were less than Paul, that He restrained the gift; (God forbid!) but in order that His doctrine might be beyond question, He granted to the former persecutor and enemy to write more, that thus we might all be made believers. *But all were amazed about Paul, and said, Is not this he who used to persecute? Did he not come hither to lead us bound unto Jerusalem?* Wonder not, says Paul, I know that it is hard for me *to kick against the pricks;* I know that *I am not meet to be called an Apostle, because I persecuted the Church of God; but I did it ignorantly;* for Acts 9, 21. 1 Cor. 15, 9. 1 Tim. 1, 13.

LECT. X.

1 Tim. 1, 14

(9.)

ἡ θεοτό-κος.

Luke 2, 29. 30.

ἐγκρα-τής.

Mark 1, 24.

Vid. sup iv. 10.

I thought that the preaching of Christ was the destruction of the Law; I knew not that He came to fulfil the Law, and not to destroy it; *but the grace of God was exceeding abundant in me.*

19. Many, my beloved, are the true testimonies concerning Christ. The Father from Heaven is Witness of the Son; the Holy Ghost is Witness, descending bodily in the shape of a dove; the Archangel Gabriel is His witness, bringing good tidings to many; the Virgin Mother of God is His witness; the blessed manger is His witness. Egypt is His witness, who received her Lord while yet young in the flesh. Symeon is His witness, who received Him in his arms, and said, *Lord, now lettest Thou Thy servant depart in peace, according to Thy word, for mine eyes have seen Thy salvation, which Thou hast prepared before the face of all people.* And Anna the prophetess is His witness, that widow of most devout and austere life. His witness is John the Baptist, the greatest among the prophets, the introducer of the new covenant, who in a manner joined in himself the two Covenants, the Old and the New. Jordan is His witness among rivers: the sea of Tiberias is His witness among seas. The blind, the maim, the dead raised to life, are His witnesses. The devils are His witnesses, saying, *What have we to do with Thee, Jesus; we know Thee who Thou art, the Holy One of God.* The winds are His witnesses, bidden and bridled by Him: the five loaves are His witnesses, multiplied to five thousand. The holy wood of the cross is His witness, which is seen among us to this day, and, by means of those who have in faith taken thereof, has from this place now almost filled the whole world. The palm-tree in the valley is His witness, which supplied branches to the children who then hailed Him. Gethsemane is His witness, which to our imaginations almost shows Judas still. Golgotha, this holy place which is raised above all others, is His witness in the sight of all. The holy Sepulchre is His witness, and the stone which lies there to this day. The sun now shining is His witness, which then at the season of His salutary Passion suffered eclipse. The darkness is His witness, which was then from the sixth to the ninth hour; the light is His witness, which shone out from the ninth hour till evening. The Mount of Olives is

His witness, whence He ascended to the Father; the clouds, laden with showers, are His witnesses, which received their Lord. The Heavenly gates which received their Lord are His witnesses; concerning which the Psalmist said, *Lift up your heads, O ye gates, and be ye lift up, ye everlasting doors; and the King of glory shall come in.* His former foes bear witness to Him, of whom the blessed Paul is one, for a little while hating Him, for a long while serving Him. The Twelve Apostles witness of Him; not in words only, but by their own tortures and deaths, heralding the truth. The shadow of Peter is His witness, which in the Name of Christ healed the sick. The handkerchiefs and aprons are His witnesses, which once by Christ's power wrought like cures by means of Paul. Persians and Goths, and all they of the Gentiles, are His witnesses, dying for His sake, whom with the eyes of their flesh they never beheld. The devils, whom believers to this day drive away, bear witness to Him.

_{Ps 24, 7.}
_{Pr. B. vers.}

20. So many and diverse, yea and more than these, are the witnesses of Christ: will any one then, henceforth, disbelieve in Him, thus witnessed? If, therefore, there be any who before believed not, let him believe now; if any was before a believer, let him take to him a greater increase of faith, believing on our Lord Jesus Christ, and understanding whose name he bears. Thou art called Christian; be tender of that Name; let not our Lord Jesus Christ, the Son of God, be blasphemed through thee, but rather let thy fair deeds shine before men; that they who see them may, in our Lord Jesus Christ, glorify the Father who is in heaven:—To whom be glory, both now, and for ever and ever. Amen.

LECTURE XI.

ON THE SON OF GOD, AS ONLY-BEGOTTEN, BEFORE ALL AGES, AND THE CREATOR OF ALL THINGS.

HEBREWS i. 1, 2.

God, who at sundry times and in divers manners spake in times past unto the Fathers by the Prophets, hath in these last days spoken unto us by His Son.

LECT. XI.

1. THAT we hope in Jesus Christ, we have shown sufficiently, according to our ability, in what we delivered to you yesterday. But we must not simply believe in Jesus Christ, nor receive Him, as if one of the many, improperly called Christs. For they were figurative Christs, but He is the true Christ, not raised by advancement from among men to the Priesthood, but having this dignity eternally from the Father. And for this cause the Faith guarding us beforehand, lest we should suppose Him to be one of the ordinary Christs, adds to the profession of the Faith, that we believe "in One Lord Jesus Christ, the Only-begotten Son of God."

χριστῶν, anointed.
ἐκ προκοπῆς. vid. sup x 14.

2. And again, when thou hearest of the Son, think Him not an adopted Son, but a Son naturally, a Son Only-begotten, having no other for His brother; for therefore is He called Only-begotten, because in the dignity of the Godhead, and in His generation of the Father, He has no brother. But we call Him the Son of God, not of ourselves, but because the Father Himself named Christ His Son; and that name is true which is given to children by their fathers.

3. Our Lord Jesus Christ then became man; but by the many He was not known. Wishing, therefore, to teach that which was not known, He assembled His disciples, and asked

them, *Whom say men, that I, the Son of Man, am?* Not from vain-glory, but wishing to show them the truth, lest dwelling with God, the Only-begotten of God, they should think lightly of Him as if He were a mere man. And when they answered, that some said He was Elias, and some Jeremias, He said to them, "They who know not are excusable, but ye, the Apostles, who have in My name cleansed lepers, and cast out devils, and raised the dead, ought not to be ignorant of Him, for whom ye do these wondrous works." And when all were silent, (for it was beyond man's reach to learn,) Peter, the leader of the Apostles, and chief herald of the Church, uttering no refinement of his own, nor persuaded by man's reasoning, but having his mind enlightened from the Father, says to Him; *Thou art the Christ;* nor only so, but *the Son of the living God.* And a blessing follows the speech, (for in truth it was above man,) and what he had said received this seal, that the Father had revealed it to him. For the Saviour says, *Blessed art thou, Simon Barjonah, for flesh and blood hath not revealed it unto thee, but My Father which is in heaven.* He therefore who acknowledges our Lord Jesus Christ, the Son of God, partakes of this blessedness; but he who denies the Son of God, is a poor miserable man.

Mat. 16, 13.

πρωτο-
στάτης,
κορυ-
φαῖος.
vid.
Lecture
11. 19.

4. Again, I say, when thou hearest of the Son, hear of Him as a Son, not merely in an improper sense, but in a true sense, as a Son by nature, unoriginate [a]; not as having come from bondage into the higher state of adoption, but as a Son eternally begotten, by an inscrutable and incomprehensible generation. And in like manner, when thou hearest of the First-born, think not that this is according to men; for the first-born among men have other brothers also. And it is somewhere written, *Israel is My Son, even My first-born;* but Israel is, as Reuben was, the rejected first-born; for Reuben

ἄναρχον,
εἰς προ-
κοπὴν
υἱοθεσίας,

πρωτότο-
κος

Exod 4, 22

---

[a] On the application of the word ἄναρχος, unoriginate, to the Son and Spirit there was great variety of opinion in the primitive Church. Clement Alex. calls our Lord ἀρχὴν ἄναρχον the unoriginate origin, but, whereas the Marcionites and Manichees expressed their tritheism under the word, and the Sabellians imputed that doctrine to the Church, the Apostolic Canons condemn those who baptize "in the name of the Three unoriginate" Athanasius also denies the Three unoriginate. Alexander of Alexandria taking a middle course ascribes to Christ an unoriginate *generation* The two Gregories explain that the difference of usage among Catholics arose only from the difference of opinion how best to avoid seeming in words to countenance heresies which they one and all abhorred. vid Petav. de Trin. v. 5

went up to his father's couch, and Israel cast the Son of his Father out of the vineyard, and crucified Him. To others also the Scripture says, *Ye are the children of the Lord your God;* and elsewhere, *I have said, Ye are gods; and all of you are children of the Most High. I have said,* not, "I have begotten." They, in that God *said,* received the sonship, which they had not ; He was not begotten to be other than He was before, but was begotten from the beginning, the Son of the Father, being above all beginning and all ages; the Son of the Father, in all things like to Him who begat Him, eternal of an eternal Father, Life of Life begotten, and Light of Light, and Truth of Truth, and Wisdom of Wisdom, and a King of a King, and God of God, and Power of Power.

5. If then thou hear the Gospel saying, *The book of the generation of Jesus Christ, the Son of David, the Son of Abraham,* understand it to mean "according to the flesh;" for He is the Son of David *in the end of the world,* but the Son of God before all worlds unoriginate. The one He received, not having it before; the other, which He hath, He hath eternally, in that He is begotten of the Father. He has two fathers: one, David, according to the flesh; one, God the Father, after a divine manner according to His Godhead. As the Son of David, He is both subject to time, and is handled, and His descent is traced; but according to His Godhead, He is subject neither to time nor place, nor has He descent; for *who shall declare His generation? God is a Spirit;* He who is Spirit hath spiritually begotten, as being immaterial, an inscrutable and incomprehensible generation. The Son Himself says of the Father, *The Lord said unto Me, Thou art My Son, to-day have I begotten Thee.* This *to-day* is not recent, but eternal; a to-day without time, before all ages. *From the womb, before the morning star, I begat Thee.*

6. Believe then on Jesus Christ, the Son of the living God; and that Son, Only-begotten; according to the Gospel, which says, *For God so loved the world, that He gave His Only-begotten Son, that whosoever believeth in Him should not perish, but have everlasting life.* And again, *He that believeth on Him is not condemned, but is passed from death unto life.* But *he that believeth not the Son, shall not see life, but the wrath of God abideth on him ;* because he hath not believed on the

Only-begotten Son of God. Concerning whom John testifying says, *And we beheld His glory, the glory as of the Only-begotten of the Father; He is full of grace and truth;* at whom the devils trembled, and said, *Let us alone; what have we to do with Thee, Jesus, Thou Son of the Most High God.*

John 3, 18.
John 1, 14.
Luke 4, 34.
Mark 5, 7.

7. He is then the Son of God by nature, and not by adoption, begotten of the Father. And he *that loveth Him that begat, loveth Him also that is begotten of Him;* but he who despises Him who is begotten, proceeds to insult Him who begat. But when thou hear of God's begetting, fall not upon bodily things: think not of a corruptible generation, lest thou be profane. *God is a Spirit;* spiritual is His generation: for bodies beget bodies, and need that time should intervene; but time intervenes not in the generation of the Son from the Father. And in the one case what is begotten, is begotten imperfect; but the Son of God was begotten perfect; for what He is now, that is He from the beginning, being begotten without beginning. And we are begotten, so as to pass from infantine ignorance to a state of reason; thy generation, O man, is imperfect, for thy increase is progressive. But think not that it is thus with Him, nor impute defect in power to Him who begat: for if that which He begat was imperfect, and in time received perfection, thou imputest defect in power to Him who begat; since that which time afterwards bestowed, this, according to thee, the Father from the beginning did not bestow.

οὐ θέσει
1 John 5, 1.
(3.)
John 4, 24.
Vid. supra, 4 note a.
ἐκ προκοπῆς.

8. Think not, therefore, that this generation is human, as Abraham begat Isaac. For when Abraham begat Isaac, he begat, not whom he would, but whom another bestowed on him. But in God the Father's begetting, there is no ignorance nor intermediate deliberation. For to say that He knew not what was begotten is the greatest impiety; and it is as great to say that after deliberation held in time, He afterwards became a Father. For God was not before without a Son, and afterwards in time became a Father; but He hath the Son eternally, having begotten Him, not as men beget men, but as Himself only knoweth, who begat Him before all ages, Very God.

9. For the Father being Very God, begat the Son like to

I

Himself, Very God. Not as teachers beget disciples, as Paul says to some, *In Christ Jesus I have begotten you through the Gospel.* For in this case he who was not a son by nature, became a son by discipleship; but in the case before us, He is a son naturally, a son truly. Not as you, the illuminated, now become the sons of God; for ye also become sons, but it is by adoption of grace, as it is written, *But as many as received Him, to them gave He power to become the sons of God, even to such as believe on His name: which were begotten, not of blood, nor of the will of the flesh, nor of the will of man, but of God.* And we indeed are begotten of water and of the Spirit; but Christ was not thus begotten of the Father; for at the time of His baptism, addressing Him with the words, "This is My Son," He said not, "This is now become My Son," but, "This is My Son:" that He might make manifest, that even before the operation of baptism, He was a Son.

[margin: ὅμοιον ἑαυτῷ. 1 Cor. 4, 15. John 1, 12 13. Mat 3, 17]

10. The Father begat the Son, not as among men mind begets thought. For the mind in us is something subsisting; but our thought, when uttered, is scattered abroad in the air and comes to an end [b]. But we know Christ to be begotten, not as a word sent forth, but a Word subsisting and living; not spoken by the lips, and dispersed, but eternally and ineffably begotten of the Father and in a Person. For *in the beginning was the Word, and the Word was with God, and the Word was God,* sitting at God's right hand;—the Word, understanding the Father's will, and creating all things at His will; the Word, which came down and went up; (for a word of utterance merely, when spoken, goes neither down nor up;) the Word speaking and saying, "I speak that which I have seen with My Father;" the Word, possessed of power, and reigning over all things; for the Father hath committed all things unto the Son.

[margin: γεννᾷ νοῦς λόγον, i. e. thought, or word. ἐνυπόστατον· προφορικόν. ἐν ὑποστάσει John 1, 1. νεύματι. προφορικός.]

(4.) 11. The Father then begat Him, not as any of men can understand, but as Himself only knoweth. For how He begat Him, we profess not to tell; only we insist upon its not being in this manner or that. Nor are we only ignorant of the

---

[b] This was the doctrine held concerning the Son by many schools of heresy, the Samosatenes, Sabellians, Photinians, &c

generation of the Son from the Father, but so is every created nature. *Speak to the earth, if it can tell thee;* and though thou inquire of all things that are upon the earth, they shall not be able to tell thee; for the earth cannot speak of the substance of Him who is its potter and fashioner. Nor is the earth only ignorant, but the sun also; for the sun was created on the fourth day, not knowing what had been in the three former days; but he, since he knows not any thing of the three days which were before him, cannot tell forth the Creator Himself. The heaven shall not declare this; for at the will of the Father *was the heaven like smoke established,* by Christ. Nor shall the heaven of heavens declare it, nor the waters that are above the heavens. Why then art thou cast down, O man, because ignorant of what not even the heavens know? Nor are the heavens only ignorant of this generation, but also every angelic nature. For should a man ascend (were it possible) to the first heaven, and perceiving the ranks of Angels there, approach them and ask, how God begat His own Son; they would perhaps say, "We have others beyond us, greater and higher than we; ask them." Ascend to the second heaven and the third; attain, if thou canst, to Thrones, and Dominions, and Principalities, and Powers; and even though one should attain unto them, which is impossible, yet would they also decline to answer; for neither do they know it.

Job 12, 8 Sept.

Is. 64, 8.

νεύματι. Is 51, 6. Sept.

12. For me, I have ever wondered at the curiosity of bold men, who through their seeming reverence fall into impiety. For knowing nothing of Thrones, and Dominions, and Principalities, and Powers, the workmanship of Christ, they attempt to be inquisitive about the Creator Himself. Tell me first, O most daring man, how a Throne differs from a Dominion, and then busily inquire into the things of Christ. Tell me, what is a Principality and what a Power, and what a Virtue, and what an Angel; and then inquire concerning their Maker; for all things were made by Him. But thou wouldest not ask Thrones or Dominions, or rather thou canst not; what other is there that knoweth the *deep things of God,* save only the Holy Ghost, who spake the Divine Scriptures?[10] But not even the Holy Ghost Himself has spoken in the Scriptures concerning the generation of the Son from the Father; why then art thou curious about things which not

1 Cor 2,

LECT. XI. even the Holy Ghost has written in the Scriptures? Thou, who knowest not what is written, why art thou inquisitive about what is not written? There are many subjects of inquiry in the Divine Scriptures; we comprehend not what is written; why do we busy ourselves about what is not written? Enough is it for us to know, that God hath begotten One Only Son.

13. Be not ashamed to confess thine ignorance, seeing that thou art ignorant with Angels. He who begat alone knows Him who was begotten; and He who was begotten of Him, knows Him who begat. He who begat knows what He begat; and the Holy Spirit of God testifies in the Scriptures, 1 Cor. 2, 11. that He who was begotten without beginning, is God. *For what man knoweth the things of a man, save the spirit of man, which is in him? even so, the things of God knoweth no* John 5, 26. *man, but the Spirit of God. For as the Father hath life in Himself, so hath He given to the Son to have life in Himself;* Ib 5, 23. *and, that all men should honour the Son, even as they honour the Father;* and as the Father quickeneth whom He will, Ib 5, 21. *even so the Son quickeneth whom He will.* Neither He who begat suffered any loss, nor lacks there any thing to Him who was begotten[c]. (I know that I have said these things many times, but they are said so often for your safety.) Neither has He who begat, a father, nor He who is begotten, a brother; neither was He who begat changed into the Son, nor did He who was begotten become the Father[d]. Of One Only Father, is One Only-begotten Son; neither two Unbegotten, nor two Only-begotten; but there is One Father, Unbegotten; (for He is unbegotten who has no father;) and One Son, eternally begotten of the Father; begotten not in πρὸ αἰώ- time, but before the worlds; not increased by advancement, ιων but having been begotten that which He is now.

ἐκ προ- κο -ῆς. (5.) 14. We believe then in the Only-begotten Son of God, begotten of the Father, Very God. For the True God, begets not a false God, as has been already said. Nor did He first resolve, and afterwards beget Him; but He begat Him eternally, and far more quickly than our words or thoughts;

---

[c] The Arians charged this upon the Catholics as legitimately following from their doctrine.

[d] This tenet was one of the forms of Sabellianism; vid Basil. Ep. 129. 1. Athan. Orat. iv. 9. Apost. Can. xli.

for we speaking in time, take up time; but in the case of the Divine Power, the generation is apart from time. And, as I have said many times, He did not bring the Son from nothing into being [e], nor take him who was not into sonship: but the Father, being Eternal, eternally and ineffably begat One Only Son, who has no brother. Nor are there two first principles; but the Father is *the head of the Son;* One is the beginning. For the Father begat His Son, Very God, called Emmanuel; and Emmanuel, being interpreted is, God with us.

ἄχρονος.

ἀρχὴ, beginning or principle.

1 Cor. 11, 3.

Mat. 1 23.

15. And wouldest thou know that He who was begotten of the Father, and afterwards made man, is God? listen to the Prophet's words, *This is our God, and there shall none other be accounted of in comparison of Him. He hath found out all the way of knowledge, and hath given it unto Jacob His servant, and to Israel His beloved. Afterwards He did show Himself upon earth, and conversed with men.* Seest thou God taking man's nature after the giving of Moses' law? Hear too a second testimony to Christ's Godhead, that which was just now read, *Thy throne, O God, is for ever and ever:* for lest, from His presence here in the flesh, He should be thought to have been advanced after this to the Godhead, the Scripture says plainly, *Therefore God, even Thy God, hath anointed Thee with the oil of gladness above Thy fellows.* Seest thou Christ, as God, anointed by God the Father [f]?

Bar. 3, 35—37.

Heb. 1, 8.

εἰς προκοπήν.

Heb. 1, 9.

16. Wouldest thou receive yet a third testimony to Christ's Godhead? Listen to Esaias, saying, *Egypt hath laboured, and the havens of Ethiopia;* and after a little, *and in Thee shall they make their prayer, because God is in Thee, and there is no God save Thee; Thou art God, and we knew it not, God of Israel the Saviour;* almost saying the very same thing which He said in the Gospel, *The Father is in Me, and I am in the Father.* He said not, *I am the Father,* but, *the Father is in Me, and I am in the Father.* And again, He said not, *I and the Father am one,* but, *I and the Father are one;* that we should neither separate them, nor so confound them, as to make the Son the Father. One they are, in respect of the attributes which belong to Godhead, since

Is 45, 14. 15 Sept.

John 14, 11.

υἱοστατοπλᾶς. vid.

above, Cat. iv. 8.

---

[e] As Arius maintained.
[f] Several Fathers consider that our Lord is called Christ apart from His human nature. vid. Petav. de Incarn. xi. 8. §. 9.

118   *The Son not the Father nor a Creature.*

LECT. XI — God hath begotten God. One, from consideration of their kingdom; for the Father reigns not over these, and the Son over those, (like Absalom, lifting himself up against his father;) but that kingdom which the Father has, the same has the Son likewise. One they are, because there is no disagreement or division between them; for the will of the Father is not one, and that of the Son another. One, because the works of Christ are not one, and the Father's other; for the creation of all things is one, the Father having created them through the Son: *He spake, and they were made; He commanded, and they were created,* saith the Psalmist; for He who speaks, speaks to One who hears; and He who bids, bids as One who is present with Him.

Ps 148, 5 Pr. B. vers.
ἐντέλλεται.

(6.)   17. The Son then is very God, having the Father in Himself, not changed into the Father; for the Father was not made man, but the Son. For let the truth be freely spoken [g]. The Father suffered not for us; but the Father sent Him who should suffer for us. Neither let us ever say, There was a time, when the Son was not [h]; nor let us admit that the Son is the Father. But let us walk in the king's highway; let us turn aside neither to the right-hand nor to the left. Neither let us, thinking to honour the Son, call Him the Father; nor, supposing to honour the Father, imagine the Son to be some one of the creatures. But let the One Father through the One Son be worshipped, and let not their worship be separated; let the One Son be proclaimed, who before the ages sitteth at the right hand of the Father; partaking in His throne eternally, not by advancement in time, after His passion.

ἐκ προκοπῆς.

John 14, 9.
ὅμοιος ἐν πᾶσιν
ἀπαράλλακτοι.
John 14, 9.

18. *He who hath seen the Son, hath seen the Father;* for the Son is in all things like to Him who begat Him, Life of Life begotten, Light of Light, Power of Power, God of God. The characteristics of Godhead are not distinct in the Son; and he who is counted worthy to behold the Son's Godhead, attains to the fruition of the Father. This is not my word, but that of the Only-begotten Son; *Have I been so long time*

[g] The Catholics were accused by the Arians of Sabellianizing Eustathius and Marcellus were both deposed from their sees, (the latter with reason,) by the Arian Councils, A D 330—340, on this charge. Cyril seems from this passage not to have been free from a like prejudice against their companions.

[h] ἦν ὅτε οὐκ ἦν, one of the Arian formulæ.

with you, and hast thou not known Me, Philip? He that hath seen Me, hath seen the Father. And to be brief, let us neither make a separation nor confusion between the Father and the Son; and neither say thou ever, that the Son is foreign to the Father, nor give way to them who say, that the Father is at one time the Father, at another, the Son; for these things are strange and impious, and not the doctrines of the Church. But the Father, having begotten the Son, remains the Father, and is not changed. He begat Wisdom, yet retained Wisdom Himself; and begat Power, yet became not weak; He begat God, He lost not His Godhead; and neither has He Himself lost aught, by diminution or change, nor has He who was begotten any thing wanting. Perfect is He who begat, perfect is That which was begotten, He who begat, is God, He who was begotten, is God,—Himself God of all things, yet styling the Father, His own God [1]; for He is not ashamed to say, *I ascend unto My Father and your Father, and to My God and your God.* [John 20, 17 vid above,]

19. But lest thou shouldest think that He is the Father of the Son and of the creatures in a like sense, He has in what follows signified a difference. For He said not, "I ascend to our Father," lest the creatures should be made fellows of the Only-begotten: but He said, "My Father, and your Father," in one way Mine, by nature,—in another yours, by adoption. And again, "to My God, and your God;" in one way Mine, as His True and Only-begotten Son; in another yours, as being His workmanship. The Son of God then is Very God, ineffably begotten before all ages; (for I say the same thing often to you, that it may be graved upon your mind). Believe also that God has a Son; but how He has, inquire not; for though thou seek, thou shalt not find. Exalt not thyself, lest thou fall; *think only upon those things which have been commanded thee.* Tell me first who He is who begat, and then learn what He begat; but if thou canst not understand His nature who begat, search not into the manner of That which was begotten. [Cat. vii. 7.] (7.) [Ecclus 3, 22.]

20. It is enough for godliness for thee to know, as we have

---

[1] "The Father is *His* God," says Hilary, as quoted by the Benedictine Editor, "because of Him He is born *to be* God," ex eo natus in Deum est De Trin iv. 53.

LECT. said, that God hath One Only Son, One, naturally begotten;
XI who began not to be when He was born in Bethlehem, but is
before all worlds. For listen to Micah the prophet, saying,
Micah *And thou, Bethlehem Ephratah, though thou be little among*
5, 2 *the thousands of Judah, yet out of thee shall He come forth
unto Me, that is to be Ruler in Israel; whose goings forth
have been of old, from everlasting.* Think not then of Him
who is now come out of Bethlehem; but worship Him who
is eternally begotten of the Father. Allow not any who say,
that the beginning of the Son is in time; but acknowledge the
Father, as that Beginning apart from time; for the Father
is the Beginning of the Son, timeless, incomprehensible,
without beginning; the Father is the fountain of the river of
righteousness, even of the Only-begotten; who begat Him as
Himself only knoweth. And wouldest thou know, that our
Lord Jesus Christ is likewise King Eternal? listen again to
John 8, Him when He says, *Your father Abraham rejoiced to see My*
56. *day, and he saw it, and was glad.* Then, when the Jews
received this hardly, He says again to them something yet
John 8, harder; *Before Abraham was, I am.* And again, He says to
58.
John 17, the Father, *And now, O Father, glorify Thou Me with Thine
5. own self, with the glory which I had with Thee before the
world was;* for He has plainly said, "before the world was,
ver. 24. I had glory with Thee." And again, when He says, *for
Thou lovedst Me before the foundation of the world,* He
evidently declares, "I have eternal glory with Thee."

(8.) 21. We believe then in One Lord Jesus Christ, the Only-
begotten Son of God; begotten of His Father, Very God
Col 1, before all worlds; by whom all things were made. *Whether*
16. *they be thrones, or dominions, or principalities, or powers,* all
things were made by Him, and there is none of things created,
which is exempted from His authority. Be every heresy
silent, which brings in different creators and framers of the
world; be silent the tongue which blasphemes Christ the Son
of God; let them be silent, who say that the Sun is Christ, for
He is the sun's Creator, not the sun which we see. Let them
be silent, who say that the world is the workmanship of Angels [k], who wish to wrest His dignity from the Only-begotten;

---

[k] The Manichees said that the Sun was Christ, and the Gnostics held that the world was created by Angels.

for whether they be things visible, or invisible, whether thrones or dominions, or any thing that is named, all things were made by Christ. He reigns over the things which have been created by Himself, not having captured as His prey what belongs to another, but ruling over His own workmanship; as the Evangelist John has said, *All things were made by Him, and without Him was not any thing made*; all things were made by Him, the Father working by the Son. [John 1, 3]

22. Now I wish to give an illustration of what I have been saying. I know that it is but feeble; for what of things visible, can be an exact emblem of Divine and Invisible Power? yet feeble as it is, be it spoken by the feeble to the feeble. For suppose a certain king, whose son was a king, wishing to form a city, should impart to his son, his partner in the kingdom, the form of the city; and he receiving the pattern, should bring his design to an accomplishment: in like manner when the Father proposed to form all things, the Son at the will of the Father, created all things, that the act of willing[1] might secure origination to the Father, and the Son in turn might be sovereign over His own workmanship,— the Father not separated from lordship over His own works, and the Son reigning over things created not by others, but by Himself. For, as I have said, neither did Angels create the world, but the Only-begotten Son, who was begotten, as I have said, before all ages; by whom all things were made, nothing being excepted from His creation. And now I finished what I had to say thus far, by the grace of Christ. [νεύματι.]

23. Let us now go back to our profession of the faith, and so finish for the present. Christ made all things, whether thou speak of Angels or Archangels, Dominions or Thrones. Not that the Father availed not to create the works Himself; but He willed the Son to reign over His own workmanship, Himself giving to Him the design of the things to be made: for the Only-begotten honouring His own Father, says, *The Son can do nothing of Himself, but what He seeth the Father do; for what things soever He doeth, these also doeth the Son* (9.) [John 5, 19.]

---

[1] νεῦμα, resolve, i e. the Almighty Father's primary expression of His will made to the Son, as a nod is the bodily expression of the will.

likewise. And again, *My Father worketh hitherto, and I work;* there being no incongruity in the things wrought, *for all Mine are Thine, and Thine are Mine,* saith the Lord in the Gospels. And this may we most certainly know from the Old and New Testaments. For when He said, *Let Us make man in Our image, after Our likeness,* it is manifest that He addressed some one present. But most decisive of all are the Psalmist's words, *He spake, and they were made; He commanded, and they were created;* as if the Father bade and spoke, and the Son created all things at His will. And this has Job mystically said: *He which alone spreadeth out the heavens, and treadeth upon the waves of the sea;* signifying to those who understand, that He who by His presence walks upon the sea, is also He who before this made the heavens. And again the Lord says, *Or hast thou taken earth and clay, and fashioned a living creature, and set it with the power of speech upon the earth?* then afterwards, *Have the gates of death opened to thee with fear; and have the porters of hell been scared when they saw thee?* thus signifying, that He who through His loving-kindness descended into hell, at the first created also man out of clay.

24. Christ then is the Only-begotten Son of God, and the Maker of the world; for *He was in the world, and the world was made by Him,* and *He came unto His own,* as the Gospel teaches us. Not only of the things which appear, but also of the things which appear not, is Christ the Maker, at the will of the Father. *For by Him,* saith the Apostle, *were all things created, that are in heaven and that are in earth, visible and invisible, whether they be thrones, or dominions, or principalities, or powers; all things were created by Him, and for Him; and He is before all things, and by Him all things consist.* Though thou shouldest mention the worlds, yet is Jesus Christ the Maker of these also, at the behest of the Father; for *in these last days God hath spoken unto us by His Son, whom He hath appointed Heir of all things, by whom also He made the worlds:*—To whom be glory, and honour, and might, with the Father and the Holy Ghost, now and always, and world without end. Amen.

LECTURE XII.

ON THE INCARNATION OF THE SON OF GOD.

ISAIAH vii. 10—14.

Moreover the Lord spake again unto Ahaz, saying, Ask thee a sign of the Lord thy God; ask it either in the depth, or in the height above. And Ahaz said, I will not ask, neither will I tempt the Lord. And he said, Hear ye now, O House of David; is it a small thing for you to weary men, but will ye weary my God also? Therefore the Lord Himself shall give you a sign; Behold, a Virgin shall conceive, and bear a Son, and shall call His Name Immanuel.

1. NURSLINGS of purity, and disciples of soberness, let us with lips full of purity hymn the praises of God, born of a Virgin. Let us, who are accounted worthy to partake of the flesh of the Spiritual Lamb, partake of the head with the feet;—vid. of the head, which means His Godhead; of the feet, that is, Exod 12, 9. His manhood. We, who are hearers of the Holy Gospels, let us attend to John the Divine; for he who has said, *In* John 1, *the beginning was the Word, and the Word was with God,* 1 *and the Word was God,* has added, *And the Word became* ver. 14. *flesh.* For neither is it religious to worship the mere man, τὸν ψιλὸν nor is it pious to speak of Him as God only, separate from ἄνθρωπον. His manhood. For if Christ, as He truly is, be God, but took not manhood, we are aliens from salvation. Be He then adored as God, but let it be believed that He became man; for it boots not to call Him man, without His Godhead, nor is it salutary, if we confess not His manhood together with His Godhead. Let us confess the presence of the King, and the Physician. For the King Jesus, when vid about to be our Physician, having girded Himself with the John 13, 4.

124   *Errors of heretics on the doctrine.*

LECT. XII.

napkin of human nature, ministered to what was sick; the perfect Teacher of babes, He hath become a babe with babes, that He might make wise the foolish. The Bread of heaven came down to the earth, that it might nourish the famishing.

'Ιουδαίων παῖδες.

2. But the Jewish race, who have set at nought Him who has come, and expect him who is to come wickedly[a], have refused the True Christ, and the deceived wait for the deceiver. And even in this is the Saviour found to be true,

John 5, 43.

who said, *I am come in My Father's name, and ye receive Me not; if another shall come in his own name, him ye will receive.* It is well also to ask the Jews a question. Is Esaias the Prophet, who says, that Emmanuel shall be born of a Virgin, true or false? If they accuse him as false, it is nothing wonderful; for it is their way not only to accuse the prophets as liars, but also to stone them. But if the Prophet is true, point out Emmanuel. Further, shall he, who is to come, who is looked for by you, be born of a virgin, or no? For if he is not to be born of a virgin, ye charge falsehood on the Prophet; but if ye expect this in the case of him who is to come, why do ye refuse Him who is come already?

(2.)

3. Let the Jews then, since they so will, go astray; but let the Church of God be glorified. For we receive God the Word, who was truly made man, not of the will of man and woman, as the heretics say[b], but made man of the Virgin and the Holy Ghost according to the Gospel, not in appearance[c], but in reality. And that He was really made man of the Virgin, now attend the time for teaching it, and thou shalt receive the proof; for heretics go wrong in many ways. Some of them altogether deny that He was born of the Virgin[d]; others say that He was born, yet not of a virgin, but of a woman married to a husband. And others say that Christ was not God made man, but that a man was made God[e]; for they have dared to say that it was not the pre-existing Word who became man, but that a certain man by advancement was crowned.

φαντασίᾳ.

προκόψας.

[a] i. e. Antichrist
[b] e. g. The Ebionites, Theodotus, &c.
[c] As the Docetæ taught.
[d] As these, mentioned in a former Lecture (iv. 9.), who said He was born, but not of the Virgin, as if διὰ σωλῆνος.
[e] Paul of Samosata.

4. But remember thou the things spoken yesterday concerning His Godhead; believe that that very same Only-begotten Son of God, was again born of the Virgin. Listen to John the Evangelist, who says, *And the Word became flesh, and dwelt among us.* For the Word was eternal, begotten before all ages of the Father; but the flesh He took lately, for our sakes. But many object, and say, "What reason was there so great, that God should descend to manhood? and, Can the nature of God have converse with men at all? and, Is it possible for a virgin to bear?" Since then there is much controversy, and the strife is various in its forms, come, let us, by Christ's grace, and the prayers of those present, explain each difficulty. [John 1, 14]

5. And first we have to inquire, wherefore Jesus came down? Now heed not any ingenious views of mine; else thou mayest be misled; but unless thou receive the witness of the prophets concerning each matter, believe not what is spoken; unless thou learn from Holy Scripture concerning the Virgin, and the place, and the time, and the manner, receive not witness from man. Any one at this time who teaches it, may possibly be suspected; but who of any sense, will suspect him who prophesied a thousand years and more ago? If then thou inquire the reason of Christ's coming, go back to the first book of the Scriptures. In six days God made the world; but the world was for man. The sun, however resplendent with bright beams, was made to give light to man. And all the living creatures were made to serve us. Herbs and trees were created for our enjoyment. All the works were good, but of these none was an image of God, save only man. The sun was fashioned at His mere command; man by God's hands. *Let Us make man in Our own image, after Our likeness.* The wooden image of an earthly king is honoured; how much more, then, the rational image of God. Yet this, the greatest of God's creation, disporting himself in Paradise, was by the devil's envy cast out. The foe exulted over the fall of him whom he had envied; wouldest thou have had the foe continue to rejoice? He, not daring to accost the man because of his strength, accosted, as being weaker, the woman, yet a virgin; for after his expulsion from Paradise, then Adam knew Eve his wife (3.) [Gen 1, 26.] [Gen 4 1.]

126   *Christ came in the flesh to restore man.*

LECT. XII.

6. Cain and Abel succeeded in the race of man; and Cain was the first murderer. Afterwards the deluge was poured abroad, because of the great wickedness of men. Fire came down from heaven on the people of Sodom, because of their transgression. After a time God chose Israel; but even he became froward, and the chosen race received a wound. For while Moses stood before God upon the mount, a calf was worshipped by the people instead of God. Under their Lawgiver Moses, who said, *Thou shalt not commit adultery,* a man entered a resort of sinners, and dared to be wanton. After Moses, the Prophets were sent to heal Israel; but, while they exercised that office, they bewailed themselves, as not getting the better of the evil; so that one of them says, alas, *The good man is perished out of the earth, and there is none upright among men;* and again, *They are all gone out of the way; they are together become unprofitable; there is none that doeth good, no, not one.* And again, *Cursing, and stealing, and adultery, and killing, are poured out on the land.* They sacrificed their sons and their daughters unto devils. They used auguries, and enchantments, and divinations; and again, *They fastened their garments with cords, and made hangings near the altar* [f].

Micah 7, 2
Ps 14, 3. quoted in Rom. 3, 12
Hos 4, 2
Sept Ps 106, 37.
Amos 2, 8 Sept.

(4.)

Is 1, 6. Sept.

Ps 13, 7. Sept 14, 11.
Pi B. vers
Ps 80, 17 18.
Ps 144, 5
1 Kings 19, 10.

7. Very great was the wound of man's nature. *From the sole of the foot even unto the head there was no soundness in it; there was no mollifying ointment, nor oil, nor bandages.* Then the Prophets, bewailing themselves, and being in trouble, said, *Who shall give salvation unto Israel out of Sion?* and again, *Let Thy hand be upon the man of Thy right hand, and upon the Son of man, whom Thou madest strong for Thyself: so will we not go back from Thee.* And another of the Prophets cries out, *Bow Thy heavens, O Lord, and come down;* the wounds of man's nature pass our skill to heal; *they have slain Thy Prophets, and digged down Thine altars;* the evil is irretrievable by us; Thou must retrieve it.

8. The Lord heard the prayer of the Prophets. The Father did not overlook our race which was perishing; He sent His

---

f The verse stands in our translation thus "They lay themselves down on clothes laid to pledge by every altar."

own Son, the Lord from heaven, to be our Physician. And
one of the Prophets says, *The Lord whom ye seek cometh,* Mal 3,
and He shall suddenly come,—whither? *to His temple,* where 1
ye stoned Him. Then, having heard this, another of the
Prophets says to Him, "When telling of God's salvation, John 8,
speakest thou low? bringing the good tidings of God's salva- 59.
tion, speakest thou in secret?" *O thou that tellest good tidings* Is 40,
to Zion, get thee up into the high mountains; say unto the 9 10.
cities of Judah—what?—*Behold your God ! Behold the Lord* (margin,
God will come with strong hand. Again, the Lord Himself as the
said, *Lo, I come, and I will dwell in the midst of thee, saith* Sept.)
the Lord. And many nations shall be joined to the Lord. Zech 2,
The Israelites have refused salvation through Me; *I come to* 10 11.
gather all the nations and the languages; for He came unto Is 66,
His own, and His own received Him not. Comest Thou, and 18 Sept.
what wilt Thou bestow on the nations? *I come to gather all* John 1,
nations; and I will leave on them a Sign. For from My 11.
conflict on the Cross, I will give to each of My soldiers a Is 66,
royal Seal to bear upon his brow! And another of the 19 Sept.
Prophets saith, *He bowed the heavens also, and came down,* σφρα-
and darkness was under His feet. For His coming down γίδα
from heaven was not known by men. Cat iv.
14

9. Then Solomon, hearing his father David saying these Ps 18, 9.
things, and having built a wondrous house, and looking
forward to Him who should come into it, says in astonishment, *But will God in very deed dwell with men on the* 2 Chron.
earth? Yea, says David, anticipating Him in the Psalm, 6, 18.
which is inscribed, *For Solomon;* in which it is said, *He shall*
come down like rain into a fleece of wool. "Like rain," he Ps 72,
says, because of His heavenly nature, "into a fleece of wool," title.
because of His manhood. For the rain coming down into a Ib ver
fleece of wool, descends noiselessly; so that, the mystery of 6 Pr B.
His birth being unknown, the wise men said, *Where is He*
who is born King of the Jews? and Herod, being troubled, Mat 2,
inquired concerning Him who was born, and said, *Where is* 2. 4.
Christ born?

10. Who is He who comes down? He says, afterwards,
He abideth with the sun and before the moon, for generations Ps 71,
of generations. And again another of the Prophets says, (72,) 5
Rejoice greatly, O daughter of Zion, shout, O daughter of Zech 9,
9

Jerusalem; behold, thy King cometh unto thee; He is just, and having salvation. There are many kings; of which of them speakest thou, O Prophet? Give us a sign which other kings have not. If thou say, He is a purple-clad king, the dignity of such apparel has been anticipated. If thou say that He is attended by spear-men, and seated on a gold-embossed chariot, this also has been anticipated by others. Give us a peculiar sign of that King, whose coming thou announcest. And the Prophet answers and says, *Behold, thy King cometh; He is just, and having salvation, lowly and riding upon an ass, and upon a colt, the foal of an ass,* not in chariots. Thou hast an incommunicable mark of the King who is to come. Alone of kings did Jesus sit upon an unharnessed foal, entering into Jerusalem, with acclamations like a king. And what does this King, who is to come? *By the blood of Thy covenant, I have sent forth Thy prisoners out of the pit, wherein is no water.*

11. But He might chance to sit upon a foal; give us rather a sign, of the place where the king who is to enter in, shall stand? And give not the sign far from the city, lest we be ignorant of it; but give it us near, and manifest to our eyes, that while in the city, we may behold the place. Again the Prophet answers, saying, *And His feet shall stand in that day upon the Mount of Olives, which is before Jerusalem on the east.* Can any one stand within the city, and not behold the place?

12. We have two signs, and we desire a third; tell us what the Lord shall do when He is come. Another Prophet says, *Behold your God,* and so on; then, *He will come and save you; then the eyes of the blind shall be opened, and the ears of the deaf shall be unstopped. Then shall the lame man leap as an hart, and the tongue of the dumb shall sing.* And let us mention another testimony also. Thou speakest, O Prophet, of the Lord coming, and doing signs such as never were; what other evident one givest thou besides? *The Lord comes into judgment with the ancients of His people, and the princes thereof.* A notable sign this; the Master judged by Ancients, His servants, and enduring it.

(5.) 13. These things the Jews, though they read, hear not; for they have stopped the ears of their heart, that they may not hear.

But let us believe in Jesus Christ, who came in the flesh, and was made man; for otherwise we had not received Him. For since we could not look on Him, or enjoy Him, as He is, He became what we are, that we might attain to the enjoyment of Him. For if we cannot look full on the sun, which was created on the fourth day, can we behold God, its Creator? The Lord came down in fire on Mount Sinai, and the people endured it not, but said to Moses, *Speak thou with us, and we will hear; but let not God speak with us, lest we die;* [Exod 20, 19.] and again, *For who is there of all flesh, that hath heard the voice of the Living God speaking out of the midst of the fire, and lived?* [Deut. 5, 26] If to hear the voice of God speaking would work death, how shall not the sight of God Himself minister death? And why wonderest thou? Even Moses himself saith, *I exceedingly fear, and quake.* [Heb 12, 21.]

14. What wouldest thou then? that He who came for our salvation, should become the minister of death, men not bearing Him? or that He should suit His grace to our level? Daniel endured not a vision of an Angel; and canst thou bear the sight of the Lord of Angels? Gabriel appeared, and Daniel fell down: of what sort was he who appeared, and what was his form? *His face was as the appearance of lightning,* not as the sun, *and his eyes as lamps of fire,* not as a furnace of fire; *and the voice of his words was like the voice of a multitude,* not as of twelve legions of angels · and yet the Prophet fell down And the Angel came to him, saying, *Fear not, Daniel; stand upright; be of good courage, thy words have been heard.* And Daniel says, *I arose trembling* yet even thus he answered not, until the likeness of a man's hand touched him. And when he who had appeared was changed into a vision of a man, then Daniel spake; and what says he? *O my Lord, by the vision my sorrows are turned upon me; and there remained no strength in me, neither is there breath left in me.* [Dan 10, 6] [ver. 12] [11 19] [ver. 11.] [ver. 16 17.] If an Angel appearing took away the voice and strength of the Prophet, would the appearance of God have allowed him to breathe? And until *there touched me one like the appearance of a man,* says the Scripture, Daniel took not courage. [ver 18] Thus a proof having been shown of our weakness, the Lord took on Him what man required. For since man sought to be addressed by one of like countenance, the Saviour took on Him

K

LECT. XII.
τὸ ὁμοιοπαθές.

τῆς ἐνσάρκου παρουσίας.
Ps. 114, 3

Rom. 7, 23.

Rom 5, 20.

1 Cor 2, 8

vid infra, Cat. xiv 17, and 19
Is 25, 8 Sept

τὴν παρακαταθήκην.

a nature of like affections, that men might the more readily be taught.

15. But receive another reason also. Christ came that He might be baptized, and that He might sanctify Baptism · He came that He might work wonders, walking upon the waters of the sea. Since then before His coming in the flesh, *the sea saw Him and fled, and Jordan was driven back,* the Lord took to Himself His body, that the sea might endure to behold Him, and that Jordan might without fear receive Him. This then is one reason : there is also a second. Since through Eve, a virgin, came death, it behoved that through a virgin, or rather from a virgin, should life appear ; that as the serpent had deceived the one, so to the other Gabriel might bring good tidings. Men, having forsaken God, made images in the form of men ; since then that which was in the form of man was untruly worshipped, God became truly man, that the untruth might be destroyed. The devil had used the flesh as an instrument against us ; and this knowing, Paul saith, *But I see another law in my members, warring against the law of my mind, and bringing me into captivity,* and the rest. By those very weapons then have we been saved, by which the devil was used to vanquish us. The Lord took of us a like nature with us, that He might save human nature. He took a like nature with us, that to that which lacked He might give the larger grace, that sinful humanity might be made partaker of God. *For where sin abounded, grace did much more abound.* It behoved the Lord to suffer on our behalf, but had the devil known Him, he had not dared to approach Him, *for had they known it, they would not have crucified the Lord of Glory.* His body then was made to bait death withal, to the end that the dragon hoping to devour Him, might cast forth those whom he had already devoured. For *Death waxing mighty devoured;* and again, *The Lord God will wipe away tears from off all faces.*

16. Was Christ made man for nought ? are our doctrines mere inventions and human sophisms ? are not Holy Scriptures our salvation ? are not the predictions of the Prophets ? Keep then, I pray, this deposit undisturbed, and let no one remove thee ; believe that God was made man. That this was possible, has been proved ; but if the Jews persist in

disbelieving, let us hold this forth to them. What strange thing do we preach, saying that God was made man, when yourselves say, that Abraham entertained the Lord? What strange thing do we preach, when Jacob says, *I have seen* Gen 32, *God face to face, and my life is preserved?* The Lord who 30 ate with Abraham, has eaten with us also What strange thing then do we preach? But we present moreover two witnesses, who were with the Lord in Mount Sinai;—Moses was in the *clift of the rock;* and Elias was once in the clift Exod of the rock. These were present with Him in Mount Tabor 33, 22 when He was transfigured, and *spake* to His disciples *of His* Luke 9, *decease, which He should accomplish at Jerusalem.* It having 30 31 then been proved possible, as I said before, for Him to be made man, the rest of the proofs may be left for the diligent to collect.

17. But I promised above to find the time also of the (7) advent of the Saviour, and the place: and I must not go away convicted of falsehood, but rather send away the Church's novices well guarded. Let us then inquire the time when the Lord came; since His advent is recent, and therefore excepted against; and *Christ Jesus is the same yesterday, to-day, and* Heb 13, *for ever.* Moses the Prophet says then, *A Prophet shall the* 8 Deut. *Lord your God raise up unto you of your brethren, like unto* 18, 15 *me.* (Let the words, *like unto me,* be reserved awhile, and quoted Acts 7, we will examine them in their proper place g.) But when 37 comes this expected Prophet? Go back, he says, to my writing; search into the prophecy of Jacob spoken to Judah *Judah, thou art he whom thy brethren shall praise,* and so Gen 49, forth, not to repeat the whole; and then, *A Ruler shall not* 8 ver. 10. *fail out of Judah, nor a Chieftain from his loins, till He* Sept *come for whom it is reserved; and He is the expectation* (not of the Jews, but) *of the Gentiles.* Thus he hath given as a sign of the coming Christ, the ceasing of the Jewish rule. If they are not now under the Romans, Christ is not yet come; if they have a Rulerof the race of Judah and David, the expected one is not yet come. For I am ashamed to speak of their recent measures relative to their Patriarchs[h], as they now

---

g This intention is not fulfilled in the sequel of these Lectures
h Concerning the Patriarchs of the West, as they were called, or Heads of the Captivity in Judæa, vid Basnage, History of the Jews, lib. iii. They

LECT XII

Gen 49, 11

call them, and what is the race of these men, and who is their mother: but I leave it to those who know. But He who is to come, the *Expectation of the Gentiles*, what further sign hath He? he saith afterwards, *binding His foal unto the vine;* thou seest that foal clearly spoken of by Zecharias.

Ps 2, 7. ver 9 Sept.

18. But thou seekest again another testimony also respecting the time. *The Lord said unto Me, Thou art My Son, this day have I begotten Thee*. and after a little, *Thou shalt rule them with a rod of iron*. I have already said that the kingdom of the Romans is plainly called a rod of iron; Daniel however will supply for us what is wanting on this point For when he relates and explains to Nebuchadnezzar the emblem of the statue, he tells him all he saw as regards it; moreover that a Stone cut out of a mountain without hands, set up not by man's contrivance, should overpower the whole world. And

Dan 2, 44 Sept.

he speaks most openly, thus, *And in the days of those kingdoms shall the God of Heaven set up a kingdom which shall never be destroyed, and the kingdom thereof shall not be left to other people.*

(8)

19 But we seek yet more evidently the proof of the times of His coming; for man, being hard of belief, unless he can clearly calculate the very years, gives no credence to what is spoken. What was the season then, and what manner of time was it? when, the kings sprung from Judah failing, a stranger, Herod, succeeds to the kingdom. Therefore the Angel talking with Daniel says, (and mark now, I pray, the

Dan 9, 25

words;) *Know therefore and understand, that from the going forth of the commandment to restore and to build Jerusalem unto Messiah the Prince, shall be seven weeks and threescore and two weeks.* Now threescore and nine weeks of years make four hundred and eighty-three years. He said then, that after the building of Jerusalem four hundred and eighty-three years having elapsed, and the princes having failed, then there comes a certain stranger king, in whose time Messiah is born. Now Darius the Mede built the city in the sixth year of his kingdom, and in the first year of the sixty-sixth

---

were of the tribe of Levi, and consisted of a succession of chief governors by lineal descent, from the time of Hadrian to the early part of the fifth century. Their residence was at Tiberias. They were called Governors of the West in contrast to the Princes of the Captivity at Babylon.

Olympiad, of the Greeks[1]. (The Greeks call an Olympiad, the games which are celebrated every four years, on account of the day which in the course of four years of the sun's motion, is made up of the three hours over in each year.) And Herod reigns in the hundred and eighty-sixth Olympiad, in the fourth year thereof. Now from the sixty-sixth to the hundred and eighty-sixth, the intervening Olympiads are an hundred and twenty, and a little more. Now the hundred and twenty Olympiads make four hundred and eighty years. For the remaining three years are accounted for by the interval between the first year and the fourth year. Thus hast thou the proof according to the Scripture, which says, *From the going forth of the commandment to restore and to build Jerusalem, unto Messiah the Prince, shall be seven weeks, and threescore and two weeks.* Of the times then thou hast for the present this proof, though there are other different interpretations of the aforesaid weeks of years spoken of in Daniel.

20. But now attend to the place of the promise. Micah says, *And thou, Bethlehem house of Ephratah, art not little among the thousands of Judah; for out of thee shall He come forth unto me, that is to be Ruler in Israel; whose goings forth have been from of old, from everlasting.* Moreover, concerning the place, thou, being an inhabitant of Jerusalem, knowest beforehand what is written in the hundred and thirty-second Psalm, *Lo, we heard of it at Ephratah, and found it in the fields of the wood.* For a few years ago the place was woody[k]. Again thou hast heard Habakkuk saying to the Lord, *When the years draw nigh, Thou shalt be known; when the time comes, Thou shalt be shown.* And what is the sign, O Prophet, of the coming of the Lord? He says presently, *In the midst of two lives shalt Thou be known;* saying this plainly to the Lord, "When Thou shalt come in the flesh, Thou shalt live and die, and having risen from the

Micah 5, 2 μὴ ὀλιγοστός μὴ omitted in Sept
(9)
Ps 132, 6.
Hab 3, 2. Sept. Ibid Sept ζώων ed Ben after Theodoret, instead of ζώων.

---

[1] e B C 516—518, but this was the sixth year of Darius Hystaspes, not of Darius the Mede, and the building of the City was begun in the twentieth of Artaxerxes Various dates are given for the commencement of the period, e g the second of Cyrus when the rebuilding of the Temple commenced, or the seventh of Artaxerxes, the date of Ezra's mission, or the twentieth of the same king when he commissioned Nehemiah

[k] Hadrian, as it appears, had planted or dedicated a grove to Adonis near the grotto of the Nativity (Hieron Ep. ad Paulin 13 ed 1684) Helena had cleared it away about sixteen years before this Lecture was delivered Ed Ben

The mode of Christ's coming

LECT. XII.

Ibid ver 3. Sept.

dead, shalt live again." And from what quarter round about Jerusalem comes He? From the East or the West, or the North or the South? tell us exactly. And he answers most plainly, and says, *God shall come from Teman,* (now Teman means south,) *and the Holy One from Mount Paran, shady, woody.* With which the Psalmist agreeing says, *We found it in the plains of the wood.*

21. Further, we seek, of whom, and how He comes. This

Is 7, 14.

Esaias tell us, *Behold, a Virgin shall conceive, and bear a Son, and shall call His name Immanuel.* Now the Jews contradict this doctrine: for it is their way of old to be wretched assailants of the truth: and they say that it is not written "virgin," but "damsel." But even granting this, still I find the same truth

παρθένις βιαζο- μένη.

here. For they must be asked, when does one who is assaulted cry out, and call for aid,—after the outrage, or before it? If now the Scripture says elsewhere, *The damsel cried, and there*

Deut. 22, 27.

was none to help her, speaks it not of a virgin? A further proof that a virgin may be meant in Holy Scripture by "damsel," is found in the book of Kings, saying of Abishag

1 Kings 1, 4.

the Shunamite, *And the damsel was very fair;* for that she had been chosen and brought to David a virgin, is confessed.

(10.)

Is 7, 11

22. But the Jews say again, This was said to Ahaz concerning Hezekiah. Read we then the Scripture, *Ask thee a Sign of the Lord thy God; ask it either in the depth, or in the height above.* Now first of all, the Sign ought to be something extraordinary: for that was a sign, when the water came from the rock; and when the sea was divided; and when the sun was turned backward, and the like. But next I observe, what is a still plainer confutation of the Jews. (I am aware that I am going into details, and that the hearers are wearied; yet suffer the multitudes of words, since it is for Christ's sake that these things are discussed, and they are not about common matters.) Now since Esaias spake this in the reign of Ahaz, and Ahaz reigned only sixteen years, and the prophecy was spoken to him within these years, it confutes the objection of the Jews that the next king Hezekiah, the son of Ahaz, was five and twenty years old when he began to reign; and the prophecy being confined within sixteen years, he must have been begotten by Ahaz full nine years before the prophecy. Now what need was there to speak the

prophecy concerning one already born, even before the reign of his father Ahaz? For he said not, *a virgin* hath conceived, but, *shall conceive*, speaking as with foreknowledge.

23. That the Lord was born of a Virgin we know for certain; now we must show, of what race the Virgin was. *The Lord hath sworn in truth unto David; He will not turn from it: Of the fruit of thy body will I set upon thy throne.* Ps 132, 11
And again, *His seed also will I make to endure for ever, and his throne as the days of heaven.* And afterwards, *Once have I sworn by My holiness that I will not lie unto David; his seed shall endure for ever, and his throne as the sun before Me, and shall be established for ever as the moon.* Ps 89, 22 ver 35 36 37
Thou seest that it is Christ, and not Solomon, who is spoken of; for Solomon's throne endured not as the sun. But if any one make it an objection that Christ sate not on the wooden throne itself of David, we may refer to the expression, *The Scribes and Pharisees sit on Moses' seat,* for this refers not to his wooden seat, but to the authority of his teaching. Thus inquire then for the throne of David, not for his wooden throne, but for his kingdom itself. And receive as witnesses of this the children crying out, *Hosanna to the Son of David, blessed is the King of Israel.* And the blind men also say, *Thou Son of David, have mercy upon us* And Gabriel testifies plainly, saying to Mary, *And the Lord God shall give unto Him the throne of His Father David.* And Paul says, *Remember that Jesus Christ, of the seed of David, was raised from the dead according to my Gospel.* And in the beginning of his Epistle to the Romans, he says, *Which was made of the seed of David, according to the flesh.* Receive thou therefore Him who is born of David, obeying the prophecy which says, *And in that day there shall be a root of Jesse; and He that shall rise to reign over the Gentiles, in Him shall the Gentiles trust.* Mat 23, 2 Mat 21, 9 John 12, 13. Mat 20, 30 Luke 1, 32 2 Tim. 2, 8. Rom. 1, 3. Is 11, 10 Sept. quoted Rom 15, 12

24. All this sorely troubles the Jews This Esaias also (11) foreknew, saying, *And they shall be willing, if they were scorched with fire; for unto us a Child hath been born,* (not to them,) *even a Son, and hath been given unto us.* But mark, that He was first the Son of God, then He was given unto us. And after a little, he says, *And of His peace there shall be no bound;*—the Romans have their bounds, but of the Is. 9, 5. 6. Sept. ver 7. Sept.

kingdom of the Son of God is there no bound; the Persians and Medes have their bounds, but the Son has none;—he proceeds, *upon the throne of David, and upon his kingdom, to order it.* The Holy Virgin therefore was sprung from David.

25. For it behoved the Purest, and the teacher of Purity, to come forth from a pure bride-chamber; for if he who fulfils well the office of Jesus' priest refrains himself from women, how should Jesus Himself be born of man and woman? *Because Thou art He,* says the Psalmist, *that drew Me out of the womb.* Mark carefully the word, *drew Me out of the womb,* which means that He was born without man, being drawn from the womb and flesh of the Virgin; for it is different in the case of them who are born of the marriage law.

26. He is not ashamed to take flesh of such members, being the framer of these very members And who tells us this? The Lord says to Jeremiah, *Before I formed thee in the belly, I knew thee; and before thou camest forth out of the womb, I sanctified thee.* He, then, who in framing men, touches them and is not ashamed, should He be ashamed, in fashioning for Himself His holy flesh, that veil of His Godhead? It is God who even now forms babes in the womb, as it is written in Job, *Hast thou not poured me out as milk, and curdled me like cheese? Thou hast clothed me with skin and flesh, and hast fenced me with bones and sinews.* There is nothing in man's frame shocking, except thou pollute it with adulteries and licentiousness. He who made Adam, made Eve also, and male and female were fashioned by the Divine hands, nothing in the body is shocking, as framed at the beginning. Let the mouths of all the heretics be stopped[1], who slander the body, yea rather, Him who formed it. but let us remember the saying of Paul, *Know ye not that your bodies are the temples of the Holy Ghost, which is in you?* And again, the Prophet, speaking in the person of Jesus, foretold, saying, *My flesh is of them.* And elsewhere it is written, *Therefore He shall give them till the time of her who beareth;* and what is the Sign? He says afterwards, *She shall bring forth, and the rest of their brethren shall return.* And what is the nuptial pledge of the Virgin, the holy Bride? *I will even betroth thee unto*

---

[1] The Manichees, &c

Me in faithfulness. And Elisabeth in like manner speaking to her says, *And blessed is she which believed; for there shall be a performance of those things which were told her of the Lord.* ^{Luke 1, 45.}

27. But both Greeks and Jews harass us with their allegation, that it was impossible that Christ should be born of a virgin. We may silence the Greeks out of their own fables. For ye who tell that stones, when thrown, became men, how say ye that it is impossible for a virgin to bear? Ye who in your legends relate that a daughter was born from the brain, how say ye that it is impossible for a son to have been born from a virgin womb? Ye who assert the fiction that Bacchus was born from the thigh of your Jupiter, how is it that ye set at nought our truth? I know that I am speaking what is unnecessary for the present hearers; but we put these things before thee, that thou mayest have the opportunity of retorting them on the Greeks, attacking them out of their own fables. (12.)

28. Meet, however, those of the circumcision with this question; which is the difficult thing, for an aged woman, barren, and past age, to bear, or for a virgin in her youth to have a child? Sarah was barren, and though it had ceased to be with her after the manner of women, yet contrary to nature she bore a child. If then it be contrary to nature for a barren woman and for a virgin to bear, either reject both or receive both; for it is the same God who wrought the one, and provided the other. For thou wilt not dare to say, that in one case it was possible for God so to do, and not in the other. And again, what kind of nature is it, for a man's hand to be changed in one hour to another appearance, and to be restored again? How then was Moses' hand made white as snow, and at once restored again? But thou sayest that God by so willing changed it. Is God, by willing, able in that instance, and is He not in this? And that was a sign which related only to the Egyptians, but this was a Sign given to the whole world. O ye Jews, which is the more difficult, for a virgin to bear a child, or for a rod to be quickened into a living creature? Ye own that in the case of Moses, a perfectly straight rod taking the form of a serpent was terrible to him who had cast it down, so

that he who had before held it as a rod, now fled from it as a dragon. For it was in truth a dragon; but he fled, not being afraid at what he had held, but being filled with terror at Him who had changed it. The rod had teeth and eyes of a dragon; shall now eyes which see be produced from a rod, and shall not a child be born from a virgin's womb at God's will? For I mention not that the rod of Aaron also in one night did that which other trees are many years in accomplishing. For who knows not, that a rod when it has lost its bark, will never sprout forth, even though it be set in the midst of streams? Yet since God follows not, but makes, the natures of trees, the fruitless and withered and barkless rod flowered and budded, and bore almonds. Has not then He, who bestowed fruit on this rod supernaturally, for the sake of the typical High-priest, granted to the Virgin to bear a son, for the sake of the True?

(13.) 29. These are good heads of argument; however, the Jews still contradict, and do not feel the force of this reference to the rod, because it is not a reference to births, like this, strange and contrary to nature. Ask them then the following questions.—Of whom at the beginning was Eve begotten? What mother conceived her, who had none? But the Scripture says that she was made from the side of Adam. Was then Eve born without a mother from the side of man, and may not a child be born without a father, from a virgin's womb? A benefit was owing to men from womankind; for Eve sprung from Adam, not conceived by a mother, but, as it were, brought forth by man alone Mary then repaid the benefit, not by man, but immaculately by herself, conceiving by the Holy Ghost, through the power of God.

30. But let us take something yet greater than this; for that bodies should be born of bodies, though it be strange, is nevertheless possible. But that the dust of the earth should be made a man, this is more wonderful; that clay mixed together should become the coats and brightness of the eye, is more wonderful. That from dust, one in its appearance, should spring at once the hardness of the bones and the delicateness of the lungs, and the other different sorts of

members, this is wonderful. That clay should be quickened, and should traverse the world, self-moved, and build houses, this is wonderful. That clay should teach, and speak, and follow crafts, and reign, this is wonderful. Whence then, O most shallow Jews, was Adam made? Did not God take dust from the earth, and mould this wondrous creature? Shall clay then be changed into an eye, and a virgin not bear a son? Does that which is, of the two, impossible among men come to pass, and not that which is possible?

31. Let us keep these things in mind, brethren; let us (14.) employ these weapons of defence. Let us not endure those heretics who teach a mere visionary advent. Let us loathe them also, who say that the birth of the Saviour was of a man and woman, and who dare to say that it was of Joseph and Mary, because it is written, *And he took unto him his wife.* Mat. 1, For let us call to mind Jacob, who before he had received 24. Rachel said to Laban, *Give me my wife;* for like as she, in Gen. 29, virtue of the promise only, was called the wife of Jacob, 21. before the marriage took place, so also Mary, in that she was betrothed, was called the wife of Joseph. And behold the exactness of the Gospel, which says, *And in the sixth* Luke 1, *month the Angel Gabriel was sent from God unto a city of* 26. 27. *Galilee, named Nazareth, to a virgin espoused to a man whose name was Joseph,* and so forth; and again, when the taxing was, and Joseph went up to be taxed, what saith the Scripture? *and Joseph also went up from Galilee, to be taxed* Luke 2, *with Mary his espoused wife, being great with child.* For 4. 5 though she was great with child, yet said he not, "with his wife," but "with his espoused wife." For *God sent forth* Gal. 4, 4. *His Son,* says Paul, *made,* not of a man and woman, but *of a woman only,* that is of a Virgin; for we have before showed, that a virgin is also called a woman; for of a virgin ὁ παρθε- was He born, who makes souls virgins. νοποιὸς
 τῶν ψυ-
32. But thou wonderest at the event; she also wondered χῶν who bore Him, for she says to Gabriel, *How shall this be,* Luke 1, *seeing I know not a man?* But he says to her, *The Holy* 34. 35. *Ghost shall come upon thee, and the power of the Highest shall overshadow thee; therefore also that Holy Thing which shall be born of thee shall be called the Son of God.* Immaculate and undefiled was His birth, for where the Holy

> Ghost breathes, there all pollution is taken away · undefiled was the birth in the flesh of the Only-begotten from the Virgin. Though heretics should deny the truth, the Holy Ghost shall convict them; that overshadowing Power of the Highest shall wax wroth with them, Gabriel shall confront them in the day of judgment; the place of the manger, which received its Lord, shall overwhelm them with shame. The shepherds shall testify, who then received the glad tidings; and the host of Angels praising and chanting and saying, *Glory to God in the highest, and on earth peace to men of good will;* and the Temple, into which He was then brought on the fortieth day; and the pair of turtle-doves, which were offered for Him[m]; and Symeon, who then took Him in his arms, and Anna the Prophetess, who was there present.

> 33. Since then God bears witness, and the Holy Ghost with Him, and Christ says, *Why go ye about to kill Me, a Man that hath told you the truth,* let the heretics be silent who speak against His manhood; for they speak against Him who said, *Handle Me, and see; for a spirit hath not flesh and bones, as ye see Me have.* Adored be the Lord the Virgin-born, and let the Virgins understand what is the crown of their condition. Also let the order of Solitaries understand the renown of chastity; for we too are allowed the same dignity. For nine months was the Saviour in the womb of the Virgin; but the Lord was a man for three and thirty years; so that if a virgin has to boast of those nine months, much more we of those many years.

> (15.) 34. But run we all by the grace of God the race of chastity, *young men and maidens, old men and children;* not going after licentiousness, but praising the name of Christ. Let us not be ignorant of the glory of chastity; for its crown is angelic, and its perfection superhuman. Let us be chary of these our bodies, which are to shine as the sun; let us not for a little pleasure, pollute a body such and so constituted; for the sin is small and only for an hour, but the shame is for many years, yea, eternal. Angels on earth are they, who follow chastity, the Virgins have their part with Mary the Virgin. Let all vain ornament be banished away, and every

LECT XII. ἔνσαρκος γέννησις

Luke 2, 14 εὐδοκίας, Cyril. bonæ voluntatis, Vulgate. εὐδοκία, rec text.

John 7, 19 and 8, 40

Luke 24, 39

Ps. 148, 12.

---

[m] This reason for the offering is commonly given by the Fathers, the text in Leviticus 12, 6. specifies only the purification of the Mother.

hurtful look, and all wanton gait, and dress, and perfumes, which are the baits of pleasure. The perfume of all of us be the prayer of sweet savour, even of good works, and the sanctification of our bodies; that the Lord Virgin-born may say of us also, both of men who keep their chastity, and of women who receive the crown, *I will dwell in them, and walk in them; and I will be their God, and they shall be My people*: 2 Cor 6, 16.
—To whom be glory for ever and ever. Amen.

LECTURE XIII.

ON THE CRUCIFIXION AND BURIAL OF CHRIST.

ISAIAH liii. 1, 7.

Who hath believed our report? and to whom is the arm of the Lord revealed? He is brought as a lamb to the slaughter, and as a sheep before her shearers is dumb, so He openeth not His mouth

LECT. XIII.

Gal 6, 14

1. EVERY deed of Christ is a boast of the Catholic Church, but her boast of boasts is the Cross; and knowing this, Paul says, *But God forbid that I should glory, save in the Cross of Christ.* For wondrous indeed it was, that he who was blind from his birth should recover his sight in Siloam; but what is this compared with the blind of the whole world? It was a great thing, and passing nature, for Lazarus to rise again after four days; but this grace extended to him alone, and what was it compared with the dead in sin throughout the world? Marvellous was it, that five loaves should issue forth into food for the five thousand; but what is that to those who are famishing in ignorance through all the world? It was marvellous that she should have been loosed who had been bound by Satan eighteen years: yet what is this to all of us,

στέφανος. who are fast bound in the chains of our sins? Now the glory of the Cross has led into light those who were blind through ignorance, has loosed all who were held fast by sin, and has ransomed the whole world of men.

ψιλός.

Rom. 5, 17.

2. And wonder not that the whole world was ransomed; for it was no mere man, but the only-begotten Son of God, who died on its behalf. And yet one man's sin, even Adam's, had power to bring death to the world; but *if by one man's offence death reigned* over the world, how shall not life much

rather reign *by the righteousness of One* ? And if because of the tree of food they were thus cast out of paradise, shall not believers now because of the Tree of Jesus, much more easily enter into paradise ? If the first man formed out of the earth brought in universal death, shall not He who formed him out of the earth bring in everlasting life, being Himself Life ? John 14, If Phinees, when he waxed zealous and slew the evil-doer, 6 stopped the wrath of God, shall not Jesus, who slew not another, but gave up Himself for a ransom, put away the 1 Tim. 2, wrath which is against men ? 6.

3. Let us then not be ashamed of the Cross of our Saviour, (2) but rather glory in it. *For the preaching of the Cross is unto* 1 Cor 1, *the Jews a stumbling-block, and unto the Greeks foolishness,* 18 23. *but to us salvation: and to them that perish it is foolishness, but unto us which are saved it is the power of God.* For it was not a mere man who died for us, as I said before, but the Son of God, God made man. Further; if under Moses a lamb kept the destroyer at a distance, did not much rather the *Lamb of God, which taketh away the sins of the world,* deliver John 1, us from our sins ? The blood of a brute animal gave 29 salvation; and shall not the Blood of the Only-begotten much rather save ? If any disbelieve the power of the Crucified, let him inquire of the devils; if any believe not words, let him believe what he sees. Many have been crucified throughout the world, but by none of these are the devils scared; but Christ having been crucified for us, when they see but the Sign of the Cross, they shudder. For those died for their own sins, but Christ for the sins of others; for He *did no sin, neither was guile found in His mouth.* It is 1 Pet. 2, not Peter who says this, for then might we suspect that he 22 from Is 53, 9. was partial to his Teacher; but it is Esaias who says it, not indeed present with Him in the flesh, but in the Spirit contemplating aforetime His coming in the flesh. Yet why now bring the Prophet only as a witness? receive the witness of Pilate himself who gave sentence upon Him, saying, *I find* Luke 23, *no fault in this Man*. and who, when he gave Him up, 14. washed his hands, and said, *I am innocent of the blood of* Mat 27. *this just person.* There is yet another witness of the sinless- 24 ness of Jesus,—the robber, the first man admitted into v Luke paradise, who rebuked his fellow, and said, " *We receive* 23, 41

LECT XIII — the due reward of our deeds; but this Man hath done nothing amiss; for we were present, both thou and I, at His judgment."

δόκησις.
4. Jesus then really suffered for all men; for the Cross was no illusion, otherwise our redemption is an illusion also. His death was not in appearance, for then is our salvation also a tale. If His death was but in appearance, they were

Mat 27, 63.
true who said, *We remember that that deceiver said, while He was yet alive, After three days I will rise again.* His passion then was real; for He was really crucified, and we are not ashamed thereat. He was crucified, and we deny it not, nay, I will rather glory to speak of it. For though I should now deny it, this Golgotha confutes me near which we

vid supr Cat iv 10. x. 19
are now assembled; the wood of the Cross confutes me, which has from hence been distributed piecemeal to all the world. I confess the Cross, because I know of the Resurrection; for if, after being crucified, He had remained as He was, I had not perchance confessed it, for I might have hidden it with my Master; but now that the Resurrection has followed the Cross, I am not ashamed to declare it.

(3.) 5. Being then in the flesh like others, He was crucified, but not for like sins. For He was not led to death for covetousness, in that He was the Teacher of poverty; nor was He condemned for concupiscence, for He Himself says plainly,

Mat 5, 28
Whosoever shall look upon a woman to lust after her, hath already committed adultery with her; not for smiting or striking hastily, for He turned the other cheek also to the smiter; not for despising the Law, for He was the fulfiller of the Law; not for reviling a prophet, for it was Himself who was proclaimed by the Prophets; not for defrauding any of their hire, for He ministered without reward and freely He

1 Pet 2, 22 23
sinned not in words, or deeds, or thoughts, *who did no sin, neither was guile found in His mouth; who when He was reviled, reviled not again; when He suffered, He threatened not;* who came to His passion, not unwillingly, but willingly,

Mat 16, 22 23
yea, should any dissuading Him say even now, *Be it far from Thee, Lord,* He will say again, *Get thee behind Me, Satan.*

6. And wouldest thou be persuaded that He came to His passion willingly? others die without their own will, in that

they know not of their death; but He spoke before of His
passion. *Behold, the Son of man is betrayed to be crucified.* Mat. 26, 2.
But knowest thou wherefore this Friend of man shunned not
death? It was lest the whole world should perish in its sins.
Behold, we go up to Jerusalem, and the Son of man shall be v. Mat
betrayed, and shall be crucified; and again, *He stedfastly set* 20, 18
His face to go to Jerusalem. And wouldest thou know cer- 51.
tainly, that the Cross is a glory to Jesus? Hear His own
words, not mine. Judas set about betraying Him, being
ungrateful to the Master of the house. Having but just now
gone forth from His table, and drunk His cup of blessing, yet
in return for that draught of salvation he sought to shed
righteous blood. *He who did eat of His bread, lifted up his* Ps 41,
heel against Him; his hands were but lately receiving the 9.
blessed gifts[a], and within a little while for the wages of
treason he was plotting His death. And being reproved, and
having heard that word, *Thou hast said,* he again went out: Mat. 26,
then said Jesus, *The hour is come, that the Son of man should* 25
be glorified. Thou seest how He knew the Cross to be His 23.
proper glory. Further, was Esaias when he was sawn asun- vid
der not ashamed, and shall Christ be ashamed when dying Cat. 11.
for the world? *Now is the Son of man glorified.* Not but 14.
that He had glory before: for He was *glorified with the glory* 31.
which was before the foundation of the world. He was glori- John 17,
fied as God ever; but now He was glorified in bearing the 5.
Crown of His patience. He gave not up His life by force,
nor was He put to death violently, but of His own accord.
Hear what He says: *I have power to lay down My life, and* John 10,
I have power to take it again: I yield it of My own choice 18.
to My enemies; for unless I chose, this could not be. He
came therefore of His own set purpose to His passion, re- ἐκ προαι-
joicing in His noble deed, smiling at the crown, cheered by ρέσεως.
the salvation of men; not ashamed of the Cross, for it saved
the world. For it was no common man who suffered, but
God in man's nature, striving for the prize of His patience.

7. But the Jews contradict, ever ready, as they are, to (iv.
cavil, and backward to believe; so that for this cause the

---

[a] τὰς εὐλογίας. The word has this meaning in Chrysostom and Cyril of Alexandria also, afterwards it came to signify consecrated bread, distinct from that of the Eucharist Vid Bingham, Antiq. xv. 4. §. 3.

Prophet in the text says, *Lord, who hath believed our report? Persians believe, and Hebrews believe not; they shall see, to whom He was not spoken of, and they that have not heard shall understand,* while they who study these things, shall set at nought what they study. They speak against us, and say, "Does the Lord then suffer? what? had men's hands power over His sovereignty?" Read the Lamentations; for in those Lamentations, Jeremias, lamenting you, has written what is worthy of lamentations. He saw your destruction, he beheld your downfall, he bewailed Jerusalem which then was; for that *which now is* shall not be lamented for; for that Jerusalem crucified Christ, but that *which now is* worships Him. Lamenting then he says, *The breath of our countenance, the Lord Christ was taken in our corruptions.* Am I stating views of my own? Behold he testifies of the Lord Christ seized by men. And what follows from this? Tell me, O Prophet. He says, *Of whom we said, Under His shadow we shall live among the heathen.* For he correctly signifies that the grace of life shall no longer dwell in Israel, but among the heathen.

8. But since their gainsayings are many, come, let me, with the help of your prayers, (as the shortness of the time may allow,) set forth through the Lord's grace some few testimonies concerning the Passion. For all things concerning Christ are put into writing, and nothing is doubtful, for nothing is without a text. All things are inscribed on the monuments of the Prophets; clearly written not on tablets of stone, but by the hand of the Holy Ghost. Since then thou hast heard the Gospel speaking concerning Judas, oughtest thou not to be furnished with the testimony to it? Thou hast heard that He was pierced in the side by a spear; oughtest thou not to see whether this also is written? Thou hast heard that He was crucified in a garden; oughtest thou not to see whether this also is written? Thou hast heard that He was sold for thirty pieces of silver; oughtest thou not to learn what prophet spake this? Thou hast heard that He was given vinegar to drink; learn where this also is written. Thou hast heard that His body was laid in a rock, and that a stone was set over it; oughtest thou not to receive this testimony also from the prophet? Thou hast heard that

He was crucified with robbers; oughtest thou not to see whether this also is written? Thou hast heard that He was buried; oughtest thou not to see whether the circumstances of His burial are any where undoubtedly written? Thou hast heard that He rose again; oughtest thou not to see whether we mock thee not, teaching these things? For *our speech and our preaching is not with enticing words of man's wisdom.* 1 Cor. 2, 4. We stir now no sophistical contrivances; for these are exposed; we do not conquer words with words, for these come to an end; but we preach Christ Crucified, who has already been preached aforetime by the Prophets. But thou, I pray, having received the testimonies, seal them in thine heart. And, since they are many, and the rest of our time is narrowed into a short space, listen now to a few, (as many as is possible,) and those the chief ones; and having received these beginnings, be diligent and seek out the remainder. Let not thine hand be only stretched out to receive, but let it be also ready to work. God bestows every thing. *For if any of you lack wisdom, let him ask of God who giveth,* and he shall receive. May He through your prayer, grant speech to us who address you, and faith to you who hear. Vid. Ecclus. 4, 31. Jam 1, 5.

9. Let us then seek the texts in proof of the Passion of Christ: for we are met together, not now to make an abstract exposition of the Scriptures, but rather to be made assured of the things which we already believe. Now thou hast received from me, first the testimonies concerning the coming of Jesus; and concerning His walking on the sea, (for *Thy way is in the sea,*) it is written, *Who walketh on the sea, as on a pavement.* And concerning divers cures thou hast elsewhere received testimony. Now therefore I begin from whence the Passion began. Judas was the traitor who came against Him, and stood, speaking words of peace, but plotting war. The Psalmist then says concerning him, *My friends and My neighbours drew near against Me, and stood.* And again, *His words were softer than oil, yet were they drawn swords.* *Hail, Master,* and he betrayed his Master to death; he was not moved with his warning, when He said, *Judas, betrayest thou the Son of man with a kiss?* saying, as it were, this to him, Recollect thine own name; Judas means confession; thou hast come to terms, thou hast received the money, make (5.) θεωρητικὴν ἐξήγησιν. Ps. 77, 19. Job 9, 8. Sept. Ps. 38, 11. Sept. Ps. 55, 21.

confession quickly. *Hold not Thy peace, O God of My praise; for the mouth of the wicked, and the mouth of the deceitful, are opened against Me; they have spoken against Me with a lying tongue, they have compassed Me about also with words of hatred.* But that some of the chief-priests also were present, and that the bonds were before the gate of the city, thou hast heard before, if thou rememberest [b] the exposition of the Psalmist, who has told the time and the place; how *they returned at evening, and hungered like dogs, and encompassed the city.*

10. Attend also in respect to the thirty pieces of silver. *And I will say to them, If it be good in your sight, give me my price, or refuse,* and the rest. One price is owing to Me from you for My healing the blind and lame, and I receive another; for thanksgiving, dishonour, for worship, insult. Beholdest thou how the Scripture foresaw these things? *And they appointed My price at thirty pieces of silver.* How exact the prophecy! how great and unerring is the wisdom of the Holy Ghost! For he said, not ten, nor twenty, but thirty, exactly as many as there were. Tell also what became of this value, O Prophet! Does he who received it keep it? or does he restore it? and after it was restored, what becomes of it? The Prophet then says, *And I took the thirty pieces of silver, and cast them into the house of the Lord, into the refining house.* Compare the Gospel with the Prophecy: *Judas,* it says, *repented himself, and cast down the pieces of silver in the temple, and departed.*

(6) 11. But now the exact solution of this seeming discrepancy shall be given. For they who make light of the prophets, allege that the Prophet says on the one hand, *And I cast them into the house of the Lord, into the refining house,* but the Gospel on the other hand, *And they gave them for the potters' field.* Listen then how they may be both true. For those conscientious Jews forsooth, the high-priests of that time, seeing Judas repenting and saying, *I have sinned, in that I have betrayed the innocent blood,* reply, *What is that to us, see thou to that.* Is it then nothing to you, the crucifiers? but shall he who received and restored the price of murder see to it, and shall ye the murderers not see to it? Then they say

---

[b] Alluding to some Homily distinct from these Lectures. Ed Ben.

among themselves, *It is not lawful to cast them into the treasury, because it is the price of blood.* Out of your own mouths is your condemnation, if the price is polluted, so is the deed polluted; but if thou art fulfilling righteousness in crucifying Christ, why receivest thou not the price of it? But the point of inquiry is, how the two do not disagree, the Gospel saying, *the potters' field,* and the Prophet, *the refining house.* But not only people who are goldsmiths, or χρυσο-brass-founders, have refining houses; but potters also have χόων παῖδες. them for their clay. For when they have sifted off the fine and delicate and useful earth from the rubbish, and separated from it the mass of the refuse matter, they first mould up the clay with water, that they may work it with ease into the forms intended. Why then wonderest thou that the Gospel says plainly *the potters' field,* whereas the Prophet spoke his prophecy like an enigma, since prophecy is in many places enigmatical.

12. They bound Jesus, and led Him to the hall of the (7.) High-priest. And wouldest thou know and be sure that this also is written? Esaias says, *Woe unto their soul, for they* Is 3, 9. *have taken evil counsel against themselves, saying, Let us* 10. Sept. *bind the Just, for He is troublesome to us.* And truly, *Woe unto their soul!* Let us see how. Esaias was sawn asunder, yet after this the people was restored. Jeremias was cast into the mire of the dungeon, yet was the wound of the Jews healed; for it was the less, in that it was a sin against man. But when the Jews sinned, not against man, but against God in man's nature, *Woe unto their soul!* He says, *Let us bind the Just;* could He not then set Himself free? some one will say; He, who freed Lazarus from the bonds of death after four days, and loosed Peter from the iron bands of his prison? Angels stood around ready, saying, *Let us burst their bands in sunder;* but they hold back, because their Lord was pleased to undergo it. Again, He was led to the judgment-seat before the Elders; thou hast already the testimony to this, *The Lord will come into judgment with the ancients of* Is. 3, 14. *His people, and the princes thereof.*

13. And the High-priest having questioned Him, and heard the truth, is wroth; and the wicked minister of wicked men smites Him; and the countenance, which had shone as

the sun, endured to be smitten with lawless hands. Others coming spat on the face of Him, who by His spittle had healed one who was blind from his birth. *Do ye thus requite the Lord, O foolish people and unwise?* And the Prophet wondering, says, *Lord, who hath believed our report?* for the thing is incredible, that God, the Son of God, and the Arm of the Lord, should suffer such things. But that they who are saved may not disbelieve, the Holy Ghost writes before, in the person of Christ, who says, (for He who then spake these things, was afterward an actor in them,) *I gave My back to the scourges;* for Pilate, having scourged Him, delivered Him to be crucified; *and My cheeks to smitings; and My face I turned not away from the shame of spittings;* saying, as it were, "Though knowing before that they will smite Me, I did not even turn My cheek aside; for how should I have nerved My disciples against death for truth's sake, had I Myself sunk under this?" I said, *He who loveth his life shall lose it:* if I had loved My life, how could I have taught, not doing what I taught? First then, being Himself God, He endured to suffer these things at the hands of men; that after this, we men, when we suffer such things at the hands of men for His sake, might not be ashamed. Thou seest that the prophets have clearly written of these things also. Many however of the Scripture testimonies must be passed over, for want of time; for if one should exactly search out all, not one of the things concerning Christ would be left without witness.

14. And having been bound, He came from Caiaphas to Pilate,—is this too written? yes; *And having bound Him, they led Him away as a present to the king of Jarim.* Here some hasty hearer will object, "Pilate was not a king," (to leave for a while the main part of the question,) "how then having bound Him, led they Him to the king?" But read thou the Gospel; *When Pilate heard that He was of Galilee, he sent Him to Herod;* for Herod was then king, and was present at Jerusalem. And now observe the exactness of the Prophet; for he says, that He was sent as a present; for *the same day Pilate and Herod were made friends together, for before they were at enmity between themselves.* For it became Him who was on the eve of making peace in earth and heaven, to

make His very judges the first to be at peace between themselves; for the Lord was there present, *who reconciles the hearts of the princes of the earth.* See the exactness and true testimony of the Prophet.

15. Look with awe then at the Lord while He was judged. He endured to be led and carried by the soldiers. Pilate sat in judgment, and He who sitteth on the right hand of the Father, stood and was judged. The people whom He had redeemed from the land of Egypt, and ofttimes from other places, shouted against Him, *Away with Him, away with Him, crucify Him.* Wherefore, O ye Jews? because He has healed your blind? or because He has made your lame to walk, and bestowed His other benefits? So that the Prophet in amazement speaks of this too, *Against whom have ye opened your mouth, and against whom have ye let loose your tongue?* and the Lord Himself says in the Prophets, *Mine heritage is unto Me as a lion in the forest; it crieth out against Me; therefore have I hated it.* I have not refused them, but they have refused Me; wherefore it follows that I say, *I have forsaken My house.*

^v Job 12, 24. Sept. where it means to alter, or prevent.

Is. 57, 4. Sept.

Jer. 12, 8

ver 7.

16. When He was judged, He held His peace; so that Pilate was moved for Him, and said, *Hearest Thou not what these witness against Thee?* Not that he knew Him who was judged, but he feared his own wife's dream of which news had been sent to him. And Jesus held His peace. The Psalmist says, *I was as a man that heareth not; and in whose mouth are no reproofs;* and again, *But I as a deaf man heard not; and I was as a dumb man that openeth not his mouth.* Thou hast before heard^c concerning this, if thou rememberest it.

Ps. 38, 14 ver 13.

17. But the soldiers who surrounded Him, mock Him, and their Lord becomes a sport to them, and their Master is turned into jest by them. *When they looked on Me, they shaked their heads.* Yet there is the figure of kingly state; for though they mock, yet do they bend the knee. And the soldiers crucify Him, having first put on Him a purple robe, and they set a crown on His head; for what though it be of thorns? Every king is proclaimed by soldiers, it became Jesus too in a figure to have been crowned by soldiers;

(9.)

Ps. 109, 25.

^c Not in any extant work.

> LECT. XIII.
> Cant. 3, 11.

so that for this cause the Scripture says in the Canticles, *Go forth, O ye daughters of Zion, and behold King Solomon in the crown wherewith His mother crowned Him.* And the crown itself was a mystery; for it was a remissal of sins, a dismissal of the curse.

> Gen 3, 17. 18.

18. Adam received the doom, *Cursed is the ground for thy sake; thorns also and thistles shall it bring forth to thee.* For this cause Jesus assumes the thorns, that He might cancel the doom; for this cause also was He buried in the earth, that the cursed earth might receive, instead of the curse, the blessing. At the time of the sin, they clothed themselves with fig-leaves; for this cause Jesus also made the fig-tree the last of His signs. For when about to go to His passion, He curses the fig-tree, not every fig-tree,

> Mark 11, 14.
> μηκέτι τις,
> Cyril,
> μηκέτι μηδεὶς εἰς τὸν αἰῶνα,
> no man for ever,
> 1ec. text.

but that one alone, for the sake of the figure; saying, *No more let man eat fruit of thee;* be the doom cancelled. And because at the former time they clothed themselves with fig-leaves, He came at a season when food is not wont to be found on the fig-tree. Who knows not that in wintertime the fig-tree bears no fruit, but is clothed with leaves only? Was Jesus ignorant of this, which all knew? No, but though He knew, yet He came as if seeking, not ignorant that He should not find, but extending the emblematical curse to the leaves only.

19. And having touched on things connected with Paradise, I am astonished truly at the truth of the types. In Paradise was the Fall, and in a Garden was our Salvation.

> Gen. 3, 8.

From the Tree came sin, and until the Tree sin lasted. *In the evening, when the Lord walked in the Garden, they hid themselves;* and in the evening the robber is brought by the Lord

> (10.)

into Paradise. But some one will say to me, "These are views of thine own; show me from some prophet the Wood of the Cross; except thou give me a testimony from a prophet, I will not be persuaded. Hear now from Jeremias,

> Jer 11, 19. Sept
> Mat. 26, 2.

and assure thyself; *I am as a harmless lamb led to be slaughtered; did I not know it?* (for in this manner read it as a question, as I have read it; for He who said, *Ye know that after two days is the feast of the passover, and the Son of Man is betrayed to be crucified,* did He not know?) *I am as a harmless lamb led to be slaughtered; did I not know it?*

Prophetical types of the Cross. 153

(but what sort of lamb? let John the Baptist interpret it, when he says, *Behold the Lamb of God, that taketh away* John 1, *the sin of the world*) *They have devised against Me a* Jer. 11, *wicked device, saying,*—(He who knows the devices, knew He 19. not the result of them? And what said they?)—*Come, and* Ibid. *let us place a beam upon His bread* ᵈ—(and if the Lord reckon thee worthy, thou shalt hereafter know, that His body according to the Gospel bore the figure of bread;)—*Come now,* τύπον *and let us place a beam upon His bread, and destroy Him* ἔφερεν *out of the land of the living;*—(life admits not of destruction, ἄρτου. why labour ye for nought?)—*And His name shall be remembered no more.* Vain is your counsel; for *before the sun His* Ps. 72, *Name* abideth in the Church. And because it was life, which 17. Sept. hung on the Cross, Moses says, weeping, *And thy Life shall* Deut. *hang before thine eyes; and thou shalt be afraid day and* 28, 66. *night, and thou shalt not trust thy life.* And so too, what Sept was just now taken as the text, *Lord, who hath believed our* ἀναγνω- *report?* σθέν.

20. This was wrought in figure by Moses, when he crucified the serpent, that whoso had been bitten by the living serpent, and looked to the brazen serpent, might be saved by believing. Does then the brazen serpent save when crucified, and shall not the Son of God incarnate save when crucified also? Throughout, life comes by means of wood. In the time of Noe the preservation of life was by an ark of wood. In the time of Moses the sea, beholding the emblematical rod, shrunk from him who smote it; is then Moses' rod mighty, and is the Cross of the Saviour powerless? I pass by the greater part (11.) of the types, to keep within compass. The wood in Moses' case sweetened the water; and from the side of Jesus the water flowed upon the wood.

21. The beginning of signs under Moses was blood and water; and the last of all Jesus' signs was the same. Moses began by changing the river into blood; and Jesus at the end gave forth from His side water with blood. This was perhaps on account of the two speeches, his who judged Him, and theirs who cried out against Him; or because of the

---

ᵈ This interpretation is acknowledged by Tertullian (in Jud. 10. in Marc iii. 19. iv 40.), S. Ambrose (in Psalm 35. præf 3), Theodoret (in loc), &c, and in the Breviaries.

believers and the unbelievers. For Pilate said, *I am innocent,* and washed his hands in water; they who cried out against Him said, *His blood be upon us :* there came therefore these two out of His side; the water perhaps, for him who judged Him; but for them that shouted against Him, the blood. And again it is to be understood in another way. The blood was for the Jews; the water for the Christians: for upon them as conspirators is the sentence of condemnation by the blood; but to thee who now believest, the salvation which is by water. For nothing happened without a meaning. Our fathers who have written comments have given another reason of this matter. For since in the Gospel the power of salutary Baptism is twofold, that namely bestowed by means of water on the illuminated, and that to holy martyrs in persecutions through their own blood, there came out of that salutary Side blood and water, to ratify the gift to confession made for Christ, whether in illumination, or on occasions of martyrdom. There is something besides meant by the Side. The woman, who was formed from the side, led the way to sin; but Jesus who came to bestow the grace of pardon on men and women alike, was pierced in the side for women, that He might undo the sin.

ἐν Εὐαγγελίοις, vid supr. Cat. iv. 4. 7.

φωτίσματι, or baptism.

22. And whoever will inquire, will find other reasons also; but what has been said is enough, because the time is limited, and my hearers may be tired. And yet one never can weary of hearing concerning our crowned Lord, and least of all in this most holy Golgotha. For while others only hear, we have sight and touch too. Let none be weary; take thine armour against the adversaries in the cause of the Cross itself; set up the faith of the Cross, as a trophy against the gainsayers. For when thou art going to dispute with unbelievers concerning the Cross of Christ, first make with thy hand the Sign of Christ's Cross, and the gainsayer will be dumb. Be not ashamed to confess the Cross; for Angels glory in it, saying, *We know whom ye seek, Jesus the Crucified.* Canst thou not say, O Angel, "I know whom ye seek, my Master"? No, but he says with boldness, "I know the Crucified." For the Cross is a crown, not a dishonour.

Mat 28, 5

(12.) 23. Now let us return to the proofs out of the Prophets which I spoke of. The Lord was crucified; thou hast received the testimonies. Thou seest this spot of Golgotha! Thou answerest with a shout of praise, as if assenting. Look to it lest thou recant it in time of persecution. Rejoice not in the Cross in time of peace only, but hold fast the same faith in time of persecution also; not being a friend of Jesus in time of peace, and His foe in time of wars. Thou receivest now the forgiveness of thy sins, and the gifts of the King's spiritual bounty; when war shall come, strive thou with high heart for thy King. Jesus, the Sinless, for thee was crucified; and wilt not thou be crucified for Him who was crucified for thee? Thou art not bestowing a favour, for thou hast first received; but thou art returning a favour, repaying thy debt to Him who in Golgotha was crucified for thee. Now Golgotha is interpreted, " the place of a skull." Who were they then, who prophetically named this Golgotha, in which Christ the true Head endured the Cross? As the Apostle says, *Who is the Image of the Invisible God;* and after a little, *and He is the Head of the body, the Church.* And again, *The Head of every man is Christ;* and again, *Who is the Head of all principality and power.* The Head suffered in " the place of the skull." O wondrous prophetic adaptation! The very name almost reminds thee, saying, " Think not of the Crucified as of a mere man; He is *the Head of all ψιλῷ principality and power.* That Head which was crucified is ἀνθρώπῳ. the Head of all power, and has for His Head the Father; *for the Head of the man is Christ, and the Head of Christ is God."* [Col 1, v. 18.] [1 Cor. 11, 3] [Col 2, 10.] [1 Cor. 11, 3.]

24. Christ then was crucified for us, having been judged in the night, when it was cold, and a *fire of coals* was laid. He was crucified at the third hour; and from the sixth hour there was darkness until the ninth hour; but from the ninth hour there was light again. Are these things then written? Let us inquire. Now the Prophet Zacharias says, *And it shall be in that day, and there shall not be light, and there shall be cold and frost one day;* (it was cold, wherefore Peter warmed himself;) *And that day shall be known unto the Lord;* (what, knew He not the other days? days are many, but *this is the day* of the Lord's patience, *which the Lord made;)—And that day shall be known unto the Lord, not day, and not night;* what is this dark saying which the [John 18, 18.] [Zech 14, 6 7. Sept.] [Ps 118, 24.]

Prophet speaks? That day is neither day nor night? what then shall we name it? The Gospel interprets it, by relating the event. It was not day; for the sun shone not uniformly from his rising to his setting, but from the sixth hour till the ninth hour, there was darkness at mid-day. The darkness therefore was in the interval; but God called the darkness night. Wherefore it was neither day nor night: for neither was it all light, that it should be day; nor was it all darkness, that it should be called night; but after the ninth hour the sun shone forth. This also the Prophet foretells; for after saying, *Not day, nor night,* he added, *And at evening time it shall be light*[e]. Seest thou the exactness of the prophets? Seest thou the truth of the things foretold?

25. But seekest thou at what hour exactly the sun was darkened? was it the fifth hour, or the eight, or the tenth? Tell, O Prophet, the certainty thereof to the indocile Jews; when shall the sun go down? The Prophet Amos answers, *And it shall come to pass in that day, saith the Lord God, that I will cause the sun to go down at noon;* (for there was darkness from the sixth hour;) *and I will darken the earth in the clear day.* What sort of season is this, O Prophet, and what sort of day? *And I will turn your feasts into mourning;* for this was done in the days of unleavened bread, and at the feast of the Passover: then afterwards he says, *And I will make Him as the mourning of an Only Son, and those with Him as a day of anguish;* for in the day of unleavened bread, and at the feast, their women mourned and wept, and the Apostles who had hidden themselves were in anguish. Wonderful then is this prophecy.

(13.) 26. But, some one will say, "Give me yet another sign; what other plain sign is there in the matter?" Jesus was crucified; and He had but one coat, and one cloak: now His cloak the soldiers shared among themselves, having rent it into four; but His coat was not rent, for when rent it would have been no longer of any use; so about this lots were cast by the soldiers; thus the one they divide, but for the other they cast lots. Is then this also written? They know, the diligent chanters of the Church, who imitate the Angel hosts,

---

[e] Theodoret (in loc.) gives the same interpretation, S. Jerome (in loc.) explains it of the second advent.

Prophecy of Christ's passion. 157

and continually sing praises to God : who are thought worthy Ps 22, to chant Psalms in this Golgotha, and to say, *They parted* 18 *My raiment among them, and for My vesture they did cast* John 19, 24 *lots.* The word " lots " expresses the very act of the soldiers κλῆρος ἦν ὁ

27. Again, when He had been judged before Pilate, He λαχμός. was clothed in red; for there they put on Him a purple robe. Is this also written ? Esaias saith, *Who is this that cometh* Is 63, 1. *from Edom? the redness of His garments is from Bosor;* Sept. (who is this who for a *dishonour* weareth purple? for Bosor hath in Hebrew this meaning [f].) *Why are Thy garments red,* v 2. *and Thy raiment as from the trodden winepress?* But He Is 65, 2. answers and says, *All day long have I stretched forth Mine* Sept. *hands unto a disobedient and gainsaying people* [g].

28. He stretched out His hands on the Cross, that He might encompass the ends of the world; for this Golgotha is the very centre of the earth. It is not my word, but it is a prophet who hath said, *Thou hast wrought salvation in the* Ps 74, *middle of the earth.* He stretched forth human hands, who 12. by His spiritual hands had established the heaven; and they were fastened with nails, that His manhood which bore the sins of men, having been nailed to the tree, and having died, sin might die with it, and we might rise again in righteous- Rom 5, ness. *For since by* one *man came death,* by One Man also 12 17. came life; by One Man, the Saviour, dying of His own αὐτοπρο- αιρέτως accord: for remember what He said, *I have power to lay* John 10, *down My life, and I have power to take it again.* 18.

29. So He endured these things, having come for the (14.) salvation of all; but the people returned Him an evil recompense. Jesus says, *I thirst,*—He who had brought forth the waters for them out of the flinty rock ; and He asks fruit of the Vine which He had planted. But what does the Vine ? This Vine, by nature indeed of the holy fathers, but of Sodom by κατὰ purpose of heart ;—(for *their Vine is of the vine of Sodom,* προκίρε- σιν. *and of the fields of Gomorrah ;*)—this Vine, when the Lord Deut was athirst, having filled a sponge and put it on a reed, offers 32, 32. Him vinegar. *They gave Me also gall for My meat, and in* Ps. 69, 21.

---

[f] S Jerome says it means *flesh* (caro) or *in distress* (in tribulatione) Ep 61 ad Pammach vol ii. p 120 ed 1684. It is now considered to mean a *fold for cattle,* as in Mic 2, 12, from בצר secuit, munivit.

[g] This passage is interpreted of the Crucifixion by Origen, Jerome, Theodoret (all in loc), &c &c not of course excluding its primary reference to God's fatherly all-embracing love.

LECT XIII
Mark 15, 23

My thirst, they gave Me vinegar to drink. Thou seest the plainness of the Prophet's description. But what sort of gall put they into My mouth? *They gave Him,* it says, *wine mingled with myrrh.* Now myrrh is of the taste of gall, and exceeding bitter. Are these things what ye recompense unto the Lord? Offerest thou these things, O Vine, unto thy Master? Rightly did the Prophet Esaias aforetime bewail you, saying,

Is 5, 1.
v 2.
Sept.

My well-beloved hath a vineyard in a very fruitful hill; and (not to recite the whole) he goes on, *I waited that it should bring forth grapes; I thirsted that it should give wine; but it brought forth thorns;* for thou seest the crown, wherewith I

v. 6.

am adorned. What then shall I now decree? *I will command the clouds that they rain no rain upon it.* For the prophets, the clouds, were removed from them, and are for

1 Cor. 14, 29.
Eph. 4, 11.

the future in the Church; as Paul says, *Let the prophets speak two or three, and let the others judge;* and again, *God gave in the Church, some, Apostles, and some, Prophets.* Agabus, who bound his own feet and hands, was a prophet.

(15.)
Is 53, 12.

30. And concerning the robbers who were crucified with Him, it was written, *And He was numbered with the transgressors.* Both of them had been transgressors, but one was so no longer. For the one was a transgressor to the end, stubborn against salvation; whose hands indeed were fastened, but who through his blasphemies smote with his tongue.

Ps 109, 25.

When the Jews passing by wagged their heads, mocking the Crucified, and fulfilling what was written, *When they looked on Me, they shaked their heads,* he also reviled with them.

Luke 23, 40. &c.

But the other rebuked the reviler; and to him the end of life was the beginning of restoration; the surrender of his soul was a preventing others in salvation. And after rebuking him, he says, *Lord, remember me;* for to Thee is my speech. Leave this man, for the eyes of his understanding are blinded; but remember me. I say not, remember my works, for of these I am afraid. Every man has a feeling for his fellow-traveller; I am travelling with Thee deathwards; remember me, Thy fellow-wayfarer. I say not, Remember me now, but, *when Thou comest into Thy kingdom.*

31. What power, O robber, enlightened thee? Who taught thee to worship that despised Man, thy companion on the Cross? O Eternal Light, which givest light to them that are

in darkness! Therefore also he rightly heard the words, *Be of good cheer;* not that thy deeds are such as should make thee be of good cheer; but that the King is here, dispensing favours. The request reached unto a distant time; but the grace is very speedy. *Verily I say unto thee, This day shalt thou be with Me in Paradise;* because *to-day* thou hast *heard My voice, and hast not hardened thine heart.* Very speedily I passed sentence upon Adam, very speedily I pardon thee. To him it was said, *In the day wherein thou eatest, thou shalt surely die;* but thou to-day hast obeyed the faith, to-day is thy salvation. Adam by the Tree fell; thou by the Tree art brought to Paradise. Fear not the serpent; he shall not cast thee out; for he is *fallen from heaven.* And I say not unto thee, This day shalt thou depart, but, This day shalt thou be with Me. Be of good courage. thou shalt not be cast out. Fear not the fiery sword; it shrinks from its Lord. O mighty and ineffable grace! The faithful Abraham had not yet entered, but the robber enters! Moses and the Prophets had not yet entered, and the lawless robber enters. Paul also wondered at this before thee, saying, *Where sin abounded, there grace did much more abound.* They who had borne the heat of the day had not yet entered; and he of the eleventh hour entered. Let none murmur against the goodman of the house, for he says, *Friend, I do thee no wrong; is it not lawful for Me to do what I will with Mine own.* The robber has a wish to work righteousness, but death prevents him; I wait not exclusively for work, I have accepted faith. I am come who *feed My sheep among the lilies,* I am come to feed My sheep in the gardens. I have *found* a *sheep,* a *lost* one, but I lay it on My shoulders, for he believes, since he himself has said, *I have gone astray like a lost sheep; Lord, remember me when Thou comest in Thy kingdom.*

^{Luke 23, 43.}
^{Ps. 95, 7. 8}
^{Gen 2, 17.}
^{Luke 10, 18.}
^{vid. Am. bros. in Ps 118. s 20 n. 12.}
^{Rom. 5, 20.}
^{v. Matt. 20, 12. &c.}
^{Cant 6, 3.}
^{Luke 15, 5 6.}
^{Ps 119, 176.}

32. Of this garden I sang of old to My spouse in the Canticles, and spake thus to her. *I am come into My garden, My sister, My spouse;* (now the place where He was crucified was a garden;) and what takest Thou thence? *I have gathered My myrrh;* having drunk wine mingled with myrrh, and vinegar. And having received these, He said, *It is finished.* For the mystery has been fulfilled; the things that

^{(16.) Cant. 5, 1.}
^{Ibid.}
^{John 19, 30.}

are written have been fulfilled; sins are forgiven. For *Christ being come an High-priest of good things to come, by a greater and more perfect tabernacle, not made with hands, that is to say, not of this building, neither by the blood of goats and calves, but by His own blood, He entered in once into the holy place, having obtained eternal redemption for us; for if the blood of bulls and of goats, and the ashes of an heifer, sprinkling the unclean, sanctifieth to the purifying of the flesh, how much more the blood of Christ?* And again, *Having therefore, brethren, boldness to enter into the holiest by the blood of Jesus, by a new and living way, which He hath consecrated for us, through the veil, that is to say, His flesh.* And because His flesh, this veil, was dishonoured, the emblematical veil of the temple was rent through, as it is written, *And, behold, the veil of the temple was rent in twain from the top to the bottom;* for not a morsel of it was left; for since the Master said, *Behold, your house is left unto you desolate,* the house has been rent into pieces.

33. These things the Saviour endured, *making peace through the Blood of His Cross, for things in heaven, and things in earth.* For we were enemies of God through sin, and God had appointed the sinner to die. There must needs therefore have happened one of two things; either that God, keeping His words, should destroy all men, or that in His lovingkindness, He should cancel the sentence. But behold the wisdom of God; He preserved both to His sentence its truth, and to His loving-kindness its exercise. Christ took our sins *in His body on the tree, that we being dead to sin, should live to righteousness.* Of no small account was He who died for us; He was not a literal sheep; He was not a mere man; He was more than an Angel; He was God made man. The transgression of sinners was not so great, as the righteousness of Him who died for them; we have not committed as much sin as He has wrought righteousness who laid down His life for us,—who laid it down when He pleased, and took it again when He pleased. And wouldest thou have proof that He laid down His life not by violence, nor against His will yielded up the ghost? He cried to the Father, saying, *Father, into Thy hands I commend My spirit;* I commend it, that I may take it again. And having said these things, *He gave*

Prophecy of the tomb.

up the ghost; but not for any long time, for He rose again from the dead speedily.

34. The Sun was darkened, because of *the Son of righteous- (17.) ness.* The rocks were rent, because of the spiritual Rock. [Mal. 4, 2] The tombs were opened, and the dead arose, because of Him νοητήν. who was *free among the dead; He sent forth His prisoners* [Ps 88, 5.] *out of the pit wherein is no water.* Be not then ashamed of [Zech. 9, 11.] the Crucified, but be thyself bold to say, *He beareth our* [Is. 53, 4. 5.] *sins, and carrieth our sorrows, and with His stripes we are healed.* Let us not be unthankful to our Benefactor. And again; *for the transgression of my people was He stricken;* [ver. 8. 9.] *and He made His grave with the wicked, and with the rich in His death.* Therefore Paul says plainly, *that Christ died* [1 Cor. 15, 3. 4.] *for our sins according to the Scriptures, and that He rose again the third day according to the Scriptures.*

35. But we seek to be told plainly where He has been buried. Is His tomb then made with hands? Is it, like the tombs of kings, raised above the ground? Is the Sepulchre made of stones joined together? And what is laid upon it? Tell us, O Prophets, the exact truth concerning His tomb also, where it is placed, and where we shall seek it? And they say, *Look unto the solid rock which ye have hewn.* [Is. 51, 1. Sept] Look and behold. Thou hast in the Gospel, *In a sepulchre* ἐν εὐαγ- *hewn in stone, which was hewn out of a rock.* And what [γελίοις, in Gos-] happens next? What kind of door has the sepulchre? [pel les-] Again another Prophet says, *They cut off My life in the* [sons v. supr.] *dungeon, and cast a stone upon Me.* I, who am *the Chief* [iv 4 &c.] *corner-stone, elect, precious,* lie for a little time within a [Luke 23, 53.] stone. I who am a stone of stumbling to the Jews, but of [Mark 15, 46.] salvation to them who believe. The Tree of Life, therefore, [Lam. 3,] was planted in the earth, that the earth which had been [53 λάκ-] cursed might enjoy the blessing, and that the dead might [κῷ 1 Pet. 2,] be released. [6.]

36. Let us not then be ashamed to confess the Crucified (18) Be the Cross our seal made with boldness by our fingers on [vid.] our brow, and in every thing; over the bread we eat, and the [Tertull. de Cor.] cups we drink; in our comings in, and goings out; before [Mil. 3.] our sleep, when we lie down and when we awake; when we are in the way, and when we are still. Great is that preservative; it is without price, for the poor's sake; without

toil, for the sick; since also its grace is from God. It is the Sign of the faithful, and the dread of devils: for He has *triumphed over them in it, having made a shew of them openly;* for when they see the Cross, they are reminded of the Crucified; they are afraid of Him, who hath *bruised the heads of the dragon.* Despise not the Seal, because of the freeness of the gift; but for this the rather honour thy Benefactor.

37. And if thou art ever led into disputation, and hast not the grounds of proof, yet let Faith remain firm in thee; or rather, become thou well learned, and then silence the Jews out of the prophets, and the Greeks out of their own fables. They themselves worship men thunderstricken [h]: but the thunder when it comes from heaven, comes not at random. If they are not ashamed to worship men thunderstricken and abhorred of God, art thou ashamed to worship the beloved Son of God, who was crucified for thee? I am ashamed to speak about their so-called Gods, and I leave them because of time; let those who know, speak. And let all heretics also be silenced. If any say that the Cross is an illusion, turn away from him. Abhor those who say that Christ was crucified to our fancy only; for if so, and if salvation is from the Cross, then is salvation a fancy also. If the Cross is fancy, the Resurrection is fancy also; but *if Christ be not risen, we are yet in our sins.* If the Cross is fancy, the Ascension also is fancy; and if the Ascension is fancy, then is the second coming also fancy, and every thing is henceforth unsubstantial.

38. Take therefore first, as an unassailable foundation, the Cross, and build upon it the rest of the faith. Deny not the Crucified; for, if thou deny Him, thou hast many to arraign thee. Judas the traitor will arraign thee first; for he who betrayed Him, knew that He was condemned to death by the chief-priests and elders. The thirty-pieces of silver bear witness; Gethsemane bears witness, where the betrayal happened; I speak not yet of the Mount of Olives, on which they were that night, praying. The moon in the night bears witness; the day bears witness, and the darkened sun; for it endured not to look on the crime of the

[h] Æsculapius.

conspirators. The fire remonstrates with thee, by which Peter stood and warmed himself; if thou deny the Cross, the eternal fire awaits thee. I say what is severe, that thou may not have experience of it. Remember the swords that came against Him in Gethsemane, that thou be not punished by the eternal sword. The house of Caiaphas will arraign thee, shewing by its present desolation the power of Him who was erewhile judged there. Yea, Caiaphas himself will rise up against thee in the day of judgment; the very servant will rise up against thee, who smote Jesus with the palm of his hand; they also who bound Him, and they who led Him away. Even Herod shall rise up against thee; and Pilate; as if saying, Why deniest thou Him who was slandered unto us by the Jews, whom we knew to have done no wrong? For I Pilate then washed my hands. The false witnesses shall rise up against thee, and the soldiers who put on Him the purple robe, and set on Him the crown of thorns, and crucified Him in Golgotha, and cast lots for His coat. Simon the Cyrenian will cry out upon thee, who bore the Cross behind Jesus.

39. There will cry out upon thee, among the stars, the darkened Sun; among the things upon earth, the Wine mingled with myrrh; among reeds, the Reed; among herbs, the Hyssop; among the things of the sea, the Sponge; among trees, the Wood of the Cross;—the soldiers, too, as was said, who nailed Him, and cast lots for His vesture; the soldier who pierced His side with the spear; the women who then were present; the veil of the temple then rent asunder; the hall of Pilate, now laid waste by the power of Him who was then crucified; this holy Golgotha, rising on high, and shewing itself to this day, and displaying even yet how because of Christ the rocks were then riven[1]; the neighbouring sepulchre where He was laid; and the stone which was laid on the door, which lies to this day by the tomb[k]; the Angels who were then present; the women who worshipped Him after His resurrection; Peter and John, who ran to the sepulchre; and Thomas, who thrust his hand into His side, and his fingers into the print of the nails. For it was for our sakes

---

[1] The martyr Lucian (ap Ruff. Hist ix. 6) says the same.

[k] Vide also Jerome, Ep. 27. ed 1684.

<small>LECT. XIII.</small>
<small>κατ' οἰκο-νομίαν.</small>

that he so carefully handled Him; for what thou who wert not there present, wouldest have sought, he being present, by God's Providence, did seek.

<small>σταυρώ-μενον.</small>

40. Thou hast Twelve Apostles, witnesses of the Cross; and the whole earth, and the world of men who believe on Him who was upon it. Let thy very presence here now persuade thee of the power of the Crucified. For who has now brought thee to this assembly? what soldiers? With what bonds hast thou been forced? What doom has driven thee here now? No, but the salutary Trophy of Jesus, the Cross, has brought you all together. This has enslaved the Persians, and tamed the Scythians; this, to the Egyptians, has given, for cats and dogs and their manifold errors, the knowledge of God; this, to this day heals diseases; this, to this day drives away devils, and overthrows the juggleries of drugs and charms.

<small>Zech 12, 10</small>

41. This shall appear again with Jesus from heaven[1]; for the trophy shall precede the king: that seeing *Him whom they pierced*, and by the Cross knowing Him who was dishonoured, the Jews may repent and mourn; (but *they shall mourn tribe by tribe*, when their season for repentance shall be no more;) and that we may glory, boasting of the Cross, worshipping the Lord who was sent, and crucified for us, and worshipping also God His Father who sent Him, with the Holy Ghost: To whom be glory for ever and ever. Amen.

<small>ver 12. Sept.</small>

---

[1] It is the common opinion of the Fathers, that "the sign of the Son of Man in heaven" will be the Cross. vid. Chrysostom and Jerome in Matt. xxiv. 30.

LECTURE XIV.

ON THE RESURRECTION, ASCENSION, AND EXALTATION OF CHRIST.

1 Cor. xv. 1—4.

Moreover, brethren, I declare unto you the Gospel which I preached unto you, which also ye have received, and wherein ye stand; by which also ye are saved, if ye keep in memory what I preached unto you, unless ye have believed in vain. For I delivered unto you first of all that which I also received, how that Christ died for our sins according to the Scriptures; and that He was buried, and that He rose again the third day according to the Scriptures.

1. *Be glad, O Jerusalem, and hold festival together, all ye who love* Jesus; *for He is risen; rejoice all ye who before mourned,* hearing the reckless deeds and enormities of the Jews. For He who was entreated of them with insult here, is risen again; and as the Lecture on the Cross was one of pain, so now let the good tidings of the Resurrection gladden all present. Let mourning be turned into gladness, and lamentation into joy; and let our mouth be filled with joy and gladness, because of Him who after His resurrection said, *Rejoice.* For I know the sorrow of the lovers of Christ during the days past; since, our words having ended at His Death and Burial, and not having told the good tidings of the Resurrection, their mind was kept in suspense to hear what they longed for. Now therefore the Dead is risen,—He who was *free among the dead,* and the deliverer of the dead. He, whose head, by reason of His patience, was bound in scorn with the crown of thorns, has now, being risen, put on the diadem of His victory over death.

[v. Is 66, 10. Sept.]

[v. Mat. 28, 9.]

[Ps. 88, 5.]

Prophecies of the Resurrection.

LECT. XIV.
ὁ παρών.
1 Cor 15, 4.

2. As then we have set before you the witnesses of His Cross, in like manner let us now ascertain the proofs of the Resurrection; since the Apostle in the text says, *He was buried, and rose the third day according to the Scriptures.* Since therefore an Apostle sends us to Scripture testimonies, it is proper for us to recognize there the hope of our salvation; and to learn, first, whether the Divine Scriptures tell us the time of the Resurrection, whether it is in summer, or in autumn, or after winter;—and from what sort of place the Saviour arises;—and what the name of the place is called in the wondrous prophets;—and whether women, who had sought Him and found Him not, afterwards found Him and rejoiced that when the Gospels are read, the narratives of these holy works may not be thought fables or legends.

(2.)
Is 57, 2. Sept.
Is 57, 1. 2. Sept
Is 53, 9. Sept
Gen 49, 9 Sept.
Num. 24, 9.
Ps. 22, 15.
Is. 51, 1 Sept.

3. Now that Christ was buried, ye have heard plainly in the foregoing discourse; since Esaias says, *His burial shall be in peace:* for in His burial He made peace in heaven and earth, bringing sinners unto God. And, *the just is taken away from the face of unrighteousness,* and, *His burial shall be in peace,* and, *I will give the wicked for His burial.* And the prophecy of Jacob in the Scriptures, saying, *He couched and lay down as a lion, and as a lion's whelp; who shall awaken Him?* And in like manner in Numbers, *He couched, He lay down as a lion, and as a great lion.* And ye have heard ofttimes the Psalm which says, *And Thou hast brought Me into the dust of death.* Also, we specified the spot, when we quoted the words, *Look unto the rock which ye have hewn.* Now therefore let the texts for the Resurrection itself follow.

Ps. 12, 5.

4. He says therefore in the eleventh Psalm, *For the oppression of the poor, for the sighing of the needy, now will I arise, saith the Lord.* But with some persons this passage is uncertain; for He often arises to wrath also, that He may take vengeance on His enemies. Come then to the fifteenth

Ps. 16, 1. Sept.
Ib v. 4.
(v Sept)

Psalm, which says plainly, *Preserve me, O God, for in Thee do I put my trust;* and after this, *Their drink offerings of blood will I not offer, nor take up their names into my lips,* since they have refused Me, and named Cæsar as their king;

Ib. v 8.

and afterwards, *I have set the Lord always before Me; because He is at My right hand, I shall not be moved;* and after a little,

Ib. v. 7.

My reins also instruct Me in the night-season; and after this it says most plainly, *For Thou wilt not leave My soul in hell,* Ib. v. 10. *neither wilt Thou suffer Thine Holy One to see corruption.* He has not said, *neither wilt Thou suffer Thine Holy One to see* death, else He had not died; but *corruption,* says He, I shall not see, and I shall not abide in death. *Thou wilt* Ib v. 11. *shew Me the path of life.* Behold, here is plainly preached life after death. Turn next to the twenty-ninth Psalm, *I will* Ps. 30, 1. *extol Thee, O Lord, for Thou hast lifted Me up, and hast not* Sept. *made My foes to rejoice over Me .* what came to pass? wert Thou rescued from Thine enemies, or wert Thou set free when about to be smitten? He himself says most plainly, *Thou,* Ib. v 3 *Lord, hast brought My soul out of hell.* In the former place (Pr. B vers and He says, *Thou wilt not leave,* speaking prophetically; and Sept.) here He speaks of what is to happen, as if it had already happened, *Thou hast brought; Thou hast kept My life from* Ibid. *them that go down to the pit.* At what time shall this be? (3.) *Weeping shall endure for the evening; but joy cometh in* Ib v 5. *the morning;* for in the evening was the mourning of the Sept. disciples, and in the morning, the gladness of the Resurrection.

5. And wouldest thou know the place also? He says again in the Canticles, *I went down into the garden of nuts.* Cant 6, For though it be now adorned and that most excellently with 11 royal gifts, yet it was before a garden, and the tokens and vid inf. traces thereof remain. *A garden enclosed* was it; *a fountain* 9 and 14. *sealed* by the Jews, who said, *We remember that that* Cant. 4, *deceiver said while He was yet alive, After three days I will* 12. *rise again; command therefore that the sepulchre be made* Mat 27, 63. 64 *sure;* and afterwards, *They went and made the sepulchre sure, sealing the stone, and setting a watch.* To whom, v 66. referring, there is one who said well, *And in rest wilt Thou judge them.* But who is the *fountain sealed,* or who is Job 7, 18. Sept. interpreted as the *well of living waters?* It is the Saviour, Cant. 4, concerning whom it is written, *With Thee is the fountain* 15. *of life.* Ps. 36, 9.

6. But what saith Zephaniah to the disciples in the person of Christ? *Prepare Thyself, rise up early, all their small* Zeph 3, *clusters are destroyed;* that is, of the Jews, with whom there 7. Sept. are left no grapes of salvation, no not even a stray cluster; for their vine is cut down. See how he says to the disciples,

LECT. XIV.

Ib v 8

Μαρτύ-
ριον vid.
Euseb.
Const.
iv 40.
&c.

Zeph 3, 9.

Ib v 10

(4.)

Ps. 88, 1.

v 4. 5.

v. 8
v. 10.
v. 13.

Prepare thyself, rise up early; at early dawn expect the Resurrection. And afterwards in the same connexion, he says, *Therefore await Me, saith the Lord, on the day of My resurrection at the Testimony.* Seest thou that the Prophet foresaw even that the place of the Resurrection should be called, the Testimony? For wherefore is this place of Golgotha and of the Resurrection not called like the other churches, a church, but a Testimony? It was perhaps because of the Prophet, who had said, *On the day of my Resurrection, at the Testimony.*

7. And who then is this, and what is the sign of Him who rises again? It is said plainly in what follows, in the same passage of the Prophet, *For then I will turn to the people a language;* (since, after the Resurrection, the Holy Ghost being sent, the grace of tongues was given;) *to serve the Lord with one consent.* And what other pledge is there in the same Prophet of their *serving the Lord with one consent? From beyond the rivers of Ethiopia, they shall bring to Me sacrifices.* Thou knowest what is written in the Acts, that an Ethiopian Eunuch came from beyond the rivers of Ethiopia. When therefore the Scriptures tell both the time and the peculiar character of the place, and also the signs following the Resurrection, be thou assured henceforth of the Resurrection, and let no one shake thee from confessing that Christ is raised from the dead.

8. Now receive yet another testimony in the eighty-seventh Psalm, where Christ speaks by the Prophets; (for He who then spoke, afterwards came to us,) *O Lord God of My salvation, I have cried day and night before Thee;* and after a little, *I am as a Man that hath no strength, free among the dead.* He said not, "I am a man without strength," but "as a Man without strength," for He was crucified, not from want of strength, but willingly; and His death was not without power or will. *I am counted with them that go down into the pit.* And what is the Sign? *Thou hast put away Mine acquaintance far from Me;* (for the disciples fled;) *wilt Thou shew wonders to the dead?* Then after a little, *But unto Thee have I cried, O Lord, and in the morning shall my prayer prevent Thee.* Seest thou how they declare the very time both of the Passion and of the Resurrection?

9. And whence did the Saviour arise? He says in the Song of Songs, *Rise up, My love, and come away*: and afterwards, *in the cleft of the rock; for the cleft of the rock* he calls the cleft which was then at the door of the salutary Sepulchre, and was hewn out of the rock itself, as it is customary here in the front of sepulchres. For now it appears not, the outer cave having been hewn away for the sake of the present adornment; for before the sepulchre was decorated by royal zeal, there was a cave in the face of the rock. But where is the rock which has in it this *cleft*? lies it in the midst of the city, or near the walls and the outskirts? and is it in the ancient walls, or in the outer walls which were built afterwards? He says then in the Canticles, *In the cleft of the rock, near to the outer wall*[a].

Cant. 2, 10.

Cant. 2, 14 Sept.

[a] A writer of great name, in a review of Dr Clarke's Travels, (who denied the accuracy of the tradition in the text concerning the site of the Sepulchre,) thus expresses himself. "Nor was it only its superior sanctity which would preserve its memory. As the private property of an opulent Christian family, it would be secured from pollution or injury, and the tomb itself was no 'hereabouts,' which tradition was to settle, but an object too visible and too definite either to be overlooked or mistaken. While a single Christian survived in the town, it could never cease to be known and venerated.... But as Dr. Clarke has shown that the present appearance of the sepulchre is at variance with the account in the Gospel, and the general character of Jewish tombs, it remains for us to examine whether the alterations of time, together with those ascribed to the bad taste and unfortunate zeal of Helena, can have been sufficient to produce this difference. His reasons for incredulity are as follows —the tomb of Christ was in a garden without the walls of Jerusalem, the structure which at present bears its name, is in the heart of, at least, the modern city, and Dr. C is unwilling to believe that the ancient limits can have been so much circumscribed to the north as to exclude its site. Further, the original sepulchre was undoubtedly a cave the present offers no such appearance, being an insulated pile, constructed or cased with distinct slabs of marble That both these arguments, however, are inconclusive will appear, we think, to Dr C himself, from a testimony which will shortly be produced," [the passage of St Cyril in the text] "It is certain that, whether probable or not, the ancient limits of the city did exclude the *present* sepulchre, and that this last, defaced and altered as it is, may be really 'the place where the Lord lay,' is likely from the following circumstances Forty yards, or thereabouts, from the upper end of the sepulchre, the natural rock is visible, and in the place which the priests call Calvary, it is at least as high as the top of the sepulchre itself. The rock then *may* have extended as far as the present entrance, and though the entrance itself is hewn into form and cased with marble, the adytum yet offers proof that it is not factitious. It is a trapezium of seven feet by six, neither at right angles to its own entrance, nor to the aisle of the Church which conducts to it, and in no respect conformable to the external plan of the tomb This last is arranged in a workmanlike manner, with its frontal immediately opposite the principal nave, and in the same style with the rest of the Church It is shaped something like a horse-shoe, and its walls, measured from this outer horse-shoe to the inner trapezium, vary from five to eight feet in thickness, a sufficient space to admit of no inconsiderable density of rock, between the outer and inner coating of marble. This, however, does not apply to the antechamber, of which the frontal at least is probably fictitious and where that indenture in the marble is found

10. At what season does the Saviour arise? Is it the season of summer, or some other? In that same Song, before the above-mentioned place, he says straightway, *The winter is past, the rain is over and gone; the flowers appear on the earth, and the time of pruning is come.* Is not the earth now full of flowers, and are they not pruning the vines? Thou seest how he says also, that the winter is now past. For in this month Xanthicus, it is now spring; and this season, which is the first month among the Hebrews, is that in which is the feast of the Passover; of the figurative Passover erewhile, but now of the true. This is the season of the creation of the world[b]: for then God said, *Let the earth bring forth grass, the herb yielding seed after his kind.* And now, as thou seest, every herb is producing seed. And as at that time, God having made the sun and moon, gave them courses of equal length, so also but a few days ago it was the season of the Equinox. At that time, God said, *Let Us make man in Our own image, after Our likeness:* and the *image* he received; but the *likeness*, by his transgression, he defaced[c]; at that very season then in which he lost this, did his restoration also come to pass. At the same season in which created man was cast out of paradise for his disobedience, was believing man brought into it again by obeying. Salvation therefore was at the very season when the fall was; when *the flowers appeared, and the time of pruning was come.*

11. The place of His burial was a garden; and that which was planted therein was a Vine; for He has said, *And I am the Vine.* It was planted then in the earth, that the curse which was on it for Adam's sake might be rooted out. The

Marginalia: LECT. XIV (5.) Cant 2, 11. καιρὸς τῆς τομῆς, Sept. Gen 1, 26. vid. infra xvii 12. v. John 15, 1.

which induced Dr C to believe that the whole thickness of the wall was composed of the same costly substance. Now these circumstances afford, we apprehend, no inconsiderable grounds for supposing, with Pococke, that it is indeed a grotto above ground the irregularity of the shape, the difference between the external and internal plan, the thickness of the walls, so needless, if they are throughout of masonry, all favour this opinion; nor is the task ascribed to Helena's workmen of insulating this rock, from that which is still preserved a few yards distant, at all incredible, when we consider that the labour, while it pleased the taste of their employer, furnished at the same time materials for her intended Cathedral" Quarterly Review, March, 1813

[b] This belief is expressed also by Ambros Hexam 1. 4. n. 13. Cosm. Topogr. v p 192 &c.

[c] This distinction is also made by Irenæus, (Hær. v. 6. and 16.) Ambrosiast (dign cond. hum. 2 and 3.) Philastrius (Hær. 98) &c. They seem to consider "image" to have reference to our *nature*, and "likeness" to our *holiness*. vid also Bp. Bull's dissertation on the Paradisiacal state of man.

earth was doomed to thorns and thistles; the true Vine sprang out of the earth, that the saying might be fulfilled, *Truth shall spring out of the earth, and righteousness shall look down from heaven.* And what will He say who is buried in the garden? *I have gathered My myrrh with My spice;* and again, *Myrrh and aloes with all the chief spices.* But these are the marks of His burial; and in the Gospels it is said, *The women came to the sepulchre, bringing the spices which they had prepared.* And there came also *Nicodemus, and brought a mixture of myrrh and aloes.* And afterwards it is written, *I have eaten My bread with My honey;* the bitter, before His Passion, and the sweet after His Resurrection. Then, being risen, He entered through the closed doors; but they believed not in Him, for they thought they saw a spirit; but He says, *Handle Me, and see;* thrust your fingers into the prints of the nails, as Thomas required. *And when they yet disbelieved for joy, and wondered, He said unto them, Have ye here any meat? and they gave Him a piece of a broiled fish, and of an honeycomb.* Thou seest how was fulfilled that Scripture, *I have eaten my bread with my honey.*

Ps. 85, 11
Cant 5, 1.
Cant 4, 14
Luke 24,
1.
John 19, 39
Cant 5, 1 Sept.
John 20, 19.
Luke 24, 36 &c

12. But before He entered in through the closed doors, the Bridegroom and the Physician of souls was sought by those most noble and courageous women. Those blessed women came to the sepulchre, and sought Him who was risen, and the tears still flowed from their eyes; though it was time rather to be glad, and to dance for Him who was risen. Mary according to the Gospel came seeking Him, and found Him not; and after this, she heard from the Angels, and at last saw Christ. Are these things also written? Yes; he says in the Song of Songs, *On my bed I sought Him whom my soul loveth;* at what time? *By night on my bed I sought Him whom my soul loveth;* (Mary, it is said, came while it was yet dark;) *On my bed I sought Him by night; I sought Him, but I found Him not.* And in the Gospel Mary says, *They have taken away my Lord, and I know not where they have laid Him.* But the Angels who were there present relieve her ignorance, saying, *Why seek ye the Living among the dead?* He is not only risen, but is risen and the dead with Him. But she knew not this, and in her person

(6.)

Cant 3, 1.
John 20,
John 20, 13.

the Song of Songs said to the Angels, *Saw ye Him whom my soul loveth? It was but a little that I passed from them,* (that is, the two Angels,) *when I found Him whom my soul loveth: I held Him, and would not let Him go.*

<small>Cant. 3, 3 4 ἕως οὗ, Sept.</small>

13. For after the vision of the Angels, Jesus came as His own Herald; and the Gospel says, *And Jesus met them, saying, All hail! and they came and held Him by the feet.* They held Him, that it might be fulfilled, *I will hold Him, and will not let Him go.* The woman was weak indeed in body, but in spirit was manful. *Many waters cannot quench love, neither can the floods drown it;* He was dead whom they sought, yet was not the hope of the Resurrection quenched. And the Angel says to them again, *Fear not;* I say not to the soldiers, *fear not*, but to you; as for them, let them be afraid, that having learned by trial, they may bear witness and say, Truly this was the Son of God; but you ought not to be afraid, *for perfect love casteth out fear; go, tell His disciples that He is risen;* and the rest. And they depart, fearful, yet with joy; is this also written? yes, the second Psalm, which relates the Passion of Christ, says, *Serve the Lord with fear, and rejoice with trembling;*—rejoice, because of the risen Lord; but with trembling, because of the earthquake, and the Angel who appeared as lightning.

<small>Mat. 28, 9.</small>

<small>Cant 8, 7.</small>

<small>1 John 4, 18</small>

<small>Ps 2, 11</small>

<small>(7.)</small>

14. Though, therefore, Chief Priests and Pharisees through Pilate's means sealed the tomb; yet the women beheld Him who was risen. And Esaias knowing the feebleness of the Chief Priests, and the women's strength of faith, says, *Ye women, who are come from beholding, come hither; for the people hath no understanding;*—the Chief Priests want understanding, while women are eye-witnesses. And when the soldiers came into the city to them, and told them all that had come to pass, they said to them, *Say ye, His disciples came by night, and stole Him away while we slept.* Well therefore has Esaias afore-time said this also, as in their persons, *But tell us, and relate to us another deceit.* He who rose again is up, and by bribes they persuade the soldiers; but they persuade not the kings of our time. The soldiers then surrendered the truth for silver; but the kings of this day have, in their piety, built this holy Church of the Resurrection of God our Saviour, inlaid with silver and

<small>Is 27, 11. Sept.</small>

<small>Mat 28, 13.</small>

<small>Is 30, 10. Sept.</small>

embossed with gold, in which we are assembled; and have embellished it with rarities of silver and gold and precious stones. *And if this come to the governor's ears,* they say, *we will persuade him.* Yea, though ye persuade the soldiers, yet ye will not persuade the world; for why, as Peter's guards were condemned when he escaped out of ward, were not they also who watched Jesus Christ condemned? It was because the former, on whom sentence was pronounced by Herod, were ignorant and had nothing to say for themselves; while the latter, who had seen the truth, and concealed it for money, were protected by the Chief Priests. Nevertheless, though but a few of the Jews were persuaded at the time, the world became obedient. They who hid the truth, have been themselves hidden; but they who received it were made manifest by the power of the Saviour, who not only rose from the dead, but also raised the dead with Himself. And in the person of these the Prophet Osee says plainly, *After two days will He revive us, and the third day will He raise us up, and we shall live in His sight.* Hos. 6, 2.

15. But since the disobedient Jews will not be persuaded by the Divine Scriptures, but forgetting all that is written gainsay the Resurrection of Jesus, it were good to meet them thus: On what ground, while you say that Eliseus and Elias raised the dead, do you gainsay the Resurrection of our Saviour? Is it that we have no living witnesses now out of that generation to what we say? Well, do you also bring forward witness of those other deeds? But that is written;—so is this also written: why then do ye receive the one, and reject the other? They were Hebrews who wrote those things; so were all the Apostles Hebrews · why then do ye disbelieve the Jews? Matthew who wrote the Gospel wrote it in the Hebrew tongue[d]; and Paul the preacher was an Hebrew of the Hebrews; and the twelve Apostles were all of Hebrew race: then fifteen Bishops of Jerusalem[e], were appointed in succession from among the Hebrews. What then is your reason for allowing your own accounts, and rejecting ours? since these also are written by Hebrews from among yourselves. (8)

---

[d] So say Papias, (apud Euseb. Hist iii. 39) Origen, (ibid vi 25) Jerom, (præf in Evang.) and Epiphanius, (Hær 51 5.)

[e] I e. till the destruction of Jerusalem by Hadrian A D. 134.

16. But it is impossible, some one will say, that the dead should arise; and yet Eliseus twice raised the dead,—when he was alive, and also when dead. Now, we believe, that when Eliseus was dead, a dead man who was cast upon him and touched him, arose; is then Christ not risen? But in that case, the dead man who touched Eliseus, arose, yet he who raised him continued nevertheless dead: now the Dead of whom we speak both arose Himself, and many dead were raised without having even touched Him. For *many bodies of the Saints which slept arose, and came out of the graves after His Resurrection, and went into the Holy City,* (evidently this, in which we now are,) *and appeared unto many.* Eliseus then raised indeed a dead man, but he conquered not the world; Elias raised a dead man, but devils are not driven away in the name of Elias. We are not speaking against the Prophets, but we are making much of their Master; for we do not exalt our own by disparaging theirs; for theirs are ours; but by what happened among them, we recommend our own.

17. But they say again, "A corpse lately dead was raised by the living; but to shew us how one three days dead can possibly arise, how a man should be buried, and rise after three days." If we seek for Scripture testimony in proof, the Lord Jesus Christ Himself supplies it in the Gospels, saying, *For as Jonas was three days and three nights in the whale's belly; so shall the Son of man be three days and three nights in the heart of the earth.* And on examining the story of Jonas, great is the force of the resemblance. Jesus was sent to preach repentance; so also was Jonas; though the one fled, not knowing what should come to pass; but the other came willingly, to give repentance unto salvation. Jonas slumbered in the ship, and was fast asleep amidst the stormy sea; and while Jesus slept, according to God's providence, the sea began to rise, to shew in the sequel the might of Him who slept. To the one they said, *Why art thou so fast in sleep? Arise, call upon thy God, that God may save us;* but in the other case they say unto the Master, *Lord, save us.*— Then they said, *Call upon thy God;* here they say, *Do thou save.* But the one says, *Take me, and cast me forth into the sea; so shall the sea be calm unto you;* the other, Himself

rebuked the winds and the sea, and there was a great calm. The one was cast into a whale's belly: but the other descended of His own accord thither, where is the invisible νοητόν whale of death. And He descended of His own accord, that death might cast forth those whom he had devoured, according to that which is written, *I will ransom them from the power of the grave; I will redeem them from death* Hos 13, 14

18. And here let us consider whether it be harder for a man after having been buried to rise again, or for a man in the belly of a whale, and in so great heat of a living creature, to escape corruption. For who among men knows not, that the heat of the belly is so great, that even bones which have been swallowed moulder away? How then did Jonas, who was three days and three nights in the whale's belly, escape corruption? And, seeing that the nature of all men is such that we cannot live without breathing, as we do, the air, how did he live without it for three days? But the Jews make this answer, The power of God, they say, descended with Jonas when he was tossed about in hell. Then, does the Lord grant life to His own servant, by sending with him His power, and can He not grant it to Himself as well? If that is credible, this is credible also; if this is incredible, that also is incredible. For to me both are alike worthy of credence. I believe that Jonas was preserved, for all things are possible with God; I believe that Christ also was raised from the dead; for I have many testimonies of this, both from the Divine Scriptures, and from the operative power even at this day of Him who arose,—who descended into hell alone, but who ascended thence with a great company; for He went down to death, and many bodies of the saints which slept arose through Him.

19. Death was struck with dismay on beholding a new (10.) visitant descending into Hades, not bound by the chains of that place. Wherefore, O ye porters of Hades, when ye saw Him, were ye scared? What unwonted fear seized you? Death fled, and his flight betrayed his cowardice. The holy prophets ran unto Him, and Moses the Lawgiver, and Abraham, and Isaac, and Jacob; David also, and Samuel, and Esaias, and John the Baptist, who bore witness when he asked, *Art Thou He that should come, or do we look for another?* Matt. 11, 3.

All the Just were ransomed, whom death had devoured; for it behoved the King who had been heralded, to become the redeemer of His noble heralds. Then each of the Just said, *O death, where is thy sting? O grave, where is thy victory? For the Conqueror hath redeemed us.*

20. Of this our Saviour, the Prophet Jonas wrought out a figure, from the belly of the whale praying and saying, *I cried by reason of my affliction,* and so on; *out of the belly of hell,* and yet he was in the whale; yet though in the whale, he says that he is in hell; for he was a figure of Christ, who should descend into Hades. And after a little, he says, in the person of Christ, prophesying most clearly, *I went down to the chasms of the mountains;* and yet he was in the belly of the whale. What mountains then encompass thee? I know, he says, that I bear the figure of Him, who is to be laid in the Sepulchre hewn out of the rock. And being in the sea, Jonas says, *I went down to the earth,* since he bore the figure of Christ, who descended to the heart of the earth. And foreseeing that the Jews would persuade the soldiers to lie, and would tell them, *Say that they stole Him away,* he says, *They that observe lying vanities forsake their own mercy.* For He who pitied them came, and was crucified, and rose again, giving His own precious blood both for the Jews and the Gentiles; yet they say, *Say that they stole Him away,* observing lying vanities. But concerning His resurrection, Esaias also says, *He who brought from the earth the great Shepherd of the sheep;* he hath added the word, *great,* lest He should be thought on a level with the shepherds who had gone before Him.

21. Since then we have the prophecies, let faith abide with us. Let them fall who fall through unbelief, since they so will; but thou hast taken thy stand on the rock of faith in the Resurrection. Let no heretic ever persuade thee to speak evil of the Resurrection. For to this day do the Manichees say, that the resurrection of the Saviour was phantom-wise, and not real, slighting Paul who says, *Who was made of the seed of David according to the flesh;* and again, *By the resurrection of Jesus Christ our Lord from the dead.* And again he aims at them, and speaks thus, *Say not in thine heart, who shall ascend into heaven; or, who shall descend*

into the deep? that is, to bring up Christ again from the dead; and in like manner warning as he has elsewhere written again, *Remember that Christ Jesus was raised from* 2 Tim. 2, *the dead;* and again, *And if Christ be not risen, then is our* $^8_1$ Cor *preaching vain, and your faith is also vain. Yea, and we* 15, 14. *are found false witnesses of God; because we have testified* 15. *of God that He raised up Christ, whom He raised not up.* But in what follows he says, *But now is Christ risen from* ver. 20. *the dead, the first fruits of them that slept;—And He was* ver. 5. *seen of Cephas, then of the twelve;* (for if thou believe not one witness, thou hast twelve witnesses;) *then He was seen of above* ver. 6. *five hundred brethren at once;* (if they disbelieve the twelve, let them admit the five hundred,) *then he was seen of James,* His own brother, and first Bishop of this diocese. Seeing παροικία. then that such a Bishop originally saw Christ Jesus when risen, πρωτο- do not thou, his disciple, disbelieve him. But thou sayest that τύπως. His brother James was a partial witness; *Then he was seen* v 8. *also of me* Paul, His foe; but what testimony is doubted, when an enemy proclaims it? " I, once the persecutor, now preach the glad tidings of the Resurrection."

22. Many are the witnesses of the Saviour's resurrection.— The night, and the light of the full moon, (for that night was the sixteenth [f];) and the rock of the sepulchre which received Him. The stone also shall rise up against the face of the Jews, for it saw the Lord; even the stone which was then vid sup. rolled away, itself testifies of the Resurrection, lying there to xiii 39. this day. The Angels of God who were present testified of the Resurrection of the Only-begotten. Peter and John, and Thomas, and the rest of the Apostles; some of whom ran to the sepulchre, and saw the burial-clothes, in which He was wrapped before, lying there after the Resurrection; and others handled His hands and His feet, and beheld the prints of the nails; and altogether enjoyed that salutary Breath, John 20 and were counted worthy to forgive sins in the power of the 22. Holy Ghost. Women too were witnesses, those who held His feet, and who beheld the mighty earthquake, and the radiance of the Angel who stood by. And the linen clothes which

---

[f] On the question of the days of the month Nisan on which the Crucifixion and Resurrection took place, vid. Gres-well's Dissertations, vol iii Diss 4 where passages from the Fathers on the subject are brought together.

LECT XIV. were rolled about Him, and which He left when He rose;— the soldiers, and the money given to them; the spot itself also, yet to be seen;—and the house of this holy Church, which out of his loving affection to Christ, was by the Emperor Constantine of blessed memory, both built, and beautified as thou seest.

23. A witness of the resurrection of Jesus is Tabitha also, who was in His name raised from the dead; for how shall we disbelieve that Christ is risen, when even His Name has raised the dead? The sea also bears witness to the resurrection of Jesus, as thou hast heard before. The draught of fishes also testifies, and the fire of coals and the fish laid thereon. Peter also bears witness, who had erst denied Him thrice, and who then thrice confessed Him; and was commanded to feed His spiritual sheep. To this day stands Mount Olivet, still to the eyes of the faithful all but displaying Him mounting on a cloud, and the heavenly gate of His ascension. For He descended from heaven to Bethlehem, but to heaven He ascended from the Mount of Olives; at the former place beginning His conflicts for men, but in the latter, crowned after them. Thou hast therefore many witnesses; thou hast this very place of the Resurrection; thou hast also the place of the Ascension towards the east; thou hast also for witnesses, the Angels which then bore witness, and the cloud on which He went up, and the disciples who came down from that place.

vid sup. 17—20

νοητά.

(13.) ᾠκονό-μησε

κατ' οἰ-κονομίαν.

24. It follows in course, in teaching the Faith, to speak of the Ascension; but the grace of God has so ordered it, that thou heard most fully concerning it, as far as our weakness allowed, yesterday, on the Lord's day; since, by the providence of divine grace, the course of the Lessons in Church, included the account of our Saviour's going up into the heavens, and though what was then said was spoken for the sake of all, and for the united body of the faithful, yet was it especially for thy sake. Now I ask, didst thou attend to what was said? Thou knowest that the words which come next in the Creed teach thee to believe in Him "who rose again the third day, and ascended into heaven, and sitteth on the right hand of the Father." Now I suppose that thou certainly rememberest the exposition; yet I will now also

cursorily put thee in mind of what was then said. Remember what is distinctly written in the Psalms, *God is gone up with a shout;* remember that the divine powers also said to one another, *Lift up your gates, ye Princes,* and the rest; remember also the Psalm which says, *Thou hast ascended on high, Thou hast led captivity captive;* remember the Prophet who says, *Who buildeth His ascension unto heaven;* and the other particulars mentioned yesterday with a view to the gainsaying of the Jews. Ps. 47, 5
Ps 24. 7.
Sept
Ps 68, 18
Amos 9, 6. Sept
(marg)

25. For when they gainsay the ascension of the Saviour, as being impossible, remember the account of the carrying away of Habakkuk. for if Habakkuk was transported by the Angel, being carried by the hair of his head, much rather was the Lord of both Prophets and Angels, powerful with His own strength to mount on a cloud from the Mount of Olives into the Heavens. It is well to bear in mind wonders like to this, but reserve thou the preeminence for the Lord, the Worker of wonders; for the others were borne up, but He bears up all things. Remember that Enoch was translated; but Jesus ascended: remember what was said yesterday concerning Elias, that Elias was taken up in a chariot of fire; but that *the chariots of* Christ *are twenty thousand, even thousands of Angels:* and that Elias was taken up, towards the east of Jordan; but that Christ ascended at the east of the brook Cedron: and that Elias went *as into heaven;* but Jesus, into heaven: and that Elias said that a double portion in the Holy Spirit should be given to his disciple; but that Christ granted to His own disciples so great enjoyment of the grace of the Holy Ghost, as not only to have it in themselves, but also, by the laying on of their hands, to impart the fellowship of it to them who believed. Bel and Dragon, v 33 &c.
Dan. 14, 35. Sept.

vid 2 Kings 2, 11
Ps 68, 17.
2 Kings 2, 11. Sept.

26. And when thou art thus wrestling against the Jews, after thou hast worsted them by parallel instances, then come further to the preeminence of the Saviour's glory. For they were servants, but He the Son of God. And this will remind thee of His preeminence, that the servant of Christ was caught up to the third heaven. For if Elias attained as far as the first heaven, but Paul as far as the third, the latter has doubtless obtained a more honourable dignity. Be not ashamed of thine Apostles; they are not inferior to (14.)

Moses, or behind the Prophets; but they are noble with the noble, yea, than the noble yet more noble. For Elias truly was taken up into heaven; but Peter has the keys of the kingdom of heaven, having received the words, *Whatsoever thou shalt loose on earth shall be loosed in heaven.* Elias was taken up only to heaven; but Paul both into *heaven*, and into *paradise;* (for it behoved the disciples of Jesus to receive more manifold grace;) and *heard unspeakable words, which it is not lawful for a man to utter.* But Paul descended again from above, not because he was unworthy to abide in the third heaven, but in order that after having enjoyed things above man's reach, and descended in honour, and having preached Christ, and died for His sake, he might in addition receive the crown of martyrdom. I pass over the rest of this argument, as I went through it yesterday in the Lord's-day service; for with understanding hearers, a recapitulation is sufficient for instruction.

(15.) 27. And remember also what I have often said concerning the Son's sitting at the right hand of the Father; because that comes next in the Creed, thus, 'And who is ascended into heaven, and sitteth at the right hand of the Father.' Let us not curiously pry into what is properly meant by the throne; for it is incomprehensible: nor endure those who falsely say, that it was after His Cross and Resurrection and Ascension into heaven, that the Son began to sit on the right hand of the Father [g]. For the Son gained not His throne by advancement; but from the time that He is, (and He is ever begotten,) He also sitteth together with the Father. And this throne the Prophet Esaias having beheld before the incarnate coming of the Saviour, says, *I saw the Lord sitting on a throne, high and lifted up*, and the rest. For the Father no man hath seen at any time, and He who then appeared to the Prophet was the Son. And the Psalmist says, *Thy throne is established of old, Thou art from everlasting.* But though many are the testimonies on this point, yet because of the lateness of the time, we will content ourselves only with these

28. Our present business is to remind you of a few out of much which I said concerning the Son's sitting at the right

---
[g] The Paulianists

hand of the Father. For the hundred and ninth Psalm says
plainly, *The Lord said unto my Lord, Sit Thou on My right* Ps. 110,
hand, until I make Thine enemies Thy footstool. And the [1.]
Saviour, confirming in the Gospel what is here said, says that
David spake not these things of himself, but by the inspiration of the Holy Ghost, saying, *How then doth David in* Mat. 22,
spirit call Him Lord, saying, The Lord said unto my Lord, [43.]
Sit Thou on My right hand, and the rest. And in the Acts of
the Apostles, Peter on the day of Pentecost standing with the
Eleven, and discoursing to the Israelites, has in very words Acts 2,
cited this testimony from the hundred and ninth Psalm. [14.]

29. A few other testimonies must also be suggested concerning the Son's sitting at the right hand of the Father.
In the Gospel according to Matthew it is written, *Neverthe-* Mat. 26,
less, I say unto you, Hereafter ye shall see the Son of Man [64.]
sitting on the right hand of power, and the rest. And following this the Apostle Peter also says, *By the Resurrection of* 1 Pet 3,
Jesus Christ, who is gone into heaven, and is on the right [22.]
hand of God. And the Apostle Paul, writing to the Romans,
says, *It is Christ that died, yea rather, that is risen again,* Rom. 8,
who is even at the right hand of God. And charging the [34.]
Ephesians, he thus speaks, *According to the working of His* Eph 1,
mighty power, which He wrought in Christ when He raised [19, 20.]
Him from the dead, and set Him at His own right hand; and
the rest. And he thus taught the Colossians, *If ye then be* Col 3.
risen with Christ, seek those things which are above, where 1
Christ sitteth on the right hand of God. And in the Epistle
to the Hebrews he says, *When he had purged our sins, He* Heb. 1,
sat down on the right hand of the Majesty on high And [3.]
again, *But unto which of the Angels said He at any time,* ver. 13.
*Sit thou at My right hand, until I make thine enemies thy
footstool?* And again, *But this Man, after He had offered* Heb 10,
one sacrifice for sin, for ever sat down on the right hand of [12.]
*God; from henceforth expecting till His enemies be made
His footstool.* And again, *Looking unto Jesus, the Author* Heb 12,
and Finisher of our faith; who for the joy that was set before 2
*Him endured the Cross, despising the shame, and is set down
on the right hand of the throne of God.*

30. And though there are many other texts concerning the
session of the Only-begotten on the right hand of God, yet

let these suffice us at present; with a repetition of my remark, that it was not after His coming in the flesh that He obtained the dignity of this seat; no, for even before all ages, the Only-begotten Son of God, who is our Lord Jesus, ever has the throne on the right hand of the Father. Now may He Himself, the God of all, who is Father of Christ, and our Lord Jesus Christ, who came down, and ascended, and sitteth together with the Father, watch over your souls; keep unshaken and unchanged your hope in Him who rose again; raise you together with Him from your dead sins, to His heavenly gift; count you worthy to be *caught up in the clouds, to meet the Lord in the air,* in His fitting time; and, until that time arrive of His glorious second advent, write all your names in the Book of the living, and having written them, never blot them out. (For many, those who fall away, have their names blotted out.) And may He grant to all of you to believe on Him who rose again, and to look for Him who is gone up, and is to come again, (to come, but not from the earth; for be on your guard, O man, because of the deceivers who are to come;) who sitteth on high, and is here present together with us, *beholding the order of each, and the steadfastness of his faith.* For think not that because He is absent in the flesh, He is therefore absent also in the Spirit. He is here present in the midst of us, listening to what is said of Him, and beholding what is in thy mind, and *trying the reins and the hearts;*—who also is now ready to present those who are coming to baptism, and all of you, in the Holy Ghost to the Father, and to say, *Behold, I and the children whom God hath given Me:*—To whom be glory for ever. Amen.

LECTURE XV.

ON THE SECOND ADVENT, THE LAST JUDGMENT, AND THE PERPETUITY OF CHRIST'S KINGDOM.

DANIEL vii. 9—14.

I beheld till the thrones were cast down, and the Ancient of days did sit, &c. . . The Judgment was set, and the books were opened, &c . . . I saw in the night visions, and behold one like the Son of Man came with the clouds of heaven, and came to the Ancient of days, and they brought Him near before Him. And there was given Him dominion, &c . . His dominion is an everlasting dominion, which shall not pass away, &c

1 WE preach not one advent only of Christ, but a second also, far more glorious than the former. For the former gave to view His patience ; but the latter brings with it the crown of the divine kingdom. For all things, to speak generally, are twofold in our Lord Jesus Christ His generation is twofold : the one, of God, before the worlds ; the other, of the Virgin in the end of the world. His descent is twofold. one was in obscurity, like the dew on the fleece, the second is ^v Ps 72, 6 vid His open coming, which is to be In His former advent, He supra was wrapped in swaddling clothes in the manger ; in His Cat xii 9 second, He *covereth Himself with light as with a garment.* Ps 104, In His first coming, *He endured the Cross, despising the* 2 Heb. 12, *shame ;* in His second, He comes attended by the Angel 2 host, receiving glory. Let us not then rest in His first advent, but look also for His second. And as we have said at His first coming, *Blessed is He that cometh in the Name* Mat 21, *of the Lord,* so will we repeat the same at His second 9 v Mat. coming ; that with the Angels meeting our Master, we may 23, 39

worship Him and say, *Blessed is He that cometh in the Name of the Lord.* The Saviour comes, not to be judged again, but to judge them who judged Him; He who before was silent when judged, shall arraign those transgressors who did those daring deeds at the Cross, and shall say, *These things hast thou done, and I kept silence.* Then, He came by a divine disposition, teaching men with persuasion; but this time they will of necessity have Him for their King, though they wish it not.

2. And concerning these two comings, Malachi the Prophet says, *And the Lord whom ye seek shall suddenly come to His temple;* behold the first coming. And again of the second coming he says, *And the Messenger of the covenant whom ye delight in. Behold, He shall come, even the Lord Almighty; but who may abide the day of His coming; and who shall stand when He appeareth? For He is like a refiner's fire, and like fuller's sope, and He shall sit as a refiner and purifier of silver.* And immediately after the Saviour Himself says, *And I will come near to you to judgment; and I will be a swift witness against the sorcerers, and against the adulterers, and against the false swearers,* and the rest. For this cause Paul warning us beforehand says, *If any man build on this foundation gold, silver, precious stones, wood, hay, stubble; every man's work shall be made manifest; for the day shall declare it, because it shall be revealed by fire.* Paul also signifies these two comings, writing to Titus and saying, *The grace of God our Saviour hath appeared unto all men, teaching us that, denying ungodliness and worldly lusts, we should live soberly, righteously, and godly in this present world; looking for that blessed hope, and the glorious appearing of the great God and our Saviour Jesus Christ.* Thou seest how he has spoken of the first, for which he gives thanks; and of the second, to which we look forward. Wherefore the words of the Faith we profess, run thus; that we should believe in Him, " who again is ascended into heaven, and sitteth on the right hand of the Father, and shall come in glory to judge the quick and dead; whose kingdom shall have no end."

(2.) 3. Our Lord Jesus Christ, then, comes from heaven; and He comes with glory at the end of this world, in the last day.

For this world shall have an end, and this created world shall be made new. For since corruption, and theft, and adultery, and every sort of sins, have been poured forth over the earth, and blood has been mingled with blood in the world, therefore, that this wondrous dwelling-place may not remain filled with iniquity, this world shall pass away, that that fairer world may be made manifest. And wouldest thou receive the proof of this out of the express words of Scripture? Listen to Esaias, saying, *And the heavens shall be rolled together as a scroll; and all their host shall fall down, as the leaf falleth off from the vine, and as a falling fig from the fig-tree.* And the Gospel says, *The sun shall be darkened, and the moon shall not give her light, and the stars shall fall from heaven.* Let us not sorrow, as if we alone died; the stars also shall die; and perhaps rise again. And the Lord shall roll up the heavens, not that He may destroy them, but that He may raise them up again more beautiful. Hear David the Prophet saying, *Thou, Lord, in the beginning hast laid the foundations of the earth, and the heavens are the work of Thy hands; they shall perish, but Thou remainest.* But some one will say, Behold, he says plainly that they shall perish. Hear in what sense he says, they shall perish; it is plain from what follows; *And they all shall wax old as doth a garment; and as a vesture shalt Thou fold them up, and they shall be changed.* For as a man is said to "perish," according to that which is written, *The righteous perisheth, and no man layeth it to heart,* and this, though the resurrection is looked for, so we look for a resurrection, as it were, of the heavens also. *The sun shall be turned into darkness, and the moon into blood.* Here let converts from the Manichees gain instruction, and no longer make those lights their gods; nor impiously think, that this sun which shall be darkened is Christ. And again hear Christ saying, *Heaven and earth shall pass away, but My words shall not pass away;* for the creatures are not equal in honour with the Master's words.

^v Hos. 4, 2.

Is 34, 4.

Mat. 24, 29.

Ps. 102, 25 &c. Heb. 1, 10.

Is 57, 1.

Joel 2, 31.

Mat 24, 35.

4. The things then which are seen shall pass away, and there shall come the things which are looked for, things fairer than these; but as to the time let no one be curious. For *it is not for you,* He says, *to know the times and the*

Acts 1, 7.

Lect. XV

Mat 24, 42 41
(3.)

κατ' οἰ-κονομίαν
Mat 24, 3.

ver 4

seasons, which the Father hath put in His own power. And venture not thou to declare when these things shall be, nor on the other hand abandon thyself to slumber. For he saith, *Watch, for in such an hour as ye think not the Son of Man cometh.* But seeing that it behoved us to know the signs of the end, and whereas we are looking for Christ, therefore, that we may not be deceived and perish, nor be led astray by that false Antichrist, the Apostles, moved by the divine will, address themselves by a providential arrangement to the True Teacher, and say, *Tell us, when shall these things be, and what shall be the sign of Thy coming, and of the end of the world?* We look for Thee to come again, but Satan is transformed into an Angel of light; put us therefore on our guard, that we may not worship another instead of Thee. And He, opening His divine and blessed mouth, says, *Take heed that no man deceive you.* And you, hearers, who now as it were see Him with the eyes of your mind, listen to Him saying the same things to you likewise; *Take heed that no man deceive you.* And this word exhorts you all to give heed to what is spoken, for it is not a tale of things gone by, but a prophecy of things future, and which will surely come. We prophesy not, for we are unworthy; but we set before you the things which are written, and tell you the signs. Observe thou, which of them have already come to pass, and which yet remain; and make thyself safe.

Mat 24, 4. 5.
First sign.

5. *Take heed that no man deceive you: for many shall come in My name, saying, I am Christ, and shall deceive many.* This has happened in part: for ere now Simon Magus said this, and Menander, and some others of the godless leaders of heresy, and others say it in our days, or shall say it after us.

Second sign.
Ib. v. 6

Luke 21, 11
χειμῶ-νες, Cyr σημεῖα, rec text
Mat. 24, 42.

6. The second sign. *And ye shall hear of wars and rumours of wars.* Is there then at this time war between Persians and Romans for Mesopotamia, or no? Does nation rise up against nation and kingdom against kingdom, or no? *And there shall be famines and pestilences and earthquakes in divers places.* These things have already come to pass; and again, *And fearful sights from heaven, and mighty storms. Watch therefore,* He says; *for ye know not what hour your Lord doth come.*

7. Next we seek our own sign of His coming; we members (4) of the Church seek the Church's sign. And the Saviour ἐκκλησι- says, *And then shall many be offended, and shall betray one* αστικοί *another, and shall hate one another.* If thou hear that Mat 24, 10 bishops advance against bishops, and clergy against clergy, Third and people against people even unto blood [a], be not troubled, sign for it has been written before. Heed not the things now happening, but the things which are written; nor even though I who teach thee perish, do thou perish with me; nay, a hearer may even become better than his teacher, and he who came last may be first, since even those of the eleventh hour the Master receives. If among the Apostles there was found treason, dost thou wonder that even among bishops there is found hatred of the brethren? But the sign concerns not only rulers, but the people also; for He says, *And because iniquity* Ib v. 12. *shall abound, the love of many shall wax cold.* Will any then among those present boast that he entertains friendship unfeigned towards his neighbour? Do not the lips often kiss, and the countenance smile, and the eyes brighten forsooth,

[a] S Cyril here describes the state of the Church, when orthodoxy was for a while trodden under foot, its maintainers persecuted, and the varieties of Arianism, which took its place, were quarrelling for the ascendancy Gibbon quotes two passages, one from a pagan historian of the day, another from a Father of the Church, which fully bear out S Cyril's words What made the state of things still more deplorable, was the defection of some of the orthodox party, as Marcellus, into opposite errors, while the subsequent secessions of Apollinaris and Lucifer, show what lurking disorders there were within it at the time when S Cyril wrote (Vid. infra. 9) The passages referred to are as follows. "The Christian Religion," says Ammianus, "in itself plain and simple, he (Constantius) confounded by the dotage of superstition Instead of reconciling the parties by the weight of his authority, he cherished and propagated, by vain disputes, the differences which his vain curiosity had excited. The highways were covered with troops of Bishops, galloping from every side to the assemblies, which they called synods; and while they laboured to reduce the whole sect to their own particular opinions, the public establishment of the posts was almost ruined by their hasty and repeated journeys" Hist xxi 16 S Hilary of Poictiers thus speaks of Asia Minor, the chief seat of the Arian troubles: "It is a thing equally deplorable and dangerous, that there are as many creeds as opinions among men, as many doctrines as inclinations, and as many sources of blasphemy as there are faults among us, because we make creeds arbitrarily, and explain them as arbitrarily. The Homoousion is rejected and received and explained away by successive synods The partial or total resemblance of the Father and of the Son is a subject of dispute for these unhappy divines Every year, nay, every moon, we make new creeds to describe invisible mysteries We repent of what we have done, we defend those who repent, we anathematize those whom we defended We condemn either the doctrine of others in ourselves, or our own in that of others, and reciprocally tearing one another to pieces, we have been the cause of each other's ruin" ad Constant ii 4 5 Gibbon's translations are used, which, though diffuse, are faithful in their matter. What a contrast do these descriptions present to Athanasius' uniform declaration, that the whole question was really settled at Nicæa, and no other synod or debate was necessary!

while the heart is planning guile, and plotting mischief with words of peace?

<small>Fourth sign
Mat 24, 41</small>

8 Thou hast this sign also. *And this Gospel of the kingdom shall be preached in all the world for a witness unto all nations, and then shall the end come* And as we see, nearly the whole world is now filled with the doctrine of Christ.

<small>Fifth sign.
Ib v. 15.</small>

9. And what comes to pass after this? *When ye therefore shall see the Abomination of Desolation, spoken of by Daniel the Prophet, stand in the Holy Place, (whoso readeth, let him*

<small>Ib. v. 23</small> *understand.) And again, Then if any man shall say unto you, Lo, here is Christ, or, there; believe it not.* Hatred of the brethren makes room next for Antichrist; for the devil prepares beforehand divisions among the people, that he who is to come may be acceptable to them. But God forbid that any of Christ's servants here, or elsewhere, should side with the enemy! Concerning this matter the Apostle Paul writing

<small>2 Thess. 2, 3-10</small> has given a manifest sign, saying, *For that day shall not come, except there come a falling away first, and that man of sin be revealed, the son of perdition, who opposeth and exalteth himself above all that is called God, or that is worshipped; so that he as God sitteth in the temple of God, showing himself that he is God Remember ye not that when I was yet with you, I told you these things? And now ye know what withholdeth, that he might be revealed in his time. For the mystery of iniquity doth already work, only he who now letteth will let, until he be taken out of the way. And then shall that wicked be revealed, whom the Lord shall consume with the spirit of His mouth, and shall destroy with the brightness of His coming. Even him, whose coming is after the working of Satan, with all power and signs and lying wonders, and with all deceivableness of unrighteousness in them that perish.* Thus wrote Paul, and now is the

<small>ἀποστασία
υἱοπατορίαν
ἐξ οὐκ ὄντων.</small> *falling away* For men have fallen away from the right faith; and some preach the identity of the Son with the Father, and others dare to say that Christ was brought into being, from a substance which had a beginning. And formerly the heretics were manifest; but now the Church is filled with heretics in disguise. For men have fallen away

<small>2 Tim. 4, 3.</small> from the truth, and *have itching ears.* Is it a plausible

Satan forestalled the Truth in paganism, to prejudice men against it. 189

theory? all listen to it gladly. Is it a word of correction? all turn away from it. Most have departed from right words, ὀρθῶν and rather choose the evil, than desire the good. This therefore is *the falling away*, and the enemy is soon to be looked for: and already he has begun to send forth his forerunners [b], that being ready, he may then come upon the prey. Look therefore to thyself, O man, and watch over thy soul. The Church now charges thee before the Living God; she declares to thee the things concerning Antichrist before they arrive. Whether they will happen in thy time we know not, or whether they will happen after thee we know not; but it is well that, knowing these things, thou shouldest be on thy guard.

10. The true Christ, the Only-begotten Son of God, comes (4.) no more from the earth. If any come seeing visions in the wilderness, go not forth; if they say, *Lo, here is Christ, lo,* Mat 24, *there,* believe it not. Downwards and to the earth look no 26. longer; for the Sovereign descends from heaven, not alone as before, but with many, attended by tens of thousands of Angels; nor secretly as the dew on the fleece; but shining v. Ps 72, forth openly as the lightning. For He hath said Himself, 6. *As the lightning cometh out of the east, and shineth even unto* Mat. 24, *the west, so shall also the coming of the Son of Man be;* and 27. again, *And they shall see the Son of Man coming in the* Ib v. 30. *clouds with power and great glory, and He shall send His Angels with a great sound of a trumpet;* and the rest.

11. But as, when formerly He was to take man's nature, and God was expected to be born of a Virgin, the devil, to create prejudice against this, craftily spread fables beforehand among the idol-worshippers, of false gods, begetting and born of women, that, the falsehood having got possession of the ground, the truth also, as he supposed, might be disbelieved; so now, since the true Christ is to come a second time, the adversary, taking advantage of the expectation of the simple, and especially of them of the circumcision, brings in a certain man who is a wizard, and most expert in the beguiling craftiness of sorceries and enchantments; who shall seize

---

[b] τοὺς ἑαυτοῦ προδρόμους The Arian troubles, this was the common opinion of the Fathers of the day Vid Athan Apol contr Arian fin Basil Ep 264 Hilar in Auxent. 5. Hence Pope Gregory calls the Bishop of Constantinople of his day a "forerunner of Antichrist," as being *ambitious* of the title of Universal Bishop, and creating *divisions* in the Church Vid. Epist. vii 33.

Antichrist a king; his reign three years and a half.

LECT. XV

upon the power of the Roman empire, and shall falsely style himself Christ; by this name of Christ deceiving the Jews, who are looking for the Anointed, and seducing those of the Gentiles by his magical illusions.

12 But this aforesaid Antichrist comes when the times of the Roman empire shall have been fulfilled, and the end of the world is now drawing near. There shall rise up together ten kings of the Romans, reigning in different parts perhaps, but all about the same time, and after these shall arise Antichrist, the eleventh king, who by his magical craft shall seize upon the Roman power; and of the kings who reigned before him, three he shall humble, and the remaining seven he shall keep in subjection to himself. At first indeed he will put on a show of mildness, (as though he were a learned and discreet person,) and of soberness and benevolence and having by the signs and lying wonders of his magical deceit, beguiled the Jews, as though he were the expected Christ, he shall afterwards characterize himself by all kinds of excesses of cruelty and lawlessness, so as to outdo all unrighteous and ungodly men who have gone before him; displaying against all men, but especially against us Christians, a spirit murderous and ruthless, merciless and crafty. And he shall perpetrate such things for three years and six months only; and then he shall be destroyed by the glorious second advent from heaven of the only-begotten Son of God, our Lord and Saviour Jesus, the true Christ, who shall slay Antichrist *with the spirit of His mouth*, and shall deliver him over to the fire of hell.

λόγιός τις καὶ συνετός

2 Thes. 2, 8

(5). 13. Now these things we teach, not of our own ingenuity, but having learned them out of the divine Scriptures of the Church, and chiefly from the prophecy of Daniel in the text; as Gabriel also the Archangel interpreted it, speaking thus: *The fourth beast shall be the fourth kingdom upon earth, which shall surpass all kingdoms.* And that this kingdom is that of the Romans, has been the tradition of the Church's interpreters. For as the first kingdom which became renowned was that of the Assyrians, and the second, that of the Medes and Persians together, and after these, that of the Macedonians was the third, so the fourth kingdom now is that of the Romans. Then Gabriel goes on to interpret, saying,

ἐκκλησιαστικῶν.

Dan 7, 23 Sept.

Antichrist will pretend to miracles, he will abhor idols.

And the ten horns out of this kingdom are ten kings that shall arise; and another king shall rise up after them, and he shall surpass in wickedness all who were before him; (he says, not only the ten, but also all who were before him,) *and he shall subdue three kings,* (manifestly out of the ten former kings, but it is plain that having subdued three, he will be the eighth king[c],) *and he shall speak great words against the Most High.* A blasphemer is he and an outrageous person, not inheriting his kingdom from his fathers, but usurping power by means of sorcery. [ver 24 Sept / v. 25.

14. And who is this, and of what sort of working? Interpret to us, O Paul. *Whose coming,* he says, *is after the working of Satan, with all power and signs and lying wonders;* implying, that Satan uses him as an instrument, working personally through him; for knowing that his judgment hath now no longer respite[d], he henceforth wages war no more by his ministers, as is his wont, but by himself more openly. And *in all signs and lying wonders;* for the father of falsehood will make a show of the works of falsehood, that the multitude may think that they see a dead man raised, when he is not raised, and the lame walking, and the blind seeing, when the cure has not been wrought. [2 Thess. 2, 9 / αὐτοπροσώπως

15. And again he says, *Who opposeth and exalteth himself* (6.) *above all that is called God, or that is worshipped;* (above *every God;* Antichrist therefore will abhor the idols,) *so that he sitteth in the temple of God.* What temple? He means, the Temple of the Jews which has been destroyed. For God forbid that it should be the one in which we are! Wherefore say we this? lest we should be supposed to favour ourselves. For since he comes to the Jews as Christ, and desires to be worshipped by the Jews, he will make great account of the Temple, that he may more completely beguile them; making it seem that he is the man of the race of David, who shall build up the Temple which was erected by Solomon[e]. And Antichrist shall come at the time when there shall not be left one stone upon another in the Temple, [2 Thess. 2, 4.

---

[c] "And the beast that was, and is not, even he is the eighth, and is of the seven, and goeth into perdition." Rev. 17, 11

[d] Vid. Iren. Hær. v. 26. 2

[e] This was the common opinion of the early Fathers vid Iren. Hær. v. 25. 30 Greg Naz Orat 47. 14 &c Cyril wrote this before Julian's attempt to rebuild the Jewish Temple.

according to the doom pronounced by our Saviour [f]; for when, either through decay of time, or demolition for the use of new buildings, or ensuing from other causes, every stone shall have been overthrown, not merely of the outer circuit, but of the shrine also, where the Cherubim were, then shall he come with all signs and lying wonders, exalting himself against all idols; at first indeed feigning a philanthropic, but afterwards displaying his relentless temper, and that chiefly against the Saints of God. For he says, *And I beheld, and the same horn made war with the saints;* and again elsewhere, *and there shall be a time of trouble, such as never was since there was a nation even to that same time.* Dreadful is that beast, a mighty dragon, unconquerable by man, ready to devour; concerning whom though we have more things to speak out of the divine Scriptures, yet we will content ourselves with thus much, in order to keep within compass.

16. Wherefore the Lord knowing the mightiness of the adversary, extends his indulgence to the religious, saying, *Then let them which be in Judea flee to the mountains.* But if any man is conscious that he is very stout-hearted, to encounter Satan, let him stand; (for I do not despair of the Church's nerves,) and let him say, *Who shall separate us from the love of Christ.* Thus, let those of us who are fearful provide for our own safety; and let those of us who are of a good courage, remain · *for there shall be great tribulation, such as was not since the beginning of the world, no, nor ever shall be.* But thanks be to God who hath confined the violence of that tribulation to a few days; for He says, *But for the elect's sake those days shall be shortened;* and Antichrist shall reign for three years and a half only. We speak not from Apocryphal books [g], but from Daniel; for he says,

Marginal references: Dan. 7, 21. Dan. 12, 1. Mat. 24, 16. Rom. 8, 35. Mat. 24, 21. v. 22. ἀποκρύφων.

[f] Even S Crysostom, after the awful defeat of Julian's attempt, which was attended by a considerable disturbance of the ground on which the Temple had stood, pronounces that the prophecy against "one stone on another" was not yet fulfilled. vid Hom. 75 in Matt. Ed Ben.

[g] "Some have thought that Cyril here alludes to the Apocalypse," (vid note a on Catech iv 33 p 48 Ibid note c on 36 p 51) "which is not improbable .. All those ancient writers, whom he follows in this Lecture, in their description of Antichrist always appeal to the Apocalypse as well as to Daniel. Vid Iren v 26 1 Hippol. de Antichr 34 &c· Cyril then must have intentionally omitted mention of the Apocalypse in treating this subject, and he here seems to give the reason of it. At the same time he may be alluding to other Apocryphal works, e. g. those of the Millenarians, &c " Ed Ben The Canonicity of the Apocalypse is sufficiently established by its general reception by the Church in the fifth century, whatever doubts before existed in particular parts of Christendom.

And they shall be given into his hand until a time and times Dan 7, 25.
and the dividing of time. A *time* is the one year in which
his coming shall have increase; and *the times* are the
remaining two years of iniquity, which make up the sum of
the three years, and *the dividing of time* is the six months.
And again in another place Daniel says the same thing, *And* Dan 12, 7.
he sware by Him that liveth for ever that it shall be for a
time, times, and a half. And some peradventure have
referred what follows also to this, namely, *the thousand two* Dan 12, 11
hundred and ninety days; and, *Blessed is he that waiteth*
and cometh to the thousand three hundred and five and v 12
thirty days. For this cause we must hide ourselves and fly;
for perhaps *we shall not have gone over the cities of Israel,* Mat 10, 23.
till the Son of Man be come.

17. Who then is that blessed man, who shall at that time (8)
devoutly witness for Christ? For I say that those Martyrs
excel all martyrs. For hitherto they have only wrestled with
men; but the Martyrs in the time of Antichrist shall do battle
with Satan in his own person. And former persecuting kings αὐτοπρο-σώπως
have only put to death; they have not pretended to raise the
dead, nor showed the appearance of signs and wonders.
But in his time there shall be the evil seductions both of fear
and of deceit, *insomuch that if it were possible they shall* Mat 24, 24
deceive the very elect. Let it never enter into the heart of
any then alive to ask, "What did Christ more? By what
power does this man work these things? Unless God had
pleased, He would not have allowed them." The Apostle
warns thee, and says beforehand, *And for this cause God* 2 Thess 2, 11 12
shall send them strong delusion; (*send,* that is, *shall allow to*
happen;) not that they might be excused, but *that they might*
be damned. Wherefore? They, he says, *who believed not the*
truth, that is, the true Christ, *but had pleasure in unrighte-*
ousness, that is, in Antichrist. But God permits these things,
as in the persecutions which happen from time to time, so
also then, not because He wants power to hinder them, but
because according to His wont He crowns His own Champions by means of patience, as He did His own Prophets and
Apostles; to the end that after having toiled for a little while
they may inherit the eternal kingdom of heaven, according
to that which Daniel says, *And at that time thy peoples hall* Dan 12, 1 2

be delivered, *every one that shall be found written in the book,* (manifestly, the book of life;) *and many of them that sleep in the dust of the earth shall awake, some to everlasting life, and some to shame and everlasting contempt; and they that be wise shall shine as the brightness of the firmament; and they that turn many to righteousness as the stars for ever and ever.*

18. Take precautions then, O man; thou hast the signs of Antichrist; do not merely keep them in mind thyself, but impart them also freely to all. If thou hast a child according to the flesh, now admonish him of this; if thou hast begotten one through catechizing, put him also on his guard, lest he receive the false one as the True. For the *mystery of iniquity doth already work.* I fear these wars of the nations; I fear the divisions of the churches; I fear the mutual hatred of the brethren. But enough on this subject; only God forbid that it should be fulfilled in our days; nevertheless, let us be on our guard. And thus much concerning Antichrist.

(9) 19. But let us wait and look for the Lord's coming upon the clouds from heaven. Then shall the Angelic trumpets sound; *the dead in Christ shall rise first,*—the religious persons, who are alive shall be caught up in the clouds, receiving as the reward of their labours, more than human honour, inasmuch as theirs was a more than human strife; according as the Apostle Paul writes, saying, *For the Lord Himself shall descend from heaven with a shout, with the voice of the Archangel, and with the trump of God: and the dead in Christ shall rise first. Then we which are left and remain shall be caught up together with them in the clouds, to meet the Lord in the air; and so shall we ever be with the Lord.*

20. This coming of the Lord, and the end of the world, was known to the Preacher; who says, *Rejoice, O young man, in thy youth,* and in what follows; *Therefore remove anger from thy heart, and put away evil from thy flesh;* . . . *and remember thy Creator* . . . . *while the evil days come not,* . . . . *while the sun, or the light, or the moon, or the stars be not darkened,* . . . . *and those that look out of the windows be not darkened;* (covertly meaning the faculty of sight;) *or ever the silver cord be loosed;* (he speaks of the assemblage of the stars, for their appearance is like silver;) *and the flower of*

gold be bruised, (thus veiling the mention of the golden sun; *and they rise up at the voice of the bird, and they see from the height, and terrors be in the way.* What shall they see? *Then shall they see the Son of man coming in the clouds of heaven; and they shall mourn tribe by tribe.* And what shall come to pass when the Lord is come? *The almond tree shall blossom, and the grasshopper shall grow in substance, and the briar shall be scattered abroad.* And as the interpreters say, the blossoming almond signifies the departure of winter; and our bodies shall after the winter blossom with a heavenly flower. *And the grasshopper shall grow in substance,* (that means the winged soul clothing itself with the body,) and *the briar shall be scattered abroad,* (that is, the transgressors who are like thorns shall be scattered.)

ἀνθέμιον, camomile. ἤδ ἄνθεμις. τοῦ στρουθίου. ver 5. Sept. Mat. 24, 30. Zech. 12, 12. Sept. Eccles. 12, 5. Sept ἡ κάππαρις.

21. Thou seest how they all anticipate the coming of the Lord. Thou seest how they know *the voice of the bird.* Let us know what sort of voice this is. *For the Lord Himself shall descend from heaven with a shout, with the voice of the Archangel, and with the trump of God.* The Archangel shall shout aloud and say to all, Rise to meet the Lord. And fearful will be that descent of our Master. David says, *Our God shall come, and shall not keep silence; a fire shall devour before Him, and it shall be very tempestuous round about Him,* and the rest. The Son of Man shall come to the Father, according to the text, *with the clouds of heaven,* and *with a stream of fire,* which is to try men[h], following as His train. Then if any man's works are of gold, he shall be made brighter, if any man's course of life be like stubble, and without substance, he shall be burned by the fire. And the Father *shall sit,* having *His garment white as snow, and the hair of His head like the pure wool.* And this is spoken after the manner of men; wherefore? Because He is the King of those who are not defiled with sins; *for,* He says, *your sins shall be as white as snow, and shall be as wool,* which is the emblem of the forgiveness of sins, or of sinlessness itself. But the same Lord

Eccles 12. 4 1 Thess 2, 16. Ps. 50, 3. Dan 7, 13 10 1 Cor 3, 12. 13. ἀνυπόστατον. Dan. 7, 9. Is 1, 18

---

[h] δοκιμαστικοῦ This is a common Greek opinion, that the fire of the last judgment will be purgatorial in its nature. Vid Ambrose (in Ps 37, 14), Hilary, (in Matth. 2. § 4) &c.

shall come from heaven in the clouds, who ascended in the clouds, for He Himself hath said, *And they shall see the Son of Man coming in the clouds of heaven, with power and great glory.*

(10.) 22. But what is the sign of His coming? lest the hostile power dare to counterfeit it. *And there shall appear*, He says, *the sign of the Son of Man in heaven*. But Christ's own true sign is the Cross; a sign of a luminous Cross shall go before the King, plainly declaring Him who was formerly crucified: that the Jews who before *pierced Him* and plotted against Him, when they see it, may *mourn tribe by tribe*, saying, "This is He who was smitten, this is He whose face they spat on, this is He on whom they put chains, this is He whom of old they crucified, and set at nought; whither, they will say, shall we flee from the face of His wrath?" But the Angel hosts shall encompass them, so that they shall not be able to flee any where. The sign of the Cross shall be a terror to His foes; but joy to His friends who have believed in Him, or preached Him, or suffered for His sake. Who then is that blessed man, who shall be found the friend of Christ? That King, so great and glorious, attended by trains of Angels, the fellow of the Father's throne, will not despise His own servants. For lest His Elect be confused with His foes, *He shall send His Angels with a great sound of a trumpet, and they shall gather together His elect from the four winds.* He despised not one, even Lot; how then shall He despise many righteous? *Come, ye blessed of My Father,* will He say to them who shall then ride on chariots of clouds, and be collected by Angels.

23. But some one present will say, "I am a poor man," or again, "I shall perhaps be found at that time sick and in bed;" or, "I am but a woman, and I shall be taken at the mill shall we then be despised?" Be of good courage, O man; the Judge is no respecter of persons; *He will not judge according to a man's appearance, nor reprove according to his speech.* He honours not the learned before the simple, nor the rich before the needy. Though thou be in the field, the Angels shall take thee; think not that He will take the landlord, and will leave thee the farmer. Though thou be a slave, though thou be poor, be not any whit distressed; He who *took the form of a servant* despises not

servants. Though thou be laid sick upon thy bed, yet it is written, *Then shall two be in one bed; the one shall be taken,* ^{Luke 17, 34} *and the other left.* Though thou be of necessity put to ^{v Judg} grind, whether thou be man or woman; though thou have ^{16, 21.} children, and sit beside the mill, yet He *who by His might* ^{v Exod} *bringeth out them that are bound,* overlooks thee not. He who ^{11, 5. Sept} brought forth Joseph out of ward and bondage to a kingdom, ^{Ps 68, 6.} redeems thee also from thy afflictions into the kingdom of ^{Sept} heaven. Only be of good cheer, only work, only strive cheerfully; for nothing is lost. Every prayer of thine, every ^{v Acts} Psalm thou singest is recorded, every alms-deed, every fast ^{10, 4} is recorded; every marriage duly observed is recorded; con- ^{ἐγκρά-} tinence kept for God's sake is recorded; but the first crowns ^{τεια, 1 e.} in record are those of virginity and purity; and thou shalt ^{widow-hood} shine as an Angel. But as thou hast gladly listened to the good things, listen without shrinking to the contrary. Every covetous deed of thine is recorded, every act of fornication is recorded against thee, every false oath of thine is recorded, every blasphemy, every sorcery, every theft, every murder. All these things are henceforth recorded, if thou do them after having been baptized; for thy former deeds are blotted out.

24. *When the Son of man,* He says, *shall come in His glory,* (11.) *and all the Angels with Him.* Behold, O man, before what ^{Mat 25, 31} multitudes thou shalt come to judgment. The whole race of ^{οἱ ἅγιοι} men will then be present. Reckon, therefore, the numbers of ^{Ἀγγελοι, holy,} the Roman nation; reckon the numbers of all the barbarian ^{rec text} tribes now living, and of those who have died within the last hundred years; reckon how many nations have been buried during the last thousand years; reckon all from Adam to this day. Great indeed is the multitude; but yet it is little, for the Angels are many more. They are *the ninety and nine* ^{v Mat} *sheep,* but mankind is the single *one.* For according to the ^{18, 12} extent of universal space, must we reckon the number of its inhabitants. The whole earth is but as a point in the midst of this one heaven, and the heaven which encircles it contains as great a multitude of inhabitants as it has extent. And the heaven of heavens contains unimaginable numbers. And it is written, *Thousand thousands ministered unto Him,* ^{Dan 7, 10.} *and ten thousand times ten thousand stood before Him;* not that the multitude was only so great, but the Prophet could

not express more than these. And then will be present at the judgment, God, the Father of all, Jesus Christ being seated with Him, and the Holy Ghost being with Them; and the angelic trumpet shall summon all of us, bearing our deeds. Ought we not then now to be sore troubled at this? Think it not a slight doom, O man, putting punishment apart, to be condemned in the presence of so many. Shall we not then choose rather to die many deaths, than be condemned by friends?

(12.) 25. Let us shudder then, brethren, lest God condemn us; who needs not inquiry or proofs, to condemn. Say not, in the night I committed fornication, or wrought sorcery, or did any other thing, and there was no man by. Out of thine own conscience shalt thou be judged, thy *thoughts the meanwhile accusing or else excusing, in the day when God shall judge the secrets of men.* The terrible countenance of the Judge will force thee to speak the truth; or rather, even though thou speak not, it will convict thee. For thou shalt rise clothed with thy own sins, or else thy righteousness. And this has the Judge Himself declared, saying, (for it is Christ who judges, *for the Father judgeth no man, but hath committed all judgment unto the Son,* not divesting Himself of His power, but judging through the Son; therefore the Son judgeth by the will of the Father; for the wills of the Father and of the Son are not different, but one and the same,) what then says the Judge, as to whether thou shalt bear thy works, or no? *And before Him shall they gather all nations* · (for in the presence of Christ *every knee must bow, of things in heaven, and things in earth, and things under the earth* ·) *and He shall separate them one from another, as a shepherd divideth his sheep from the goats.* How does the shepherd make the separation? Does he examine out of a book which is a sheep and which a goat? or does he distinguish by their plain marks? Does not the wool show the sheep, and the hairy and rough skin the goat? In like manner, if thou hast now been cleansed from thy sins, thy deeds shall be henceforth as pure wool; and thy robe shall remain unstained, and thou shalt even say, *I have put off my coat, how shall I put it on?* By thy vesture shalt thou be known for a sheep. But if thou be found hairy, like Esau, who was rough with hair, and wicked in mind, who for food lost his birth-right and sold his privilege, thou shalt be among those on the left hand. But God forbid that any here present should be an outcast from grace, or for his evil deeds be found on the left hand among the ranks of the sinners!

26. Terrible in good truth is the judgment, and terrible is the news of it. The kingdom of heaven is before us, and everlasting fire is made ready. How then, some one will say, should we escape the fire? And how should we enter into the kingdom? *I was an hungred,* He says, *and ye gave Me meat.* Learn now the way; there is here no need of allegory, but to fulfil what is said. *I was an hungred, and ye gave Me meat; I was thirsty, and ye gave Me drink; I was a stranger, and ye took Me in, naked, and ye clothed Me; I was sick, and ye visited Me; I was in prison, and ye came unto Me.* These things if thou do, thou shalt reign together with Him, but if thou do them not, thou shalt be condemned. At once then begin to work these things, and abide in the faith; lest, like the foolish virgins, tarrying to buy oil, thou be shut out. Be not confident because thou merely possessest the lamp, but constantly keep it burning. Let the light of thy good works shine before men, and let not Christ be blasphemed on thy account. Wear thou the garment of incorruption[1], resplendent with good works; and that which thou hast received from God to dispense as a steward, dispense thou profitably. Hast thou been put in trust with riches? Dispense them well. Hast thou been entrusted with the word of teaching? Be a good steward thereof. Canst thou bring over to the Church the souls of the hearers? Do this diligently. There are many doors of good stewardship. Only let none of us be condemned and cast out; so we may with boldness meet Christ the Everlasting King, who reigns for ever. For He reigns for ever, who having died for quick and dead, shall be judge of quick and dead. And as also Paul says, *For to this end Christ both died and rose and revived, that He might be Lord both of the dead and living.* (13.) Mat. 25, 35. Rom. 14, 9.

27. And shouldest thou ever hear any say that the kingdom of Christ shall have an end, abhor thou the heresy; it is another head of the dragon, lately sprung up in Galatia. (14.)

---

[1] Vid Greg Naz. Orat 42, n 26 Const. Apost. viii. 6.

A certain one [k] has dared to affirm, that after the end of the world Christ shall reign no longer; and he has dared to say, that the Word which came forth from the Father shall be again absorbed into the Father, and shall be no more; uttering such blasphemies to his own perdition. For he has not listened to the Lord, saying, *The Son abideth for ever.* He has not listened to Gabriel, saying, *And He shall reign over the house of Jacob for ever, and of His kingdom there shall be no end.* Consider this text. Heretics of this day teach in disparagement of Christ, while Gabriel the Archangel taught the eternal abiding of the Saviour; whom then wilt thou rather believe? wilt thou not rather give credence to Gabriel? Listen to the testimony of Daniel in the text, *I saw in the night visions, and behold, one like the Son of Man came with the clouds of heaven, and came to the Ancient of days. .... And there was given Him dominion, and glory, and a kingdom, that all people, nations, and languages should serve Him, and His dominion is an everlasting dominion, which shall not pass away, and His kingdom that which shall not be destroyed* Hold fast this in preference, these things believe, and cast away the words of heresy; for thou hast heard most explicitly concerning the endless kingdom of Christ.

28. Thou hast the like doctrine in the interpretation of the Stone, *which was cut out of the mountain without hands,* which is Christ according to the flesh; *And [His] kingdom shall not be left to other people.* And David says in one place, *Thy throne, O God, is for ever and ever;* and in another place, *Thou, Lord, in the beginning hast laid the foundation of the earth, and the heavens are the work of Thy hands,* and then, *they shall perish, but Thou remainest,* and what follows; *but Thou art the same, and Thy years shall not fail.* Which words Paul has interpreted of the Son.

29. And wouldest thou know, how they who teach the contrary arrived at such madness? They read wrongly that good word of the Apostle, *For He must reign, till He hath put all enemies under His feet,* and they say, when His enemies shall have been put under His feet, He shall cease to reign, wrongly and foolishly alleging this. For He who is king before He has subdued His enemies, how shall He

[k] This was Marcellus, Bishop of Ancyra, Soci Hist ii 19 p 99

not the rather be king, after He has gotten the mastery over them?

30. They have also dared to say that the Scripture, *When* (15.) *all things shall be subdued unto Him, then shall the Son also* 1 Cor 15, *Himself be subject unto Him that put all things under Him,* 28 that this Scripture shows that the Son shall be absorbed into the Father. Shall ye then, O most impious of all men, ye the creatures of Christ, continue? and shall Christ, by whom both you and all things were made, perish? Such a word is blasphemous. But further, how shall all things be made subject unto Him? Shall they perish, or continue? Shall then the other things, when subject to the Son, abide, and shall the Son, when subject to the Father, not abide? For He shall be subject, not because He shall then begin to be accord- πειθαρ-ant to the Father, (for He *doth* always *those things that* χεῖν John 8, *please Him,*) but because, then as before, He obeys the 29. Father, yielding, not a forced obedience, but a self-chosen ὑπακούει εὐπει-accordance, for He is not a servant, that He should be θείαν subject by force, but a Son, that He should comply of His προαιρέ-free choice and natural love. σει φιλο στοργίᾳ

31. But let us examine them; what is the meaning of "until" or "as far as"? For with this very word will I close with them, and try to expose their error. Since they have dared to say that the words, *till He hath put His enemies under His feet,* show that He Himself shall have an end, and have presumed to set bounds to the eternal kingdom of Christ, and to bring to an end, as far as words go, His never-ending sovereignty, come now, let us read the like expressions in the Apostle. *Nevertheless, death reigned from Adam till* Rom. 5, *Moses.* Did men then die up to this time, and did none 14. die any more after Moses, or after the Law was there no more death among men? Well then, thou seest that the word "unto," is not to limit time, but that Paul rather signified this,—" And yet, though Moses was a righteous and wondrous man, the doom of death which was sent forth against Adam, reached even unto him, and them that came after him; and this, though they had not sinned like Adam, in the disobedience concerning the eating of the Tree."

32. Take again another similar phrase. *For until this day* 2 Cor 3 . . . *when Moses is read, the vail is upon their heart.* Does 14. 15.

"until this day" mean only "until Paul"? Is it not "until this day" present, and even to the end? And if Paul say to the Corinthians, *For we are come as far as unto you also in preaching the Gospel of Christ, having hope to preach the Gospel in the regions beyond you*, thou seest manifestly that "as far as" implies not the end, but has something following it. In what sense then shouldest thou remember to take that Scripture, *till He hath put all enemies under His feet?* According as Paul says in another place, *But exhort each other daily, while it is called to-day;* meaning, "continually." For as we may not speak of the "beginning of the days" of Christ, so neither endure thou any one who at any time speaks of the end of His kingdom. For it is written, *His kingdom is an everlasting kingdom.*

33. And though I have many more texts out of the divine Scriptures, that the kingdom of Christ has no end ever, I will be content with those above alleged, because of the advance of the day. But thou, O hearer, worship Him only as thy King, fleeing all heretical error. And if the grace of God permit us, the remaining Articles also of the Faith shall be in good time declared to you. And may the God of all keep you all, as ye bear in mind the signs of the end, and remain unsubdued by Antichrist. Thou hast received the tokens of that Deceiver who is to come; thou hast received the proofs of the true Christ, who shall openly come down from heaven. Fly therefore the one, the False one; and look for the other, the True. Thou hast learnt the way, how in the judgment thou mayest be found among the company on the right hand; guard *that which is committed to thee* concerning Christ, and be conspicuous in good works, that thou mayest stand with a good confidence before the Judge, and inherit the kingdom of heaven:—Through whom, and with whom, be glory to God with the Holy Ghost, for ever and ever. Amen.

Margin references: Lect XV. 2 Cor. 10, 14 15. 16. 1 Cor. 15, 25. Heb. 3, 13. v Heb 7, 3. Dan. 7, 27. (16.) 1 Tim. 6, 20.

LECTURE XVI.

ON THE ONE HOLY GHOST, THE COMFORTER, WHICH SPAKE IN THE PROPHETS.

1 Corinthians xii. 1, 4.

Now concerning spiritual gifts, brethren, I would not have you ignorant. . . . Now there are diversities of gifts, but the same Spirit.

1. NEED have we truly of spiritual grace, that we may discourse concerning the Holy Spirit; not that we may speak suitably to His dignity, for this is impossible, but that in alleging the words of the divine Scriptures, we may not put ourselves in jeopardy. For surely a very fearful thing is written in the Gospels, where Christ says plainly, *Whosoever speaketh a word against the Holy Ghost, it shall not be forgiven him, neither in this world, neither in the world to come.* Mat. 12, 32. And there is often fear, lest a man, either from ignorance, or from what is considered religion, speaking what he ought not concerning Him, should receive this doom. The Judge of quick and dead, Jesus Christ, has declared that he hath no forgiveness; if then any man stumble, what hope has he?

2. To Jesus Christ's very grace, therefore, it must belong to grant both to us to speak without deficiency, and to you to hear with discretion; for discretion is needful not to them only who speak, but also to them that hear, lest they hear one thing, and receive a different impression. Let us then speak nothing concerning the Holy Ghost but what is written; and if any thing be not written, let us not busy ourselves about it. The Holy Ghost Himself spake the Scriptures;

204   *There is but One Holy Ghost.*

LECT XVI.

He has also spoken concerning Himself as much as He pleased, or as much as we could receive. Be those things therefore spoken, which He has said; for whatsoever He has not said, we dare not say

(2.)   3. There is One Only Holy Ghost, the Comforter; and as there is One God the Father, and no second Father,—and as there is One Only-begotten Son and Word of God, who hath no brother;—so is there One Only Holy Ghost, and no second spirit equal in honour to Him. The Holy Ghost then is Power most mighty, of a divine and unsearchable nature; for He is a living and intelligent Being, and is the sanctifying principle of all things made by God through Christ. He it is who illuminates the souls of the just; He was in the Prophets, He was also in the Apostles in the New Testament. Abhorred be they who dare to separate into parts the active power of the Holy Ghost! There is One God, the Father, Lord of the Old and of the New Testament; and One Lord, Jesus Christ, who was prophesied of in the Old Testament, and came in the New; and One Holy Ghost, who through the Prophets preached of Christ, and when Christ was come, descended, and manifested Him.

4. Let no one then divide the Old from the New Testament[a]; let no one say that the Spirit in the former is one, and in the latter another, for thus he offends against the Holy Ghost Himself, who together with the Father and the Son is honoured, and at the observance of Holy Baptism is included with them in the Holy Trinity. For the Only-begotten Son of God said plainly to the Apostles, *Go ye, and teach all nations, baptizing them in the name of the Father, and of the Son, and of the Holy Ghost.* Our hope is in the Father, and the Son, and the Holy Ghost. We preach not three Gods; let the Marcionites be mute; but we preach One God, by One Son, with the Holy Ghost. The Faith is indivisible, religious worship is undistracted. We neither divide the Holy Trinity, like some; nor do we as Sabellius introduce confusion. But we know according to godliness One Father, who sent His Son to be our Saviour; we know One Son, who promised that He would send the Comforter from the Father; we know the Holy Ghost, who spake in the Prophets, and

Mat 28, 19.

εὐσέβεια

συναλοιφήν.

---

[a] As did the Gnostics and Manichees. Philast. Hær. 126.

who on the day of Pentecost descended on the Apostles in the form of fiery tongues, here, in Jerusalem, in the Upper Church of the Apostles [b]; for all the choicest privileges belong to us. Here Christ came down from heaven; here the Holy Ghost came down from heaven. And in truth it were most fitting, that as we discourse concerning Christ and Golgotha, upon this Golgotha, so also we should speak concerning the Holy Ghost in the Upper Church; yet since He who descended there jointly partakes of the glory of Him who was crucified here, we here speak concerning Him also who descended there · for religious worship is indivisible.

5. We would now say somewhat concerning the Holy Ghost; not to declare with exactness His substance, for this (3) were impossible; but to speak of the diverse mistakes of some ὑπόστα- concerning him, (lest we unawares fall upon them,) and to σιν block up the paths of error, that we may journey on the King's one highway. And if we now for caution's sake repeat any of the statements of these heretics, let it recoil on their heads, and let us be guiltless, both we who speak, and ye who hear.

6. For the heretics, who are most profane in all things, have *sharpened their tongue* against the Holy Ghost also, Ps 140, and have dared to utter atrocious things; as Irenæus the ὁ ἐξηγη- teacher has written in his directions against heresies. For τῆς. some of them have dared to say that they were the Holy προστά- Ghost;—of whom the first was Simon, the sorcerer spoken of γμασι in the Acts of the Apostles · for when he was cast out, he presumed to teach such doctrines; and they who are called Gnostics, impious men, have spoken other things against the Spirit, and the abandoned Valentinians again something else; and the profane Manes dared to call himself the Comforter sent by Christ. Others again have taught that the Spirit is different in the Prophets and in the New Testament. Great then is their error, or rather their blasphemy. Abhor therefore such, and flee from them who blaspheme the Holy Ghost, and have no forgiveness. For what fellowship hast thou with the desperate, thou, who art to be baptized now, and into the Holy Ghost also? If he who attaches himself to a thief, and

[b] On Mount Sion, and divided into two parts, the Upper and the Lower Vid Epiphan. de Mens 14.

concurs with him, is punishable, what hope shall he have, who offends against the Holy Ghost?

7. And abhor the Marcionists also, who tear away from the New Testament the text of the Old. For Marcion first, that most impious of men, who first asserted three Gods, knowing that in the New Testament are contained testimonies concerning Christ from the Prophets, cut out those taken from the Old Testament, that the King might be left without witness. Abhor those above-mentioned Gnostics, men of knowledge by name, but fraught with ignorance; who have dared to say such things of the Holy Ghost, as I dare not repeat.

(4.) 8. Let the Cataphrygians also be thy abhorrence, and Montanus, their ringleader in evil, and his two so-called prophetesses, Maximilla and Priscilla. For this Montanus, who was out of his mind and really mad, (for he would not have said such things, had he not been mad,) dared to say that he was the Holy Ghost,—he, miserable man, and filled with all uncleanness and lasciviousness [c]; for it suffices but to hint at this, out of respect for the women who are present. And having fixed his abode at Pepuza, a most insignificant hamlet of Phrygia, he falsely named it Jerusalem; cutting the throats of wretched little children, and chopping them up into horrid food, for the purposes of their so-called mysteries,—(wherefore till but lately in the time of persecution, we were suspected of doing this, because these Montanists were called, falsely indeed, by the common name of Christians,)— yet he dared to call himself the Holy Ghost, filled as he was with all impiety and savage cruelty, and condemned by a sentence beyond mitigation.

9. And he was seconded, as was said before, by that most impious Manes also, who blended together what was bad in every heresy; who being the very lowest pit of destruction, collected the doctrines of all the heretics, and wrought out and set forth a yet more novel error. And he dared to say that he himself was the Comforter, whom Christ promised to send. But the Saviour when He promised Him, said to the Apostles, *But tarry ye in the city of Jerusalem, until ye be endued with power from on high.* What then?

Luke 24, 49

[c] These charges against the Montanists are not satisfactorily borne out by other writers.

did the Apostles who had been dead two hundred years, wait for Manes, *until they should be endued with power*, and will any dare to say, that they were not from that time full of the Holy Ghost? And in truth it is written, *Then they laid* Acts 8, *their hands on them, and they received the Holy Ghost;* was 17. not this before Manes, yea, many years ago, when the Holy Ghost descended on the day of Pentecost?

10. Wherefore was Simon the sorcerer condemned? Was it not that he came to the Apostles, and said, *Give me also* Acts 8, *this power, that on whomsoever I lay hands, he may receive* 19 *the Holy Ghost?* For he said not, "Give me also the fellowship of the Holy Ghost," but " Give me the power;" that he might sell to others that which might not be sold, of which he had not himself possession. And he brought money to them who had nothing; and this, seeing men bringing the prices of the things sold, and laying them at the Apostles' feet. And he considered not that they who trod under foot the wealth which was brought for the maintenance of the poor, were not likely to give the power of the Holy Ghost for a bribe. But what say they to Simon? *Thy money perish with thee,* Ib. v 20. *because thou hast thought that the gift of God may be purchased with money;* thou art a second Judas, who for money hast expected to buy the grace of the Spirit. If then Simon, who wished to get this power for a price, is to *perish*, how impious is Manes, who said that he was the Holy Ghost? Let us hate them who are worthy of hatred; withdraw we from them whom God withdraws from; let us also say unto God with all boldness concerning all heretics, *Do not I hate* Ps 139, *them, O Lord, that hate Thee, and am not I grieved with* 21. *them that rise up against Thee?* For there is also an enmity which is right, according as it is written, *I will put enmity* Gen 3, *between thee and her seed;* for friendship with the serpent 15 works enmity with God, and death.

11. Let then thus much suffice concerning those outcasts; (5.) and now let us return to the divine Scriptures, and let us *drink waters out of our own cisterns,* (that is, the holy Prov 5, Fathers,) *and running waters out of our own wells.* Drink 15. we of that *living water, which springs up into everlasting* John 4, *life;* but this spake the Saviour *of the Spirit, which they that* Ib 7, 38. *believe on Him should receive.* For observe what He says, 39.

LECT XVI

He that believeth on Me, (not simply this, but,) *as the Scripture hath said,* (thus He hath sent thee back to the Old Testament,) *out of his belly shall flow rivers of living water,* rivers, not perceived by sense, and merely watering the earth with its thorns and trees, but bringing light to the soul. And in another place He says, *But the water that I shall give him, shall be in him a well of water springing up into everlasting life,*—a new water, living and springing up, springing up to them who are worthy.

αἰσθητοί.

John 4, 14.

12. And why has He called the grace of the Spirit by the name of water? because by water all things subsist; because of water are herbs and animals created; because the water of the showers comes down from heaven; because it comes down one in form, yet manifold in its working. For one fountain watered the whole of the Garden, and one and the same rain comes down upon all the world, yet it becomes white in the lily, and red in the rose, and purple in the violets and pansies, and different and varied in each several kind: so it is one in the palm-tree, and another in the vine, and all in all things; being the while one in nature, not diverse from itself; for the rain does not change, when it comes down, first as one thing, then as another, but adapting itself to the nature of each thing which receives it, it becomes to each what is suitable. Thus also the Holy Ghost, being one, and of one nature, and undivided, divides to each His grace, *according as He will :* and as the dry tree, when it partakes of water, puts forth shoots, so also the soul in sin, when it has been through repentance made worthy of the Holy Ghost, brings forth clusters of righteousness. And He, being One in nature, yet at the will of God and in the Name of Christ works many excellencies. For He employs the tongue of one man for wisdom; the soul of another He enlightens by Prophecy; to another He gives power to drive away devils; to another He gives to interpret the divine Scriptures. He invigorates one man's self-command; He teaches another the way to give alms; another He teaches to fast and exercise himself; another He teaches to despise the things of the body; another He trains for martyrdom · diverse in different men, yet not diverse from Himself, as it is written, *But the manifestation of the Spirit is given to every man to profit withal.* For to

v Gen. 2, 10.

μονοειδές.
1 Cor 12, 11.

νεύματι.

1 Cor 12. 7—11

one is given by the Spirit the word of wisdom; to another the word of knowledge by the same Spirit; to another faith by the same Spirit; to another the gifts of healing by the same Spirit; to another the working of miracles; to another prophecy; to another discerning of spirits; to another diverse kinds of tongues; to another the interpretation of tongues · but all these worketh the self-same Spirit, dividing to every man severally as He will.

13. But since concerning that which is called Spirit, many (6.) and diverse things are written in the divine Scriptures, and there is reason to fear lest some out of ignorance fall into confusion, not knowing what sort of spirit is spoken of; it will be well now to certify you, of what kind the Scripture declares the Holy Spirit to be. For as Aaron is called Christ, and David and Saul and others are called Christs, i. e. Anointbut there is only one true Christ, so, since the name of the ed. v. Spirit is given to different things, it is right to see what is supr x. meant in particular by the Holy Spirit. For many things are 11. xi. 1. called spirits. Thus an Angel is called spirit, and our soul is called spirit, and this wind which is blowing is called spirit; and great excellence is spoken of as spirit; and an unclean deed as spirit; and a devil our adversary is called spirit. Beware therefore when thou hearest these things, lest from their having a common name thou mistake one for another. For concerning our soul the Scripture says, *His spirit shall go* Ps 146, *forth, and he shall return to his earth:* and of the same soul 4. Sept. it says, again, *Which formeth the spirit of man within him.* Zech. 12, 1. And of the Angels it is said in the Psalms, *Who maketh His* Ps 104, *Angels spirits, and His ministers a flaming fire.* And of the 4 Ps. 48, wind it saith, *Thou shalt break the ships of Tarshish with a* 7. Sept. *violent spirit;* and, *As the tree in the wood is moved by the* Is 7, 2. *spirit;* and, *Fire, hail, snow, ice, spirit of storm.* And of Sept Ps. 148, good doctrine the Lord Himself says, *The words that I speak* 8 *unto you, they are spirit, and they are life;* instead of, " are John 6, 63. spiritual " But the Holy Spirit is not pronounced by the tongue; but He is Living, and He it is who gives to speak wisely, speaking and discoursing Himself.

14. And wouldest thou know that He discourses and speaks? Philip by revelation of an Angel went down to the way which leads to Gaza, when the Eunuch was coming;

210   *Instances of the Holy Ghost speaking.*

Lect XVI
Acts 8, 29.
Ezek. 11, 5.
Acts 13, 2.

and the Spirit said to Philip, *Go near, and join thyself to this chariot.* Seest thou the Spirit talking to one who hears Him? And Ezekiel speaks thus, *And the Spirit of the Lord fell upon me, and said unto me, Speak; Thus saith the Lord.* And again, *The Holy Ghost said,* unto the Apostles who were in Antioch, *Separate me Barnabas and Saul for the work whereunto I have called them.* Beholdest thou the Spirit living, separating, calling, and with authority sending forth?

Acts 20, 23.

So Paul said, *Save that the Holy Ghost witnesseth in every city, saying that bonds and afflictions await me.* For this the good Sanctifier of the Church, and her Helper, and Teacher, the Holy Ghost, the Comforter, of whom the Saviour

John 14, 26

said, *He shall teach you all things,* (and He said not only, *He shall teach,* but, *He shall bring to your remembrance whatever I have said unto you;* for the teachings of Christ and of the Holy Ghost are not different, but the same;) He, I say, testified before to Paul what should befall him, that he might be the more stout-hearted, from knowing them previously.—I have been led to make these remarks in consequence of the text, *The words which I speak unto you, they are spirit;* that thou mayest understand this, not of the utterance of the lips, but of good doctrine.

(7.)

Hos 4, 12.

15. In Scripture too sin also is called spirit, as I have already said; but in another and opposite sense, as when it is said, *The spirit of whoredoms caused them to err.* The name "spirit" is given also to the *unclean spirit,* the devil; but with the addition of, "unclean;" for to each is joined its distinguishing name, to mark its proper nature. When the Scripture uses "spirit" in reference to the soul of man, it is with the addition, "of man;" if it mean the wind, it says, the "spirit of storm;" if sin, it says, the "spirit of whoredoms;" if the devil, it says, "an unclean spirit:" that we may know which particular thing is spoken of, and thou mayest not suppose that it means the Holy Ghost; God forbid! For this word spirit is common to many things; and every thing which has not a gross body is in a general way called spirit. Since, therefore, the devils have not such bodies, they are called spirits: but great is the difference; for the unclean devil, when he comes upon the soul of a man, (may the Lord deliver from him every soul that hears me, yea, and that is away¹) he comes

like a wolf upon a sheep, ravening for blood, and ready to devour. His presence is most cruel, the sense of it most oppressive; the mind is darkened; his attack is an injustice also, and the usurpation of another's possession. For he tyrannically uses another's body, another's instruments, as his own property; he throws down him who stands upright; (for he is akin to him who *fell from heaven,*) he perverts the tongue and distorts the lips. Foam comes instead of words; the man is filled with darkness; his eye is open, yet the soul sees not through it; and the miserable man quivers convulsively before his death. The devils are truly foes of men, using them basely and pitilessly. ^{Luke 10, 18.}

16. Such is not the Holy Ghost; God forbid! For His doings tend the contrary way, to what is good and salutary. First, His coming is gentle; the perception of Him is fragrant; most light is His burden; beams of light and knowledge gleam forth before His coming. He comes with the bowels of a true guardian; for He comes to save, and to heal, to teach, to admonish, to strengthen, to exhort, to enlighten the mind, first of him who receives Him, and afterwards of others also, through him. And as a man, who having been previously in darkness, on a sudden beholds the sun, receives light in his bodily sight, and sees plainly things which he saw not, so in like manner he who is vouchsafed the Holy Ghost, is illuminated in his soul, and sees things beyond man's sight, which he knew not; his body is on earth, yet to his soul are mirrored forth the heavens. He sees, like Esaias, *the Lord sitting upon a throne high and lifted up;* he sees, like Ezekiel, *Him who is above the Cherubim;* he sees, like Daniel, *thousand thousands, and ten thousand times ten thousand;* and the man, little though he be, beholds the beginning of the world and the end of the world, and the times intervening, and the successions of kings, —things which he had not learnt: for the True Enlightener is present with him. The man is within walls; but the power of his knowledge reaches far and wide, and he sees even what other men are doing. (8) Is. 6, 1. Ezek. 10, 1. &c. Dan. 7, 10.

17. Peter was not with Ananias and Sapphira when they sold their possessions, but he was present by the Spirit; *Why,* he says, *hath Satan filled thine heart to lie to the* Acts 5, 3.

Holy Ghost? There was no accuser; there was no witness; whence knew he what had happened? *Whiles it remained was it not thine own? and after it was sold, was it not in thine own power? why hast thou conceived this thing in thine heart?* The *unlettered* Peter, by the grace of the Spirit, learnt what not even the sages of the Greeks had known. Thou hast the like, in the case also of Elisseus. For when he had freely healed the leprosy of Naaman, Gehazi received the reward, the reward of another's achievement; and took the money from Naaman, and bestowed it in a dark place. But *the darkness is no darkness* to the Saints. And when he came, Elisseus asked him; and like Peter, when he said, *Tell me whether ye sold the land for so much?* he also inquires, *Whence comest thou, Gehazi?* Not in ignorance, but in sorrow ask I *whence comest thou?* From darkness art thou come, and to darkness shalt thou go; thou hast sold the cure of the leper, and the leprosy shall be thy heritage. I have fulfilled, he says, the bidding of Him who said to me, *Freely ye have received, freely give;* but thou hast sold this grace; receive now the terms of thy purchase. But what says Elisseus to him? *Went not mine heart with thee?* I was here shut in by the body, but the spirit which has been given me of God, saw even the things afar off, and showed me plainly what was doing elsewhere. Thou seest how the Holy Ghost not only rids of ignorance, but invests with knowledge; thou seest how He illuminates souls.

18. Esaias lived nearly a thousand years ago; and he beheld Sion *as a cottage.* The city was still standing, and beautiful with public places, and robed in majesty; yet he says, *Zion shall be ploughed as a field,* foretelling what is fulfilled in our days. And observe the exactness of the prophecy; for he said, *And the daughter of Zion shall be left as a cottage in a vineyard, as a lodge in a garden of cucumbers.* And now the place is filled with gardens of cucumbers. Seest thou how the Holy Spirit illuminates the holy ones? Be not therefore carried away to other things, by the force of a common term, but keep fast what is exactly meant.

19. And if ever, while thou hast been sitting here, thoughts concerning chastity or virginity have come into my mind, it

has been His teaching. Has not often a maiden, already at the bridal threshold, fled away, He teaching her the doctrine of virginity? Has not often a man high in court, spurned wealth and rank, being taught by the Holy Ghost? Has not often a young man, at the sight of beauty, closed his eyes, and fled from the sight, and escaped the defilement? Askest thou whence it came to pass? The Holy Ghost taught the soul of the young man. Many ways of covetousness are there in the world; yet Christians refuse possessions: wherefore? by the instigation of the Holy Ghost. Awful in truth is that Spirit, holy and good; and fittingly are we baptized into Father, Son, and Holy Ghost. A man, still with a body about him, wrestles with many fiercest demons; and often the demon, whom many men could not master with iron bands, has been mastered by him with words of prayer, through the power which is in him of the Holy Ghost; and the mere breathing of the Exorcist becomes as fire to that unseen foe. A mighty Succour and Protector, therefore, have we of God; a great Teacher of the Church, a mighty Champion on our behalf. Let us not be afraid of the demons, nor of the devil; for our Champion is mightier. Only let us open to Him our doors; *for He goes about seeking such as are worthy*, and searching on whom He may confer His gifts. [Wisd 6, 16.]

20. And He is called the Comforter, because He comforts (10.) us, and encourages us, and *helpeth our infirmities; for we know not what we should pray for as we ought; but the Spirit itself maketh intercession for us, with groanings which cannot be uttered*, that is, to God. Oftentimes, a man for Christ's sake has been outraged and injuriously dishonoured; martyrdom is at hand; tortures on every side, and fire, and sword, and savage beasts, and the deep pit. But the Holy Ghost softly whispers to him, "Wait thou for the Lord, O man; what is now befalling thee is a small matter; that which is bestowed on thee is great. Suffer thou a little while, and be with Angels everlastingly; *the sufferings of this present time are not worthy to be compared with the glory which shall be revealed in us.*" He portrays to the man the kingdom of heaven; He almost shows him even the paradise of delight; and the martyrs, whose bodily countenances [Rom 8, 26.] [Rom. 8, 18.]

LECT. XVI.
τῇ δυνά- μει.
παροι- κίας ἐπαρ- χίας.
ἀκτημο- σύνην.

are of necessity turned to their judges, but who in spirit are already in Paradise, despise those hardships which are seen.

21. And wouldest thou be sure that through the power of the Holy Ghost the Martyrs bear their witness? The Saviour says to His disciples, *And when they bring you unto the synagogues, and unto the magistrates, and powers, take ye no thought how ye shall answer, or what ye shall say; for the Holy Ghost shall teach you in the same hour, what ye ought to say.* For it is impossible to suffer martyrdom for Christ's sake, except a man suffer by the Holy Ghost; for if *no man can say that Jesus is the Lord, but by the Holy Ghost*, how shall any man give his own life for Jesus' sake, but by the Holy Ghost?

Luke 12, 11. 12

1 Cor 12, 3

(11.) 22. Great indeed, and all-powerful in gifts, and wonderful, is the Holy Ghost. Consider, how many of you are now sitting here, how many souls of us are present. For each He is working as is suitable, and being in the midst, He beholds the temper of each. He beholds also his thoughts and his conscience, and what we say, and what we imagine. What I have now said is great indeed, yet is it small. For consider, I pray, with thoughts illuminated by Him, how many Christians there are of this diocese, and how many in the whole province of Palestine, and carry forward thy mind from this province, to the whole Roman empire; and after this, consider the whole world; races of Persians, and nations of Indians, Goths and Sarmatians, Gauls and Spaniards, and Moors Libyans and Ethiopians, and the rest for whom we have no names; for of many of the nations not even the names have reached us. Consider, I pray, of each nation, Bishops, Priests, Deacons, Solitaries, Virgins, and other laity; and then behold the great Protector, and Dispenser of their gifts; —how throughout the world He gives to one chasity, to another perpetual virginity, to another almsgiving, to another voluntary poverty, to another power of repelling hostile spirits. And as the light with one gleam sheds radiance on all things, so also the Holy Ghost enlightens those who have eyes; for if any from blindness is not vouchsafed His grace, let him not blame the Spirit, but his own unbelief.

(12.) 23. Thou hast seen His power, which is throughout the

world; tarry now no longer upon earth, but ascend on high. Ascend, I say, in imagination even unto the first heaven, and behold how many uncounted myriads of Angels are there. Rise up in thy thoughts, if thou canst, yet higher; do but consider the Archangels, do but consider the Spirits; consider the Virtues, consider the Principalities, consider the Powers, consider the Thrones, consider the Dominions;—the Comforter is of all these the Ruler from God, and the Teacher, and the Sanctifier. Of Him has Elias need, and Elisseus, and Esaias, among men; of Him Michael and Gabriel have need among Angels. Nought of things created is equal in honour to Him · for the families of the Angels, and all their hosts assembled together, have no equality with the Holy Ghost. All these the all-excellent power of the Comforter overshadows. And they indeed are sent forth to minister; but He searches even the deep things of God, according as the Apostle says, *For the Spirit searcheth all things, yea, the deep things of God. For what man knoweth the things of a man, save the spirit of man which is in him? even so the things of God knoweth no man, but the Spirit of God.* 1 Cor. 2, 10.11.

24. He preached concerning Christ in the Prophets; He wrought in the Apostles; He to this day seals the souls in Baptism. And the Father indeed gives to the Son; and the Son shares with the Holy Ghost. For it is Jesus Himself, not I, who says, *All things are delivered unto Me of My Father;* and of the Holy Ghost He says, *When He, the Spirit of Truth, shall come,* and the rest . . . . *He shall glorify Me; for He shall receive of Mine, and shall show it unto you.* Mat 11, 27 John 16, 13 14. The Father through the Son, with the Holy Ghost, bestows all things; the gifts of the Father are none other than those of the Son, and those of the Holy Ghost; for there is one Salvation, one Power, one Faith; One God, the Father; One Lord, His only-begotten Son; One Holy Ghost, the Comforter. And it is enough for us to know these things; but inquire not curiously into His nature or substance: for had it been written, we would have spoken of it; what is not written, let us not venture on; for it is sufficient for our salvation to know, that there is Father, and Son, and Holy Ghost. ὑπόστα-σιν

25. This Spirit descended upon the seventy Elders in the days of Moses. (Now let not the length of the discourse, (13.)

beloved, produce weariness in you: but may He of whom our discourse is, grant strength to every one, both to us who speak, and to you who listen!) This Spirit, as I said, came down upon the seventy Elders in the time of Moses, and I say this to thee, that I may set before thee, that He knows all things, and worketh *as He will.* The seventy Elders were chosen; *And the Lord came down in a cloud, and took of the Spirit that was upon Moses, and gave it unto the seventy Elders;* not that the Spirit was divided, but His grace, according to the vessels of it, and the capacity of the recipients. But there were present sixty and eight, and they prophesied; but Eldad and Medad were not present: therefore that it might be shown that it was not Moses who bestowed the gift, but the Spirit who wrought, Eldad and Medad, who had been called, but had not as yet presented themselves, prophesy.

26. Jesus the Son of Nun, the successor of Moses, was amazed; and coming to him he says, "Hast thou heard that Eldad and Medad prophesy? They were called, and they came not; *my lord Moses, forbid them.*" "I cannot forbid them," he says, "for this grace is from Heaven; nay, so far am I from forbidding them, that I even think it a mercy. I think not, however, that thou hast said this in envy; yet hast thou not rivalry *for my sake,* because that they prophesy, and thou prophesiest not yet? wait for the proper season; *and O that all the Lord's people were prophets, whenever the Lord shall put His Spirit upon them!"* saying this also prophetically, *Whenever the Lord shall put;* "However He has not as yet given it; so thou hast it not yet."—Had not then Abraham this, and Isaac, and Jacob, and Joseph? And they of old, had they it not? Nay, but the words plainly mean, "*when He shall put it* upon all; as yet indeed this grace is partial, then it shall be given lavishly." And he secretly alluded to what was to happen on the day of Pentecost among us; for He descended among us, yet He had before also descended upon many. For it is written, *And Jesus the son of Nun was full of the Spirit of wisdom; for Moses had laid his hands upon him.* Thou seest the same figure in the Old and New Testament;—in the days of Moses, the Spirit was given by the laying on of hands; and Peter also gives

the Spirit by the laying on of hands. And on thee also, who art about to be baptized, shall His grace come; yet in what manner I say not, for I will not anticipate the proper season.

27. He also came upon all the just, and the Prophets; Enos, I mean, and Enoch, and Noah, and the rest; upon Abraham, Isaac, Jacob; for as regards Joseph, even Pharaoh understood that he had the Spirit of God within him. And of Moses, and the wonderful works wrought by the Spirit in his days, thou hast heard often. This Spirit had Job, that most enduring man, and all the saints, though we repeat not all their names. He also was sent when the tabernacle was in making, and filled with wisdom the wise-hearted men who were with Bezaleel. ^{v. Gen. 41, 38.} ^{Exod 31, 1—6. and 36, 1. &c.}

28. In the might of this Spirit, as we have it in the Book of Judges, Othniel judged; Gideon was made strong; Jephtha conquered; Deborah, a woman, waged war; and Samson, so long as he wrought righteousness, and grieved Him not, achieved things beyond man's power. And as for Samuel and David, we have it plainly in the Books of Kings, that by the Holy Ghost they prophesied, and were the chiefs of the prophets;—and Samuel was called, *the Seer*; and David says distinctly, *The Spirit of the Lord spake by me*, and in the Psalms, *And take not thy Holy Spirit from me*, and again, *Let thy good Spirit lead me forth into the land of righteousness*. And as we have it in the Books of Chronicles, Azariah, in the time of King Asa, and Jahaziel in the time of King Jehoshaphat, partook of the Holy Ghost, and again, another Azariah, he who was stoned. And Ezra says, *Thou gavest also Thy good Spirit to instruct them*. But as touching Elias, who was taken up, and Elisseus, those spirit-instinct [b] and wonder-working men, it is manifest, without our saying so, that they were full of the Holy Ghost. ^{Judg. 3, 10. Ib 6, 34. Ib. 11, 29.} ^{1 Sam. 9, 9. 2 Sam. 23, 2. Ps. 51, 11.} ^{Ps. 143, 10. (Pr. B. vers.) 2 Chron. 15, 1. Ib. 20, 14. vid 24, 20, 21. Neh. 9, 20}

29. And if a man peruse all the books of the Prophets, both of the twelve, and of the others, many will he find the texts to be concerning the Holy Ghost; as when Micah says in the person of God, *Unless I fulfil might by the Spirit of the Lord*; and Joel cries, *And it shall come to pass after*- (15.) ^{Mic. 3, 8. Sept. Joel 2, 28.}

---

[b] πνευματοφόρων. "Used in a bad sense, as belonging to false prophets, in Hos 9, 7 Zeph 3, 4. Sept. but applied to holy men by ecclesiastical writers." Ed Ben.

218 Texts from the Old Testament concerning the Holy Spirit.

LECT. XVI

Hag 2, 4. 5.

Zech 1, 6. Sept.

Is 11, 2. Sept.

Is. 42, 1.
Is 44, 3.
Ib 48, 16.
Ib 59, 21
Ib. 61, 1

Ib. 63, 10
v. 11.

Ezek. 11, 5.

v. Gen. 46, 29.

Luke 15, 20.

Ezek. 11, 24.

vid. sup. Cat. iii. 16.
Ezek. 36, 25—27.

Ezek. 37, 1

(16.)
Susanna
of Dan.
13, 22.

wards, *that I will pour out My Spirit upon all flesh;* and Haggai, *For I am with you, saith the Lord of Hosts; My Spirit remaineth among you;* and in like manner Zechariah, *But receive My words and My statutes which I command by My Spirit, to My servants the Prophets;* and the rest.

30. And Esaias too, with his majestic voice, says, *And the Spirit of the Lord shall rest upon Him, the spirit of wisdom and understanding, the spirit of counsel and might, the spirit of knowledge and godliness; and the fear of the Lord shall fill Him;* signifying that the Spirit is one and undivided, but His operations various. So again, *Behold My servant,* and the rest; *I have put My Spirit upon Him.* And again, *I will pour My Spirit upon thy seed;* and again, *And now the Lord God and His Spirit hath sent Me;* and again, *This is My covenant with them, saith the Lord, My Spirit which is upon thee;* and again, *The Spirit of the Lord God is upon Me, because He hath anointed Me,* and the rest; and again in his charge against the Jews, *But they rebelled and vexed His Holy Spirit,* and, *where is He that put His Holy Spirit within Him?* Also thou hast in Ezekiel, (if thou be not now weary of listening,) what has already been quoted, *And the Spirit of the Lord fell upon me, and said unto me, Speak; Thus saith the Lord.* But the words, *fell upon me* we must understand in a good sense, that is "lovingly;" as Jacob also, when he had found Joseph, fell upon his neck; and as the loving father, in the Gospels, on seeing his son who had returned from his wandering, *had compassion, and ran and fell on his neck, and kissed him.* And again in Ezekiel, *And he brought me in a vision by the Spirit of God into Chaldæa, to them of the captivity.* And other texts thou heardest before, in what was said about Baptism; *Then will I sprinkle clean water upon you,* and the rest; *a new heart also will I give you, and a new spirit will I put within you;* and then immediately, *And I will put My Spirit within you.* And again, *The hand of the Lord was upon me, and carried me out in the Spirit of the Lord.*

31. He endued with wisdom the soul of Daniel, that young as he was he should be judge of Elders. The chaste Susanna was condemned as a wanton; there was none to plead her cause; for who should deliver her from the rulers?

She was led away to death, she was now in the hands of the executioners. But her Helper was at hand, the Comforter, the Spirit who sanctifies every intelligent nature. Come hither to me, He says to Daniel; young though thou be, convict those elders who labour under the sins of youth; for it is written, *God raised up the Holy Spirit upon a young stripling;*—in a word, (to cut the subject short,) by the sentence of Daniel that chaste lady was saved. We bring this forward as an instance; for this is not the season for expounding. Nebuchadnezzar also knew that the Holy Spirit was in Daniel; for he says to him, *O Belteshazzar, master of the magicians, because I know that the Spirit of the Holy Gods is in thee.* One thing is said truly, and one falsely; for that he had the Holy Spirit was true, but he was not the *master of the magicians,* for he was no sorcerer, but was wise through the Holy Ghost. And before this also, he interpreted to him the vision of the Image, which he who had seen it himself knew not; for he says, Tell me the vision, which I who saw it know not. Thou seest the power of the Holy Ghost; that which they who saw it know not, they who saw it not know and interpret.

32. And indeed it were easy to collect very many texts out of the Old Testament, and to discourse more largely concerning the Holy Ghost. But the time is short; and we must confine ourselves to a hearing of suitable length. Wherefore, being now content awhile with passages from the Old Testament, we will, if it be God's pleasure, proceed in the next Lecture to what remains to bring out of the New Testament. And may the God of peace, through our Lord Jesus Christ, and through the love of the Spirit, count all of you worthy of spiritual and heavenly gifts:—To whom be glory and power for ever and ever. Amen.

LECTURE XVII.

ON THE HOLY GHOST.

1 CORINTHIANS xii. 8.

For to one is given by the Spirit the word of wisdom; to another the word of knowledge by the same Spirit; &c.

LECT. XVII

1. In the preceding Lecture, we set forth according to our ability to the ears of your love some small portion of the testimonies concerning the Holy Ghost; and on the present occasion, we will, if it be God's pleasure, proceed to treat, as far as may be, of those which remain out of the New: and as then we restrained our eagerness within bounds in what you heard, (for there is no satiety in discoursing concerning the Holy Ghost,) so now we must say but a small part of what remains. For now, as well as then, we freely own that our weakness is overwhelmed by the multitude of what is written. Neither to-day will we use the subtleties of men, for that were not convenient; but merely call to mind what comes from the divine Scriptures; for this is the safest course, ac-

1 Cor. 2, 13.

cording to the blessed Apostle Paul, who says, *Which things also we speak, not in the words which man's wisdom teacheth, but which the Holy Ghost teacheth, comparing spiritual things with spiritual.* Thus we act like travellers or voyagers, who having one goal to a very long journey, though they with diligence hasten on, yet by reason of human weakness, are wont to take in their way divers cities or harbours.

(2.) 2. Therefore though the discourses concerning the Holy Ghost are divided, yet He Himself is undivided, being one and the same. For as in speaking concerning the Father, at one time the subject of our teaching was how He is the one only Cause; and at another, how He is called Father, or Almighty; and at another, how He is the Creator of all things; the division of the Lectures making no division of the Faith, in that He, the Object of devotion, both was and is, One;—and again, as in discoursing concerning the Only-begotten Son of God, we taught at one time concerning His Godhead, and at another concerning His manhood, dividing into many discourses the doctrine concerning our Lord Jesus Christ, yet proclaiming without division faith towards Him;—so now also though the Lectures concerning the Holy Spirit are divided, yet we preach faith undivided towards Him. For it is One and the Self-same Spirit who *divides* His gifts *to every man severally as He will*, Himself the while abiding undivided. For the Comforter is not different from the Holy Ghost, but one and the self-same, called by various names; who lives and subsists, and speaks, and works; and of all rational natures made by God through Christ, both of Angels and of men, He is the Sanctifier.

περὶ μον-αρχίας.

1 Cor. 12, 11.

ὑφεστώς.
λογικῶν.

3. But lest any from lack of learning, should suppose from the different titles of the Holy Ghost that these spirits are divers, and not one and the self-same, who is alone, the Catholic Church guarding thee beforehand hath delivered to us in the profession of the faith, to "believe in one Holy Ghost the Comforter, who spake by the Prophets;" that thou mightest know, that though His names be many, the Holy Spirit is but one;—of which names, we will now rehearse a few out of many.

4. He is called the Spirit, according to the Scripture just now read, *For to one is given by the Spirit the word of wisdom*. He is called the Spirit of Truth, as the Saviour says, *When He, the Spirit of Truth, is come*. He is called also the Comforter, as He said, *For if I go not away, the Comforter will not come unto you*. But that He is one and the same, though called by different titles, is shown plainly from the following. For that the Holy Spirit and the Comforter are the same, is declared in those words, *But the Comforter, which is the Holy Ghost;* and that the Comforter is the same as the Spirit of Truth, is declared, when it is said, *And I will give you*

(3.)

1 Cor. 12, 8.
John 16, 13.

Ib. v. 7.

Ib 14, 26 16. &c.

δώσω,
Cyr. δώ.

222 *The Spirit of God, of the Father, of the Lord, of Christ, of the Son,*

LECT XVII.
σει, He shall give,
1 ec text.
Ib 15, 26
Mat. 3, 16.
cf John 1, 32.
Rom. 8, 14.
Mat. 10, 20.
Eph. 3, 14, 16.

another Comforter, that He may abide with you for ever, even the Spirit of Truth; and again, But when the Comforter is come whom I will send unto you from the Father, even the Spirit of Truth. And He is called the Spirit of God, according as it is written, And I saw the Spirit of God descending; and again, For as many as are led by the Spirit of God, they are the sons of God. He is called also the Spirit of the Father, as the Saviour says, For it is not ye that speak, but the Spirit of your Father which speaketh in you; and again Paul saith, For this cause I bow my knees unto the Father of our Lord Jesus Christ; . . . that He would grant you to be strengthened by His Spirit. He is also called the Spirit of the Lord, according to that which Peter spake,

Acts 5, 9.

Why is it that ye have agreed together to tempt the Spirit of the Lord? He is called also the Spirit of God and Christ, as

Rom. 8, 9.

Paul writes, But ye are not in the flesh, but in the Spirit, if so be that the Spirit of God dwell in you. Now if any man have not the Spirit of Christ, he is none of His. He is called

Gal. 4, 6.

also the Spirit of the Son of God, as it is said, And because ye are sons, God hath sent forth the Spirit of His Son. He is

1 Pet. 1, 11.

called also the Spirit of Christ, as it is written, Searching what or what manner of time the Spirit of Christ which was

Phil. 1, 19

in them did signify; and again, Through your prayer, and the supply of the Spirit of Jesus Christ.

5. Thou wilt find many other titles of the Holy Ghost besides. Thus He is called the Spirit of Holiness, as it is

Rom. 1, 4.
Rom. 8, 15.

written, According to the Spirit of Holiness. He is also called the Spirit of adoption, as Paul saith, For ye have not received the spirit of bondage again to fear, but ye have received the Spirit of adoption, whereby we cry, Abba, Father. He is also called the Spirit of revelation, as it is written,

Eph 1, 17.

May give you the Spirit of wisdom and revelation in the knowledge of Him. He is also called the Spirit of promise,

Eph. 1, 13.

as the same Paul says, In whom also after that ye believed, ye were sealed with that Holy Spirit of Promise. He is also

Heb. 10, 29.

called the Spirit of grace, as when he says again, And hath done despite to the Spirit of grace. And by many other suchlike titles is He named And thou heardest in the foregoing

v. Cat xvi 28
Ps 143, 10 51, 12 Sept.

Lecture, that in the Psalms, He is called at one time the good Spirit, and at another the princely Spirit; and in Esaias

He was styled the Spirit of wisdom, and of understanding, and of counsel, and of might, and of knowledge, and of godliness, and of the fear of God. By all which Scriptures both those before and those now alleged, it is established, that though the titles of the Holy Ghost be different, He is one and the same; living and subsisting, and always present *ὑφεστὼς* together with the Father and the Son; not uttered or breathed *συμπαρόν.* by the mouth and lips of the Father and the Son, nor dispersed into the air, but having a real substance, speaking *ἐνυπόστατον.* Himself, and working, and dispensing, and sanctifying; the saving dispensation which is to usward from the Father and the Son and the Holy Ghost, being consistent and harmo- *οἰκονομίας.* nious and one, as we have also said before. For I wish you to keep in mind those things which were lately spoken, and to know clearly that there is not one spirit in the Law and the Prophets, and another in the Gospels and Apostles; but that it is One and the Self-same Spirit, which both under the Old and under the New Testament, spake the divine Scriptures.

6. This is the Holy Ghost, who came upon the Holy Virgin (4.) Mary; for since He who was born was Christ the Onlybegotten, the *power of the Highest overshadowed her*, and the Luke 1, *Holy Ghost coming upon her*, sanctified her, that she might 35, be able to receive Him, *by whom all things were made* John 1, I have no need of using many words for thee to learn that 3. that birth was without defilement or taint, for thou hast learned it. It is Gabriel who says to her, I am the herald of what shall be done, but I have no part in it. Though an Archangel, I know mine place; and though I joyfully bid thee All hail, yet how thou shalt bring forth, is not of any grace of mine. *The Holy Ghost shall come upon thee,* Luke 1, *and the power of the Highest shall overshadow thee; there-* 35. *fore also that Holy Thing which shall be born of thee shall be called the Son of God.*

7. This Holy Spirit wrought in Elisabeth; for He has in knowledge not virgins only, but acknowledges matrons also, so that their marriage be lawful. And Elisabeth was filled with the Holy Ghost, and prophesied; and that noble handmaiden says of her own Lord, *And whence is this to me, that* Luke 1, *the Mother of my Lord should come to me?* For Elisabeth 43. counted herself blessed. Filled with this Holy Spirit, Zacharias

also, the father of John, prophesied, telling how many good things the Only-begotten should procure, and that John should be His harbinger through baptism. By this Holy Ghost also it was revealed to just Symeon, that he should not see death, till he had seen the Lord's Christ; and he received Him in his arms, and bore clear testimony in the Temple concerning Him.

8. But John moreover, who had been filled with the Holy Ghost from his mother's womb, was for this cause sanctified, that he might baptize the Lord; not giving the Spirit himself, but preaching glad tidings of Him who gives the Spirit. For he says, *I indeed baptize you with water to repentance, but He that cometh after me is mightier than I,* and the rest; *He shall baptize you with the Holy Ghost and with fire.* With fire, wherefore? because the descent of the Holy Ghost was in fiery tongues; concerning which the Lord says joyfully, *I am come to send fire on the earth; and what will I, if it be already kindled?*

(5.) 9. This Holy Ghost descended on the Lord at His baptism, that the dignity of Him who was baptized might not be hidden; as John says, *But He which sent me to baptize with water, the same said unto me, Upon whomsoever thou shalt see the Spirit descending and remaining upon Him, the same is He which baptizeth with the Holy Ghost.* But see what saith the Gospel; *the heavens were opened;* they were opened because of the dignity of Him who descended; for, *lo,* he says, *the heavens were opened, and he saw the Spirit of God descending like a dove, and lighting upon Him* : that is, with voluntary motion in His descent. For it behoved, as some have interpreted, that the handsel and first-fruits of the Holy Spirit in the baptized, should be given to the manhood of the Saviour, who confers such grace. But perhaps He came down in the form of a dove, as some say, to exhibit a figure of one who is pure and innocent and undefiled, and also helps in the prayers for the children she has begotten, and for forgiveness of sins; as it was emblematically foretold that Christ should be thus manifested in the appearance of His eyes; for in the Canticles she cries concerning the Bridegroom, and says, *His eyes are as the eyes of doves by the rivers of water.*

10. Of this dove, the dove of Noe, according to some, was in part a figure. For as in his time by means of wood and of water salvation came to men, and the beginning of a new creation, and the dove returned to him towards evening with an olive branch, thus, say they, the Holy Ghost also descended upon the true Noe, the Author of the second birth, who draws together into one the wills of all nations, of whom the various sorts of animals in the ark were a figure:—Him at whose presence the spiritual wolves feed with the lambs, in whose Church the calf, and the lion, and the ox, feed in the same pasture, as we behold to this day the rulers of the world guided and taught by Churchmen. The spiritual dove therefore, as some interpret, came down at the season of His baptism, that He might show that it is He who by the wood of the Cross saves them who believe, who should at eventide through His death vouchsafe to them salvation. προαιρέ-
σεις.

ἐκκλη-
σιαστι-
κῶν.

11. And of these things perhaps there may be another (6.) exposition; and now too we ought to hear the words of the Saviour Himself concerning the Holy Ghost. For He says, *Except a man be born of water and of the Spirit, he cannot* John 3, *enter into the kingdom of God.* And because this grace is 5. from the Father, He says, *How much more shall your heavenly* Luke 11, *Father give the Holy Spirit to them that ask Him.* And 13. because we ought to worship God in the Spirit, He says, *But the hour cometh and now is, when the true worshippers* John 4, *shall worship the Father in spirit and in truth; for the* 23. *Father seeketh such to worship Him. God is a Spirit; and they that worship Him must worship Him in spirit and in truth.* And again, *But if I cast out devils by the Spirit of* Mat. 12, *God; and* immediately afterwards, *Wherefore I say unto you,* 28. *All manner of sin and blasphemy shall be forgiven unto men;* v. 31. *but the blasphemy against the Holy Ghost shall not be forgiven. And whosoever speaketh a word against the Son of man, it shall be forgiven him; but whosoever speaketh a word against the Holy Ghost, it shall not be forgiven him, neither in this world, neither in the world to come.* And again He says, *And I will pray the Father, and He shall give you another* John 14, *Comforter, that He may be with you for ever, the Spirit of* 16. *Truth; whom the world cannot receive, because it seeth Him* μένῃ, *not, neither knoweth Him; but ye know Him, for He dwelleth* abide, ἣ Cyr. rec. text.

226 *Texts from the New Testament concerning the Holy Ghost.*

LECT. XVII.
ver. 25.

with you, and shall be in you. And again He says, *These things have I spoken unto you being yet present with you. But the Comforter, which is the Holy Ghost, whom the Father will send in My name, He shall teach you all things, and bring all things to your remembrance, whatsoever I have said unto you.*

Ib. 15, 26.

And again He says, *But when the Comforter is come, whom I will send unto you from the Father, even the Spirit of Truth, which proceedeth from the Father, He shall testify of Me.*

Ib. 16, 7

And again the Saviour says, *For if I go not away, the Comforter will not come unto you. . . . . And when He is come, He will reprove the world of sin, of righteousness, and of judgment;*

ver. 12.

and afterwards again, *I have yet many things to say unto you, but ye cannot bear them yet. Howbeit, when He the Spirit of Truth is come, He will guide you into all truth; for He shall not speak of Himself; but whatsoever He shall hear that shall He speak, and He will show you things to come. He shall glorify Me, for He shall receive of Mine, and shall show it unto you. All things that the Father hath are mine; therefore said I, That He shall take of Mine, and shall show it unto you.* I have read to thee now what the Only-begotten Himself has uttered, that thou mayest not give heed to human words.

(7.) 12. The fellowship of this Holy Spirit He bestowed on the

John 20, 22

Apostles; for it is written, *And when He had said this, He breathed on them, and saith unto them, Receive ye the Holy Ghost; whose soever sins ye remit, they are remitted unto them; and whose soever sins ye retain, they are retained.*

vid. supr. xiv. 10.

This was the second time He breathed, (His first breath having been stifled by wilful sins;) that the Scripture might

Nahum 2, 1. Sept

be fulfilled, *He went up breathing upon thy face, and delivering thee from affliction.* But whence went He up? From Hades; for thus the Gospel relates, that after His resurrection then He breathed on them. But though He bestowed His grace then, He was to lavish it yet more bountifully; and He says to them, "I truly am ready to give it even now, but the vessel cannot yet hold it; for a while therefore receive ye grace, according as ye can bear it; but look forward for even more;

Luke 24, 39.

but tarry ye in the city of Jerusalem, until ye be invested with power from on high. Receive it in part now; then, ye shall bear it in its fulness. For he who receives often, possesses the gift but in part; but he who is invested, is completely enfolded by his robe. "Fear not," He says, "the weapons and darts of the devil; for ye bear with you the power of the Holy Ghost." But remember that the Holy Ghost is not divided, but the grace which is by Him.

13. Jesus therefore went up into heaven, and fulfilled the promise. For He said to them, *I will pray the Father, and He shall give you another Comforter.* They were accordingly sitting, looking for the coming of the Holy Ghost; and when *the day of Pentecost was fully come,* here, in this city of Jerusalem,—(for this honour also belongs to us; and we speak not of good which has happened among others, but of that which has been vouchsafed among ourselves,)—on the day of Pentecost, I say, they were sitting, and the Comforter came down from heaven, the Guardian and Sanctifier of the Church, the Ruler of souls, the Pilot of the tempest-tossed, the Enlightener of the lost, who presides in the combat, and crowns the victors. _{John 14, 16. Acts 2, 1.}

14. But he came down to invest the Apostles with power, and to baptize them; for the Lord says, *ye shall be baptized with the Holy Ghost not many days hence.* His grace is not in part, but His power is in full perfection; for as he who plunges into the waters and is baptized is encompassed on all sides by the waters, so were they also baptized completely by the Holy Ghost. The water however envelopes but outwardly, but the Spirit baptizes also the soul within, and that perfectly. And wherefore wonderest thou? Take an example from matter; poor indeed and common, yet useful for the simpler sort. If the fire penetrating the mass of the iron makes the whole of it fire, so that what was cold becomes burning and what was black is made bright,—if fire which is a body thus penetrates and works without hindrance in iron which is also a body, why wonder that the Holy Ghost enters into the very inmost recesses of the soul? (8.) Ib. 1, 5.

15. And lest men should be ignorant of the greatness of that mighty gift, which was coming down to them, there sounded as it were a heavenly trumpet. For *suddenly there came a sound from heaven as of a rushing mighty wind,* signifying the presence of Him who was to grant unto men, to seize with violence the kingdom of God; that both their Ib 2, 2. &c.

LECT.
XVII
νοητοῦ.

eyes might see the fiery tongues, and their ears hear the sound. *And it filled all the house where they were sitting;* for the house became the vessel of the spiritual water; as the disciples sat within, the whole house was filled. Thus they were entirely baptized according to the promise, invested soul and body with a divine and saving garment. *And there appeared unto them cloven tongues like as of fire, and it sat upon each of them; and they were all filled with the Holy Ghost.* They partook of fire, not of burning but of saving fire; of fire which consumes the thorns of sins, and gives lustre to the soul. This is now coming upon you also, and that, to strip away and devour your sins which are like thorns, and to brighten that precious possession of your souls, and to give you grace; for He gave it then to the Apostles. And He sat upon them in the form of fiery tongues, that by fiery tongues their heads might be encircled with new and spiritual diadems. The fiery sword barred of old the gates of Paradise; the fiery tongue which brought salvation restored the gift.

(9.)
Acts 2, 4.

16. *And they began to speak with other tongues, as the Spirit gave them utterance.* The Galilean Peter or Andrew spoke Persian or Median. John and the rest of the Apostles spake every tongue to those of Gentile extraction; (for it has not arisen in our time that multitudes of strangers assemble here from all quarters, but they have done so since that time.) What teacher can be found so great as to teach men things at once which they have not learned? So many years are they in learning by grammar and the other arts to speak well Greek only; nor do all speak even this equally well; the Rhetorician perhaps succeeds in it, and the Grammarian sometimes not, and the Grammarian is ignorant of the subjects of philosophy. But the Holy Spirit taught the Apostles many languages at once, languages which all their life long they had not known. This is in truth vast wisdom, this is power divine. What a contrast is their long ignorance in time past, and their sudden utterance of these divers and strange languages!

17. The multitude of the hearers was confounded;—it was a second confusion, in the room of that first evil one at Babylon. For in that confusion of tongues, there was division of

purpose, because their feelings were ungodly; but here minds were restored and united, because the object of interest was godly. The means of falling were the means of recovery. Wherefore they marvelled, saying, *How hear we them speaking?* No marvel if ye be ignorant; for even Nicodemus was ignorant of the coming of the Spirit, and to him it was said, *The Spirit breatheth where it listeth, and thou hearest the* John 3, *voice thereof, but canst not tell whence it cometh, and* 8. *whither it goeth;* but if even though hearing His voice, I know not whence He cometh, how can I explain, what ὑπόστα-He is in substance? σιν.

18. *But others mocking said, These men are full of new* (10.) *wine,* and they spoke truly though in mockery. For in truth the wine was new, even the grace of the New Testament; but this new wine was from the spiritual Vine, which had νοητῆς. oftentimes ere this borne fruit in Prophets, and had budded in the New Testament. For as in things sensible, the vine ever remains the same, but bears new fruits in its seasons, so also the self-same Spirit continuing what it is, as it had often wrought in Prophets, now manifested a new and marvellous work. For though His grace had been extended on the Fathers also, yet it came at this time exuberantly; for before they but partook of the Holy Ghost, but now they were baptized wholly.

19. But Peter who had the Holy Ghost, and who knew what he possessed, says, " *Men of Israel,* ye who preach Joel, Acts 2, but know not the things which are written, *these men are not* 15. &c. *drunken as ye suppose.* Drunken they are, not however as ye suppose, but according to that which is written, *They* Ps 36, 8. *shall be drunken with the fatness of thy house; and thou* Sept. *shalt make them drink of the river of thy pleasures.* They are drunken, yet sober; their drunkenness is a death to sin and a quickening of heart, a drunkenness contrary to that of the body; for this last even causes forgetfulness of what was known, but that even bestows the knowledge of what was not known. They are drunken, for they have drunk the wine of the spiritual vine, which says, *I am the vine and ye are* νοητῆς. *the branches.* But if ye are not persuaded by me, understand John 15, what I tell you from the very time of the day; for it is the 5 third hour of the day. For He who, as Mark relates, was

230   *St Peter's speech at Pentecost.*

LECT XVII. crucified at the third hour, has now at the third hour sent down His grace. For His grace is not other than the Spirit's grace, but He who was then crucified, who also gave this promise, has now made good that which He promised. And if ye would receive a testimony also of this, Listen," he says: "*But this is that which was spoken by the prophet Joel; And it shall come to pass in the last days, saith God, I will pour of My Spirit*"—(and this word, *I will pour*, implied

John 3, 34. a rich gift; *for God giveth not the Spirit by measure, for the Father loveth the Son, and hath given all things into His hand;* and He has given Him the power also of bestowing the grace of the All-holy Spirit on whomsoever He will;) —*I will pour of My Spirit upon all flesh, and your sons and your daughters shall prophesy;* and afterwards, *And on My servants and on My handmaidens I will pour out in those days of My Spirit, and they shall prophesy.*" The Holy Ghost is no respecter of persons; for He seeks not dignities, but piety of soul. Let not either the rich be puffed up, or the poor dejected, but only let each prepare himself for the reception of the Heavenly gift.

(11.) 20. We have said much to-day, and perchance you are weary of listening; yet more still remains. And in truth for the doctrine of the Holy Ghost there were need of a third lecture; and of many besides. But we must have your indulgence on both points. For as the Holy Festival of Easter is at hand, we have this day lengthened our discourse; yet we had not room to bring before you all the testimonies from the New Testament, which we ought. For much is still to come from the Acts of the Apostles, in which the grace of the Holy Ghost wrought mightily in Peter and in all the Apostles together; much also from the Catholic Epistles, and the fourteen Epistles of Paul; out of all which we will now endeavour to gather a few, like flowers from a large meadow, merely by way of remembrance.

βούλησις. 21. For in the power of the Holy Ghost, by the will of Father and Son, Peter standing with the Eleven, and lifting
Is. 40, 9. Sept. up his voice, (according to the text, *Lift up thy voice with strength, thou that bringest good tidings to Jerusalem,*)
νοητῷ. captured in the spiritual net of his words, *about three thousand souls.* So great was the grace which wrought in all the

Apostles together, that, out of the Jews, the crucifiers of
Christ, this great number believed, and were baptized in the
Name of Christ, and *continued steadfastly in the Apostles'* Acts 2,
doctrine and in prayers. And again in the same power of the ⁴².
Holy Ghost, Peter and John as they went up into the Temple
at the hour of prayer, which was the ninth hour, in the Name
of Jesus healed the lame man at the Beautiful gate, who had
so been from his mother's womb for forty years; that it might
be fulfilled which was spoken, *Then shall the lame man leap* Is. 35, 6.
as an hart. And thus, as they swept into the spiritual πνευμα-
meshes of their doctrine five thousand believers at once, so τικῇ.
they confuted the bewildered rulers of the people and chief
priests, and that, not by their own wisdom, for *they were* Acts 4,
unlearned and ignorant men, but by the mighty power of the ¹³.
Holy Ghost; for it is written, *Then Peter filled with the Holy* Acts 4, 8.
Ghost said to them. So great also was the grace of the Holy
Ghost, which wrought by means of the Twelve Apostles in
them who believed, that *they were of one heart and of one soul,* v. 32.
and their enjoyment of their goods was common, the possessors
piously offering the prices of their possession, and no one
among them wanting aught; while Ananias and Sapphira,
who attempted to lie to the Holy Ghost, underwent their
befitting punishment.

22. *And by the hands of the Apostles were many signs and* Acts 5,
wonders wrought among the people. And such spiritual grace ¹². &c.
was shed around the Apostles, that gentle as they were, they πνευμα-
were the objects of dread; for *of the rest durst no man join* τικῇ.
himself to them; but the people magnified them. And *multitudes were added of them who believed in the Lord, both of
men and women;* and the streets were filled with sick on
beds and couches, that at least *the shadow of Peter, passing
by, might overshadow some of them.* And *the multitude also
of the cities round about came* unto this holy Jerusalem,
*bringing sick folks, and them which were vexed with unclean
spirits, who were healed every one* in this might of the Holy
Ghost.

23. Again, when the Twelve Apostles, after having been (12.)
cast into prison by the chief priests for preaching Christ, and
having been marvellously delivered from it at night by an
Angel, were brought to the judgment hall to them out of the

Lect. XVII

Acts 5, 32 &c.

Temple, they fearlessly rebuked them, in their discourse to them concerning Christ. And when they added this, that *God hath given His Holy Spirit to them that obey Him*, and had been beaten, they went their way rejoicing, and ceased not to *teach and preach Christ Jesus*.

24. Nor in the Twelve Apostles only wrought the grace of the Holy Ghost, but also in the first-born children of this once barren Church, I mean the seven Deacons; for these

Acts 6, 3.

also were chosen, as it is written, being *full of the Holy Ghost and of wisdom*. Of whom Stephen, rightly so named, the first-fruits of the Martyrs, a man *full of faith and of the Holy Ghost, did great wonders and miracles among the people*, and vanquished those who disputed with him; *for they were not able to resist the wisdom and the Spirit by which he spake*. And when he was maliciously accused and brought to the judgment hall, he was radiant with angelic effulgence; for *all they who sat in the council, looking steadfastly on him, saw his face, as it had been the face of an Angel*. And having by his wise defence confuted the Jews,

Acts 7, 51 &c

those *stiffnecked men, uncircumcised in heart and ears, ever resisting the Holy Ghost*, he beheld *the heavens opened*, and saw *the Son of Man standing on the right hand of God*. He saw Him, not by his own power, but, as the Divine Scripture says, *being full of the Holy Ghost, he looked up steadfastly into heaven, and saw the glory of God, and Jesus standing on the right hand of God*.

25. In the same power of the Holy Ghost, and in the Name

Acts 8, 5. &c

of Christ, Philip at one time drove away in the city of Samaria the unclean spirits, which cried out with a loud voice; and he healed the palsied and the lame, and brought to Christ great multitudes of believers. To whom Peter and John came down, and imparted with prayer, and the laying on of hands, the fellowship of the Holy Ghost, from which Simon Magus alone was declared an alien, and that justly. And at another time Philip was called by an Angel of the Lord in the way, for the sake of that most godly Ethiopian Eunuch, and heard distinctly the Spirit Himself, saying, *Go near, and join thyself to this chariot*. He instructed the Eunuch, and baptized him, and so having sent into Ethiopia a

Ps 68, 31.

herald of Christ, according as it is written, *Ethiopia shall soon* stretch out her hands unto God, he was caught away by the Angel, and preached the Gospel in the cities in succession.

26. With this spirit was Paul also filled after his calling (13) by our Lord Jesus Christ. Let godly Ananias come as a witness to what we say, he who in Damascus said to him, *The Lord, even Jesus who appeared to thee by the way as thou camest, hath sent me, that thou mightest receive thy sight, and be filled with the Holy Ghost.* And He straightway, mightily working, changed the blindness of Paul's eyes into restored sight; and having vouchsafed His seal unto his soul, made him *a chosen vessel* to *bear the Name* of the Lord who had appeared to him, *before kings and the children of Israel,* and out of the former persecutor, fashioned an ambassador and good servant,—one, who *from Jerusalem, round about unto Illyricum, fully preached the Gospel of Christ,* and instructed even imperial Rome, and carried the earnestness of his preaching as far as Spain, undergoing conflicts innumerable, and performing signs and wonders. Of him for the present enough.

Acts 9, 17

Rom 15, 19.

27. In the power of the same Holy Spirit, Peter also, the chief of the Apostles, and the bearer of the keys of the kingdom of heaven, healed Æneas the paralytic in the Name of Christ at Lydda, which is now Diospolis, and at Joppa raised from the dead the charitable Tabitha. And being on the housetop in a trance, he saw heaven opened, and the vessel like a sheet let down, full of beasts of every shape and sort, and learnt plainly through this to call no man common or unclean, though he should be of the Greeks. And when he was sent for by Cornelius, he heard clearly the Holy Ghost Himself saying, *Behold, men seek thee; arise therefore, and get thee down, and go with them, doubting nothing; for I have sent them.* And that it might be fully ascertained that those of the Gentiles also who believe are made partakers of the Holy Ghost, the Scripture speaks thus concerning Cornelius and them who were with him, when Peter was come to Cesarea, and taught the things concerning Christ; *While Peter yet spake these words, the Holy Ghost fell on all them which heard the word, and they of the circumcision which believed were astonished, as many as came with Peter, because that on the Gentiles also was poured the gift of the Holy Ghost.*

πρωτοστάτη, vid sup. Catech.

ii. 19. xi 3.

Acts 10.

Lect. XVII.	28. And when in Antioch, the most renowned city of Syria, the preaching of Christ took effect, Barnabas was sent hence as far as Antioch to help on the good work, being
Acts 11, 24.	*a good man, and full of the Holy Ghost, and of faith;* who seeing a great harvest of believers in Christ, brought Paul from Tarsus to Antioch, as his fellow-combatant. And when by them crowds were instructed and assembled in the Church,
v. 26.	*it came to pass that the disciples were called Christians first in Antioch;* the Holy Ghost, I consider, bestowing on the believers that new Name, which had been promised before by the Lord. And the grace of the Spirit being shed forth by God more abundantly in Antioch, there were there prophets
Acts 13, 3.	and teachers, with whom was Agabus also. And *as they ministered to the Lord and fasted, the Holy Ghost said, Separate Me Barnabas and Saul for the work whereunto I have called them.* And after the laying on of hands, *they were sent forth by the Holy Ghost.* Now it is manifest, that the Spirit which speaks and sends, is a living Spirit, sub-
ὑφεστώς	sisting, and effectual, as we have said.
(14.)	29. This Holy Spirit, who in unison with Father and Son, has established the New Testament in the Church Catholic, has set us free from the grievous burdens of the law,—those ordinances, I mean, concerning things common and unclean, the meats, and sabbaths, and new moons, and circumcision, and sprinklings, and sacrifices; which were given for a
Heb. 10, 1.	season, and *had the shadow of good things to come,* but which when the truth had come, were rightly abrogated. For when Paul and Barnabas were sent to the Apostles, because of the question moved at Antioch by them who said that it was necessary to be circumcised and to keep the customs of Moses, the Apostles who were here at Jerusalem by a written Epistle set free the whole world from all legal and typical observances; yet they attributed not to them- selves the full authority in this matter, but acknowledge in
Acts 15, 28. 29.	their Epistle, writing thus, *For it hath seemed good unto the Holy Ghost and to us to lay upon you no greater burden than these necessary things; that ye abstain from meats offered to idols, and from blood, and from things strangled, and from fornication;* showing evidently by what they wrote, that though the writing was by the hands of men, even the

Apostles, yet the decree was universal because of the Holy οἰκουμε-
Ghost: which decree Paul and Barnabas took and confirmed νικόν.
through the universal Church.   οἰκουμέ-
                                  νην.

30. And now, having proceeded thus far, I must ask (15.)
indulgence from your love, or rather from the Spirit who
dwelt in Paul, if I be not able to rehearse every thing, by
reason of my own weakness, and your weariness who listen.
For when shall I in terms suitable declare the marvellous
deeds wrought by the operation of the Holy Ghost in the
Name of Christ? Those wrought in Cyprus upon Elymas the
sorcerer, and in Lystra at the healing of the cripple, and
those done in Cilicia and Phrygia and Galatia and Mysia
and Macedonia? or those at Philippi; the preaching, I
mean, and the driving out of the unclean spirit in the Name
of Christ; and the salvation by baptism of the jailer with his
whole house at night after the earthquake? or the events at
Thessalonica; or the address at Areopagus in the midst of the
Athenians; or the instructions at Corinth, and in all Achaia?
How shall I worthily recount the mighty deeds which at
Ephesus by the hands of Paul, were wrought by the Holy
Ghost? whom they of that city knew not before, but came Acts 19,
to know Him by the doctrine of Paul; and they when Paul[1.]
had laid his hands on them, and the Holy Ghost had come
upon them, *spake with other tongues, and prophesied.* And
so great spiritual grace was upon him, that not only his
touch wrought cures, but even *handkerchiefs and napkins,* v. 12.
brought from his body, healed diseases, and scared away the
spirits of evil; and moreover *they also who used curious* v. 19.
*arts brought their books together, and burned them before
all men.*

31. I pass by the work wrought at Troas on Eutychus, who
*sinking down with sleep fell down from the third loft, and
was taken up dead;* yet was saved alive by Paul. I also
pass by the prophecy addressed to the Elders of Ephesus τὰ[τῆς?]
assembled at Miletus, in which he openly said, *That the* προφη-
                                                          τείας
Holy Ghost witnesseth in every city, saying,—and the rest; for
by saying, *in every city,* Paul made manifest that the marvellous works done by him in every city, were of the operative
power of the Holy Ghost, at the will of God, and in the νεύματι.
Name of Christ who spake in him. By the power of this

LECT. XVII

Holy Ghost, the same Paul hasted to this holy city Jerusalem, and this, though Agabus by the same spirit foretold what should befall him; and he spoke to the multitudes with confidence, telling them concerning Christ. And when brought to Cesarea, and encompassed by the seats of judges, Paul at one time before Felix, and at another before Festus the governor and King Agrippa, obtained of the Holy Ghost grace so great, and of such overcoming wisdom, that at last Agrippa himself the king of the Jews said, *Almost thou persuadest me to be a Christian.* This Holy Spirit granted to Paul, when he was in the island of Melita also, to receive no harm when bitten by the viper, and to effect divers cures on the diseased. This Holy Spirit guided him, the persecutor of old, even as far as imperial Rome, a herald of Christ; and there he persuaded many of the Jews to believe in Christ, and to them who gainsaid he said plainly, *Well spake the Holy Ghost by Esaias the Prophet, saying unto your fathers,* and the rest.

Acts 28, 25.

32. And that Paul was full of the Holy Ghost, and his fellow Apostles, and they who after them have believed in Father, Son, and Holy Ghost, hear his own plain words in his Epistles; *And my speech,* he says, *and my preaching was not with enticing words of man's wisdom, but with demonstration of the Spirit and of power.* And again, *Who hath also sealed us, and given us the earnest of the Spirit.* And again, *He that raised up Jesus from the dead shall also quicken your mortal bodies by His Spirit which dwelleth in you.* And again, writing to Timothy, *That good thing which was committed to thee keep by the Holy Ghost which is given to us.*

1 Cor. 2, 4.

2 Cor. 1, 22.

Rom. 8, 11.

2 Tim 1, 14 δο-θέντος, Cyr ἐνοι-κοῦντος ἐν, dwelling in, rec text (16.)

33. And that the Holy Ghost subsists, and lives, and speaks, and foretells, I have often said already, and Paul writes it plainly to Timothy. *Now the Spirit speaketh expressly, that in the latter times some shall depart from the faith,*—which we see in the divisions not only of former times but of our own; so motley and diversified are the errors of the heretics. And again the same Paul says, *Which in other ages was not made known unto the sons of men, as it is now revealed unto the Holy Apostles and Prophets by the Spirit.* And again, *Wherefore, as the Holy Ghost saith;* and again,

1 Tim. 4, 1.

Eph 3, 5.

Heb. 3, 7.

The Holy Ghost also witnesseth to us. And again he calls [Heb. 10, 15.] unto the champions of righteousness, saying, *And take the* [Eph 6, 17.] *helmet of salvation, and the sword of the Spirit, which is the Word of God, by all prayer and supplication.* And again, *And be not drunk with wine, wherein is excess; but be filled* [Ib 5, 18. 19.] *with the Spirit, speaking to yourselves in psalms, and hymns, and spiritual songs.* And again, *The grace of our Lord* [2 Cor. 13, 14.] *Jesus Christ, and the love of God, and the communion of the Holy Ghost.*

34. By all these proofs, and by more which have been passed over, is the personal, and hallowing, and effectual ἐνυπό- power of the Holy Ghost established in them of understand- στατος. ing; for the time would fail my discourse, did I set about alleging what yet remains from the fourteen Epistles of Paul, wherein he has taught with such variety, completeness, and piety. And to the power of the Holy Ghost it must belong, to grant to us forgiveness for our deficiencies by reason of the scantiness of the time, and upon you the hearers to impress the more perfect knowledge of what yet remains; while from the frequent reading of the sacred Scriptures you who are diligent come to understand these things, and by this time hold more steadfastly, both from those present Lectures, and what has before been told you, the Faith in the "One God the Father Almighty; and in our Lord Jesus Christ, His Only-begotten Son; and in the Holy Ghost the Comforter." Though the word itself, and the title of Spirit, is used widely in the sacred Scriptures,—for it is said of the Father, *God is a Spirit,* [John 4, 24.] as it is written in the Gospel according to John; and of the Son, *A Spirit before our face, Christ the Lord;* and of the [Lam 4, 20.] Holy Ghost, *the Comforter, the Holy Ghost,* as was said;—yet the very arrangement of articles observed in the Faith, if religiously understood, disproves the error of Sabellius also. Now therefore return we to the point which now presses and is profitable to you.

35. Beware lest by any means thou come to the dispensers (17.) of Baptism, like Simon, in pretence, thy heart the while not seeking the truth. It is ours to warn, but it is thine to secure thyself. If *by faith thou standest,* blessed art thou; if thou [Rom. 11, 20.] hast fallen by unbelief, from this day forward cast away thine unbelief, and take up an undoubting faith. For, at the season

of baptism, when thou goest to the Bishops, or Presbyters, or Deacons,—(for its grace is every where, in villages and in cities, on them of low as on them of high degree, on bondsmen and on freemen, for this grace is not of men, but the gift is from God through men,)—approach the Minister of Baptism, but approaching, think not of the face of him thou seest, but remember that Holy Ghost of whom we are now speaking. For He is present in readiness to seal thy soul, and He shall give thee that Seal at which evil spirits tremble,
Eph. 1, 13. a heavenly and sacred seal, as also it is written, *In whom also after that ye believed, ye were sealed with the Holy Spirit of promise.*

36. Yet He tries the soul. He casts not pearls before
vid. sup. Introd. Lect. 2. swine; if thou pretend, though men baptized thee, the Holy Spirit will not. But if thou approach with faith, while men minister outwardly, the Holy Ghost bestows that which is unseen. Thou art coming to a great trial, to a great muster, in that one hour, which if thou throw away, thy disaster is irretrievable; but if thou be counted worthy of grace, thy soul will be illuminated, thou wilt receive a might which thou hadst not, thou wilt receive weapons terrible to the evil spirits; and if thou cast not away thine arms, but keep the Seal upon thy soul, no evil spirit will approach thee; for he will be cowed; for by the Spirit of God are the evil spirits cast out.

37. If thou believe, thou shalt not only receive remission of
(18.) sins, but do also things which pass man's power. And mayest thou be worthy of the gift of prophecy also! For thou shalt receive grace according to the measure of thy capacity and not of my words; for I may possibly speak of but small things, yet thou mayest receive greater. For faith is a wide field. All thy life long will the Comforter abide with thee; He will care for thee, as for his own soldier, concerning thy goings out, and thy comings in, and thy plotting foes. And He will give gifts of grace of every kind, if thou grieve Him not by sin;
Eph 4, 30. for it is written, *And grieve not the Holy Spirit of God, whereby ye have been sealed unto the day of redemption.* What then, beloved, is it to preserve grace? Be ye ready to receive grace, and when ye have received it, cast it not away.

38. And may the God of All, who spake by the Holy Ghost through the prophets, who sent Him forth upon the Apostles on the day of Pentecost, in this place send Him forth at this time also upon you; and by Him keep us also, imparting His benefit in common to all of us, so that we may ever render up the fruits of the Holy Ghost, *love, joy, peace, long-suffering, gentleness, goodness, faith, meekness, temperance,* in Christ Jesus our Lord :—By whom and with whom, together with the Holy Ghost, be glory to the Father, both now, and ever, and for ever and ever. Amen.

Gal. 5, 22. 23.

LECTURE XVIII.

ON THE RESURRECTION OF THE FLESH, THE CATHOLIC CHURCH,
AND THE LIFE EVERLASTING.

EZEKIEL xxxvii. 1.

The hand of the Lord was upon me, and carried me out in the Spirit of the Lord, and set me down in the midst of the valley which was full of bones.

LECT. XVIII.

1. THE root of all good works is the hope of the Resurrection; for the expectation of recompence nerves the soul to good works. For labourers of every kind are ready to undergo toils, if they see their reward in prospect; but when men weary themselves for nought, their heart as well as their body sinks early. The soldier who expects a prize is ready for war, but no one is forward to die for a king who is indifferent about those who serve under him, and bestows no honours on their toils. In like manner every soul believing in the Resurrection, is, as is natural, careful of itself; but, disbelieving it, abandons itself to perdition. He who believes that his body shall remain to be raised again, is careful of his robe, and defiles it not with fornication; but he who disbelieves the Resurrection, gives himself to fornication, and misuses his own body, as though it were not his own. Faith therefore in the Resurrection of the dead, is a great doctrine and lesson of the Holy Catholic Church; a great and most necessary point gainsaid by many, but surely warranted by the truth. Greeks contradict it, Samaritans disbelieve it, heretics disparage it; the contradiction is manifold, but the truth is uniform.

v. Cat. iv 2.

2. Now Greeks and Samaritans together reason with us thus. The dead man falls, and moulders away, and is all

turned into worms; and the worms perish also; so great is the decay and destruction, which is the portion of the body; how then is it to be raised? The shipwrecked are devoured by fishes, which are themselves devoured. Of them who fight with wild beasts, the very bones are ground to powder and consumed by bears and lions. Vultures and ravens feed on the flesh of the unburied dead, and then fly abroad over all the world; from what places then is the body brought together? For of the fowls who have devoured it, some may chance to die in India, some in Persia, some in the land of the Goths; other men again are consumed by fire, and their very ashes scattered by the rain or wind; whence is the body brought together again?

3. To thee, poor feeble man, India is far from the land of (2) the Goths, and Spain from Persia; but to God who holds the whole *earth in the hollow of His hand*, all things are near at Isa 10, hand. Impute not then weakness to God, from a comparison 12 of thy feebleness, but rather dwell on His power. Moreover, does the sun, a small work of God, by one glance of his beams give warmth to the whole world; does the atmosphere, which God has made, encompass all things in the world; and is God then, who is the Creator both of the sun, and of the atmosphere, removed very far off from the earth? Imagine a mixture of seed of different plants; (for as thou art weak as concerning the faith, the examples which I allege are such also;) and that these different seeds are contained in thy single hand; is it then to thee who art a man, a difficult or an easy matter to distinguish what is in thine hand, and to bring each seed together according to its nature, and to assign it to its own kind? Canst thou then distinguish between things in thine hand, and cannot God distinguish between the things in His hand, and assign them their proper place? Consider what I say; is it not impious to deny it?

4. Further, attend to the very principle of justice, and consider with thyself. Thou hast different sorts of servants: and some are good and some bad; thou honourest therefore the good, and smitest the bad And if thou art a judge, to the good thou awardest praise, and to the transgressors, punishment. Is then justice by thee observed a mortal man;

R

and with God, who is the ever-enduring King of all, is there no retributive justice? To deny it is impious. For consider what I say. Many murderers die in their beds unpunished; where then is the righteousness of God? Yea, ofttimes a murderer guilty of fifty murders, is beheaded once; how then shall he suffer punishment for the forty and nine? Unless there is a judgment and a retribution after this world, thou chargest God with unrighteousness. Marvel not, however, because of the delay of judgment; no combatant is crowned or disgraced, till the contest is over, and no president of the games ever crowns men while yet striving, but he waits till all the combatants are finished, that then deciding between them, he may dispense the prizes and the chaplets. Even thus God also, so long as the strife in this world lasts, succours the just but partially, but afterwards He assigns to them their rewards fully.

(3) 5. But if, according to thee there is no resurrection of the dead, wherefore condemnest thou the violators of graves? For if the body perishes, and there is no resurrection to be hoped for, why does the violator of the tomb undergo punishment? Thou seest that though thou deny the resurrection with thy lips, there yet abides with thee an indestructible instinct in its behalf?

6. Further, does a tree after it has been cut down blossom again, and shall man not blossom again when cut down? And does the corn sown and reaped remain to the threshing floor, and shall man when reaped from this world not remain for the threshing? And do shoots of vine or other trees, when clean cut off and transplanted, come to life and bear fruit; and shall man then, for whose sake all these are, fall into the earth and not rise again? Comparing efforts, which is greater, to mould in the outset a statue which was not, or to recast it after the same model when fallen to pieces? Cannot God then, who created us out of nothing, raise us again, who are and who decay? But thou believest not what is written of the resurrection, being a Greek: then from the analogy of nature consider these matters, and understand them from what is seen at this day. Wheat, it may be, or some other kind of grain, is sown, and when it is cast, it dies and rots, and is henceforth useless for food. But that which has

rotted, springs up in verdure; and that which was cast small, springs up most beautiful. Now wheat was made for us, for wheat and all seeds were not created for themselves, but for our use; are things which were made for us quickened when they die, and do we for whom they were made, not spring up again after our death?

7. The season is now winter, as thou seest; the trees now stand as if they were dead: where are the leaves of the fig-tree? where are the clusters of the vine? These in winter time are dead, but in the spring green, and when the season is come, there is given them as it were a quickening from a state of death. For God, knowing thine unbelief, works a resurrection year by year in these visible things; that, beholding what happens to things inanimate, thou mayest believe concerning things animate and intelligent. Further, flies and bees are often drowned in water, yet after a while revive; and dormice, after remaining motionless during the winter, are $\mu\nu o\xi\hat{\omega}\nu$ $\gamma\acute{\epsilon}\nu\eta$. restored in the summer, (for to thy low thoughts like examples are offered,) and shall He who to irrational and despised creatures grants a supernatural life, not vouchsafe it to us, for whose sake He made them?

8. But the Greeks ask for a yet more evident resurrection, (4.) and say, that even if these creatures are raised, yet that they have not utterly mouldered away; and they require to see distinctly some creature rising again after complete decay. God knew men's unbelief, and provided for this purpose a bird, called a Phœnix[a]. This bird, as Clement writes, and as Clem Rom many more relate, the only one of its race, going to the land of Ep 1. the Egyptians at revolutions of five hundred years, shows[c] 25. forth the resurrection; and this, not in desert places, lest the mystery which comes to pass should remain unknown, but in a notable city[b], that men might even handle what they disbelieve. For it makes itself a nest of frankincense and myrrh and other spices, and entering into this when its years are fulfilled, it evidently dies and moulders away. Then from the mouldering flesh of the dead a worm springs, and this

---

[a] The existence of the Phœnix is believed by Tertullian, Epiphanius, &c as well as by Clement; as was till a comparatively late date the doctrine of four elements, or of the motion of the sun round the earth In like manner the existence of megatheria and ichthyosauri was not known till lately, nor the connection between magnetism and electricity.
[b] Heliopolis.

worm when grown large is transformed into a bird;—and do not disbelieve this, for thou seest the offspring of bees also fashioned thus out of worms, and from eggs which are most moist thou hast seen the wings and bones and sinews of birds issue. Afterwards this Phœnix, becoming fledged and a perfect Phœnix, as was the former one, soars up into the air such as it had died, showing forth to men a most evident resurrection from the dead. The Phœnix indeed is a wondrous bird, yet it is irrational, nor sings psalms to God; it flies abroad through the sky, but it knows not the Only-begotten Son of God. Is then a resurrection from the dead given unto this irrational creature which knows not its Maker, and to us who ascribe glory to God and keep His commandments, shall there no resurrection be granted?

(5.)   9. But since the sign of the Phœnix is remote and uncommon, and men disbelieve our resurrection still, take again the proof of this from what is seen every day. A hundred or two hundred years ago, we all, speakers and hearers, where were we? Know we not the groundwork of the substance of our bodies? Knowest thou not how from weak and shapeless and simple elements we have our beginning, and that from what is simple and weak is shaped the living man? and how that weak element being made flesh is changed into strong nerves, and bright eyes, and sensitive nose, and hearing ears, and speaking tongue, and beating heart, and busy hands, and swift feet, and into members of all kinds? and how weak elements become a shipwright, and a mason, and a master-builder, and a craftsman of various arts, and a soldier, and a ruler, and a lawgiver, and a king? Cannot God then, who has made us of rude materials, raise us up when we have fallen into decay? He who frames a body out of what is vile, cannot He raise it again when destroyed? And does not He who fashions that which is not, raise up that which is and is fallen?

10. Take further a manifest proof of the resurrection of the dead, witnessed month by month in the sky and its luminaries. The face of the moon vanishes completely, so that no part of it is any more seen, yet it fills again, and is restored to its former state; and for the perfect demonstration of the matter, the moon at certain revolutions of years suffering eclipse and

from the law of Moses. 245

becoming changed into blood, yet recovers its luminous body. God having provided this, that thou, O man, who art formed of blood, mightest not refuse credence to the resurrection of the dead, but mightest believe concerning thyself also what thou beholdest in respect of the moon. These arguments therefore use thou against the Greeks ; for with them who receive not what is written, fight thou with unwritten weapons, by reasonings only and demonstrations, for these men know not who Moses is, nor Esaias, nor the Gospels, nor Paul.

11. Turn now to the Samaritans, who, receiving the Law (6.) only, allow not the Prophets. To them the text just now read from Ezekiel appears of no force, for, as I said, they admit not the Prophets; whence then shall we persuade the Samaritans also? Let us go to the writings of the Law. Now God says to Moses, *I am the God of Abraham, and of Isaac, and* Exod 3, *of Jacob;* this must mean of what is and subsists. For $\overset{6}{\overset{}{\underset{}{ὑφεστη}}}$- if Abraham be dead, and Isaac, and Jacob, He is the God of κότων. what is nothing When did a king ever say, that he was the king of soldiers whom he had not ? When did any display wealth of which he was not the owner ? Therefore Abraham and Isaac and Jacob must truly subsist, that God may be the ὑφεστά- God of things which are, for He said not, " I was their God," ναι. but *I am* And that there is a judgment, Abraham shows, saying to the Lord, *He who judgeth the earth, shall He not* Gen 18, *execute judgment ?* 25 Sept.

12 But to this the foolish Samaritans answer by way of objection, that the souls possibly of Abraham and Isaac and Jacob continue, but that it is impossible that their bodies should arise. Was it then possible that the rod of righteous Moses should become a serpent, and is it impossible that the bodies of the righteous should live and rise again ? And was that done contrary to its nature, and shall they not be restored according to their nature ? Again, the rod of Aaron, though cut off and dead, budded, *without the scent of waters,* sprouting Job 14, forth into blossoms as in the fields, though under a roof; and ⁹ though set in dry places, yielding in one night the flowers and fruit of plants watered for many years. Did Aaron's rod, as it were, rise from the dead, and shall not Aaron himself be raised ? And did God work wonders in wood, to secure to

him the high-priesthood, and will He not vouchsafe to Aaron himself a resurrection? A woman also was made salt contrary to nature; and flesh was turned into salt; and shall not flesh be restored to flesh? Was Lot's wife made a pillar of salt, and shall not Abraham's wife be raised again? By what power was Moses' hand changed, which in one hour became as snow, and then was restored? Simply by God's command. Had it force then, has it not force now?

13. And whence in the beginning came man into being at all, O ye Samaritans, most shallow of men? Go to the first book of the Scripture, which even you receive; *And the Lord God formed man of the dust of the ground.* Is dust transformed into flesh, and shall not flesh be again restored to flesh? You must be asked too, whence the heavens had their being, and the earth, and the seas? Whence the sun, and the moon, and the stars? How from the waters were made things which fly and swim? And how from the earth all beasts? Were so many thousands brought from nothing into being, and shall we men, who bear God's image, not be raised up? Truly this course is mere unbelief, and an ample condemnation of the unbelievers; considering Abraham addresses the Lord as *the Judge of all the earth,* and the learners of the Law disbelieve; when it is written that man is of the earth, and the readers disbelieve it also.

(7.) 14. To them therefore, the unbelievers, we say these things; but the words of the Prophets are for us, who believe. But since some who also use the Prophets believe not what is written, and allege against us that passage, *The ungodly shall not rise up in judgment,* and, *He that goeth down to the grave shall come up no more,* and, *The dead praise not Thee, O Lord,*—using ill, what is written well,—it will be well in a cursory manner, as far as is now possible, to meet them. For if it is said, that *the ungodly shall not rise up in judgment,* this shows that they shall rise, not in judgment, but in condemnation; for God needs not long scrutiny, but close on the resurrection of the ungodly follows their punishment. And if it is said, *The dead praise not Thee, O Lord,* this shows, that since in this life only is the appointed time for repentance and pardon, for which they who enjoy it shall *praise the Lord,* it remains after death for them who have died in sins,

not to give praise as the receivers of a blessing, but to bewail themselves; for praise belongs to them who give thanks, but to them who are under the scourge, lamentation. Therefore the just shall then offer praise; but they who have died in sins will have no further season for acknowledgment.

15. And respecting that passage, *He that goeth down to* *the grave shall come up no more,* observe what follows, *He shall return no more to his house, neither shall his place know him any more.* For since the whole world shall pass away, and every house shall be destroyed, how shall he return to his own house, there being henceforth a new earth? But they ought to have heard Job, saying, *For there is hope of a tree, if it be cut down, that it will sprout again, and that the tender branch thereof will not cease. Though the root thereof wax old in the earth, and the stock thereof die in the ground; yet through the scent of water it will bud, and bring forth boughs like a plant. And man when he dies, departeth; but when mortal man falls, is he no longer?* As it were remonstrating and reproving; (for thus ought we to read the words, with an interrogation;) for since a tree falls and revives, he says, shall not man revive, for whom all trees were made? And that thou mayest not suppose that I am forcing the words, read what follows, for after saying by way of question, *When mortal man falls, is he no longer?* he says, *If a man die, he shall live again;* and immediately he adds, *I will wait till my change come;* and again elsewhere, *Who shall raise up on the earth my skin, which endures these things.* And Esaias the Prophet says, *Thy dead men shall live, together with my dead body shall they arise.* And the Prophet Ezekiel, now before us, says most plainly, *Behold, I will open your graves, and cause you to come up out of your graves.* And Daniel says, *Many that sleep in the dust of the earth shall awake, some to everlasting life, and some to shame and everlasting contempt.*

[margin: ἐξομολογήσεως supr 11. Job 7, 10 Job 14, 7. &c. v Sept δυσωπῶν Ib. Sept Job 19, 26 Sept. Is 26, 19. Ezek. 37, 12. Dan 12, 2.]

16. And many Scriptures are there which testify the Resurrection of the dead, for there are other and many more sayings on this matter. But now, by way of remembrance only, we will make a passing mention of the raising of Lazarus after four days; and just allude, because of the shortness of the time, to the widow's son also who was raised Now also let

248   *The power residing in the bodies of Saints departed.*

LECT.   me just remind you of the ruler's daughter; and mention the
XVIII. rending of the rocks, and how there arose many bodies of the
saints which slept, their graves having been opened. But
specially let us call to mind that Christ was raised from the
dead. I speak but in passing of Elias, and the widow's son
whom he raised; of Elisseus also, who raised the dead twice;
once when living, and once after his death. For when alive
he wrought the resurrection by means of his soul; but that not
the souls only of the just might be honoured, but that it
might be believed that in the bodies also of the just there
is power, the corpse which was thrown into the grave of
Elisseus, when it touched the dead body of the prophet,
was quickened, and the dead body of the prophet did the
work of the soul, and that which was dead and buried gave
life to the dead, and while imparting life, yet continued itself
among the dead. Wherefore? Lest if Elisseus should rise
again, the work should be ascribed to his soul alone; and to
show, that even though the soul is not present, a virtue resides
in the body of the saints, because of the righteous soul which
has for so many years tenanted it, and used it as its minister.
And let us not foolishly disbelieve, as though this thing had
Acts 19, not happened; for if handkerchiefs and aprons, which are
15.   from without, touching the bodies of the diseased, have raised
up the sick, how much more should the body itself of the
Prophet raise the dead?

(9)   17. And with respect to these instances we might say
much, rehearsing in detail the marvellous circumstances of
each event; but as you have been already wearied both by the
ὑπερ-   prolonged fast of the Preparation, and by the watchings, let
θέσεως. what has been cursorily spoken concerning them suffice for
a while; these words having been as it were sown thinly,
that you, receiving the seed like richest ground, may in bearing
fruit increase them. But be it remembered, that the Apostles
also raised the dead; Peter raised Tabitha in Joppa, and
Paul raised Eutychus in Troas; and thus did all the Apostles,
even though the wonders wrought by each have not all been
written. Further, remember all that is said in the first
Epistle to the Corinthians, which Paul wrote against them
1 Cor   who said, *How are the dead raised, and with what body do*
15, 35 *they come?* And how he says, *For if the dead rise not, then*
ver 16

is not Christ raised; and how he called them *fools,* who believed not, and remember the whole of his teaching there concerning the resurrection of the dead, and how he wrote to the Thessalonians, *But I would not have you to be ignorant, brethren, concerning them which are asleep, that ye sorrow not, even as others which have no hope,* and all that follows : but chiefly that, *And the dead in Christ shall rise first.*   ver 36.

1 Thess 4, 13

ver 16.

18. But especially mark this, how very pointedly Paul says, *For this corruptible must put on incorruption, and this mortal must put on immortality.* For this body shall be raised, not remaining weak as now; raised, I say, the very same body, but putting on incorruption it shall be fashioned anew,— as iron blending with fire becomes fire, or rather as He knows how, the Lord who raises us. This body therefore shall be raised, but it shall abide not such as it now is, but an eternal body, no longer needing for its life nourishment as now, nor stairs for its ascent, for it shall be made spiritual, a marvellous thing, such as we cannot worthily speak of. *Then,* it is said, *shall the righteous shine forth as the sun,* and the moon, *and as the brightness of the firmament.* And God, foreknowing men's unbelief, has given to little worms in the summer to dart beams of light from their body, that from what is seen, that which is looked for might find credence; for He who gives in part is able to give the whole also, and He who makes the worm radiant with light, will much more illuminate a righteous man.

1 Cor. 15, 53.

v Matt. 13, 43 cf Dan. 12, 3.

19. We shall be raised therefore, all with our bodies eternal, but not all with bodies alike · for if a man is righteous, he will receive a heavenly body, that he may be able duly to hold converse with Angels, but if a man is a sinner, he shall receive an eternal body, fitted to endure the pains of sins, that it may burn eternally in fire, nor ever be consumed. And righteously will God assign this portion to either company; for we do nothing without the body. We blaspheme with the mouth, and with the mouth we pray. With the body we commit fornication, and with the body we keep our chastity. With the hand we rob, and by the hand we bestow alms, and in like manner the rest. Since then the body has been our minister in all things, it shall also share with us what befalls us hereafter.

(10)

20. Therefore, brethren, let us be tender of our bodies, nor let us misuse them as though not our own. Let us not say like the heretics, that this vesture of the body belongs not to us[c], but let us be careful of it as our own; for we must give account to the Lord of all things done through the body. Say not, no one sees me; think not that there is no witness of the deed. Human witness oftentimes there is not; but He who fashioned us, an unerring witness, abides faithful in heaven, and beholds what thou doest. And the stains of sin remain in the body; for as when a wound has gone deep into the body, the scar remains even after healing, even so sin wounds soul and body, and the marks of its scars remain in all; and they are effaced only by receiving the Baptismal laver. The past wounds therefore of soul and body God heals by Baptism; against future ones let us one and all jointly guard ourselves, that keeping the vestment of the body pure, we may not by fornication and sensual indulgence or other sin for a short season, lose the salvation of heaven, but may inherit the eternal kingdom of God,—which may God vouchsafe to all of you of His own grace.

(11) 21. Thus much in proof of the Resurrection of the dead; and now recite ye and go through with all diligence word by word the profession of the faith, when I have again said it to you. . . . . . .

22. The Faith which we rehearse contains in order the following, "And in one Baptism of repentance for the remission of sins; and in one Holy Catholic Church; and in the resurrection of the flesh; and in eternal life." Now of Baptism and repentance I have spoken in the foregoing Lectures; and my present remarks concerning the resurrection of the dead have been made with reference to the Article "In the resurrection of the flesh." Now then let me finish what remains to be said, in consequence of the Article, "In one Holy Catholic Church," on which, though one might say many things, we will speak but briefly.

23 Now it is called Catholic because it is throughout the world, from one end of the earth to the other; and because it teaches universally and completely one and all the doctrines

[c] e g the Gnostics, Manichees, &c.

which ought to come to men's knowledge, concerning things both visible and invisible, heavenly and earthly; and because it subjugates in order to godliness every class of men, ὑποτάσσειν εἰς. governors and governed, learned and unlearned; and because it universally treats and heals every sort of sins, which are committed by soul or body, and possesses in itself every form of virtue which is named, both in deeds and words, and in every kind of spiritual gifts.

24. And it is rightly named Church, because it calls forth and assembles together all men; according as the Lord says in Leviticus, *And assemble thou all the congregation to the doors of the tabernacle of witness.* And it is to be noted, that the word *assemble*, is used for the first time in the Scriptures here, at the time when the Lord puts Aaron into the High-priesthood. And in Deuteronomy the Lord says to Moses, *Assemble to Me the people, and I will make them hear My words, that they shall learn to fear Me.* And he again mentions the name of the Church, when he says concerning the Tables, *And on them was written according to all the words which the Lord spake with you in the mount of the midst of the fire in the day of the Assembly;* as if he had said more plainly, in the day in which ye were called and gathered together by God. And the Psalmist says, *I will give Thee thanks in the great Assembly; I will praise Thee among much people.* [ἐκκλησία, as-sembly v. Heb. 12, 23 Lev 8, 3. Sept. ἐκκλησίασον. Deut 4, 10 Deut 9, 10 ἐκκλη- οἵας or Church. Ps 35, 18 v. Heb. 2, 12]

25. Of old the Psalmist sung, *Bless ye God in the Church, even the Lord, from the fountain of Israel.* But since the Jews for their evil designs against the Saviour have been cast away from grace, the Saviour has built out of the Gentiles a second Holy Church, the Church of us Christians, concerning which He said to Peter, *And upon this rock I will build My Church, and the gates of hell shall not prevail against it.* And David prophesying of both, said plainly of the first which was rejected, *I have hated the Church of the evil doers;* but of the second which is built up he says in the same Psalm, *Lord, I have loved the habitation of Thine house;* and immediately afterwards, *In the Churches will I bless the Lord.* For now that the one Church in Judæa is cast off, the Churches of Christ are increased throughout the world; and of them it is said, *Sing unto the Lord a new song, and His praise in the Church of the Saints.* Agreeably to which the Prophet also [Ps 68, 26. Mat. 16, 18. Ps 26, 5. ver 8 ver 12 Ps 149, 1.]

said to the Jews, *I have no pleasure in you, saith the Lord of Hosts;* and immediately afterwards, *For from the rising of the sun even unto the going down of the same, My name shall be great among the Gentiles.* Concerning this Holy Catholic Church Paul writes to Timothy, *That thou mayest know how thou oughtest to behave thyself in the House of God, which is the Church of the Living God, the pillar and ground of the truth.*

26. But since the word Church or Assembly is applied to different things, (as also it is written of the multitude in the theatre of the Ephesians, *And when he had thus spoken, he dismissed the Assembly,* and since one might properly and truly say that there is a *Church of the evil doers,* I mean the meetings of the heretics, the Marcionists and Manichees, and the rest,) the Faith has delivered to thee by way of security the Article, "And in one Holy Catholic Church," that thou mayest avoid their wretched meetings, and ever abide with the Holy Church Catholic in which thou wast regenerated. And if ever thou art sojourning in any city, inquire not simply where the Lord's House is, (for the sects of the profane also make an attempt to call their own dens, houses of the Lord,) nor merely where the Church is, but where is the Catholic Church. For this is the peculiar name of this Holy Body, the mother of us all, which is the spouse of our Lord Jesus Christ, the Only-begotten Son of God, (for it is written, *As Christ also loved the Church, and gave Himself for it,* and all the rest,) and is a figure and copy of Jerusalem *above, which is free, and the mother of us all;* which before was barren, but now has many children

27. For when the first Church was cast off, God, in the second, which is the Catholic Church, *hath set first Apostles, secondarily Prophets, thirdly teachers, after that miracles, then gifts of healings, helps, governments, diversities of tongues,* and every sort of virtue; I mean wisdom and understanding, temperance and justice, alms-doing and loving-kindness, and patience unconquerable in persecutions. She, *by the armour of righteousness on the right hand and on the left, by honour and dishonour,* in former days amid persecutions and tribulations crowned the holy martyrs with the varied and blooming chaplets of patience, and now in times

of peace by God's grace receives her due honours from princes and nobles, and from every rank and kindred of man. And while the kings of particular nations have bounds set to their dominion, the Holy Church Catholic alone extends her illimitable sovereignty over the whole world, *for God*, as it is written, *hath made her border peace*. But I should need many more hours for my discourse, would I speak of all things which concern her.

_{Ps 147, 14 Sept.}

---

28. In this Holy Catholic Church receiving instruction and behaving ourselves virtuously, we shall attain the kingdom of heaven, and inherit eternal life; for which also we endure all toils, that we may be made partakers of it from the Lord. For ours is no trifling aim; eternal life is our object of pursuit. Wherefore in the profession of the Faith, after the words, "And in the resurrection of the flesh," that is, of the dead, (of which we have discoursed,) we are taught to believe, " And in the life everlasting," for which as Christians we are striving. (13)

29 The Father is the real and true life; and He through the Son in the Holy Spirit pours forth as from a fountain His heavenly gifts to all; for through His love to man, the blessings of everlasting life are promised without fail even to us men. We must not disbelieve the possibility of this, but having an eye not to our own weakness but to His power, we must believe, *for with God all things are possible*. And that this is possible, and that we may look for everlasting life, Daniel declares, *And they that turn many to righteousness as the stars for ever and ever*. And Paul says, *And so shall we be ever with the Lord*: now the being for ever with the Lord implies life everlasting. But most plainly of all the Saviour Himself says in the Gospel, *And these shall go away into everlasting punishment, but the righteous into life eternal*.

_{Dan 12, 3 (v Sept) 1 Thess. 4, 17. Mat 25, 46.}

30. And many are the proofs concerning the life everlasting. And when we desire to gain this eternal life, the sacred Scriptures suggest to us the ways of gaining it; of which, because of the length of our discourse, the texts we set before you shall be but few, the rest being left to the search of the diligent. They declare at one time that it is by faith, for it is written, *He that believeth on the Son hath everlasting life*, and what follows; and again He says Himself, *Verily,*

_{John 3, 36. John 5, 24.}

verily, I say unto you, He that heareth My words, and believeth on Him that sent Me, hath everlasting life, and the rest. At another time, it is by the preaching of the Gospel; for He says, that *He that reapeth receiveth wages, and gathereth fruit unto life eternal.* At another time, by martyrdom and confession in Christ's name; for He says, *And he that hateth his life in this world, shall keep it unto life eternal.* And again, by preferring Christ to riches or kindred; *And every one that hath forsaken brethren, or sisters,* and the rest, *shall inherit everlasting life.* Moreover it is by keeping the commandments, *Thou shalt not commit adultery, Thou shalt not kill,* and the rest which follow; as He answered to him that came to Him, and said, *Good Master, what shall I do that I may have eternal life?* Further, it is by departing from evil works, and henceforth serving God; for Paul says, *But now being made free from sin, and become servants to God, ye have your fruit unto holiness, and the end everlasting life.*

<small>Lect XVIII</small>
<small>John 4, 36.</small>
<small>John 12, 25.</small>
<small>Mat. 19, 29</small>
<small>v. Mat 19, 16—18.</small>
<small>v also Mark 10, 17.</small>
<small>Rom 6, 22</small>

31. And the ways of finding eternal life are many, though I have passed over them by reason of their number. For God in His loving-kindness has opened, not one or two only, but many doors, by which to enter into the life everlasting, that, as far as lay in Him, all might enjoy it without hindrance. Thus much have we for the present spoken within compass concerning the life everlasting, which is the last doctrine of those professed in the Faith, and its termination; which may we all, both teachers and hearers, by God's grace enjoy!

(14.) 32. It remains, brethren beloved, to exhort you all by the word of teaching, to prepare your souls for the reception of the heavenly gifts. As regards the Holy and Apostolic Faith delivered to you to profess, we have spoken as many Lectures, as was possible, in the past days of Lent; not that this is all we ought to have said, for our omissions are many; and these perchance have been thought out better by more excellent teachers. And now the holy day of Easter is at hand, and your love in Christ is to be illuminated *by the Laver of regeneration.* Ye shall therefore again be taught what is requisite, if God so will; with how great piety and order you must enter in when summoned, for what purpose each of the holy

<small>Tit 3, 5.</small>

mysteries of Baptism is performed, and with what reverence and order you must go from Baptism to the Holy Altar of God, and enjoy its spiritual and heavenly mysteries; that your souls being previously illuminated by the word of doctrine, ye may discover the greatness of each particular gift bestowed on you by God.

33. And after the Holy and Salutary Day of Easter, beginning from the second day of the week, ye shall come all the days of the following week after the assembly into the Holy Place of the Resurrection, and there ye shall hear other Lectures, if God permit; in which ye shall again be taught the reasons of every thing which has been done, and shall receive the proofs thereof from the Old and New Testaments,—first, of the things done just before Baptism,—next, how ye have been cleansed from your sins by the Lord, *with the* Eph. 5, *washing of water by the word*,—and how by being Priests 26 Comp. ye have become partakers of Christ's Name,—and how the x 16. 4. Seal of the fellowship of the Holy Ghost has been given xxi. 5. 6 you,—and concerning the mysteries at the Altar of the New Testament, which had their beginning in this place, what the Divine Scriptures have delivered to us, and what is the power of these mysteries, and how ye must approach them, and when and how receive them,—and finally, how for the time to come ye must behave yourselves worthily of this grace both in works and words, that you may all be enabled to enjoy the life everlasting. And these things shall be spoken, if it be God's pleasure.

34. *Finally, my brethren, rejoice in the Lord alway; and* (15.) *again I say, Rejoice: for your redemption hath drawn nigh,* Phil 3, and the heavenly host of the Angels is waiting for your 1 and 4, 4. salvation. And there is now the voice *of one crying in the* v Luke *wilderness, Prepare ye the way of the Lord;* and the Prophet 21, 28 Is 40, 3. cries, Ho, *every one that thirsteth, come ye to the waters;* Is. 55, 1. and immediately afterwards, *Hearken diligently unto me,* v. 2. *and eat ye that which is good, and let your soul delight itself in fatness.* And within a little while ye shall hear that excellent lesson which says, *Be light, be light, O thou new* Is 60, 1. *Jerusalem; for thy light is come.* Of this Jerusalem the Sept (v marg) prophet hath said, *And afterwards thou shalt be called the* Is 1, 26. *city of righteousness, the faithful city Zion; for out of Zion* Is 2, 3.

shall go forth the law, and out of Jerusalem the word of the Lord, which from hence has been showered down on the whole world. To her the Prophet also says concerning you, *Lift up thine eyes round about, and behold* thy children *gathered together;* and she answers, saying, *Who are these that fly as a cloud, and as doves with their young ones to me?* (She calls them, *clouds,* because of their spiritual nature, and *doves,* from their purity) And again she says, *Who hath heard such a thing? who hath seen such things? shall the earth be made to bring forth in one day? or shall a nation be born at once? for as soon as Zion travailed, she brought forth her children.* And all things shall be filled with joy ineffable, because of the Lord who hath said, *Behold, I create Jerusalem a rejoicing, and her people a joy*

35. And may these words also apply to you, and at this time, *Sing, O heavens, and be joyful, O earth; for the Lord hath comforted His people, and will have mercy on His afflicted* And this shall come to pass through the loving-kindness of God, who says to you, *I will blot out as a cloud thy transgressions, and as a thick cloud thy sins.* But ye who have been counted worthy of the name of Faithful, (of whom it is written, *The Lord God shall call His servants by another name which shall be blessed on the earth,*) ye shall say with gladness, *Blessed be the God and Father of our Lord Jesus Christ, who hath blessed us with all spiritual blessings in heavenly places in Christ; in whom we have redemption through His blood, the forgiveness of sins, according to the riches of His grace,* and what follows; and again, *But God who is rich in mercy, for His great love wherewith He loved us, even when we were dead in sins, hath quickened us together with Christ,* and the rest. And again in like manner praise ye the Lord of all good things, saying, *But after that the kindness and love of God our Saviour towards man appeared, not by works of righteousness which we had done, but according to His mercy He saved us, by the washing of regeneration, and the renewing of the Holy Ghost, which He shed on us abundantly through Jesus Christ our Saviour, that being justified by His grace, we should be made heirs according to the hope of eternal life.* And may God Himself and Father of our Lord Jesus Christ, give unto *you*

the spirit of wisdom and revelation in the knowledge of Him, the eyes of your understanding being enlightened; and keep you ever in good works and words and thoughts.—To whom be glory and honour and might through our Lord Jesus Christ with the Holy Ghost now and ever, and for all the infinite ages of eternity. Amen.

CATECHETICAL LECTURES

OF

S. CYRIL,

ARCHBISHOP OF JERUSALEM,

ADDRESSED TO PERSONS RECENTLY BAPTIZED, CONCERNING THE SACRED MYSTERIES.

LECTURE XIX.
(ON THE MYSTERIES. I.)

ON THE RITES BEFORE BAPTISM.

1 Peter v. 8—14.

Be sober, be vigilant; because your adversary the devil, as a roaring lion, walketh about, seeking whom he may devour, &c.

Lect. XIX. Myst. 1.

1. I long ago desired, true-born and dearly beloved children of the Church, to discourse to you concerning these spiritual and heavenly Mysteries; but knowing well, that seeing is far more persuasive than hearing, I waited till this season; that finding you more open to the influence of my words from this your experience, I might take and lead you to the brighter and more fragrant meadow of this present paradise; especially as ye have been made fit to receive the more sacred Mysteries, having been counted worthy of divine and life-giving Baptism. It remaining therefore to dress for you a board of more perfect instruction, let us now teach you exactly about these things, that ye may know the deep meaning to you-ward of what was done on that evening of your baptism [a].

[a] On Easter Eve, which was the most common time of Baptism. Vid. Bingh. Antiqu. xi 6 §. 7

2. First, ye entered into the outer hall of the Baptistery, (2.) and there facing towards the West, ye heard the command to stretch forth your hand, and as in the presence of Satan ye renounced him. Now ye must know that this figure is found in ancient history. For when Pharaoh, that most cruel and ruthless tyrant, oppressed the free and high-born people of the Hebrews, God sent Moses to bring them out of the evil thraldom of the Egyptians. Then the door-posts were anointed with the blood of the lamb, that the destroyer might flee from the houses which had the sign of the blood; and the Hebrew people was marvellously delivered. The enemy, however, after their rescue, pursued them, and saw the sea wondrously parted for them; nevertheless he went on, following in their footsteps, and was all at once overwhelmed and engulphed in the Red Sea.

3. Now turn from the ancient to the recent, from the figure to the reality. There we have Moses sent from God to Egypt; here, Christ, sent by His Father into the world: there, that Moses might lead forth an oppressed people out of Egypt; here, that Christ might rescue mankind who are whelmed under sins: there, the blood of a lamb was the spell against the destroyer; here, the blood of the unblemished Lamb Jesus Christ is made the charm to scare evil spirits: there, the tyrant pursued even to the sea that ancient people; and in like manner this daring and shameless spirit, the author of evil, followed thee, even to the very streams of salvation. The tyrant of old was drowned in the sea; and this present one disappears in the salutary water.

4. However, thou art bidden with arm outstretched to say to him as though actually present, "I renounce thee, Satan." I wish to say, wherefore ye stand facing to the West; for it is necessary. Since the West is the region of sensible darkness, and he being darkness, has his dominion also in darkness, ye therefore, looking with a symbolical meaning towards the West, renounce that dark and gloomy potentate. What then did each of you standing up say? "I renounce thee, Satan," thou wicked and most cruel tyrant! meaning, "I fear thy might no longer; for Christ hath overthrown it, having partaken with me of flesh and blood, that through these He might *by death destroy death*, that I might not for ever be Heb. 2, 14.

subject to bondage. I renounce thee, thou crafty and most subtle serpent. I renounce thee, plotter as thou art, who under the guise of friendship didst work all disobedience, and bring about the apostasy of our first parents. I renounce thee, Satan, the artificer and abettor of all wickedness."

(3.) 5. Then in the second sentence thou art told to say, "and all thy works." Now the works of Satan are all sin, which it is necessary to renounce also;—just as if a man has escaped a tyrant, he would have doubtless escaped his instruments also. All sin therefore, according to its kinds, is included in the works of the devil. Only know this; that all that thou sayest, especially at that most thrilling hour, is written in God's books; when therefore thou doest any thing contrary to these, thou shalt be judged as *a transgressor*. Thou renouncest therefore the works of Satan; I mean, all deeds and thoughts which are against thy better judgment.

Gal. 2, 18

παρὰ λόγον.

(4) θεατρομανίαι.

Ps. 119, 37.

6. Then thou sayest, "And all his pomp." Now the pomp of the devil is the madness of shows, and horse-races, and hunting, and all such vanity: from which that holy man praying to be delivered, says unto God, *Turn away mine eyes from beholding vanity*. Be not interested in the madness of the shows, where thou wilt behold the wanton gestures of players, carried on with mockeries and all unseemliness, and the frantic dancing of effeminate men;—nor in the madness of them who in hunts expose themselves to wild beasts, that they may pamper their miserable appetite; who, that they may indulge their belly with meats, become themselves truly meat for the belly of ravenous beasts; and to speak justly, they for the sake of their proper god, their belly, cast away their life headlong in single combats. Shun also horse-races, that frantic spectacle, which subverts souls. For all these are the pomp of the devil.

7. Moreover, things also hung up at idol festivals, either meat or bread, or other such things which are polluted by the invocation of the unclean spirits, are reckoned in the pomp of the devil. For as the Bread and Wine of the Eucharist before the holy invocation of the Adorable Trinity was simple bread and wine, while after the invocation the Bread becomes the Body of Christ, and the Wine the Blood of Christ, so in like manner, such meats belonging to the pomp

ἐπικλήσεως λιτός. γίνεται

Renunciation of idolatry—Recital of the Creed. 261

of Satan, though in their own nature plain and simple, become profane by the invocation of the evil spirit.

8. And after this thou sayest, "and all thy service." Now the service of the devil is prayer in idol temples; things done to the honour of lifeless idols; the lighting of lamps, or burning of incense by fountains or rivers, (for some cheated by dreams or by evil spirits, have passed to these places, thinking to find a cure even for their bodily ailments,) and the like. Go not therefore after them. The watching of birds, divination, omens, or amulets, or charms written on leaves, sorceries, or other evil arts, and all such things, are services to the devil; therefore shun them. For if after renouncing Satan and ranging thyself with Christ, thou fall under their influence, thou shalt find the tyrant more bitter in his temptations; perchance, because he treated thee of old as his own, and has let thee off from severe slavery, and has been greatly exasperated against thee; so thou wilt be bereaved of Christ, and be tempted by him. Hast thou not heard the old history which tells us of Lot and his daughters? Was not he himself saved with his daughters, because he gained the mountain, while his wife became a pillar of salt, set up as a beacon for ever, as the memorial of her depraved will and her $προαιρέ-$ turning back. Take heed therefore to thyself, and turn not $σεως$ again to *what is behind*, going back after having put thine hand to the plough, to the salt savour of this life's doings; but escape to the mountain, to Jesus Christ, that stone hewn without hands, which has filled the world. (5.)

Phil 3, 13.
v. Dan. 2, 35 45

9. When therefore thou renouncest Satan, utterly breaking all covenant with him, that ancient league with hell, there is opened to thee the paradise of God, which He planted towards the East, whence for his transgression our first father was exiled; and symbolical of this was thy turning from the West to the East, the place of light. Then thou wert told to say, I believe in the Father, and in the Son, and in the Holy Ghost, and in one Baptism of repentance. Of which things we spoke at length in the former Lectures, as God's grace allowed us. (6.)

10. Therefore, guarded by these considerations, be sober. *For* our *adversary the devil*, as was just now read, *as a roaring lion, walketh about, seeking whom he may devour.*

1 Pet 5, 8

LECT.
XIX.
Myst 1
Is. 25, 8.
and Rev.
7, 17
πανηγυ-
ρίσεις.

In former times death was mighty and devoured; but at the holy Laver of regeneration, God has *wiped away every tear from off all faces.* For thou shalt no more mourn, now that thou hast put off the old man; but thou shalt keep holyday, clothed in the garment of salvation, even Jesus Christ.

11. And these things were done in the outer chamber. But if God will, when in the succeeding expositions of the Mysteries we have entered into the Holy of Holies, we shall then know the symbolical meaning of what is there accomplished. Now to God the father, with the Son and the Holy Ghost, be glory, and power, and majesty, for ever and ever. Amen.

LECTURE XX.

(ON THE MYSTERIES. II.)

ON THE RITES OF BAPTISM.

ROMANS VI. 3—14.

Know ye not, that so many of us as were baptized into Jesus Christ, were baptized into His death? &c . . . . for ye are not under the Law, but under grace.

1. THESE introductions into the Mysteries day by day, and these new instructions, which are the announcements of new truths, are profitable to us; and most of all to you, who have been renewed from oldness to newness. Therefore, as is necessary, I will lay before you the sequel of yesterday's Lecture, that ye may learn of what those things, which were done by you in the inner chamber, were the emblems.

2. As soon, therefore, as ye entered in, ye put off your (2) garment; and this was an image of *putting off the old man* Col 3, 9. *with his deeds.* Having stripped yourselves, ye were naked; in this also imitating Christ, who hung naked on the Cross, and by His nakedness *spoiled principalities and powers, and* Col. 2, *openly triumphed over them on the tree.* For since the powers 15. of the enemy made their lair in your members, ye may no longer wear that old vestment; I do not at all mean this visible one, but that *old man, which is corrupt according* αἰσθητόν *to the deceitful lusts.* May no soul which has once put him Eph. 4, off, again put him on, but say with the Spouse of Christ in 22 the Song of Songs, *I have put off my coat, how shall I put* Cant 5, *it on?* O wondrous thing! ye were naked in the sight of all, 3 and were not ashamed; for truly ye bore the likeness of the first-formed Adam, who was naked in the garden, and was not ashamed.

3. Then, when ye were stripped, ye were anointed with (3) exorcised oil, from the very hairs of your head, to your feet,

> LECT.
> XX.
> *Myst.* 2.

and were made partakers of the good olive-tree, Jesus Christ. For ye were cut off from the wild olive-tree, and grafted into the good one, and were made to share the fatness of the true olive-tree. The exorcised oil therefore was a symbol of the participation of the fatness of Christ, the charm to drive away every trace of hostile influence. For as the breathing of the saints, and the invocation of the Name of God, like fiercest flame, scorch and drive out evil spirits, so also this exorcised oil receives such virtue by the invocation of God and by prayer, as not only to burn and cleanse away the traces of sins, but also to chase away all the invisible powers of the evil one.

> Introd.
> Lect. IX.

(4.) 4. After these things, ye were led to the holy pool of Divine Baptism, as Christ was carried from the Cross to the Sepulchre which is before our eyes. And each of you was asked, whether he believed in the name of the Father, and of the Son, and of the Holy Ghost, and ye made that saving confession, and descended three times[a] into the water, and ascended again; here also covertly pointing by a figure at the three-days burial of Christ. For as our Saviour passed three days and three nights in the heart of the earth, so you also in your first ascent out of the water, represented the first day of Christ in the earth, and by your descent, the night; for as he who is in the night, sees no more, but he who is in the day, remains in the light, so in descending, ye saw nothing as in the night, but in ascending again, ye were as in the day. And at the self-same moment, ye died and were born; and that Water of salvation was at once your grave and your mother. And what Solomon spoke of others will suit you also; for he said,

> Eccles 3, 2

There is a time to bear and a time to die; but to you, on the contrary, the time to die is also the time to be born; and one and the same season brings about both of these, and your birth went hand in hand with your death.

(5.) 5. O strange and inconceivable thing! we did not really die, we were not really buried, we were not really crucified and raised again; but our imitation was but in a figure, while our salvation is in reality. Christ was actually crucified, and actually buried, and truly rose again; and all these things have been vouchsafed to us, that we, by imitation commu-

---

[a] This was the ancient practice, vid Tertull. in Prax. 26. de Cor. Mil. 3. Can. Apost 42 Bingham gives the history of it, Antiqu. xi. 11. §. 6—8.

nicating in His sufferings, might gain salvation in reality. O surpassing loving-kindness! Christ received the nails in His undefiled hands and feet, and endured anguish; while to me without suffering or toil, by the fellowship of His pain He vouchsafes salvation.

6. Let no one then suppose that Baptism is merely the grace of remission of sins, or further, that of adoption; as John's baptism bestowed only the remission of sins. Nay we know full well, that as it purges our sins, and conveys to us the gift of the Holy Ghost, so also it is the counterpart of Christ's sufferings. For for this cause Paul, just now read, cried aloud and says, *Know ye not that as many of us as were baptized into Christ Jesus, were baptized into His death? Therefore we are buried with Him by baptism into death.* These words he spake to them who had settled with themselves that Baptism ministers to us the remission of sins, and adoption, but not that further it has communion also in representation with Christ's true sufferings. ^{vid sup. iii. 7. πρόξενον. ἀντίτυ- τον. vid. Heb. 9, 24 Rom. 6, 3}

7. In order therefore that we may learn, that whatsoever things Christ endured, He suffered them for us and our salvation, and that, in reality and not in appearance, we also are made partakers of His sufferings. Paul cried with all exactness of truth, *For if we have been planted together in the likeness of His death, we shall be also in the likeness of His resurrection.* Well has he said, *planted together.* For since the true Vine was planted in this place, we also by partaking in the Baptism of death, *have been planted together with Him.* And fix thy mind with much attention on the words of the Apostle. He has not said, "For if we have been planted together in His death," but, *in the likeness of His death.* For upon Christ death came in reality, for His soul was truly separated from His body, and His burial was true, for His holy body was wrapt in pure linen; and every thing happened to Him truly; but in your case only the likeness of death and sufferings, whereas of salvation, not the likeness, but the reality. (6.) ^{Rom 6, 5.}

8. Of these things then having been sufficiently instructed, keep them, I beseech you, in your remembrance; that I also, unworthy though I be, may say of you, *Now I love you, brethren, because ye remember me in all things, and keep the* ^{1 Cor. 11, 2. ἀγαπῶ, Cyr.}

LECT.
XX.
Myst 2.
ἐπαινῶ,
praise,
rec. text.

ordinances, *as I delivered them unto you.* And God, who has presented you as it were alive from the dead, is able to grant unto you to walk in newness of life; because His is the glory and the power, now and for ever. Amen.

LECTURE XXI.

(ON THE MYSTERIES. III.)

ON THE HOLY CHRISM.

1 JOHN ii. 20—28.

But ye have an unction from the Holy One, &c. . . . that, when He shall appear, we may have confidence, and not be ashamed before Him at His coming.

1. HAVING been *baptized into Christ*, and *put on Christ*, ye have been made conformable to the Son of God; for God having *predestinated us to the adoption of sons*, made us *share the fashion of Christ's glorious body*. Being therefore made *partakers of Christ*, ye are properly called Christs, and of you God said, *Touch not My Christs*, or anointed. Now ye were made Christs, by receiving the emblem of the Holy Ghost; and all things were in a figure wrought in you, because ye are figures of Christ. He also bathed Himself in the river Jordan, and having imparted of the fragrance of His Godhead to the waters, He came up from them; and the Holy Ghost in substance lighted on Him, like resting upon like. In the same manner to you also, after you had come up from the pool of the sacred streams, was given the Unction, the emblem of that wherewith Christ was anointed; and this is the Holy Ghost; of whom also the blessed Esaias, in his prophecy respecting Him, says in the person of the Lord, *The Spirit of the Lord is upon Me, because He hath anointed Me to preach glad tidings to the poor*. Gal 3, 27. Eph 1, 5. Phil 3, 21 Heb 3, 14 Ps. 105, 15 ἀντίτυ- ποι. οὐσιώδης ἐπιφοίτη- σις. ἀντίτυ- πον Is. 61, 1.

2. For Christ was not anointed by men with oil or material ointment, but the Father having appointed Him to be the Saviour of the whole world, anointed Him with the Holy Ghost, as Peter says, *Jesus of Nazareth, whom God anointed* Acts 10, 38.

(2)

268   *Oil in Baptism typifies the gift of the Spirit*

Lect. XXI.
Myst 3.
Ps 45, 6. 7.

νοητῷ.

Ps 45, 7.

(3.)
ψιλόν.
λιτός.
χάρισμα.

πνεύματος ἐνεργητικόν.

2 Cor 3, 3.

Is. 50, 4.

Mat. 11, 15.

2 Cor. 2, 15

Eph. 6, 14 and 11.

with the Holy Ghost. And David the Prophet cried, saying, *Thy throne, O God, is for ever and ever; a sceptre of righteousness is the sceptre of Thy kingdom; Thou hast loved righteousness and hated iniquity; therefore God even Thy God hath anointed Thee with the oil of gladness above Thy fellows.* And as Christ was in truth crucified, and buried, and raised, and you in likeness are in Baptism accounted worthy of being crucified, buried, and raised together with Him, so is it with the unction also. As He was anointed with the spiritual oil of gladness, the Holy Ghost, who is so called, because He is the author of spiritual gladness, so ye were anointed with ointment, having been made partakers and *fellows* of Christ.

3. But beware of supposing this to be plain ointment. For as the Bread of the Eucharist, after the invocation of the Holy Ghost, is mere bread no longer, but the Body of Christ, so also this holy ointment is no more simple ointment, nor (so to say) common, after the invocation, but the gift of Christ; and by the presence of His Godhead, it causes in us the Holy Ghost. It is symbolically applied to thy forehead and thy other senses; and while thy body is anointed with visible ointment, thy soul is sanctified by the Holy and life-giving Spirit.

4. And ye were first anointed on your forehead, that ye might be delivered from the shame, which the first man, when he had transgressed, bore about with him every where; and that *with open face ye might behold as in a glass the glory of the Lord.* Then on your ears; that ye might receive ears quick to hear the Divine Mysteries, of which Esaias has said, *The Lord wakened mine ear to hear;* and the Lord Jesus in the Gospel, *He that hath ears to hear let him hear.* Then on your nostrils, that receiving the sacred ointment ye may say, *We are to God a sweet savour of Christ, in them that are saved.* Then on your breast; that having put on the breastplate of righteousness, ye may stand against the wiles of the devil. For as Christ after His baptism, and the descent of the Holy Ghost, went forth and vanquished the adversary, so likewise, having, after Holy Baptism and the Mystical Chrism, put on the whole armour of the Holy Ghost, do ye stand against the power of the enemy, and vanquish it,

saying, *I can do all things through Christ which strength-* Phil. 4, *eneth me.* 13

5. When ye are counted worthy of this Holy Chrism, ye (4.) are called Christians, verifying also the name by your new birth. For before you were vouchsafed this grace, ye had properly no right to this title, but were advancing on your way towards being Christians.

6. Moreover, you should know that this Chrism has its symbol in the old Scripture. For what time Moses imparted to his brother the command of God, and made him High-priest, after bathing in water, he anointed him; and Aaron was called Christ or Anointed, from the emblematical Chrism. So also the High-priest raising Solomon to the kingdom, anointed him after he had bathed in Gihon. To them how- 1 Kings ever these things happened in a figure, but to you not in a 1, 39. figure, but in truth; because ye were truly anointed by the Holy Ghost. Christ is the beginning of your salvation; He is truly the First-fruit, and ye the mass; but if the First-fruit v Rom. be holy, it is manifest that Its holiness will pass to the mass 11, 16. also.

7. Keep This unspotted · for It shall teach you all things (5.) if It abides in you, as you have just heard declared by the blessed John, who discourses much concerning this Chrism. For this holy thing is a spiritual preservative of the body, and safeguard of the soul. Of this in ancient times the blessed Esaias prophesying said, *And in this mountain,—* Is. 25, 6. (now he calls the Church a mountain elsewhere also, as when he says, *In the last days the mountain of the Lord's house* Is. 2, 2. *shall be established,)—in this mountain, shall the Lord make unto all people a feast; they shall drink wine, they shall* Sept. *drink gladness, they shall be anointed with ointment.* And that he may make thee sure, hear what he says of this oint-ment as being mystical; *Give all these things to the nations,* Is. 25, 7. *for the counsel of the Lord is unto all nations.* Having been Sept. anointed, therefore, with this holy ointment, keep it unspotted and unblemished in you, pressing forward by good works, and becoming well-pleasing to the Captain of your salvation, Christ Jesus, to whom be glory for ever and ever. Amen.

LECTURE XXII.

(ON THE MYSTERIES. IV.)

ON THE BODY AND BLOOD OF CHRIST.

1 COR. xi. 23.

I have received of the Lord that which also I delivered unto you, That the Lord Jesus, the same night in which he was betrayed, took bread, &c.

LECT. XXII.
Myst. 4.
Eph. 3, 6.

1. THIS teaching of the Blessed Paul is alone sufficient to give you a full assurance concerning those Divine Mysteries, which when ye are vouchsafed, ye are of *the same body* and blood with Christ. For he has just distinctly said, *That our Lord Jesus Christ the same night in which He was betrayed, took bread, and when He had given thanks He brake it, and said, Take, eat, this is My Body : and having taken the cup and given thanks, He said, Take, drink, this is My Blood.* Since then He Himself has declared and said of the Bread, *This is My Body,* who shall dare to doubt any longer? And since He has affirmed and said, *This is My Blood,* who shall ever hesitate, saying, that it is not His blood?

2. He once turned water into wine, in Cana of Galilee, at His own will[a], and is it incredible that He should have turned wine into blood? That wonderful work He miraculously wrought, when called to an earthly marriage; and shall He not much rather be acknowledged to have bestowed the fruition of His Body and Blood on the children of the bride-chamber?

3. Therefore with fullest assurance let us partake as of

---

[a] Οἰκείῳ νεύματι, Milles, οἰκεῖον αἵματι, "which is akin to blood." Ed. Ben.

The Eucharist signified in the Shew-bread and in the Psalms. 271

the Body and Blood of Christ: for in the figure [b] of Bread is ἐν τύπῳ. given to thee His Body, and in the figure of Wine His Blood; that thou by partaking of the Body and Blood of Christ, mightest be made of the same body and the same blood with Him. For thus we come to bear Christ in us, χριστο- because His Body and Blood are diffused through our mem- φόροι. bers; thus it is that, according to the blessed Peter, *we be-* μένου. *come partakers of the divine nature.* 2 Pet. 1, 4.

4. Christ on a certain occasion discoursing with the Jews said, *Except ye eat My flesh and drink My blood, ye have no* John 6, *life in you.* They not receiving His saying spiritually were 53. offended, and went backward, supposing that He was inviting ἐπὶ σαρ- them to eat flesh. κοφα- γίαν.

5. Even under the Old Testament there was shew-bread; (2) but this as it belonged to the Old Testament, came to an end; but in the New Testament there is the Bread of heaven, v. Ps. and the Cup of salvation, sanctifying soul and body; for as 78, 24. the Bread has respect to our body, so is the Word appropriate 116, 12. to our soul.

6. Contemplate therefore the Bread and Wine not as bare ψιλοῖς. elements, for they are, according to the Lord's declaration, the Body and Blood of Christ; for though sense suggests this to thee, let faith stablish thee. Judge not the matter from taste, but from faith be fully assured without misgiving, that thou hast been vouchsafed the Body and Blood of Christ.

7. The blessed David also shall advise thee the meaning of this, saying, *Thou hast prepared a table before me in the* Ps 23, 5. *presence of mine enemies.* What he says, is to this effect. Before Thy coming, evil spirits prepared a table for men, foul and polluted and full of all devilish influence; but since Thy coming, O Lord, *Thou hast prepared a table before me.* When the man says to God, *Thou hast prepared before me a table,* what other does he mean but that mystical and spiritual νοητήν. Table, which God hath prepared *over against,* that is, contrary Sept. and in opposition to the evil spirits? And very truly; for

---

[b] Ἐν τύπῳ. The word τύπος sometimes means that which stands for a thing present, sometimes that which stands for a thing absent, either 1 a *type,* as when Joshua is said to be a type of Christ. vid sup. Lect x. 11. and as τυπικῶς and ἀληθῶς are contrasted in xxi 6 or 2 an *index,* as Lect iii 6 where S. John Baptist's dress, &c is spoken of as a type of his inward character, and xiii 18.

LECT. XXII. that had fellowship with devils, but this, with God. *Thou hast anointed my head with oil.* With oil He anointed thine head upon thy forehead, 'by the seal which thou hast of God; that thou mayest be made *the impression of the seal, Holiness of God.* And *my cup runneth over.* Thou seest that cup here spoken of, which Jesus took in His hands, and gave thanks, and said, *This is My blood, which is shed for many for the remission of sins.*

Myst 4 ver 5.
v Exod 28, 32. Sept
Ps 23, 5.
Mat 26, 28.

8. Therefore Solomon also, pointing at this grace, says in Ecclesiastes, *Come hither, eat thy bread with joy,* (that is, the spiritual bread; *Come hither,* calling with words of salvation and blessing,) *and drink thy wine with a merry heart;* (that is, the spiritual wine;) *and let thy head lack no ointment,* (thou seest he alludes even to the mystic Chrism;) *and let thy garments be always white, for God now accepteth thy works;* for before thou camest to Baptism, thy works were *vanity of vanities.* But now, having put off thy old garments, and put on those which are spiritually white, thou must be continually robed in white; we mean not this, that thou must always wear white raiment; but with truly white and glistering and spiritual attire, thou must be clothed withal, that thou mayest say with the blessed Esaias, *My soul shall be joyful in my God; for He hath clothed me with the garments of salvation, He hath covered me with the robe of gladness.*

Eccles. 9, 7. v. Sept.
πνευμα-
τικόν.

πνευμα-
τικῶν,
emblematically.

Is. 61, 10. Sept

9. These things having learnt, and being fully persuaded that what seems bread is not bread, though bread by taste, but the Body of Christ; and that what seems wine is not wine, though the taste will have it so, but the Blood of Christ; and that of this David sung of old, saying, *And bread which strengtheneth man's heart, and oil to make his face to shine,*" strengthen thine heart," partaking thereof as spiritual, and " make the face of thy soul to shine." And so having it unveiled by a pure conscience, mayest thou *behold as in a glass the glory of the Lord,* and proceed from *glory to glory,* in Christ Jesus our Lord :—To whom be honour, and might, and glory, for ever and ever. Amen.

τῇ γεύσει
αἰσθητός.

Ps 104, 15.

2 Cor. 3, 18.

LECTURE XXIII.

(ON THE MYSTERIES. V.)

ON THE COMMUNION SERVICE.

1 Pet. ii. 1.

Wherefore laying aside all malice, and all guile, and hypocrisies, and envies, and evil speakings, &c.

1. On former times of our meeting together, ye have heard sufficiently, by the loving-kindness of God, concerning Baptism, and Chrism, and the partaking of the Body and Blood of Christ; and now it is necessary to pass on to what is next in order, meaning to-day to give the finish to your spiritual edification.

2. Ye saw then the Deacon give to the Priest water to wash, and to the Presbyters who stood round God's altar. He gave it, not at all because of bodily defilement; no; for we did not set out for the Church with defiled bodies. But this washing of hands is a symbol that ye ought to be pure from all sinful and unlawful deeds; for since the hands are a symbol of action, by washing them we represent the purity and blamelessness of our conduct. Hast thou not heard the blessed David opening this mystery, and saying, *I will wash my hands in innocency, and so will I compass* Ps. 26, 6. *Thine Altar, O Lord?* The washing therefore of hands is a symbol of immunity from sin.

3. Then the Deacon cries aloud, "Receive ye one another; (2.) and let us kiss one another." Think not that this kiss ranks with those given in public by common friends. It is not

274   *The kiss of peace.—The Offering of praise and thanksgiving.*

LECT.
XXIII
Myst 5

such: this kiss blends souls one with another, and solicits for them entire forgiveness. Therefore this kiss is the sign that our souls are mingled together, and have banished all remembrance of wrongs. For this cause Christ said, *If thou bring thy gift to the altar, and there rememberest that thy brother hath ought against thee; leave there thy gift upon the altar, and go thy way; first be reconciled to thy brother, and then come and offer thy gift.* The kiss therefore is reconciliation, and for this reason holy: as the blessed Paul has in his Epistles urged; *Greet ye one another with a holy kiss;* and Peter, *with a kiss of charity.*

Matt. 5, 23

1 Cor 16, 20.
1 Pet. 5, 14.

(3.)   4. After this the Priest cries aloud, "Lift up your hearts." For truly ought we in that most awful hour to have our heart on high with God, and not below, thinking of earth and earthly things. The Priest then in effect bids all in that hour abandon all worldly thoughts, or household cares, and to have their heart in heaven with the merciful God. Then ye answer, "We lift them up unto the Lord" assenting to him, by your avowal. But let no one come here, who with his lips can say "We lift up our hearts to the Lord," but in mind employs his thoughts on worldly business. God indeed should be in our memory at all times, but if this is impossible by reason of human infirmity, at least in that hour, this should be our earnest endeavour.

(4.)   5. Then the Priest says, "Let us give thanks to the Lord." For in good sooth are we bound to give thanks, that He has called us, unworthy as we are, to so great grace; that He has reconciled us who were His foes; that He hath vouchsafed to us the Spirit of adoption. Then ye say, "It is meet and right:" for in giving thanks we do a meet thing and a right; but He did, not a right thing, but what was more than right, when He did us good, and counted us meet for such great benefits.

(5.)   6. After this, we make mention of heaven, and earth, and sea; of the sun and moon; of the stars and all the creation, rational and irrational, visible and invisible; of Angels, Archangels, Virtues, Dominions, Principalities, Powers, Thrones; of the Cherubim with many faces: in effect repeating that call of David's, *Magnify the Lord with me.* We make mention also of the Seraphim, whom Esaias by the Holy Ghost beheld

Ezek. 10, 21
Ps. 34, 3

encircling the throne of God, and with two of their wings veiling their countenances, and with two their feet, and with two flying, who cried, *Holy, Holy, Holy, Lord God of Sabaoth.* For for this cause rehearse we this confession of God, delivered down to us from the Seraphim, that we may join in Hymns with the hosts of the world above. $^{τῆς\ παραδοθεῖσαν\ θεολογίαν.}$

7. Then having sanctified ourselves by these spiritual Hymns, we call upon the merciful God to send forth His Holy Spirit upon the gifts lying before Him; that He may make the Bread the Body of Christ, and the Wine the Blood of Christ; for whatsoever the Holy Ghost has touched, is sanctified and changed. $^{ἐπὶ\ τὰ\ προκείμενα}$

8. Then, after the spiritual sacrifice is perfected, the Bloodless Service upon that Sacrifice of Propitiation, we entreat God for the common peace of the Church, for the tranquillity of the world; for kings; for soldiers and allies; for the sick; for the afflicted; and, in a word, for all who stand in need of succour we all supplicate and offer this Sacrifice. (6.) $^{δεομένων\ δεόμεθα.}$

9. Then we commemorate also those who have fallen asleep before us, first, Patriarchs, Prophets, Apostles, Martyrs, that at their prayers and intervention God would receive our petition. Afterwards also on behalf of the holy Fathers and Bishops who have fallen asleep before us, and in a word of all who in past years have fallen asleep among us, believing that it will be a very great advantage to the souls, for whom the supplication is put up, while that Holy and most Awful Sacrifice is presented.

10. And I wish to persuade you by an illustration. For I know that many say [a], what is a soul profited, which departs (7.)

---

[a] So Tertullian, as regards the doctrine of the Trinity. "Simplices enim quique, ne dixerim imprudentes et idiotæ, quæ major semper credentium pars est, quoniam et ipsa regula fidei a pluribus diis sæculi, ad unicum et verum Deum transfert, non intelligentes unicum quidem, sed cum sua œconomia esse credendum, expavescunt ad œconomiam" In Prax 3. There is a close parallel between the two passages. Tertullian professes the Catholic doctrine of the Trinity, notices the *objections* which private Christians brought against it, and commits himself in answer to a private and erroneous explanation (in Prax. 5. 6. &c). So S. Cyril here bears witness as to what was done in the Eucharistic Rite, alludes to doubts and inquiries raised about it, and, by way of answer, *comments* on it in words which may be taken to countenance the idea of a Purgatory. S. Cyril by himself as little proves the latter, as Tertullian that the Son of God is not from eternity.

from this world either with sins, or without sins, if it be commemorated in the prayer? Now surely if, when a king had banished certain who had given him offence, their connexions should weave a crown and offer it to him on behalf of those under his vengeance, would he not grant a respite to their punishments? In the same way we, when we offer to Him our supplications for those who have fallen asleep, though they be sinners [b], weave no crown, but offer up Christ, sacrificed for our sins, propitiating our merciful God both for them and for ourselves.

ἁμαρτω-
λοί.

(8.)   11. Then, after these things, we say that Prayer which the Saviour delivered to His own disciples, with a pure conscience styling God our Father, and saying, *Our Father, which art in heaven.* O most surpassing loving-kindness of God! On them who revolted from Him and were in the very extreme of misery has He bestowed such complete forgiveness of their evil deeds, and so great participation of grace, as that they should even call Him Father. *Our Father, which art in heaven;* they also too are a heaven who bear the image of the heavenly, in whom God is, *dwelling and walking in them.*

2 Cor. 6, 16.

(9.)   12. *Hallowed be Thy Name.* The Name of God is in its own nature holy, whether we say so or not; but since it is sometimes profaned among sinners, according to the words, *Through you My Name is continually blasphemed among the Gentiles,* we pray that in us God's Name may be hallowed; not that it becomes holy from not being holy, but because it becomes holy in us, when we become holy, and do things worthy of holiness.

(10.)   13. *Thy kingdom come.* The clean soul can say with boldness, *Thy kingdom come;* for he who has heard Paul saying, *Let not sin reign in your mortal body,* but has cleansed himself in deed, thought, and word, will say to God, *Thy kingdom come.*

Rom. 6, 12.

(11.)   14. *Thy will be done as in heaven so in earth.* The divine and blessed Angels do the will of God, as David in a Psalm has said, *Bless the Lord, ye His Angels, that excel in strength,*

Ps. 103, 10.

---

[b] It may be added to the last note that S. Cyril, in saying that the Eucharist avails for ἁμαρτωλοί, "sinners," contradicts the Roman doctrine, which considers Purgatory to be conceded to none but imperfect believers.

that do His commandments. So then, thou meanest by thy prayer, "as Thy will is done by the Angels, so be it done on earth also by me, Lord."

15. *Give us this day our super-substantial bread*[c]. This common bread is not super-substantial bread, but this Holy Bread is super-substantial, that is, appointed for the substance of the soul. For this Bread *goeth* not *into the belly and is cast out into the draught,* but is diffused through all thou art, for the benefit of body and soul. But by *this day,* he means, "each day," as also Paul has said, *While it is called to-day.* Mat. 15, 17, ἀναδίδο- ται σύ- στασιν. Heb 3,

16. *And forgive us our debts as we forgive our debtors.* For we have many sins. For we offend both in word and in thought, and very many things do we worthy of condemnation; and *if we say that we have no sin,* we lie, as John says. And we enter into a covenant with God, entreating Him to pardon our sins, as we also forgive our neighbours their debts. Considering then what we receive and for what, let us not put off, nor delay to forgive one another. The offences committed against us are slight and trivial, and easily settled; but those which we have committed against God are great, and call for mercy such as His only is. Take heed therefore, lest for these small and inconsiderable sins against thyself, thou bar against thyself forgiveness from God for thy most grievous sins. 13. 1 John 1, 8.

17. *And lead us not into temptation, O Lord.* Does then the Lord teach to pray thus, viz. that we may not be tempted at all? And how is it said elsewhere, "the man who is not tempted, is unproved[d];" and again, *My brethren, count it all joy when ye fall into divers temptations;* or rather does not the entering into temptation mean the being whelmed under the temptation? For the temptation is like a winter-torrent difficult to cross. Some then, being most skilful swimmers, pass over, not being whelmed beneath temptations, nor swept down by them at all; while others who are not such, Jam. 1, 2.

---

[c] Ἐπιούσιος is so explained by Jerome, who for the panem quotidianum of the old Latin version, substituted panem super-substantialem. Others explain the word to mean *future,* or *to come,* i e. the new or spiritual bread, the bread of the new kingdom which is promised us. vid. Athan. de Incarn. 16. Damasc. de Fid. Orth. iv. 13 Others to mean *sufficient,* or *necessary.* vid. Theophylact. in Matt. vi. Basil Reg Brev 252

[d] This is not in Scripture, but seems rather to be a proverb giving the sense of Scripture. It is referred to by Nazianzen, (Ep 215) &c. Ed. Ben

entering into them sink in them. As for example, Judas entering into the temptation of covetousness, swam not through it, but sinking beneath it was choked both in body and spirit. Peter entered into the temptation of the denial; but having entered it, he was not overwhelmed by it, but manfully swimming through it, he was delivered from the temptation. Listen again, in another place, to the company of unscathed saints, giving thanks for deliverance from temptation, *For Thou, O God, hast proved us; Thou hast tried us like as silver is tried. Thou broughtest us into the net; Thou laidest affliction upon our loins. Thou hast caused men to ride over our heads; we went through fire and through water; but thou broughtest us out into a wealthy place.* Thou seest them speaking boldly, because they passed through and were not pierced. *But Thou broughtest us out into a wealthy place;* now their coming into a wealthy place, is their being delivered from temptation.

[margin: Ps 66, 10—12]

(15.)   18. *But deliver us from the evil.* If *Lead us not into temptation* had implied the not being tempted at all, He would not have said, *But deliver us from the evil.* Now the evil is the Wicked Spirit who is our adversary, from whom we pray to be delivered. Then, after completing the prayer, Thou sayest, *Amen;* by this Amen, which means, "So be it," setting thy seal to the petitions of this divinely-taught prayer.

19. After this the Priest says, "Holy things to holy men." (16.) Holy are the gifts presented, since they have been visited by the Holy Ghost; holy are you also, having been vouchsafed the Holy Ghost; the holy things therefore correspond to the holy persons. Then ye say, "One is Holy, One is the Lord, Jesus Christ." For truly One is holy, by nature holy; we too are holy, but not by nature, only by participation, and discipline, and prayer.

[margin: ἐπιφοίτησιν, vid. supr. xxi 1]
[margin: μετοχῇ.]
[margin: ἀσκήσει.]

(17.)   20. After this ye hear the chanter, with a sacred melody inviting you to the communion of the Holy Mysteries, and saying, *O taste and see that the Lord is good.* Trust not the decision to thy bodily palate; no, but to faith unfaltering; for when we taste we are bidden to taste, not bread and wine, but the sign [e] of the Body and Blood of Christ.

[margin: Ps. 34, 9.]

---

[e] Ἀντιτύπου σώματος. vid. above, Lect. xxi. 1 where oil is said to be the ἀντίτυπον of the Holy Ghost in Confirmation, and xx. 6. where Baptism is said

21. Approaching therefore, come not with thy wrists extended, or thy fingers open; but make thy left hand as if a throne for thy right, which is on the eve of receiving the King. And having hollowed thy palm, receive the Body of Christ, saying after it, Amen. Then after thou hast with carefulness hallowed thine eyes by the touch of the Holy Body, partake thereof; giving heed lest thou lose any of it, for what thou losest, is a loss to thee as it were from one of thine own members. For tell me, if any one gave thee gold dust, wouldest thou not with all precaution keep it fast, being on thy guard against losing any of it, and suffering loss? How much more cautiously then wilt thou observe that not a crumb falls from thee, of what is more precious than gold and precious stones? (18.)

22. Then after having partaken of the Body of Christ, approach also to the Cup of His Blood, not stretching forth thine hands, but bending and saying in the way of worship and reverence, Amen, be thou hallowed by partaking also of the Blood of Christ. And while the moisture is still upon thy lips, touching it with thine hands, hallow both thine eyes and brow and the other senses. Then wait for the prayer, and give thanks unto God, who hath accounted thee worthy of so great mysteries. (19.) $\tau\rho\acute{o}\pi\wp$ $\pi\rho o\sigma\kappa u$-$\nu\acute{\eta}\sigma\epsilon\omega s$ $\kappa\alpha\grave{\iota}\ \sigma\epsilon$-$\beta\acute{a}\sigma\mu a$-$\tau os$.

23. Hold fast these traditions unspotted, and keep yourselves free from offence. Sever not yourselves from the Communion; deprive not yourselves, by the pollution of sins, of these Holy and Spiritual Mysteries. *And the God of peace sanctify you wholly; and may your whole spirit, and soul, and body be preserved blameless unto the coming of our Lord Jesus Christ:*—To whom be glory and honour and might, with the Father and the Holy Spirit, now and ever, and world without end. Amen. 1 Thess. 5, 23

---

to be not only pardon and adoption, but also the ἀντίτυπον of the sufferings of Christ. vid Theod. Inconfus p 125. Damascene, however, maintains the word cannot be applied to the elements after consecration. vid. de Fid. Orthod. iv. 13 fin.

INDEX

AARON called Christ, xvi 13. type of Christ's priesthood, x. 11. xii 28 his rod blossoming as strange as Christ's birth, xii 28. and suggests our resurrection, xviii 12 his forgiveness an encouragement to the penitent, ii 10.

Abomination of desolation, iv 15 xv 9

Abraham justified not by works only but by faith, v. 5 perfected by faith, ib Father of Christians, v 6. his faith a type of ours, ib example of reverence to God, vi 3. beheld the Lord, xii 16.

Adam, his creation as strange as Christ's birth, xii 30 first and second Adam, xiii 2. instance of the efficacy of repentance, ii. 7 represented in his innocence by the Baptized, xx. 2.

Adoption of men to be sons of God, vii. 7 by the Father's grace, through the Son and Spirit, ib. in Baptism, Introd. 16. 1 2 iii 14 xx 6 not of necessity, but our free choice, vii. 13. Christ's Sonship not by adoption, x. 4 xi 7. (vide *Son*) Spirit of Adoption, xvii 5

Advent of Christ twofold, xv. 1. First in humiliation, ib.

Second in glory from heaven, xv 1, 3 foretold by Malachi, xv. 2 Ecclesiastes, xv 20 St. Paul, xv 2. time unknown, yet to be expected, xv. 4. signs of it given us by Christ, ib

Object of our hope, xv 1, 2, 33 not from the Earth, xv 10. shall destroy Antichrist, xv. 9, 12. changes accompanying it, xv. 3 shall bring in a new world, xv 4.

Æons of Valentinus, vi 17. why said to be thirty, ib.

Agabus, xiii. 29 xvii. 28.

Ahab, instance of the efficacy of repentance, ii. 13.

Almighty, vide x 5. note. denied of God by Greeks, vii. 1, 2 and Heretics, viii. 3. blasphemies against Him, viii. 8.

Almsdeeds, fruits of repentance, and preparation for Baptism, iii 8 iv. 37. taught by the Holy Ghost, xvi. 12

Altar of God, xxiii 2 of the New Testament, xviii 33

Ambition conquered through the Holy Ghost, xvi 19

Angels made by God, iv 4 made by Christ, xi 23 their orders, iv 16 xi 12 have no equality with the Holy Ghost, xvi 23 governed and sanctified by Him, iv. 16 xvi 23 forgiven by God, ii. 10. vide note fearful to behold, ix 1 xii 14 but little known of them by us, xi 12

Christ their Lord, x. 10 xii 14 not the makers of the world, xi. 21, 22. know not God as He is, vi. 6 vii 11. nor our Lord's generation, xi 11, 12.

Ministered to Christ, x 10 present at Baptism, iii 3 rejoice there, Introd. 15 iii 1, 3, 16. know its Seal, i. 3 (vide *Seal*) glory in the cross, xiii. 22 minister at the judgment, xv 19,22, 28 innumerable there present, xv 24.

Anointing of Christ, x 4, 14. eternally from the Father, ib as God, xi. 15. with the Holy Ghost at His Baptism, xxi 1, 2 vide *Chrism*

Anthropomorphism, vi 8 ix 1

Antichrist, iv. 15. Christ's counterfeit, xv 33 raised up by Satan to discredit truth, xv 11 a sorcerer, ib. Satan shall be in him personally, xv. 14, 17 expected by the Jews, xii 2 foretold by our Lord, xv 9 S Paul, ib Daniel, xv 13 signs of him, xv 9, 18 by sorcery shall gain the Roman Empire, and deceive the Gentiles, xv. 11, 12 the Eleventh King, xv 12, 13 for three years and a half, xv 12, 16. shall be received by the Jews as Christ, xv. 11, 12, 15 rebuild the temple, xv. 15 abhor idols, ib first mild, then persecuting, xv. 12, 15 especially to the Saints, ib shall pretend to miracles, xv 13 shall be destroyed by Christ's Advent, xv 9, 12.

Martyrs under him most glorious, xv 17 we must watch against him, xv 18, 33.

Antediluvians, instance of God's longsuffering, ii. 8.

Apelles, his heresy, iv. 20. note

Apocalypse, not reckoned in the Canon by S. Cyril, iv. 36 perhaps referred to, x 3 xv 27. vide note xv. 16

Apocryphal or doubtful books not to be studied, iv 33, 35 proofs not drawn from them, xv 16

Apostasy foretold by S Paul, in S Cyril's day, xv 9.

U

282   INDEX.

Apostles correspond to the Prophets, xiv. 26. xvi. 4, 24. more favoured than they, xiv 26.

Holy Ghost in them, xvi. 3, 4, 9, 24. partially before Pentecost, xvii 12, 13 baptized fully at Pentecost, xvii 14, 18 supernaturally enlightened, xvi 17

Witnesses of the Cross, xiii 40. and Resurrection, xiv 22 received power to forgive sins in the Holy Ghost, xiv. 22 their deeds by Him, xvii 21 &c.

Send us to the Old Testament for proofs of Christ, xiv. 2 handed down the Scriptures to us, iv 35.

Typified by Joshua's twelve officers, x 11

Apparel, to be simple, iv 29.

Archelaus, a Bishop of Mesopotamia, disputes with Manes, vi. 27—30

Arianism, iv 7 x 5, 6, 9, 14 xi 14. and *Sabellianism* alike to be shunned, iv 8 xi. 13, 16, 17. the "falling away" spoken of by S Paul, xv. 9

As far as, vide *Until.*

Ascension of Christ, iv. 13, 14. foretold by the Prophets, xiv. 24 compared with the translation of Enoch and Elias, xiv 25 preceded the full gift of the Spirit, xvii 12, 13.

Astrologers, iv 18.

Azariah, xvi. 28.

B.

Babel, its confusion contrasted with the gift of tongues at Pentecost, xvii 17

Banker, "be thou a faithful banker," vi 36

Baptism, end of the Old Testament, beginning of the New, iii 6 of John, gave remission of sin, iii 7. xx. 6 preceded by confession, ib. inferior to Christian Baptism, iii 9.

Of our Lord, sanctified ours, iii 11 xii 15 Holy Ghost descended on Him after it, xvii 9 xxi 1. in it He vanquished the Dragon in the waters, iii 11 preparatory to His Temptation, and Ministry, iii. 13, 14 xxi. 4

Christian, offered to all, Intr. 3, 4. iii 1, 2. a trial, xiv 30 xvii. 36 not to be approached lightly, or hypocritically, Introd 2—4. 1 3. (vide *Faith, Hypocrisy, Purpose*) to the faithless a curse, Introd 3, 4. like the parable of the Marriage Feast, Introd. 3 iii 2 the impenitent though washed, not accepted, ib 2, 4 xvii 36 case of Simon Magus, Introd. 2 xvii 35 preparation for it, Introd 16 i 6 iv 37 during Lent, Introd 4 i 5 iv 5. Catechizing and Exorcisms, Introd. 9—14 i 5 Repentance, Introd 4 ii. 5, &c iii. 2, 7, 8 Confession, i 2, 5. men must bring Faith, and look to God for more, Introd 17. v. 9 not the purpose of Baptism, but evil motives to be laid aside, Introd 4, 5.

Given in the name of the Holy Trinity, iii 3 xvi 4, 19 Waters of Baptism, Introd 16 iii 3, 4 contain Christ, Introd 15 why by water, iii 5 One, iv 37 but once to be received, Introd 7 xvii 36 by Heretics not Baptism, ib. Sanctified by our Lord's Baptism, iii 9, 11 xii 15 no salvation without it, iii 4, 10 except to Martyrs, ib

Freely given to faith only, Introd 8. i 4 v 10 conveys remission of sins, Introd 8, 15, 16 iii 15. to all equally, i 5. xvii. 37 xviii 20. the gift of the Holy Ghost, iii 2, 4, 14, 16 iv. 16 but not equally to all, i 5. xvii 37.

Glory and blessing of Baptism, Introd 6, 15, 16 though despised by the world, ib Regeneration, ib i 2 iii 4. iv 37 xx 4 Illumination, xiii 21. Adoption, Introd 16 iii 14 xi 9 titles of, Introd 16 called " Seal indelible," Intr 17 (vide *Seal*) transplants into spiritual Paradise, grafts in the Holy Vine, i 5. xix 9 xx 7 imparts supernatural gifts, i 13 xvii 37 Death of sin, new life, Introd 5, 16 iii. 12 xx 1 makes us members of Christ, xxi. 1 prepares for the resurrection, iv 32. destroys the sting of death, iii 11 Fellowship with Christ's sufferings, iii 12. xx. 5—7 called the "Gift," i 6 ii 9 iii 2, 4, 5, 13, &c of God, through men, xvii 35, 36 Its twofold grace of Water and the Spirit, iii 4, 16 inseparable, ib typified by Circumcision, v 6 to be diligently cherished, i 4 xv 26 xvii. 37. works after it recorded, xv 23.

Names of Candidates enrolled, Introd 1, 4 i. 5 of the Baptized written in the book of the living, xiv. 30 many who fall away blotted out, ib sins after it recorded against the Judgment, xv. 23. xviii. 20. scoffing at, Intr. 16

Baptism of Martyrs in blood, iii 10. xiii. 21. typified by the blood from our Lord's side, ib water of Baptism, by the water, ib.

Baptism of fire, xvii 8 of the Holy Ghost, xv 12, 14.

Administered by Bishops, Priests, or Deacons, xvii 35

Rites previous to, xix. 2, &c. Renunciation of Satan and his works, ib 2—9 Profession of Faith, xix 9. symbolical putting off of garments, xx. 2 anointing with exorcised oil, xx 3 Confession of the Trinity, xx

INDEX.

4 Trine immersion, ib symbolical of Christ's three-days' burial, ib. our death and birth, ib representation of Christ's sufferings, xx 5—7 followed by the Chrism, xxi vide *Chrism*
Baptism of the Manichees, vi 33
Baptistery, xix 2
Barnabas, his preaching in the Holy Ghost, xvii 28
Baruch, accounted in the Canon, iv 35. quoted xi 15
Basilides, his heresy, vi 17.
Basilisk, ix 14
Bath, of Baptism, not common water, Introd 16 iii. 2
Beasts, witnesses of God's power and glory, ix 13 emblems of human tempers, ib in the Ark, xvii 10
Bees, display God's power and wisdom, ix 13 emblematical lessons to man, ib
Beginning (ἀρχή,) only One the Father, xi 14, 20, 22
Believer, vide *Faithful*
Bishops, ministers of Baptism, xvii 35 order of, xvi 22 xvii 35 reverence due to them, iv 35 first Bishop of Jerusalem, S James, iv 28 xiv 21. first fifteen of Jerusalem Hebrews, xiv 15 Ancient Bishops settled and handed down the Canon, iv 35 strife among them a sign of Antichrist, xv 9.
Birds show forth God's glory, ix 12
Birth, New, Christ its author, xvii 10 the gift of Baptism, vide *Baptism, Regeneraton*.
Blasphemy against the Holy Ghost, danger of it, iv 16 xvi 1
Blood and water from Christ's side typical, iii 10 xiii 21 Baptism of Blood, iii 10 river changed into it by Moses corresponds with the Passion, xiii. 21 blood of the Paschal Lamb, xix 2, 3 blood not to be eaten, iv 28 vide xvii 29. Blood of Christ, vide *Eucharist*
Body, work of God, not of the evil one, iv 4, 22 viii 3 xii 26 vilified by Heretics, ib instrument not cause of sin, iv. 23 true part of man, iv 18, 22 xviii 20 its excellence shows God's glory, ix 15 to be cleansed by penitence, iv 23 cleansed by the water of Baptism, iii. 4 yet may be washed without the soul being enlightened, Introd 2 of Christians, temple of the Holy Ghost, iv 23 to be kept pure for its resurrection, iv 26, 30 xviii 20 resurrection of, encouragement to holiness, xviii 1. shown from analogies of nature, &c iv 30. xviii 6, &c shares with the soul, as its deeds, so its reward, xviii 19. (vide *Resurrection*.)

Christ's, (vide *Incarnation, Manhood,*) a bait to Death, xii. 15. veil of His Godhead, xii 26 typified by bread, xiii 19 received under the figure of bread, xxii 3 truly received in the Eucharist, xxii 1—6 Christians made one with His body, and blood, xxii 1—3 (vide *Eucharist, Flesh*)
Book of life, names of the Baptized written in, xiv 30. book of the Angels, iv. 24 our renunciation of sin recorded in God's Book, xix 5
Bread, a prophetic symbol of Christ's body, xiii 19 of the Eucharist, Christ's body, xxii. 1—6, 9 xxiii 7. signified by the show-bread, xxii 5 Supersubstantial bread, xxiii. 15 the Bread has respect to the body, the Word to the soul, xxii 5.
Breath of Christ gave power to forgive sin, xiv 22 xvii 12 and the Holy Ghost partially, xvii 12 Breathing on Candidates for Baptism, Introd 9. of Exorcism, xvi 18 xx 3
Burial of Christ, iv 11 in the Earth to bless the Earth, xiii 18, 35 xiv 11 foretold by the Prophets, xiii 34 xiv 3. in a garden, xiv 11 with Christ in Baptism, Introd 2 iii. 12. xx 4, 5.

C.

Caiaphas, his desolate house a witness, to the Cross, xiii 38.
Cain, an instance of God's mercy, ii 7
Candidates for Baptism, φωτιζόμενοι, Intr 1 xi 9 distinct from Catechumens, and from Believers, Introd 12, 13 must bring a true heart, Introd 1—4 the careless or hypocritical must not forego Baptism but their sin, ib. 4 seriousness becoming their awful situation, ib 13—15
Canon of Scripture settled and handed down by Apostles and Ancient Bishops, iv 35 to be received from the Church, iv 33.
Carpocrates, his heresy, vi 16
Cataphrygians or Montanists, xvi 8
Catechizings previous to Baptism, to be diligently attended, Intr 9, 10. i 5 their importance, ib. guard against error, ib iv. 1. planting, or building up of the Faith, Introd. 11 Creed their subject, ib. iv 2, 3. not to be revealed to Catechumens or Gentiles, Introd 12. (v. end of Introd. Lect)
Catechumen, meaning of the name, Intr. 6. distinct from the Faithful, ib i 4 v. 1 not to be informed of mysteries, Intr 12 nor of the Creed, v 12 vi 29
Catholic Church, vi. 2 xvi. 22 xvii 29 xviii 1.

Meaning of the word, xviii. 23
The name a mark of the true Church, xviii 26. to distinguish it from Heretical assemblies, ib.
Ceremonies of the Law abolished in the Church, xvii. 29
Cerinthus, his heresy, vi 16
Chaff mingled with water by the Manichees, vi. 31.
Chanting of Psalms, xiii. 26. xxiii. 20 imitation of Angels, xiii. 26.
Charms forbidden, iv. 37
Chastity, iv. 24 taught by the Holy Ghost, xvi. 19, 22.
Cherubim, ii 17 ix. 3.
Children, Song of the Three Children — instance of Confession, ii. 16.
Chrism, or Holy Ointment, typical of Christ's unction by the Holy Ghost, xxi 1, 2 after the invocation of Christ's name, by the presence of His Godhead, conveys the Holy Ghost, xxi. 3. the gift of Christ, ib symbolically applied to the different parts of the body, xxi 3, 4. gives the name of Christians, xxi 1, 5. types of it in the Old Testament, xxi 6, 7 to be kept unspotted, xxi 7. prepares us for our conflict, xxi 4
Christ, meaning of the word, x. 4, 11, 14. many so called typically, xi. 1 xxi. 1, 2
    Aaron, x 11 xvi. 13. Saul and David, xvi. 13 Christians, xxi. 1.
    Name shared by the Baptized, Intr 15 xxi. 1
    Christ Jesus the true Christ, x 14 xi. 1.
    One, x. 3, 4 though with many titles, ib His name separated by the Valentinians, vi. 17, 18
    His twofold Nature in One Person, iv 9. xii 1. xv 1. Son of God, and Son of David, xi. 5
    God, iv. 7. very God, x 6 xi 9, 14. proved from the Prophets, xi 15, &c. God of God, begotten, iv 7 xi. 4, 16, 18. Son of God, iv 7. vi 1. vii 1, &c. xii 24 (v. *Son*) only-begotten, iv 7. vii. 4 (v.*Only-begotten*) Eternally, xi 4, 7, 8, 13, 17, 20. Unoriginate, xi. 4, 5, 7. Partaker of the Father's Godhead, together with the Holy Ghost, vi. 6 (v *Trinity*) of the Father, xi 14, 20. xiii 14 begotten not made, xi 14, 17, 19, 20, 21 (v. *Arius*) Like in all things to the Father, iv. 7. xi 4, 9, 18. not the same as the Father, xi 17, 18 (v *Sabellius*.) how subordinate to the Father, x. 9. how one with the Father, xi 16 with the Father before His Incarnation, x 6 8.
    Word Personal of the Father, iv 8 xi 10 Wisdom and Power of the Father, xi 4 Maker of all things, by the will of the Father, iv. 7. x 6 xi 11, 12, 21—24 and their Lord, ib. (v. *Lord*.) His Throne Eternal, iv. 7 xi 17 (v. *Session, Throne*) Anointed Priest before all ages, x 4, 14 xi. 1.
    As Creator so restorer of the world, vi. 11. only way to the Father, x 1, 2. God made man, xii 3, 15 xiii 33 truly made man, iv 9 God dwelling with man, xi 3 Emmanuel, xi 14. Son of David, xi. 5 xii. 23. His incarnation, its reasons, xii 1, &c. xiii. 33 (v. *Incarnation*.) not a deified man, vii. 3 was with the old Fathers, x 7. xii 16 God seen in Him, xiv 27 His various names, express His various offices, x. 3, 4, 11, 13, &c
    Every thing concerning Him written in the Prophets, xii 16. xiii 8 v Lect. x —xv passim (v *Prophets*) Witnesses of Him, x. 17—20 xiii 38—40 xiv 22, 23
    The glory of Baptism, iii 9, 11 sanctified it, ib xii 15 preached not till Baptized, iii. 14 the Holy Ghost came upon Him, xvii. 9 xxi. 2, 3 like but far higher than the Prophets, xiv. 26. alone sinless, ii 10 iii 11 xiii 3, 5 His righteousness greater than our sin, xiii 33
    Died for us, xiii. 2 (v *Crucifixion, Death*) truly, xiii 4, 37 voluntarily, xiii 3, 5, 6, 33.
    Delivered the old Fathers from Hades, iv. 11 (v. *Hades*)
    His appearance after the Resurrection, xiv 11, 12 (v. *Resurrection*)
    His ascension, xiv. 24
    Sits at God's right hand, xiv. 27 present in the Church, xiv 30.
    His second coming in glory, as His first in humiliation, xv 1. (v. *Advent*) warned us against being deceived about it, xv. 4 comes no more from the Earth, xv. 10 our Judge, xv 25. His Kingdom shall have no end, xv 26, 27.
    We are made partakers of Him by the Holy Chrism, xxi 1, 6. and the Eucharist, xxii 1 (v *Father, God, Jesus, Son, Trinity, Word*.)
Christians, so called by the Holy Ghost, xvii 28. partakers of Christ's name, x 16. xxi 1. honour of this, x. 20. the new name spoken of by the Prophets, x 16
    Spread over the world, x 16 xvi 22 slandered through the crimes of heretics, xvi 8 who falsely share their name, ib vi. 12 to be espe-

INDEX. 285

cially persecuted by Antichrist, xv. 12, 15. figures of Christ, xxi 1

Church Catholic throughout the world, xvi 22 xviii. 23 (v *Kingdom*) governed and sanctified by the Comforter, xvi 14, 19, 22 xvii 13. Christ present in her assemblies, xiv 30 ever present witness of Christ, xiii. 40. (v *Creed*, *Faith*) New Covenant established in her by the blessed Trinity, xvii 29 Baptism plants in her, Intr 17. xviii 26. witness and keeper of Holy Writ, iv. 33, 35 xv. 13 (v *Scripture*) her teaching guard from error, iv 1, 2 xi. 18 xii 17 xvii. 3

Her order, Intr 4, 13 contrasted with heresy, vi 35, 36. reverence in Church, Intr 14, 15 due to her ancient Bishops from her children, iv 35 to be diligently attended before and after Baptism, i 6 xviii 28 meaning of the word ἐκκλησία, xviii 24, 25 Christian has succeeded the Jewish, ib why called Catholic, ib 23, 26 her glories, xviii 28

Falling away in it a sign of Christ's coming, xv 7. makes way for Antichrist, xv 9, 18 existed in S Cyril's day, ib lurking heretics in it, ib.

Church of the Apostles, xvi 4. of Golgotha, xiv 6 (v *Golgotha*) of the Resurrection, ib adorned by Kings, xiv 9, 14 Constantine, ib 22. Witness of the Resurrection of the Lord, ib 23 the last five Lectures delivered there, xviii 33

Circumcision, a seal—type of the seal of the Spirit in Baptism, v. 5, 6 of the Spirit, v. 6.

Clement of Rome, quoted, xviii 8.

Clouds show God's glory, ix 9

Comforter, not diverse from the Holy Ghost, xvii 2 xvi. 3, 4 why so called, xvi 20 governs and sanctifies the Church, xvi. 22 Angels and Prophets, xvi 23 abides for ever with the Faithful after Baptism, xvii 37 (v *Spirit*.) Manes called himself the Comforter, vi 25 xvi 6 9 and Montanus, xvi 8

Communion in Christ's mysteries, i. 1. in the Holy Ghost given according to each man's faith, i 5 Communion Service, xxiii. 1, &c.

Confession, ἐξομολόγησις, v ii 15 note. before Baptism, i 2, 5 takes away sin, as in David's case, ii 11, 12 Hezekiah's, ib 15 can quench fire, and tame lions, ib 16. made before John's Baptism, iii 7 by Martyrs, iii 10.

of the Trinity in Baptism, xx 4

of the seraphim ; θεολογία, xxiii 6.

Confessors comforted by the Holy Ghost, xvi 20, 21

Consecration of the Bread and Wine, xxiii 7.

Constantine, xiv 22

Continence, or widowhood, ἐγκράτεια, iv 26 x. 19 xv 23.

Controversy an evil, though necessary, vi 13 how to be engaged in, xiii 22, 37 (v *Heresy*)

Cornelius though regenerated, yet baptized with water, iii 4 xvii. 27.

Covenant New in the Church, xvii 29, of Noah and Moses not made without water, iii 5

Covetousness conquered through the Holy Ghost, xvi 19

Creation, how to be ascribed to the Father and Son, vi 9. xi. 21, 22. of all things by God denied by Heretics, iv. 4 of the world in spring-time answered by the Resurrection at the same time, xiv 10. material creation, good in itself, marred by the creature, ii. 1 blasphemed by Manichees, vi 31. God seen in it, ix 2 glorifies Him, ix 5, &c we know but little of it, ix 13, 14 should teach us reverence to Him, ix. 16

Creator of all things God, iv 4. vi 7. not the author of evil, ii 1, 4 blasphemed by Heretics, ix 4. Creator of the world its Restorer, vi 11

Creed, πίστις, (v. *Faith*) to be received from the Church, v 12 collected and proved from Scripture, ib. iv 17. epitome of necessary doctrine for the weak, ib provision for our way, ib. safeguard against error, iv 2 vii 1, 4 viii. 1 ix. 4 x 4 xi 1 xv 2, 27. xvii 3 xviii 1. confutes Sabellius, xvii. 31 not to be written down, or divulged to Catechumens, v. 12, its Articles briefly expounded, iv.

Cross, chief boast of the Church Catholic, xiii 1, 22 redeemed and enlightened the world, ib. we must not be ashamed of it, xiii 3, 36, 37. glorified by the Resurrection, xiii. 4. glory to Christ, xiii 6 foretold by Jeremiah, xiii 19. and Moses, ib. if an illusion, so is our salvation, xiii. 37 foundation of the Faith, xiii 38.

Sign of it to be used on all occasions, iv 14 xiii 22, 36 scares devils, iv 13 xiii. 3, 36. its power and virtue, xiii. 40 Christ's royal sign, iv. 14. xii 8 trophy, xiii. 40. "Sign of the Son of Man," xiii 41 xv. 22

Cross, wood of it dispersed through the world, iv. 10, note. x. 19 xiii. 4 witness of Christ through the world, x 19. of His real Passion, xiii 4

286   INDEX.

Cross, Basilica of the Holy Cross, Pref p xxiv (v. *Golgotha*)
Crown of thorns, signified the cancelling of Adam's curse, xiii 17, 18
Crucifixion not in appearance, but real, iv 10 xiii. 4 if an illusion, so is Salvation, xiii. 37 for our sins, iv 10. xiii 3, 5, 33 its time the same as that of the descent of the Spirit, xvii. 19 this and its other circumstances foretold, xiii. 24, &c. its witnesses, xiii 38—40
The Crucified, xiii 3, 22, 23, 36, 40
Curiosity, about mysteries of Baptism fearful, Intr. 2, 4. iii 7.
To be limited by what is written, xi. 12. xvi 1, 2 to give place to faith, xi 19, 20.

D.

Daniel, his power in the Holy Ghost, xvi 31 prophesied of the Romans, xii 18 xv 13 of the time of the Messiah, xii. 19 of Antichrist, xv 9—16. explanation of his prophecy, ib endured not the sight of the Angel, xii 14 (v *Confession*)
Darkness made by the author of Light, ix 7. denied by heretics, ib (v *Night*) of the Crucifixion foretold, xiii 24
David, (v. *Christ, Spirit*) spake of Christ by the Holy Ghost, x. 15 xiv. 28. Christ his Son, and Heir of his throne, xii. 23 not the exclusive object of the Psalms, ib vii 2
Saved by Confession, ii. 10 yet refused not penitence, though forgiven, ii 11
Deacons the first seven, firstborn children of the Church of Jerusalem, xvii 24 may administer Baptism, xvii 35
Dead, how Christ so called, x 4 raised by Elijah and Elisha, xiv 15, 16 by Christ without touching them, xiv 16. in His name, witness His resurrection, xiv. 23 (v *Resurrection, Judgment*)
Death, invisible whale of death, xiv 17. brought by the First man, as Life by the Second, xiii 2 v. xii. 15 doom of sins, xiii 33 vanquished by Christ's death, xii 15 xiv. 19 sting destroyed in Baptism, iii 11 death in Baptism, Intr 5. iii 12 xx 4
Of Christ real not illusory, xiii 4. not for His sin, but ours, xiii 5, 33 voluntary, ib 6, 28 foretold by Himself, xiii 6 God's sentence, and His mercy reconciled in it, xiii. 33
Demetrius of Phalerum, iv 34.
Descent into Hell, iv. 11. xiv. 19.
Of the Spirit on Christ, how explained, xvii 9.

Despair, its evils, ii 5.
Devil, meaning of the word, ii 4 the dragon, Intr 16 apostate Serpent, iv 37 first work of God, viii 4 fallen Archangel, ii 4 viii 4 impenitent, iv. 1 author of evil by this free choice, ii 14 not the Lord of the world, viii 6, 7 his envy against man, xii 5 xix 4. prompts not forces to sin, ii 3, 4 iv 21, 37 men have freely chosen him their Father, vii. 13 knew not Christ, xii 15. tries to prejudice truth by his counterfeits in idolatry, xv 11. shall work personally in Antichrist, xv 14 and war with the Martyrs, xv. 17 vanquished and cast out through the Holy Ghost, xvi 19. endured by God that man may conquer him, viii. 4. watches the Candidates for Baptism, Intr 16 renounced with his works in Baptism, xix 2-9 what his works are, ib pursues us to Baptism, xix 2, 3
Devils tremble at the seal of Baptism, i 3. xvii 35, 36 and the sign of the Cross, xiii 3. possession by them fearful, xvi 15 power against them given by the Holy Ghost, xvi 12, 22 acknowledge Christ, while Jews knew Him not, x. 15 lurked in our members till Baptism, xx 2 driven away by the Exorcised oil, xx 3
Devotion, end of religious knowledge, vi 7. xi 12, 20 *seu* l, 2.
Diocese, xiv 21 xvi 22. (v. παροικία)
Dispensation, from the Father and the Son One, xvii 5. (v οἰκονομία)
Divination, to be shunned by Christians, iv 37.
Divisions in the Church make way for Antichrist, xv 7, 9, 18
Docetæ, iv 9 vi 14 xii 3
Doctrines to be withheld from Catechumens, Intr 12 true, equally necessary with good works, iv 2 to be proved from Scripture, iv 17. xii 5 xiii. 8. (v *Faith, Scripture*) not fully comprehended by us, xi 12, 19 xvi 1 fondness for ingenious rather than practical ones, an evil sign, xv. 9
Door, Christ, x 1, 3
Dove, why a symbol of the Holy Spirit, xvii 9 of Noah, xvii 10.
Dragon, xii. 15 head of the Dragon, heresy, xv 27
In the waters, Intr 16 iii 11

E

Earth freed from Adam's curse by Christ's burial, xiii 18, 35 xiv 11
East, symbolical turning towards it in Baptism, xix. 9

INDEX. 287

Easter, xvii: 20. xviii 33. season of Baptism, ib.
Ebionites, vi 16 xii 4.
Egypt, Christ went there to destroy its idols, x 10 His witness, x 19, deliverance from, typical of Baptism, xix 3, 4
Elder, seventy Elders had the Holy Spirit, xvi 25
Elijah full of the Holy Spirit, xvi. 28. saw Christ in Sinai and Tabor, xii 16. his raising the dead answers objections against Christ's resurrection, xiv 15 compared with it, ib 16 his translation compared with Christ's ascension, xiv 25 not so favoured as the Apostles, xiv 26 typical passing of Jordan, iii 5
Elisha full of the Holy Ghost, xvi. 28. supernaturally enlightened, ib 17 his raising the dead, xiv 15, 16. compared with Christ's, ib
Elizabeth full of the Holy Ghost, xvii 7
Emmanuel v *Immanuel*
End of the world not end of Christ's kingdom or person, xv. 27—32.
Enlighten, said of Baptism, Intr 1 xiii 21 Simon Magus not enlightened though baptized, Intr 2. the Holy Ghost enlightens, xvi. 16—18. xvii 13 (v *Illuminate*)
Enmity, there is a righteous enmity, vi 35 xvi 10 against blasphemers of God, taught by the world's wonders, ix 16
Epistles of St Paul final seal of the Scripture, iv 36 why most numerous, x. 18 their completeness and variety of teaching about the Holy Ghost, xvii 34
Epistle of the Apostles on the observance of the Jewish Law by Gentiles, iv 28 xvii 29 Universal, ib
Eternity of the Son of God xi 20 of His generation, iv. 7 of His Priesthood, x 14 of His throne, xiv 27
Ethiopia, Church there, xvi 22 taught by the Eunuch, xvii 25 xvi 14
Eucharist, Christ's blessed gift, xiii 6 The Body and Blood of the Lord truly there, xxii 1, 2 under the figure of Bread and Wine, xxii 3 The Bread and Wine after invocation not simple elements, but the Body and Blood of Christ, xix 7 xxii 2, 6, 9 xxiii 7 not bread and wine, but the sign of Christ's Body and Blood, xxiii. 20 analogy of Idol-sacrifices, xix 7. of the Holy Chrism, xxi 3. we must not judge by sense of this mystery, xxii 6, 9 but believe that we have received Christ's Body and Blood, ib. 1—6 xxiii. 20 a spiritual mystery, xxii 4, 8
The Bread and Wine after the invocation of the Holy Trinity, xix. 7. made the Body and Blood of Christ, xxiii 7. sanctified and changed by the Holy Ghost, ib gifts hallowed by the Holy Ghost, xxiii 19
Spiritual Sacrifice of propitiation, xxiii 8, 9 supplications after it for the Living, ib. 8 and the Dead, xxiii 9
The Super-substantial Bread, xxiii 15 nourishment of Soul and Body, ib xxii 5
Typified by the Show-Bread, xxii 5 foretold by David, ib 7 and Ecclesiastes, ib 8
By it we bear Christ in us, xxii 3 Mode of Communicating in Christ's Body, xxiii 21 and Blood, xxiii 22.
Eve a virgin in Paradise, xii. 5 death through her, as through Mary, life, xii 15 her birth as strange as our Lord's, ib 29
Evil the creature's work, not the Creator's, ii 1 evil God believed by the Manichees and Gnostics, vi. 12, 13. physical evil, ix 14
Exercise, ἄσκησις, previous to Baptism, i 5 iii 7
Exorcisms previous to Baptism, Intr 9. expel evil spirits, ib cleanse the soul, ib collected from the Scriptures, ib to be diligently attended, i. 5 power through the Holy Ghost, xvi 19 22.
Exorcised oil, xx 3
Ezekiel saw but the likeness of God's glory, ix 1 his vision, ix 3 prophecy of Baptism, iii. 16. xvi. 30.

F.

Faith, ground and bond of human action, v 3 principle of holiness, v 4, 7 exemplified in Abraham, v 5 power of faith, ii 16 v 7, 8 in one man for another, v 8, 9 partly our own, but chiefly God's gift to those who ask, v 9 two kinds of faith; one, our assent to doctrines, saves at once, v 10 another, a gift of the Spirit, reward of the former, working miracles, v 11
Alone wanted to cure our worst sins, ii 6 in Baptism, i 1 v. 2 xvii 35 necessary to our New Birth, i 2 iii 1. enables us to receive the gift of Baptism, v 6 purifies the soul, iii 2. makes sons of God, vii 13 without works saved the robber, v 10 xiii 31. God can give faith to the faithless if he but asks, Intr 17 v 9 To be tried by false miracles as well as persecution, xv 17 and by false doctrine, xiii 37.
Faith, πίστις, i.e the Creed—one, Intr 7. xvi. 4, 24 delivered by the Church

INDEX.

and proved from Scripture, iv 17 v 12 guard against error, iv. 2. outline of teaching, iv. 3. v. 1. note. xiv 24, 27. a deposit, and treasure, v. 13 (v *Creed.*)

Faithful, i. e. Baptized Christians, Intr. 13. dignity of the title, Intr 6 v 1, 2 new name given in Baptism, i. 4. must not presume, ii 3

Fall of Adam corresponded to in its circumstances by the Passion, xiii 19

Fasting taught by the Holy Ghost, xvi. 12. means towards salvation, ii. 9. preparatory to Baptism, iii 7. part of repentance, ib. 16. iv 37. David's, ii. 12. reason of fasting, iv 27. those who cannot not to be despised, ib fast of the Preparation, xviii 17 (v *Meats*)

Fatalism of heretics, iv 18--20 vii 13

Fate not cause of sin, iv. 18—21 vii. 13 nor of our Sonship to God, vii 13. God not subject to it, iv. 5

Father, One God the Father, vii 1 xi 13. to be included in our notion of God, vi. 1. Father, by the Son, with the Holy Ghost bestows all things, xvi. 4, 24 xviii. 28 (v *Trinity.*) One in glory with the Son and Holy Ghost, vi 1. the God of the Old Testament, vii 6. Maker of the World, ib. through the Son, vi. 9 xi. 11, 12, 21—24

The Father in respect of the Son, vii 1—5 viii 1. as opposed to Jewish unbelief, vii. 2. properly and by nature the Father of Christ, iv 4 vi 1. vii. 5, 7, 10 how He begat the Son, He, with the Son and Holy Ghost, alone knows, xi 8, 11 we know but negatively, ib heresies as to how God is Father, vi. 6. vii 5 xi 4 7—10, 14, 18 not changed into the Son, xi. 13, 17, 18. distinct, yet not to be separated from the Son, iv. 8 (v *Arius, Sabellius*) suffered not for us, xi. 17 Father from Eternity, vii. 5 xi. 4, 8 never not the Father, iv 5 vii 5, 11 —The beginning (ἀρχὴ ἄναρχος,) of the Son, xi 14, 20 xiii 23 apart from time, xi 20 in the Son, xi. 17 one with the Son, xi 16 called by the Son His God, xi. 18 fountain of life, and good, vi 9. xi. 18, 20. xviii. 29. worshipped through, xi 17. xii 15 and with the Son, x. 1, 2. only known to the Son and Holy Ghost, vi. 6 vii. 11 ix 1,2 xi 12 revealed by the Son, through and with the Holy Ghost, vi 6 x 1. seen only in the Son, x 7, 8 xi 18 xiv. 27 (v *Angels*)

How called " My Father " by Christ, vii 7 xi 18, 19.

Father of men by adoption, vii 8 by faith, and their own choice, vii. 13 in Baptism, xi 9 —inconceivable honour for man to have God for his Father, vii. 12 xxiii. 11.

Other metaphorical senses of the word, vii. 8—10

Satan chosen by men for their father, vii. 13.

Father, earthly Fathers receive their prerogative from the Heavenly Father, vii. 3 to be honoured by the Sons of God, vii 15 duty to them, the first Christian duty, vii 15, 16.

Fathers of the Old Testament delivered by Christ from Hades, xiv. 19 fountains of truth to us, xvi 11.

Fig-tree cursed for the sake of the type, xiii 19

Figure, τύπος, Bread and Wine of Christ's Body and Blood, xxiii 3.

Figure, ἀντίτυπον, Baptism, of Christ's sufferings. xx 6 Chrism, of the Anointing of the Holy Ghost, xxi 1. Bread and Wine, xxiii 20

Fire, Exorcism compared to it, Introd 9. Baptism of, xvii 8 of the Holy Ghost like it, xvii 12, 14 fiery tongues at Pentecost, xvii. 15. opened Paradise, which the fiery sword had guarded, ib.

First-born, Christ in an exclusive sense, xi 4. Israel so called, ib.

Fishes show God's glory, ix 11

Flesh framed by God, xii 26, not unholy as heretics say, ib Christ not ashamed of it, ib hallowed by our Lord's incarnation, xii. 15 His weapon to conquer the devil, and death, ib. His flesh the veil of His Godhead, xii. 26 xiii 32. " eating the flesh of Christ," not understood spiritually by the Jews, xxii 4.

Flowers, their varied beauty show forth God's glory, ix 10

Forgiveness of sins, Christ's free gift, ii. 15 power of conferring it granted to the Apostles, xiv. 22. xvii. 12. how typified, xv 21

Of injuries required in Baptism, i 6 case of David and Shimei, ii 11. Even Angels forgiven, ii 10.

Forgiveness of injuries required from sinners in the Holy Communion, xxiii. 16. (v *Remission, Sin*)

Fornication defiles the temple of the Holy Ghost, iv 23

Freedom of the soul, ii. 1, 2. iv 18, 21.

G.

Gabriel, his appearance too bright for Daniel, xii 14. Messenger to the blessed Virgin, xvii 6 witnessed of the endless kingdom of Christ, xv 27

Galatia, heresy of Marcellus arose there, xv. 27.

INDEX. 289

Garment of incorruption, xv. 26 of Salvation, xix. 10. putting off of garments in Baptism, xx. 2.

Gaul, the Church there, xvi 22

Generation of Christ twofold, xi. 5 xv. 1 His Divine generation spiritual, xi 5, 7, 8. mysterious, xi 7, 8 not metaphorical, xi 9. not as mind begets thought, xi. 10 incomprehensible, iv. 7. known to no creature, xi. 11, 13. only to the Holy Ghost, xi 12. declared only negatively by the Church, xi. 11. not to be examined but believed, xi. 19, 20.—eternal, iv 7. without beginning, vii 4 xi. 4, 5, 7, 19. timeless, xi. 7, 8, 14, 17, 20. (v. *Father, Son.*)

Gethsemane, x 19.

Ghost, Holy (v *Spirit.*)

Gift, name of Baptism, i. 6. heavenly gift, ii 20. Gifts of the Father, Son, and Holy Ghost, same, xvi. 24 (v. *Baptism*)

Chrism, gift of Christ, xxi 3

Gifts of the Eucharist, hallowed by the Holy Ghost, xxiii. 19

Glory of Christ, eternal, as God, in time, as crucified, xiii. 6.

Gnostics, their heresies about the generation of the Son, vii 5, note. against the Holy Ghost, xvi 4, 7 separated the two Testaments, xvi 4 abhorred flesh and wines, iv. 27, note. v. iv 20. 22.

God, (v. *Creator, Father, Trinity,*) knowledge of Him foundation of religion, iv. 4. ignorance about Him source of heresy and idolatry, iv. 6. viii 1.

One, iv. 4 vi. passim, viii. 1, 8. xi. 17 unoriginate, unchangeable, iv. 4, 5 vi. 7 one first principle, vi 12, 13, 36 xi. 28. incorporeal, vi 7, 8 ix. 1 uniform in substance, vi. 7 like to Himself, vi. 7 infinite, iv. 5 vi 8 viii. 2. incomprehensible, vi 2, 4, 7. even to angels, vi 6. to all but the Son and Spirit, ib. x. 1. unspeakable in beginning, form, nature, vi. 7. yet we must, not indeed declare, but glorify Him, as far as we know, vi. 5. ix. 3, 16. our best knowledge to know our ignorance of Him, vi. 2. invisible, ix 1, 2 seen partially by angels, vii. 11 to man in Christ, x. 6, 7, 8. xii 16. xiv. 27. dimly in His works, ix. 2, &c

Both Just and Good, iv 4, vi 7 and full of all perfection, vi 7, 8, 9 Father of Christ, vii 5 Maker of all things, iv. 4. ix. 1, &c of darkness as well as light, ix 7. Almighty, and Sovereign over all things, though long-suffering, viii 1, &c. is in all things, vi 8, 9. all things serve Him, save the Son and Spirit, viii 5

Forsaken by idolaters, vi. 10, 11. xii 5, &c His great mercy, ii. 7, 10 pardons worst of sinners who believe, ii 5, 6

Present in Baptism, Intr. 15.

Lord both of soul and body, iv 4, 22. viii. 3

Blasphemed by heretics, vi. 12 viii 8 ix 16. not two Gods, vi. 13 viii. 3 not the soul of the world, viii. 2. various heresies concerning Him, iv 4, 5 vi. 14, &c.

" *God of Abraham, Isaac, and Jacob*," xviii. 11, 12.

God of God, (v. *Christ.*) made man, xi 15. xii. 3. xiii 33.

" *God of this world*," the words perverted by Manes, vi. 28 how explained by Archelaus, and S. Cyril, vi 28, 29.

God the Son, the Word, xii 3. (v *Christ, Son*)

God, the Holy Ghost, (v. *Spirit*)

Golgotha, St. Cyril's first xviii Lectures spoken in the Church there, iv. 10 xiii 22 vide xviii. 33. name typically prophetic of Christ, xiii 23 witness of the Crucifixion, iv. 10, 14. x. 19 xiii. 4, 39.

Gospel, only four genuine, iv. 36. forged ones, ib. Manichæan Gospel according to Thomas, iv. 36. vi 31. our Gospels attested by the Old Testament, xiv. 2 that according to S Matthew written in Hebrew, xiv. 15.

All may hear, but not understand the Gospel, Intr. 6 vi 29.

Phrase "in the Gospel," ἐν εὐαγγελίοις, vi 4, 7. xiii. 21, 35.

Grace, God's to give, ours to use, i 4 necessary that we may receive the truth, xvi. 2. requires honesty and faith, i 3 to be received and cherished, xvii. 37 given through Christ at the New Birth, i. 2.

Gift of grace, ii. 9

Spirit of grace, xvii. 5.

Greeks, dangerous because of their plausible words, iv 2. deny the resurrection, xviii 1 limit God's power, viii. 2 believe things as hard as Christ's birth, xii 27. to be silenced out of their own fables, xiii. 37 to be answered by reasoning, as the Jews by Scripture, xviii 10. their shameful idolatry, iv 6. vi. 11.

H.

Habakkuk, carried by the angel to Daniel, xiv. 25. compared with Christ, ib.

Hades. (v. *Hell.*)

X

Hands of Christ stretched on the Cross typical, xiii. 27, 28 laying on of, conveys the Spirit in both Testaments, xvi. 26
Head v. xiii. 23
Heathenism counterfeits truth to discredit it, xv 11 (v *Idolatry*)
Hearers, danger lest they receive false impressions of truth, xvi 2.
Heavens, vi. 3 the abode of angels, iii. 5. made of water, ib. ix 5. Heaven distinguished from the Third Heaven, xiv 26 its wonders shew God's glory, ix 5 shall perish but be renewed, xv. 3 Christians, a heaven, xxiii. 11.
Hell, Christ descended thither to redeem the just, iv 11 xiv. 19.
Herbs, men changed into them, who plucked them, according to Manes, vi 31.
Heresy, manifold, iv. 2 vi. 13. xvii 33. xviii. 1 contrasted with the Church, vi. 35 a knowledge of it necessary, vi. 34. xvi 5. yet an evil, vi 13, 33 arising from presumption, xi 12 from a mistaken thought of honouring the Father or the Son, xi. 17 v x 2 not to be curiously inquired into, vi 19.
Heresies alluded to by S Cyril —of Apelles; Arius; Basilides, Carpocrates; Cataphrygians; Cerinthus; Docetæ; Ebionites; Gnostics, Manes, Marcellus; Marcion; Menander; Montanus; Noctus; (iv 8 note) Paul of Samosata, (iv.8.x 5 xii 4 xiv 27) Sabellius; Simon Magnus; Valentinus.
Heretics perverted Holy Scripture, iv 19. vi 27 their assemblies to be shunned, iv. 37 how to be treated, vi 36 to be avoided, xvi. 6. why they should be hated, xvi 10. falsely called Christians, vi 12, on whom they brought discredit, xvi 8 blasphemous to God, xi 16 a sign of Christ's coming, xv. 5. formerly manifest, now lurking in the Church, xv. 9 divided attributes into persons, iv. 4 x 1, 3 xvii. 2.
Hermas a disciple of Manes, vi 31.
Hezekiah shewed the efficacy of Confession, ii. 15 not the object of Isaiah's prophecy of Immanuel, xii. 21, 22.
High Priest, reason of his bathing, iii. 5. Christ our High Priest, x. 4, 5, 11, 14 xii 28.
Holiness, all through the Holy Ghost, iv. 16 Faith, its ground, v 4. Spirit of, xvii. 5. (v *Sanctification*)
Hope support to Candidates for Baptism, Intr 9, 10.
Hour, third, that of the Crucifixion, and of the descent of the Spirit at Pentecost, xvii 19 of the Crucifixion foretold, xiii 24, 25
Human conceptions not to be intruded into the mysteries of the Gospel, xi. 7, 8
Human nature of our Lord, (v. *Incarnation*)
Hyssop, symbolical, iii 1.

I.

Idols, offerings to, become polluted by the invocation of the idol's name, iii. 3 xix. 7. not to be touched, iv. 28.
Idolatry, worship of God's gifts, vi. 10. its madness, iv. 6 and degradation, vi. 10, 11. will be abhorred by Antichrist, xv. 15
Ignorance of all creatures concerning God, vi 2 – 6. xi. 11. check to presumption, not to praise, vi 5 should repress our curiosity, xi. 11. knowledge of it our highest wisdom, vi. 2 of what is written should make us silent about what is not written, xi. 12 xvi. 1 and guarded in speaking, xvi. 1.
Illuminated, Intr. 1, 2. xviii 33. alone know the glory of the Gospel, vi. 29
Illumination of the just by the Holy Ghost, xvi. 3, 11 its power, xvi 16—18. same as Baptism, φώτισμα, xiii 21
Image, Christ the true Image of God to subvert the false one, xii. 15. man, God's image, xii. 5 soul, made in God's image, iv. 18. meaning of the "Image of God," xiv. 10. "our Image," argument from the words, x. 6.
Immortality of the soul, God's gift, iv 18.
Immanuel, prophecy of, xii 3, 21, 22. meaning of the word, xi. 14.
Impersonal, (ἀνυπόστατος,) words, iv. 8.
Incarnation of our Lord, real not illusory, iv 9. xii. 3 salvation depends on its reality, xiii. 4. denied by Simon Magus, vi 14. v. xii. 31

Must be believed as well as Christ's Godhead, xii. 1. heretical and infidel objections à priori, from its needlessness, xii. 4 reasons for it, vi. 11. Creator of the world its Restorer, ib to restore man, xiii. 5. proved from the prophets, xiii 8 &c. that man might see God, x. 7. xii. 13, 14 to sanctify the waters,—that God might be worshipped,—that man might be made partaker of God;—that the Lord might suffer for us, xii. 15. objection to its possibility, xii. 4. answered, xii. 27—30

Christ Lord and God before it, x. 6, 12. xi. 20 of a Virgin, iv. 9 xii. 2, 5, 21. why, xii 25, 33, 34. blasphemies of heretics respecting it, ib. xii 31. without taint because of the Holy Ghost, xii. 29, 32. xvii. 6 signs of its time, place and manner given

INDEX

by the Prophets, xii 5, 10—12, 17—24 implied in the histories of Abraham, Jacob, Moses, and Elias, xii 16. witnesses of it, xii 32, 33
  Satan's counterfeits among idolaters to discredit it, xv 11
Indians, converts to the Church, xvi 22
Inspiration contrasted with possession by devils, xvi 15, 16
Interpretation of Scripture, xiii 9 gift of the Spirit, xvi 12 (v. *Scripture*)
Interpreter, viii 7 xiii. 21. xvi. 6. vide xv 13
Invocation of the Holy Trinity gives a sanctifying power to the water of Baptism, iii 3. to the exorcised oil, xx 3. analogy of the invocation of the idols' name on offerings to them, iii 3 xix 7. of Christ on the Holy Ointment, causes it to convey the Holy Ghost, xxi 3 of the most Holy Trinity on the Bread and Wine, xix. 7 makes them the Body and Blood of Christ, xxiii 7
Irenæus quoted, xvi 6
Isaiah prophesied of Christ, xii 2 of His birth of a virgin, xii 2 this explained, ib 21, 22. beheld Christ, xiv 27 and in the Spirit foresaw His coming, xiii 3. witness of His innocence, ib foreknowledge given Him by the Holy Ghost, xvi 18.
  Sawn asunder, ii 14. xiii 6.

J.

Jacob saw the Lord, xii 16 prophesied of the time of His coming, ib 17.
Jeremiah, his prophecy of the Lord's sufferings, xiii 7 of gentile faith, ib
Jericho, x 11.
Jerusalem, its exclusive privileges. iii 7 xiii 22 xvi 4 xvii 13 Christian opposed to Jewish, xiii 7 St James its first Bishop, iv 28 xv 21 first fifteen Bishops Hebrews, xiv 15.
Jesus, so named because He saves, x 11, 12, 13 and heals us, x 4, 13 meaning in Hebrew, and Greek, x 12, 13 Joshua a type of Him in His kingly office, x. 11 (v *Christ*) His name hinted at by the Prophets, x 12 not more distinctly because of the Jews, x 12
Jews study and know the Scriptures without understanding them, iv 2. xii 13 to be silenced from the Prophets, xiii. 37 xviii 10 despise the testimony of the Prophets in rejecting the Lord, vii 2. x. 2 xii 2 xiv 15 deny that Jesus is Christ, x. 14 while devils acknowledge Him, x 15
  Misinterpret the Prophets, xii 21, 22 infidel objections to the Incarnation, xii. 4, 27. absurdly apply the prophecies of Christ's eternal kingdom to men, vii. 2. gainsay our Lord's sufferings, xiii 7 their subjection to Rome a proof that Christ is come, xii 17. vain attempt to discredit the Resurrection, xiv 14. their objections confuted by the examples of Elijah and Elisha, xiv 15
  Their Patriarchs, xii 17
  Are looking for Antichrist, xii 2 will receive him, xv. 11, 12, 15 will be favoured by him, xv 15 their observances and sabbaths to be shunned, iv 37
Job had the Holy Ghost, xvi 27
St John Baptist—his high office, baptism, and character, iii 6 (v *Baptism*) link between the two covenants, x 19 delivered from Hades and death by Christ, iv 11 xiv 19
  Sanctified by the Holy Ghost to baptize Christ, xvii 8.
St John the Divine, xii 1
Jonah a type and proof of Christ's resurrection, xiv 17 compared with Christ, xiv. 17, 18 in the whale, a type of Christ in Hades, xiv 20. his prayer fulfilled only in Christ, ib.
Jordan, typical, iii 5 x. 11 xiv 25
Joseph, his ill-treatment turned to good by God's providence, viii 4 full of the Holy Ghost, xvi 27.
Joseph, how called the Father of Christ, vii 9. not really so, xii 3, 31
Judas, xiii 6 his treason foretold, xiii 9 meaning of the name, ib. explanation of Zechariah's prophecy relating to him, ib 10, 11
Judge, Christ, of quick and dead, xv 26.
Judgment, day of, xv 21 its glories and terrors, xv 22, 26 hope of the poor and desolate, xv 23 God and all Angels present, xv 24 How Christ bids us prepare for it, xv 26
  Judgment of our Lord by His people, a sign foretold, xii 12 xiii 12
Just, "the Just" delivered by Christ from Hades, (v *Hell*)
  illuminated by the Holy Ghost, xvi 3, 27.
  The Just God blasphemed by heretics, iv. 4
Justification given in Baptism, Intr 16 1. 4 of Abraham by faith, vi 5 even by riches, viii 6

K

Keys of heaven given to St Peter, xiv 26.
Kings reign through God, viii 5 in the latter days honour the Gospel, xiv. 14 taught by the Church, xvii 10
Kingdom of Christ, universal foretold by Daniel, xii. 18 without bound, xii 24. unwittingly acknowledged in

INDEX.

the soldiers' mockery, xiii 17 never to end, iv. 15. xv. 27 heresy of Marcellus regarding it, ib &c. God's kingdom, in the Lord's Prayer, xxiii. 13. Four great kingdoms, xv. 13. kingdom of Antichrist, xv. 12, 13.

Kiss of Peace, xxiii. 3.

Knowledge not for curiosity but devotion, vi 5, 7. supernaturally given by the Holy Ghost, xvi 16 in the Apostles and Prophets, ib. 17, 18.

L.

Lamentations of Jeremiah refer to the second captivity of the Jews, xiii 7

"*Lamp*," meaning of in Psalm 132, x 15.

Laver of Baptism, (λουτρόν,) Intr 2, 7, 11. i. 2. iii. 3, 5. iv. 32 v 6, &c one salvation of the Laver, iv 37. of Regeneration, xix 10 repentance of the Laver, iv. 32 Laver (λουτήρ,) in the Tabernacle an emblem of Baptism, iii. 5

Law, inspired by the Holy Ghost, iv 16. blasphemed by heretics, iv. 33. fulfilled in Christ, iv 33 xiii. 5. its ceremonies now abrogated by the Holy Trinity in the Church, xvii. 29 our schoolmaster, iv. 33

Lazarus, his resurrection an earnest of our deliverance from sin, ii 5. and resurrection, xviii. 16. raised through the faith of others, v. 9.

Lent, preparation for Baptism during it, iv. 3. xviii. 32 (v. *Baptism*.)

Lessons from Scripture, Intr. 4. iv. 1 xiv 24, &c. guard against error, iv. 1. mark canonical books, iv. 33, 36

Libyans in the Church, xvi. 22

Life, the Father is true Life, xviii. 29. given us in Baptism by Him who is Life, iii 11, 12 Christ, who is Life, brought Life, as Adam Death, xiii 2. (v. *Eve*, *Tree*) Eternal Life God's gift, xviii. 28, 29. ways of entering into it, ib. 30, 31

"*Life of Life* begotten," iv. 7 xi 4, 18.

Light made by Him who made Darkness, ix 7

The Father is Light eternal, vi 9. light given to souls by the Cross, xiii. 1 by the Holy Ghost, xvi. 3, 11. (v *Baptism, Enlighten, Illuminate*)

"*Light of Light* begotten," iv. 7 xi 4, 18

"*Like* in all things to the Father," iv 7 xi. 4, 9, 18 v. xi. 19.

"*Like* to Himself," vi 7.

"*Likeness* of God," xiv. 10.

Lion of the tribe of Judah, x. 3.

Living Spirit (v *Spirit*)

Living Word (v. *Word*)

Lord, Christ Lord of all because Maker of all, x. 5, 6 xi. 21, &c. not by advancement, but by nature, x 5. before His Incarnation, x 6 from eternity, x 9 v note by the will of the Father, x 9. illustration of this, xi. 22. Lord of Angels, x. 10.

Lot, xix. 8.

M.

Macedonian empire, iv. 34.

Magic to be shunned by Christians, iv 37 service of the devil, xix 8

Maker of all things, iv 4 visible and invisible, Christ, xi 21-24 (v *Creator*)

Man work of Christ as well as of the Father, x 6. of God's own hands, xii 5, 26 in God's Image, xii 5 retained God's Image but lost His Likeness, xiv. 10. his twofold nature, iii. 4 iv 18. world made for him, xii 5

First man brought death, xiii 2. his fall, xii 5 man's miserable condition before the Incarnation, xii. 6, 7. forsook God, for the devil, ii 1 vi 10 vii. 13

Christ came to restore him, xii. 5, &c by Christ hallowed, and made partaker of God, xii. 15 allowed to call God, Father, vii. 7, 12 partaker of His name, Intr. 6. and of Christ's, x. 16

Power of man in faith, v 11 by the Holy Ghost, xvi 16 can wrestle with the Devil through the Holy Ghost, viii 4. xvi 19.

his wants met by Christ's various offices, x. 3—5. (v. *Incarnation*) his ministry used to convey God's gifts, xvii 35, 36.

Manasseh, saved through repentance, ii 14.

Manes blended all previous heresies, vi. 20. xvi. 9. History, vi. 24, &c a slave, vi 24 changed his name, ib did not arise from among Christians, vi 21. connection with the Greek philosophy, of Alexandria, vi. 22—24 and with Persian, vi 24 his disputatious spirit, vi. 24 claims to be the Paraclete, vi. 25. xvi 6, 9. fails to cure miraculously the Persian king's son, vi. 25. Flies from prison, vi. 26. disputes with Archelaus before heathen judges, vi. 27. seized and put to death by the Persian king, vi 30.

His influence, vi. 25. his disciples, vi 31.

Manichæan doctrines, vide xi 4, note Two principles, iv. 4, 5. vi 12, 13, 27, 28. perversion of Scripture for this doctrine, vi 28. they blaspheme the generation of the Son, vii. 5 the God of the Old Testament, vi. 27. xvi. 4. call the Sun Christ, vi. 13. xi. 21. abhorrence of the material

INDEX 293

world, iv. 22, 27, vi 31, 32, 34. deny the reality of Christ's Resurrection, xiv 21 fatalism, iv 18—21 baptism and offering, vi. 33. forged gospels, iv 36 vi 31 pollutions and blasphemy, vi 30—32

Manes worse than Simon Magus, xvi 10. his followers to be carefully shunned, vi 36 knowledge of their doctrines almost pollution, vi 13, 34 carefully enquired into by S. Cyril, vi. 34

Marcellus, his heresy about Christ's kingdom, iv 15. xv 27 combated, xv. 29—32 denied the personality of the Word, iv 8 note. a Sabellian, xi 17, note.

Marcion, his heresy, iv 4. vi 16 divided the Justice and Goodness of God, ib held three Gods, xvi. 4,7 v. xi 4 note. removed all texts of the Old Testament from the New, vi. 16 xvi 7.

Marriage though inferior to Virginity yet honourable, iv. 25. not to be despised by the unmarried, ib. acknowledged by the Holy Ghost. xvii. 7 second marriage permitted to the weak, iv 26.

Martyrs alone saved without Baptism of water, being baptized with blood, iii. 10 xiii. 21. make confession, iii 10. trained by the Holy Ghost, xvi. 12. strengthened by the Comforter, xvi. 20, 21. only by Him can they suffer, ib. under Antichrist, xi 17.

Mary the Virgin-Mother of God, x 19 v. xii. 33, 34. how called the wife of Joseph, xii. 31 sanctified by the Holy Ghost, xii. 29, 32. xvii. 6 sprung from David, xii. 24. the witness of Christ, x. 19. type of Virgins, xii. 33. repaired the loss caused by Eve, xii 29 Christ truly born of her, iv 9. xii 3.

Mary Magdalene, her visit to the Sepulchre foretold, xiv. 12 her noble love, xiv. 13.

Matthew wrote in Hebrew, xiv. 15.

Meats abstained from, not as unclean, but for self-denial, iv. 27, 37. vi 35. Jewish distinctions not to be observed, iv 37 offered to idols forbidden, iv 28 vide xvii. 29.

Meekness of Christ in judgment foretold, xiii 16.

Menander, his heresy, vi 16.

Mercy of God to sinners, ii. 5, 6, 10. even to Angels, ii 10.

Miracles of Christ as God, iv 9 claimed by Antichrist, xv 14 false ones permitted trial of Christian faith, stumbling-blocks of the unfaithful, xv. 17.

Mithras, worshipped in Persia, vi. 23 his ministers oppose Terebinthus and Manes, ib 24.

Montanus condemned second marriage, iv 26, note. called himself the Holy Ghost, xvi. 8 charged by S. Cyril with profligacy, and with horrid mysteries, ib.

Moon, her changes an intimation of the Resurrection, xviii 10

Moors in the Church, xvi 22

Moses the good schoolmaster, vii 8 had the Holy Ghost, xvi. 27 beheld Christ, x 6, 7 xii 16. intercession for the people and Aaron an encouragement to penitents, ii. 10 change of his rod as hard as Christ's birth, xii. 28 his rod, type of the wood of the Cross, xiii 20 sweetening the water by trees, a type of the Passion, ib river changed into blood by him corresponds with Christ's water and blood, xiii 21

Mysteries of Christ, i 1 of Baptism and the Eucharist, of the Altar, xviii. 32, 33 xix 1. not to be pried into, Intr. 2, 4. iii 7 nor divulged to Catechumens or strangers, Intr. 12. vi 29 glory of the Church, xv. 29. our account of them negative not positive, vi 2. xi. 11. xvi 5. not to be interpreted by human conceptions, xi. 7, 8. for praise not curiosity, vi. 5. we must not be silent about them, ib

"*Mystery* of iniquity," xv. 18.

N.

Name of God, vi 9 xxiii. 12. many names of Him, vi 7 of our Lord, x 3. name of Jesus, its meaning, x 4, 11, 13. of Christ, x 4, 14 virtue of the name of Christ, iv. 13 names of the Holy Ghost, xvii 2, 4, 5 various names of God, Christ, and the Holy Ghost, not to be profanely distinguished into persons, vi. 7. x 3. xvii. 2, 3. Christians partakers of God's name, Intr. 6 v. 1 of Christ's, x. 16. new name of Christians, i. 4 x 16.

Typical names given to Joshua and Aaron, x. 11. significant names of Judas, xiii 9. Samuel, Intr 14.

Name of Manes, vi. 20, 24. of the Gnostics, xvi 7.

Napkin with which Christ girded Himself symbolical of His human nature, xii 1.

Nathan, ii. 11.

Nations all subject to Christ, xvi. 22. xvii 10.

Nativities, iv 5. ix 8.

Nature not cause of righteousness or sin, iv 18—21. nor of salvation or ruin, vii 13

Nature of God, vi. 7. God by nature Father of Christ, vii. 4

Natural world, its wonders witness for God, ix 2, &c
Nebuchadnezzar an instance of the efficacy of repentance, ii 17, 18.
Necessity, none with God, iv. 5 nor upon man, iv. 18—21 not the reason of men's salvation or ruin, vii 13.
Night, its religious uses, ix 7
Noah, his ark of wood type of the Church, xxvii. 10 of the wood of the Cross, xiii 20. Example of decent order in the Church, Intr 14 his dove a type of the dove of the Holy Ghost, xvii 10.
  Himself a type of Christ, as author of a new birth, xvii. 10.

O.

Obedience of Christ, xiii 5, as a Son, not a servant, to the Father, x 9 xv 30.
Offering of Christ sacrificed for us in the Eucharist, xxiii. 10
Oil, exorcised of Baptism, xx 3. symbolical, and powerful to drive away devils, ib.
Old Fathers delivered by Christ from Hades, iv 11 xiv 19
Old Testament, its books, iv 35 document of appeal for Christian truth, xiv. 2 (v *Father, Prophet, Scripture, Testament*) blasphemed by heretics, iv 33 impiously separated by them from the New, xvi 4
Old man put off by Confession and Baptism, i 2 xix 10 xx 2.
Olives, the spiritual olive-trees, i. 4 v. xx. 3
Olives, mount of, xii 11 witnesses of the Resurrection, xiv 23 scene of the Ascension, xiv. 25. why passed by David, when flying from Absalom, ii 11.
One, how Christ is one with the Father, xi. 16.
Only-begotten, meaning of the word, x 3 xi 1, 2, &c. 13, 14
Order commended by our Lord's example, iii 11, 13, 14 of the Church, Intr 4, 13 vi 35, 36.
Orders of the ministry, xvi 22 xvii 35

P.

Parable of the marriage garment applied to Baptism, Intr 3 iii 2 of the wise and foolish Virgins, xv 26 of the Labourers, xiii. 31 of the Lost Sheep, xv 24
Paradise Adam in Paradise, xii 5 his fall, ii 4 v xiii 19 placed in Adam's view when fallen, ii 7 Invisible Paradise opened in Baptism, Intr. 15, 16 i 4. xix 1, 9 by Faith, v 10 distinguished from heaven, xiv. 26 restored by the Cross, xiii 30 The penitent thief the first to enter it, ib
Parent, (v. *Father*)
Passion of Christ real, xiii 4 witnesses of it, ib 38, 39 gainsaid by the Jews, xiii 7 witnessed by the Prophets, xiii 8, 9, &c even in its details, ib. answers circumstantially to the Fall, xiii 18, 19, its place, time, &c prophesied, xiii. 23, &c. represented in Baptism, xx 5 fellowship with it therein, ib 5, 6, 7.
Passion, "without passion," ἀπαθῶς, Christ's generation, vi 6. vii. 5
Passover, the eating of the Paschal Lamb a type of Christ's twofold nature, xii 1
Patience of Christ foretold, xiii 6, 13. gives force to His teaching, ib His Divine glory not the reward of it, iv. 7 God's appointed way to glory for man. xv. 17
Patriarchs, Jewish, of the West, xii 17.
S *Paul*, ruler and chief of the Church, vi. 15 with S Peter laid Simon Magus dead, ib The former persecutor a witness of Christ, x 17 why his Epistles most numerous x. 18 witness of the Resurrection, xiv. 21 descended from the third heaven that he might receive martyrdom, xiv 26. his labours in the Holy Ghost, xviii 26—31. completeness and variety of his teaching concerning the Holy Ghost, xvii 34
Paulianists denied the eternity of Christ's throne, xiv 27
Peace made by Christ first among His foes, xiii. 14 by His death, xiii 33
Penitence of forty days before Baptism, Intr. 4. i 5 gift of God, Intr. 9. preparatory to Baptism, ii passim iii 2, 7, 8 not declined by David after forgiveness, ii 12 cleansing of penitence, i 5 iii 2
Penitents must not despair, ii. 5
Pentecost, xvi 4, 9 Spirit descended not fully till then, xvi. 26 xvii 12, 13 His descent then, xvii 15
Perfections of God, vi. 7, 8 of the Father and the Son, xi 18
Persecution, xiii 23 the Baptism of blood in it, iii 10. xiii 21 under Antichrist, the fiercest, yet short, xv. 16
Persia, converts there witnesses of Christ, x. 19 worship of Mithras, vi. 23 origin of Manicheism, vi 24 wars with Rome, xv 6.
Person, distinction of, not implied in various names (v. *Name*)
Personality of the Word, iv 8 xi 10 of the Holy Ghost, xvi 3. xvii 2, 5, 28, 29
S *Peter* chief ruler of the Church, ii 19.

INDEX. 295

vi. 15. xi 3 xvii. 27. Chief of the Apostles, ii 19 xvii 27. His inspired confession of Christ, xi. 3 has the keys of Heaven to which Elias but went, xiv 26 xvii 27 speech at Pentecost, xvii 19. supernatural knowledge, xvi. 17 his works in the Holy Ghost, xvii. 20, 27. an example of the power of repentance, ii. 19 and of faith, v. 7. with S Paul punishes Simon Magus, vi 15.

Pharaoh, Israel rescued from him, as we from Satan, by water, iii 4. emblem of Satan, xix. 2, 3

Philip the Deacon, xvi 14 xvii. 25.

Phineas, his zeal, xiii. 2.

Phœnix, analogy of it, a proof of the resurrection, xviii. 8

Physician, Christ, Physician of the soul, ii 6 x 4, 13 xii. 1

Place of Christ's birth foretold, xii. 20 of His crucifixion xiii. 23, 28 of his burial, xiii 35. resurrection, xiv 2, 5—11.

Pomps of the Devil, xix 6.

Pontius Pilate, his treatment of Christ, xiii 15, 16 reconciled through Him to Herod, xiii. 14 witness of Christ's sinlessness, xiii. 3, 38.

Possession by Devils—contrasted with Inspiration, xvi 15.

Potters' field, xiii 10, 11.

Poverty of Christians, v. 2. xvi. 19. gift of the Holy Ghost, xvi. 22. taught by Christ, xiii. 5.

Power, the Father is Power, vi 9 Christ, God's Power personally subsisting, iv. 7. of the Godhead one, xvi. 24.

Prayer, preparatory to Baptism, Intr. 16. i 5. iv. 37 recorded, xv. 23 at night, ix. 7 for all men in the Communion Service, xxiii. 8 of the Saints departed for us, xxiii. 9. for the dead, xxiii 10. Lord's prayer, expounded, xxiii. 11, &c.

Preaching not to be attempted before Baptism, iii. 13

Preparation necessary for Baptism, Intr. 1, &c. iii. 7. how to behave during it, Intr. 13. for forty days, ib 4. i. 5. complete abstraction from the world, Intr. 6, 13, 16. i 5.

Fast of the Preparation, xviii. 17.

Presumption may be indulged under seeming reverence, xi. 12 xvi 1.

Priesthood of Christ eternal, x. 14 xi 1 (v *High Priest*, *Christ*, *Anointing*) order of, xvii. 35. he who fulfils it well abstains from marriage, xii. 25.

Principles, not two, xi. 14. (v. *Beginning* *Father*)

Promise, Spirit of, xiii 5

Prophecy, gift of the Holy Ghost, v. x 12. xvi 12 given in Baptism, xvii. 37 every thing concerning Christ the subject of it, xiii 8, 9. often enigmatical, xiii. 11.

Gives the signs of His coming, xii 10—12. (v *Psalms*, *Scripture*, *Testament*) prophecies of the time of His coming, xii 17—19 of Daniel, ib the place, xii 20 whence ib of His birth of a Virgin, xii. 21—23 of the Virgin's race, xii 23, 24 of the sufferings of the Christ, xiii. 7 of Judas, ib 9 of the thirty pieces of silver, ib 10 and the potter's field, ib. 11 of Christ's judgment, ib 12, 14, 16. of His mockery, ib 13, 15, 17. of the crown of thorns, ib. 17. and wood of the Cross, xiii. 19. of the place, xiii. 23, 28, 32 and time of the Crucifixion, ib. 24 of the darkness, ib 25 of Christ's vesture, ib. 26, 27. of His thirst, ib. 29 of the robbers, ib 30 of the tomb, ib. 35 xiv 3, 11 of the Resurrection, xiv. 2, 4, 8, 14, 17, 20, 21 its time, ib 4, 8 and place, ib 5, 6, 9, 11. of the signs following, ib 7. of our Lord's appearances, ib 11, 12 of His ascension, ib 24. and sitting at the Father's right hand, ib 28, 29. at the end of the world, xv. 3 of Antichrist, ib 9, 13 Christ's Prophecy concerning His second coming, xv 3, 4, &c of Malachi concerning it, xv. 2.

Prophets enlightened by the Holy Ghost, xvi 17, 18 Holy Ghost in them, ib. 3, 28 not partially, xvii 18 correspond to, but are inferior to the Apostles, xvi 4, 24 xiv. 26. witness all things concerning Christ, x 2 xiii. 8, 9, 13. xiv 19. nothing to be received without their testimony, xii. 5, 16. xiii 8. xiv. 2 our faith rests on them, xiv 21. xviii. 14. own the Father and the Son, vii 2. teachers of the Faith in the Old Testament, vii. 8, 10. xii 6—9, 29 owned Christ as Lord, x 7, 8 testified of His Godhead, xi. 15, 16 of the name Jesus, but covertly, x. 12. longed for His coming, xii. 7, &c testified of the Holy Ghost, xvi. 28, 29.

are ours as well as the Jews', iii. 6. xiv. 16. removed from the Jews to the Church, xiii. 29. slighted by the Jews, x. 2.

Providence of God, (οἰκονομία,) instances of Joseph, viii. 4. Peter's confession, xi. 3. Christ's prophecy of His coming, xv. 4. Thomas, xiii. 39.

Province, ἐπαρχία, xvi. 12.

Psalms, chanted in Divine Service, xiii 26 xxiii. 20. at night, ix 7. Psalms prophetical of Christ cannot be applied

INDEX.

to David or Solomon, vii 2 xii. 23 (v. *Prophecy*.)
Ptolemy, Philadelphus, iv. 34.
Punishment of the wicked, after the Resurrection, iv. 31. xviii. 19, 20.

Q

Quick and dead to be judged by Christ, xv 26.

R

Race of Christ according to the flesh, xi. 5. foretold, xii. 23.
Rahab, instance of power of repentance, ii. 9 type of the freeness of Gospel grace, x. 11.
Reading, Intr 14 1. 6. of the Scriptures recommended, iv. 37. ix 7. public, in the Church mark of a canonical book, iv 35, 36
Rebaptize, Heretics to be rebaptized, Intr. 7.
Red Sea typical of Baptism, iii 5.xix 2,3
Redemption of the world by the cross, xiii. 1, 4 wrought not by a mere man, but the Son of God, ib. 2, 33 by its Creator, vi. 11.
Regeneration, ἀναγέννησις, of souls in the Laver of Baptism through Faith, i. 2 iii. 4 in the case of Cornelius before Baptism, iii 4. Death and Birth, xx 4 in the Catholic Church, xviii 26. παλιγγενεσία, Baptism so called, Introd. 16. Laver of, Introd. 11. xviii. 34, 35. xix. 10.
Religion consists of true doctrines and good works, iv. 2. founded on belief in one God, iv. 4, 6 false views of it leading to presumption, xi 12. xvi. 1. awe requisite in speaking of its doctrines, xvi. 1. its worship indivisible, xvi 4.
Remission of sins in Baptism, xx. 6 freely given to all who believe, i. 5. iv. 32. xvii. 37.
Renunciation of Satan and his works in Baptism, xix 2—9.
Repentance, its efficacy in putting away sin, ii. 1. iv. 23 no sin beyond its power, ii 5. instances of, ii. 7. &c its temporal benefits, ii. 13 exemplified in Ahab, ib. and Jeroboam, ib 14 of the Laver, iv. 32 Baptism of, xix. 9. its fruits, mercy, and almsdeeds, iii. 8
Resurrection of Christ, iv. 12 answer to objectors from the cases of Elisha, iv. 12. xiv. 16. Jonah iv 12 xiv. 17, 18. Elijah xiv. 16. witnessed by the Old Scriptures, xiv. 2, 15, 21 all its circumstances written in the Psalms and Prophets, xiv 2, &c. (vide *Prophecy*) not discredited by the soldiers' tale, xiv. 14 Rock of our faith, xiv. 7, 21. glorifies the Cross, xiii. 4. denied by the Manichees, xiv. 21.
Its former witnesses, iv. 12. (vide *Church*) the dead who rose with Him, xiv. 16, 18, 20. its present witnesses, xiv. 22, &c.
Baptism a resemblance of it, iii. 12 xx 4.
Resurrection of the body; analogies for it in nature, iv. 30. xviii. 6. faith in it principle of holiness, iv. 30. xii. 34. xviii. 1, 20. prominence given to it by the Church, ib. and opposition of heresy, ib. objections to its possibility, xviii. 2 answered by God's power, ib. 3. justice, ib. 4 man's instinct, ib. 5 analogies of nature, ib. 6, 7. the Phœnix, ib. 8 man's origin, ib 9. God's ordering of the heavenly bodies an intimation of it, ib. 10 proved against Samaritans, ib 11—13. objections from the Prophets answered, &c. ib 14, 15. its fitness proved from the Old and New Testaments, 15—18. xviii. 19.
Revelation, Spirit of, xvii 5.
Reverence to parents, vii. 16 to God, taught by His works, ix. 16. in the Church, Intr 13, 15 vi 35 to the ancient Bishops, iv. 35. xiv 21. in religious discourse, vi 3. &c. xvi. 1 seeming, may cloak impiety, xi 12, 17
Reward given according to men's labours, i. 5. iv. 24, 27.
Riches, not as heretics thought, the devil's but God's, viii. 6, 7. evil only in their abuse, vii. 7 we may even be justified by them, viii. 6. belong to the faithful man, v. 2. viii. 6. who despises them, v. 2.
Righteous, "the Righteous," v. 10.
Righteousness of Christ greater than our sin, xiii. 33. we gain righteousness in Baptism, i. 4. Christ God's Righteousness personally subsisting, iv. 7.
Rock, riven for Christ the Rock, xiii 34. still seen, ib. 39. that followed Israel, x. 7, note.
Rod of Aaron, xii. 28. of Moses, ib. vide *Moses.*
Romans, conquest of Judæa by them proof of Christ, xii. 17, 18. empire succeeded by Antichrist, xv. 11, 12. wars with Persia, xv. 6.

S.

Sabbaths, Jewish not to be observed, iv. 37.

INDEX. 297

Sabaoth, a name of God, vi. 7 viii 8
Sabellius, v. iv xi 10 confounds the Holy Trinity, xvi 4 confuted by the very arrangement of the Creed, xvii 34. his heresy and Arianism alike to be avoided, iv 8, xi 13, 16, 17, 18 are marks of the falling away, xv 9.
Sacrifice of Christ, x 3, 5 Sacrifice of the Eucharist, xxiii 8, 9 Christ sacrificed offered in the Eucharist, xxiii. 10
Saints of the Old Testament delivered by Christ from Hades, iv 11 xiv. 19 rose with Him, xiv. 16, 18. according to Prophecy, xiv 17
Salvation depends on the truth of Christ's manhood, iv 9 xiii 37 one, xvi 24 of the Laver, iv. 37 xix 10 given to none without Baptism, iii. 10 to be despaired of by none, ii 5 (vide *Christ, Baptism, Man*)
Samaritans, iv. 37 vi 33 xviii 1
Samuel, meaning of the name, Intr 1.
Sanctification of all things by the Holy Ghost, iv 16 xvi. 3. of the Church, xvi. 14, 22. of Angels and Prophets, xvi 23 (vide *Spirit*.)
Sarah, her bearing a son as hard as the Virgins, xii. 28.
Sarmatians, xvi 22
Satan, meaning of the word, ii. 4
Scripture, its canon to be received from the Church, iv 33 as read in the Church, iv. 35 xv 13 and settled and handed down by Apostles and ancient Bishops, iv. 35 consists of Old and New Testaments, iv 33 (vide *Testament*) number and names of its books, ib 35, 36 history of the Septuagint version, iv 34. mutilated by Marcion, xvi 7 adulterated with forgeries by the Manichees, iv 36 vi 31. spoken by the Holy Ghost, xi. 12 xvi 1, 2

Nothing to be received as of the Faith unless proved by it, iv 17 its teaching embodied in the Creed, iv 33 v 12 faith grounded on it, xii 16, 17 xiii 8, 9 xiv 2 reveal all we know, or may speak of the generation of the Son, xi. 12 of the nature of the Holy Ghost, xvi 1, 2, 24. we may not speak beyond them, xii 5 variously interpreted, e g. iii 16 vi 28, 29 x 15 xi 19. xvii 9—11 perverted by heretics, e g. iv 19 vi. 17, 27, 28, 29 vii 9, 13 xv 3 danger of alleging it wrongly should teach us reverence and fear, xvi 1 we know not all its meaning, ib xi 12

Its abundance, xv 15. xvi. 32 xvii. 1, 20, 34, &c. witnesses every thing concerning Christ, xiii 8, 13.

To be diligently searched, iv 37 ix. 7. xiii. 8.

Scythianus the Saracen, forerunner of Manes, vi. 22.
Sea, witness of God's glory, ix. 11 of Christ's coming, x. 19 passion, xiii. 39 resurrection, xiv. 17—20, 23.
Seal, the Faith so called, iv. 17
Baptism, seal indissoluble, Intr 16 marks us for Christ's, i 2. through water, iii 4. Seal of Salvation, i 3 Of the Holy Ghost given in Baptism, iii 3, 4, 12. iv 16. v. 6 xvi 24 xvii 35, 36. xxii 7.
Of Circumcision, v. 5
Of the Cross, xiii. 36
Seasons, their order glorifies God, ix 6 of the Resurrection, that of Creation, xiv 10 foretold, xiv. 2, 10.
Semiarians, v note to iv. 7 Pref p. ii, iv, ix.
Septuagint version, its history, iv. 34. held inspired, ib. note
Sepulchre of Christ prophesied of, xiii. 35 xiv 9. his witness, x. 19. account of, xiv 9
Serpent, the devil, watches candidates for Baptism, Intr. 16 apostate Serpent, iv 37. brazen, a type of the Crucifixion, xiii 20
Session of Christ at God's right hand, xiv 27 proved from Scripture, ib 28. eternal, iv 7. xiv. 27, 30.
Sheep, x. 3, 5
Shew-bread, a type of the Eucharist, xxii 5.
Sick even yet healed by Christ, x 13 must not have recourse to amulets or sorcery, iv 37 xix 8.
Side of Christ typically pierced. xiii. 21. in respect of Baptism, iii 10
Signs of Christ given by the Prophets, xiii 10 (vide *Prophecy*) given to Ahaz explained, xii 22 signs of Moses correspond to Christ's acts, xiii 20, 21 of the Son of Man, the Cross, xiii 41. of the Second Advent given by Christ Himself, xv 4, &c lying signs of Antichrist, xv 11—15 a trial of faith, xv 17 of the Cross, (vide *Cross*) God's free but great gift, xiii 36.
Simon Magus, was baptized but not enlightened, Intr. 2 xvii. 35 Father of all heresy, vi 14. His blasphemies against the Father and Holy Ghost, ib xvi 6 His fate, vi. 15 compared with Manes, xvi 10
Sin, ailment of the soul, ii 1 man's choice, not God's work, ii 1 not of necessity, iv 18—21 not a thing external but from within, and our own nature, ii 2 prompted not forced by the Devil who is its chief author, ii. 3, 4. iv 21 death by sin, xiii 2. makes us enemies to God, and slays

Y

us, xiii. 33. leagues us with Satan, xix 9 marred God's world, xii 5 and ruined man, xii 6, &c all men bound by it, xiii. 1, 2 dead in it, iii. 12. Christ came to destroy it, xii 8 died for our sins and purged them, ii. 10 iii. 12. xiii. 1, 2, 4, 6, 23, 33 being Himself sinless, ii 10 iii 12. xiii 3, 5, 23 sin came by one man, died with one man, xiii 2, 28 iii 12. Fearful yet not incurable to the penitent, ii 1—5 readiness of God to forgive the believing, ii 6 efficacy of repentance, ii. 7, &c Instances, ib. collective sin pardoned, ii 10. obstinate sin alone not pardoned, iii 8. Completely and freely remitted to all in Baptism by faith, Intr. 8. i 5. iii 11, 12, 15. iv. 32 xvii. 37 xviii 20 xx. 6. Baptism its remedy, iv 32 remitted even in John's Baptism, iii. 7. Baptism a death to sin, Intr. 5 sin cleansed by Exorcisms, Intr 9 and the exorcised oil, xx 3 by the power of the Holy Ghost, xvii 15

Overcome by Faith, v. 4. steals on us, ii 3 after Baptism recorded against the Judgment, xv. 23. Its scars remain, xviii 20

Sin against the Holy Ghost, xvi. 1.

Sion, its desolation revealed by the Spirit to Isaiah, xvi 18

Sodom, Christ wrought with the Father in its destruction, x. 6.

Soldiers, their tale about the sepulchre presignified by Isaiah and Jonah, xiv. 14, 20. Its vanity, xiv. 14.

Solitaries, order of, iv. 24 xii. 33. xvi. 22. Christ their example, xii 33.

Solomon, instance of the efficacy of repentance, ii. 13.

Son, Christ the Son of God, with the Father and the Holy Ghost, Introd. 15. (vide *Trinity*.)

Implied in the mention of the Father, vii 4 glorified and worshipped with Him, and the Holy Ghost, vi 1. x. 2 with the Holy Ghost partaker of His Godhead, vi 6 (vide *Christ*)

In a singular sense, only-begotten, vii 5, 10. x. 3. xi. 2, 4. so called by the Father, xi. 2. by nature, not adoption, vii. 10 x. 4. or advancement, xi. 4, 7, 13, 15, &c not after the manner of human generation, xi 4, 8. nor as Christians are God's Sons, iii 14. vii 7. xi 9, 19. nor as mind begets thought, xi 10 begotten not made, xi. 4, 14 xv. 9 God, xi 13 incomprehensibly, iv 7. xi 4, 5, 11. as God only knoweth, xi 11, 12, 13 from eternity, iv. 7. vii. 5. xi 4, 8. 13, 14, 17, 19, 20 apart from time, xi 5, 7, 14 spiritually, xi. 5, 7 unoriginate, xi. 4, 7, 13 the Son never was not, xi. 8, 14, 17.

Like in all things to the Father, iv 7. xi 4, 9, 18, 19 of the Father as His beginning, xi. 14, 20 xiii 23. wanting nothing to the glory of the Godhead, iv 7 xi 13 was with the Father, x 6—8 One with the Father, xi 16 neither to be separated from nor confounded with the Father, iv. 7. xi. 16, 17, 18, 20 did not become the Father, xi. 13 abides for ever, not absorbed into the Father, xv. 27, 30 how subject to the Father. x. 9. xv 30. not numbered among the servants of the Father, viii 5 glorified with the Father, vi. 1 The Father's Word, and Wisdom, and Power, iv 7, 8 Maker of all things at the Father's will, xi 22 Lord over them, ib &c. alone with the Holy Ghost, knows and sees the Father, vi 6 vii 11 xi 12, 13

Makes known the Father, vii 11. only way to the Father, vii 2. x 1, 3. Incarnate to restore the Father's worship, vi 11. xii 15 and save the world, xii. 4, 5, &c Father seen only in Him, x 6, 7 xi. 15 Son before born in Bethlehem, xi. 20 became Son of Man, x. 4. Son of David, xi 5 xii 23

Sons of God, Christians, by adoption, iii 14 vii 7 xi 9, 19 by Water and the Spirit, ib. not of necessity, but of one faith, vii 13. works meet for them, vii 14.

Soul, free, ii 1 iv 18 God's fairest work, immortal by God's will, made in His image, ib diseased and destroyed by its own sin, ii 1 originally sinless, wilfully sinned, iv 19 did not sin in another state, ib purified by penitence, alms, reading of Scripture, iv. 37 cleansed by exorcism, Introd 9. sealed, iii 3, 4 baptized, xvii 14 and brightened by the Holy Ghost, xvii 16 its illumination by faith, v 11. possession by devils, xvi 15 contrasted with the influence of the Holy Ghost, xvi 16.

Soul of the world, viii. 2.

Spaniards in the Church, xvi. 22

Spectacles of the heathen to be shunned, iv. 37

Speculation taking the place of soberness in S Cyril's time, xv. 9 not to intrude beyond what is written, xi 12. xvi 1, 2.

Spirit, the word variously used, xvi. 13, 15 yet with a distinguishing term, xv 15

INDEX. 299

Holy Spirit, various names, xvii 2, 3, 4 yet one only, iv. 16 xvi 12. xvii 2, 3. included in the Holy Trinity, xvi 4 vide iv 16 vi 1, 6 xvi. 19. in the form of Baptism, xix 9 xx 4
A living Person, iv 16 xvi 3, 13, 14 xvii 2, 5, 28, 29, 33 incomprehensible, xvi. 1, 2. alone with the Son, beholds, and reveals the Father, vi. 6. vii 11 xi. 12. not numbered among the Father's servants, viii. 5 partaker of the Father's Godhead, vi 6 far above all creatures, xvi 23 shares the Father's glory, vi 1 and Christ's, xvi. 4 sanctifies and deifies all intelligent beings, iv. 16 xvi 3 the Church, xvi 14, 22 xvii 14 Angels, xvi 23. xvii 2 Prophets, xvi 23.
Indivisible yet manifold in working, iv 16 xvi 12 xvii. 2, 12
He was in the Law and the Prophets, iv 16 dictated the Scriptures, iv 16, 33 xi 12 xvi 1, 2, 3, 4, 24 same Spirit witnessed of Christ in the Old Testament, manifested Him in the New, xvi 3, 16, 24 spake by the Prophets, iv 16 was in the Old Testament Saints, xvi. 26—28 on the seventy Elders, xvi 25, 26. illuminated the Prophets, xvi 17, 18. witnessed of by them, xvi 28, 29. given partially before Pentecost, xvi. 26 xvii. 12, 13, 18.
Descended visibly on our Lord, iii. 14 why, xvii 9 xxi 1. The Comforter, xvi 20 xvii 4 given partially to the Apostles before the Ascension, xvii. 12 fully at Pentecost, xvi 26 xvii 12 His Baptism, xvii 14, 15 given to us in Baptism, iii 5, 8, 14, 16 (vide note) iv. 16 xx 6 proportionably to each man's faith, i 5 iii. 1, 2 more than the remission of sins, iii 7, 15, xxii. 17 illuminates, Introd 2 seals the souls in Baptism, iii 4 iv. 16 xvii 35, 36 perfects Baptism, yet requires water, iii 4, 16 not given to hypocrites, Introd 2, 4. iii 1 xvii 35. conveyed symbolically in the Chrism after the Washing, xxi 1—5 obliterates sin and brightens the soul, xvii. 15 trains and comforts the Martyrs, xvi 12, 20, 21 gives all graces, xvi. 12 His inspiration, xvi 16. and illumination, ib. gives power over the flesh, world, and the Devil, xvi 19. gives grace to all who believe, xvi. 22 sanctifies and changes the Bread and Wine, xxiii. 7, 19
Teaching concerning Him in the New Testament, xvii 1. of our Lord, xvii 11. in the Epistles of St. Paul, xvii. 33.

His teaching one with Christ's, xvi. 14 His operations by the will of the Father recorded in the Acts, xvii. 21, 31. with the Father and the Son has established the New Covenant in the Church, xvii 29.
Danger of speaking amiss concerning him, xvi. 1, 2, 6 blasphemies against Him of the Gnostics, xvi 6, 7. Manes, vi 25 xvi. 6, 9. Marcion, xvi. 9 Montanus, xvi. 8. Sabellius, xvi. 4 xvii 34 Simon Magus, vi. 14. Valentinus, xvi. 6

Stars have no influence, iv 18 not to be heeded by Christians, iv. 37 ix 8. glorify God, ix 5, 6 their uses to man, ix 8. shall perchance have a resurrection, xv. 3.

Stephen, xvii 3, 4.

Stone of the Sepulchre, xiii 39. xiv. 22

"*Stone* cut out without hands," xii. 18. xv 28

Strangled things forbidden, iv. 28.

Subjection of the Son to the Father, x 9 xv 30.

Susannah, xvi. 31.

T.

Table, spiritual Table of the Lord, xxii. 7. vide i 6.

Taverns to be shunned by Christians, iv 37

Temple of Jerusalem, vii 6. to be rebuilt by Antichrist, xv 15. failure of Julian's attempt to rebuild it, declared by S Cyril, Preface, p. v.

Temptation, reason of our Lord, iii 13. xxi 4 meaning of " Lead us not into temptation," xxiii. 17.

Terebinthus, successor of Scythianus and forerunner of Manes, vi. 23.

Testaments, the two Testaments make up the Scripture, iv 33 impiously separated by heretics, vii 5 xvi 4 Christ the object of Prophecy in the Old, of History in the New, xvi 3. same Spirit in both, (vide *Spirit*.) iv. 16. xvi. 4, 6 xvii. 5 both announce the gift of Baptism, iii. 16. harmony of their doctrine, ii 4.
Old Testament necessary as a witness to Christ, xvi. 7. God of it the Father of Christ, vii. 5 (vide *Prophecy*.)—Christ, xvi 11 and His Apostles refer us to it, xiv. 2. blasphemed by heretics, iv. 33 e g. Manes, vi 27. texts of it erased by Marcion from the New, vi. 16 xvi 7. its witness to the Spirit, xvi 28-32 to the Resurrection of the Body, xviii 10, &c. History of its translation into Greek, iv. 34.

300 INDEX.

Old Testament or Covenant ended, New began in the Baptism of John, iii. 6. Old abolished, New established in the Catholic Church by the Holy Trinity, xvii. 29.

Thief on the cross first-fruits of Christ's death, and first to enter Paradise, xiii. 30, 31. saved by faith, without works, ib. v. 10. witness of Christ's sinlessness, xiii. 3.

Thirty pieces of silver, prophecy of them, xiii. 10 thirty Æons of Valentinus, his argument for the number, vi 17.

Thomas doubted for our sakes through God's providence, xiii. 39.

Thomas the disciple of Manes his forged Gospel, iv. 36. vi. 31.

Thorns, crown of, cancelled Adam's curse of thorns, xiii. 17, 18.

Throne of Christ eternal, not by advancement, iv. 7 xi. 17. He had it before His suffering, ib at the Father's right hand, xiv 27, 30 not to be curiously disputed of, ib has no end, xv 27 —of David, xii 23.

Till, (vide *Until*)

Time has no place as regards God and Christ, iv. 4, 7, &c of Christ's coming, &c. prophesied of, (vide *Prophecy*); of Christ's second coming unknown, and not to be curiously examined into, xv 4

"Time" means a year in the Prophets, xv 16

"*To-day*," meaning of, in Ps 110, xi 5 timeless and eternal, ib. in the Lord's Prayer, xxiii. 15

Tongues, fiery tongues, xvii 15 gift of Pentecost, xvii 16 instead of the confusion of Babel, xvii 17 A Sign foretold of Christ's Resurrection, xiv 7

Tradition of the Creed, v 12, 13

Tradition of interpretations, xiii 21 xv 13.

Transfiguration of the Lord, xii 16 a glimpse of His awful glory, x 7

Tree of the Cross corresponds to the Tree of knowledge, xiii 19 planted in the earth, to bless it, and release the dead, xiii 26

Trinity, iv. 16 xvii 34 doctrine of, acknowledged in Baptism, xvi 4, 19 xx 4 profession of Faith in, xix 9. not to be revealed to Catechumens or Gentiles, vi 29 Heretics divide or confuse it, xvi 4 (vide *Arius, Sabellius*) not Tritheism, ib not a matter for curious speculation, xvi 24

Holy Trinity present in Baptism, Introd. 15. have established the New Covenant in the Church, xvii 29 Adoption given us by the Father's grace, through the Son and Holy Ghost, vii 7. the Son with the Holy Ghost, sees the Father, vi 6. vii 11. with and through the Holy Ghost reveals Him, vi. 6. all things serve the Father save the Son and Spirit, viii. 5. the Father through the Son, with the Holy Ghost, bestows all things, xvi 24. the saving Dispensation to usward from the Father, Son, and Holy Ghost, xvii. 5. Father spake by the Holy Ghost, xvii. 38. the Father through the Son in the Holy Ghost gives all things, xviii 29. Glory to be ascribed indivisibly to Father and Son with the Holy Ghost, vi 1. "in the power of the Holy Ghost, by the will of Father and Son," xvii 21. v. xvii. 31.

Tritheism, xvi 4 v. xi 4. note.

Truth counterfeited by Satan, that it may be disbelieved, xv 11. grace necessary lest it be received falsely, xvi 2. Hatred of it cause of error, xv. 17

Types, their wonderful truth, xiii 19. instances, ib. 17—23 different persons, types of different offices in the One Antitype, e g. Joshua and Aaron of Jesus Christ, x. 11. Joshua how a type, ib. type of Moses' rod (vide *Moses*), of Aaron, xii. 28. types of Baptism, iii 5 xix 2, 3.

Jonah, xiv 17—20

John the Baptist a type of the ascetic life, iii 6. the dove, xvii 9, 10

Typical exposition of Eccles. 12, 1—6. xv 20

U.

Unalterable, iv 4

Unbegotten, said of God, iv 4 vi. 7 xi 13

Unbelief, mars the power of Baptism, Introd 2 (vide *Faith*) only reason why men are not enlightened by the Holy Ghost, xvi 22

Unchangeable, iv 4

Unity of God (vide *God*)

Unlearned, the Creed a help to them, v 12

Unoriginate, said of the Father, iv 4 xi 20 ἀρχὴ ἄναρχος, of the Son, xi 4, (v. note,) 5, 13.

"*Until*" "*Unto*," does not limit, xv 29. 31, 32 (vide *Hooker*, E P.V. 45 § 2)

Usury forbidden, iv 37.

V

Valentinus, vi 17—19 argues from the number of our Saviour's years that there are thirty Æons, ib. his blasphemies against the Holy Ghost, xvi. 6.

INDEX. 301

Veil of Christ's flesh, xiii. 32.
Veiling of the face in Exorcisms, Introd. 9.
"*Very God*," Christ begotten, x. 6. xi 9, 14, 21.
Vesture of Christ parted, a sign foretold, xiii. 26.
Vine of Judah, xiii. 29. Christ the true Vine, x 5. xiv. 11 xvii 19. with which we have communion in Baptism, i. 4. the Holy Spirit so called, xvii. 18.
Virgin, meaning of the word in Is. 7, 14. gainsaid by the Jews, xii 21. prophecy that Christ should be born of one, xii. 2. objections, xii. 4. not harder than things believed by Jews and Pagans, xii 27—30 God born of a Virgin, xii. 1 x 19 to do honour to purity, xii. 25. to repair the loss of the virgin Eve, xii. 15, 29 (vide *Mary the Virgin*.)
Christ makes souls virgins, xii 31. Order of Virgins, iv 24 xii. 33 xvi 22. have their part with Mary, xii 34. must not despise married persons, iv 25.
Parable of the ten virgins, xv 26
Virginity, its excellence, and glory, xii. 33 xv. 23. an angel life on earth, iv 24. vi 35 xii. 34. gift of the Holy Ghost, xvi 19.

W.

Wars, signs of Christ's coming, xv. 6.
Washing of hands before the Communion, xxiii. 1
Watchfulness against first approaches of sin, ii. 3 against deceivers and Antichrist, xv. 4, 18. for Christ's coming, xv 4
Watching, preparatory to Baptism, xviii 17
Water, one in nature and manifold in operation, shews forth God's glory, ix 9, 10. and is a fit emblem of the Holy Ghost, xvi 11, 12 principle of plants, things flying and creeping, ix 10 heavens are of water, iii. 5 ix 5. why chosen as the instrument of Baptism, iii 5 its uses in the Old covenant, ib. means of rescue to Israel, ib xix. 3 sanctified by Christ's Baptism and miracles, iii. 11. xii 15.
Waters of Baptism gain a sanctifying power by the invocation of the Holy Ghost, iii 3 though despised by the world, Intr. 16 Water and the Spirit answer to Man's double nature, iii 4 vide iii 16 inseparable, iii. 4. Waters of Baptism have Christ in them, Χριστοφόρα, Intr. 15. "the grave and the mother" of the Baptized, xx. 4
Water and blood from Christ's side, its symbolical meaning, xiii. 21.
Waters of Life, xvi 11.
Way, Christ the Way, x. 3.
West, the region of darkness, xix. 4. symbolical meaning of facing it, when renouncing Satan, ib.
White raiment, v xxii. 8
Widowhood, iv. 26. x. 19. xv. 23.
Wife, meaning of the word in Matt. i. 24 xii. 31.
Will (θέλημα, νεῦμα,) of God the Father, Christ made all things by it, x. 5 9, &c (v. *Son*) v. xvii 21, 31.
Wine, new, the grace of the Holy Ghost, xvii. 18 water turned into it, compared with the Eucharist, xxii. 2. Spiritual Wine, xxii 8. becomes Christ's blood, xxii. 1—6 xxiii. 7.
Wisdom, Christ God's Wisdom personally subsisting, iv 7.
Witchcraft, forbidden, iv. 37.
Witnesses to Christ, x. 17—20. of the Crucifixion, xiii 38. of the Resurrection, xiv 22 to be sought for in the Prophets, xiii 8 xvi. 7.
Woman, life, as death, through a woman, xii 15, 29 piercing of Christ's side has reference to woman, xiii 21 conduct of the women who sought Christ, xiv 12—14.
Works, good works and true doctrines make up religion, iv 2 without Baptism of no avail, iii 4 after Baptism, our works recorded against the Judgment, xv. 23 xviii 20. vid. xix 5. good works must follow Baptism, xvii. 37, 38 vii. 14. a preparation for Judgment, xv. 25, 26.
Of Satan, xix. 5
Word, Christ the Personal Word of God, iv 8. xi 10. Himself God, xi 3, 16 in all reasonable creatures, iv. 8. not like human words conceived in the mind or spoken, iv 8 xi. 10.
World, the work of God, iv 4 made by the evil God according to the Manichees, vi 13 made by the Son, xi. 21, 22 for man, xii. 5. mirrors forth God's glory, ix. 2, &c its lessons, ix. 16. marred by man's sin, xv. 3 shall perhaps be renewed at the last day, ib "God of this world," vi 28, 29. Soul of the world, viii. 2.

X.

Xanthicus, the month, season of the Creation, Passover, Resurrection, xiv. 10.

INDEX OF GREEK WORDS.

Ἀδυσώπητος, iii. 7.
Αἰσθητός, x. 13. xiii. 33. xv. 11. xix. 2. xxii. 9
Ἀκτημοσύνη, xiii. 5. xvi. 22.
Ἀμάρτυρος, xvi. 7.
Ἀναγέννησις, Introd. 16. vii 9.
Ἀναγινωσκόμενος, iv. 33. vide xiii. 7, 19.
Ἀνάγνωσμα, x 10
Ἀναδιδόμενος, xxii 3. xxiii. 15.
Ἀναλύεσθαι, xv 27, 30.
Ἄναρχος, iv. 4. xi. 4, note. v. xi. 20. vi. 13.
Ἀνόμοιον, iv. 7, note.
Ἀντιγεννῆσαι, vii 16.
Ἀντίτυπον, xx. 1. xxi. 1. xxiii 20.
Ἀνυπόστατος, iv. 8. xiii. 37. xv. 21.
Ἀπαθῶς γεννηθείς, vi 6.
Ἀπαράλλακτος, xi. 18.
Ἀπόκρυφα, iv. 33, 35 xv. 16.
Ἀπορρεύσας, vii 5.
Ἀποστασία, xv. 9.
Ἁρπάσας τὸ κυριεύειν, x. 9.
Ἀρχή, xi 14, 20.
Ἀσαγής, xii 16
Ἄσκησις, i. 5. iv. 27. xxiii 19
Αὐτεξούσιος, ii. 1. iv. 18. vii. 13.
Αὐτοπροαίρετος, x 9.
Αὐτοπροσωπῶς, xv. 14, 17.
Ἄχρονος, xi. 14
Ἀχύρων ὕδατα, vi. 31.

Γένεσθαι, πρὸ τοῦ γένεσθαι ἦν, x 12.
Γεννηθεὶς ἀπαθῶς, vi. 6.
Γίνεται, xix. 7.

Δογματικόν, v. 10.
Δόκησις, iv 9. vi 14 xiii 4, 37.
Δόκιμος τραπεζίτης, vi. 36
Δυνάμει, xvi. 20.

Ἐγκράτεια, x 19 xv. 23.
Ἐκκλησία, xviii 24, 25.
Ἐκκλησιαστικοί, xv. 7, 13. xvii. 10.
Ἔνδοξος, xiv 30.
Ἐνεργεία, ix. 9.
Ἐνεργητικὸν πνεύματος, xxi. 3.
Ἔνσαρκος γέννησις, xii. 32.
Ἔνσαρκος παρουσία, iii 11. xii 15 xiv. 27, 30
Ἐνυπόστατος, xi 10 xvii. 5, 34.
Ἐξ οὐκ ὄντων, xv 9
Ἐξήγησις θεωρητική, xiii. 9.
Ἐξητητής, xvi. 6.
Ἐξομολόγησις, ii. 15, note. xviii. 14.
Ἐξουσία, xi. 22. vide x. 5, note.

Ἐπαρχία, xvi. 22.
Ἐπίκλησις, iii 3, 12. xix. 7.
Ἐπιούσιος, xxiii 15.
Ἐπιστήμη, Introd. 4. vi. 35.
Ἐπιφοίτησις, xxi. 1. xxiii. 19
Εὐαγγελία, iv. 4, 7. xiii. 21, 35.
Εὐλογία, xiii. 6.
Εὐπειθής, x. 9. xv. 30.
Εὐσέβεια, xvi. 4.

Ζωῶν, for ζώων, xii. 20.

Ἦν ὅτε οὐκ ἦν, xi. 18.

Θεατρομανίαι, xix. 6.
Θεικῶς, xi. 5.
Θέλημα, x. 5.
Θεολογία, xxiii. 6.
Θεοποιός, iv. 16.
Θεοτόκος, x. 19.
Θέσει, xi 7.
Θυσιαστήριον, vi. 33. xviii. 32. xxiii 2.

Ἴασις, x 4.
Ἴσχας, vi. 33.
Ἰώμενος, x. 13.

Κανονικοί, Introd. 4
Κορυφαῖος, xi. 3.

Λιτός, xix 7. xxi 3
Λογικός, iv. 8 x. 3 xvii. 2

Μαρτύριον, xiv 6.
Μέλη, ix. 15. xii. 26.
Μοναρχία, vi. 36. vii. 1. xvii. 2.
Μονογενής, xii. 10.
Μονοειδής, vi. 7 xvi. 12.

Νεῦμα, x 5 xi. 10, 11, 22, 23, 24 xv. 25 xvi 12, 31. xvii 31.
Νοήματα, vi 29
Νοητός, i. 4. xiii. 34 xiv. 17, 23 xvii. 15, 18, 19, 21. xxii. 7.

Οἰκονομία, viii. 4 x 18. xiii. 39 xiv 17, 24 xv 1, 4. xix 5.
Οἰκουμενικός, xvii 29.
Ὁμοιοπαθής, iv. 9. xii 15.
Ὅμοιος ἑαυτῷ, xi 9 vide vi. 7.
Ὅμοιος κατὰ πάντα, iv. 7 ἐν πᾶσιν, xi. 4, 9, 18.
Ὁμοούσιον, v. Pref. p. ii, iv. vii. 6.
Οὐσιώδης ἐπιφοίτησις, xxi 1.

INDEX.

Πάθει, vii 5.
Παῖδες, vi. 12. viii 8. xii. 2. xiii. 11.
Πανηγυρίζω, xix. 10.
Παντοκράτωρ, x 5.
Παρακαταθηκή, v. 13 xii. 16
Παρθενοποίους τῶν ψυχῶν, xi. 31.
Παρθένος, xii 21.
Παροικία, xiv 21 xvi. 22
Παρών, xiv. 2 xv. 27
Παρουσία, vide Ἔνσαρκος.
Πειθαρχεῖν, xv 30.
Πιστός, Introd 6. vi. 1.
Πνευματικός, xvii. 21, 22 xxii. 8.
Πνευματοφόρος, xvi 28.
Πρὸ αἰώνων, xi. 13
Προαίρεσις, Introd 1. vii. 16 ix 13 xiii. 6, 29 xv 30. xvii 10 xix 8.
Προθεσμία, Introd. 4 xviii 14
Προκείμενα, xxiii 7
Προκοπή, x. 5. xi 1, 3, 7, 13, 15, 17. xiv 27.
Προκόψας, xii 3
Πρόξενος, xii. 14 xx. 6.
Προστάτης, iv 35. vi. 15.
Πρόσωπον, x. 7.
Προφορικός, iv. 8. xi. 10.
Πρωτοστάτης, ii 19. xi. 3. xvii. 27.
Πρωτότοκος, xi. 4.
Πρωτοτύπως, xiv 21.

Σαρκοφαγία, xxii 4.
Συγκατάθεσις, v 10.

Συμπλοκή, vii 5.
Συναλοιφή, iv. 8 xvi 4.
Σύναξις, i 6 x. 14 xiv 26.
Σφρᾶγις ἀνεξάλειπτος, Introd. 17 μυστικός, i. 2, 3 iii 3, 4
Σχολάζω, Introd. 13 i 5.
Σωζόμενοι, Introd. 15. xiii. 13.

Τύπῳ, ἐν, xxii 3

Υἱοθεσίας προκοπή, xi 3.
Υἱοπατορία, iv 8 xi. 16 xv 9.
Ὑπακούειν, xv. 30.
Ὑπερθέσις, xviii 17.
Ὑπόστασις, vi. 7 vii 5. ix. 9, 11 x 3. xvi 5, 24 xvii 17
Ὑφεστώς, xvii. 2, 5, 28.

Φαινόμενοι, x. 13
Φαντασίᾳ, xii. 3 xiii. 37.
Φιλοστοργία, xv. 30
Φυσικῶς, x 9
Φωτιζόμενοι, Introd. 1, 2.
Φώτισμα, xiii 21.

Χάρισμα, xxi. 3.
Χρίστοι, xi 1 xvi 13
Χριστοφόρος, Introd 15 xxii. 3

Ψευδεπίγραφα, iv. 36
Ψιλὸς ἄνθρωπος, xii. 1. xiii 2, 24, 33. xxi. 3. xxii 6.

INDEX OF TEXTS.

GENESIS.

1, 2.	III 5.
6.	IX. 5.
14.	IX. 8.
24 25.	IX 13.
26.	X 6 XII. 5. XIV. 10.
27.	X. 6.
31.	XII 5.
2, 7.	XII 30. XIII 2. XVII. 12.
	XVIII. 13.
8.	XIX 9.
17.	XIII 31.
22.	XII. 29.
25.	XX 2
3, 7. 8.	XXI. 4.
15.	XVI 10.
17. 18	XIII 18. XIV 11.
23	XIX. 9
24.	II. 7.
4, 1.	XII 5.
8, 8. 10.	XIII 10
11, 30.	XII 28.
18, 3. 8.	XII 16
25	XVIII. 11, 13.
27.	VI 3
19, 15—30.	XIX. 8.
24.	X. 6.
27, 37.	VII. 16.
29, 21.	XII 31.
32, 30.	XII 16
49, 8—11.	XII 17
49, 9.	XIV. 3

EXODUS.

3, 6.	XVIII. 11.
4, 22.	XI 4.
12, 9	XII 9.
23.	XIII 3.
20, 12.	VII 15
19	XII. 13.
21, 17.	VII. 16.
29, 4.	III 5.
33, 13—22.	X 7 XII. 16
34, 5—9	X 8
40, 6. 7 28.	III 5

LEVITICUS.

4, 5.	X. 11 XIV. 10.
8, 3.	XVIII. 24.

NUMBERS.

11, 24—29.	XVI. 25, 26.
13, 17.	X. 11.
20, 17.	vid XI. 17. XVI 5.
24, 9.	XIV. 3.

DEUTERONOMY.

4, 10.	XVIII. 24.
15.	VI. 7.
24.	VI 27.
5, 26.	XII. 13.
9, 10.	XVIII 24.
20.	II. 10
14, 1.	XI. 4
18, 15	XII 17.
22, 27	XII. 21.
28, 66	XIII. 19.
32, 6.	VII. 8
22.	VI 27.
32	XIII. 29.
34, 9.	XVI. 26.

JOSHUA

2, 11	II 9
3, 1	X 11
6, 5 20	X 11
14, 1	ib

1 SAMUEL.

2, 6.	VI 27
9, 9 11.	XVI 28

2 SAMUEL

12, 10—18.	II. 11, 12
16, 10 11	II 12
23, 2.	XVI 28.

INDEX OF TEXTS.

1 KINGS.

1, 4	xii. 21.
13, 1 &c.	ii 14
19, 10.	xii 7
13.	xii 16.
21, 29	ii 13

2 KINGS.

2, 9—11.	xiv 25, 26
5, 24 &c	xvi 17.
16, 2	xii 22

2 CHRONICLES.

6, 18	xii. 9.
33, 12. 13.	ii. 14

EZRA.

6, 15.	xii 19

NEHEMIAH.

9, 20.	xvi. 28.

JOB

5, 8. 9	viii. 8
7, 9	xviii 14, 15
18.	xiv. 5
9, 8	xi. 23 xiii 9
10, 11	ix. 15
12, 8	xi 11
24	xiii. 14
14, 7 &c	xviii. 15.
19, 25. 26.	ib
26, 8	ix. 9
29, 16.	vii 9.
36, 27.	vi 4
37, 16 22.	viii. 8 ix 9.
38, 2 3.	ix. 1, &c
11	ix. 11
14 17	xi. 23
28 37	ix 9.
39, 26.	ix. 12.
40, 19.	viii 4.
23.	iii 11
41, 13	iii 11

PSALMS

1, 5	xviii 14.
2, 3.	xiii 12
7	vii. 2 x. 2. xi 5. xii 19
9.	xii 18.
2, 11	xiv 13
7, 9.	i. 3 v. 2.
12, 5.	xiv 4
14, 3—7	xii. 6, 7.
16, 1—10.	xiv. 4
17, 8	vi. 8.
18, 9.	xii. 8
19, 2 5	ix 6.
22, 10	xii 25.
15	xiv 3
18.	xiii 26
23, 1—3	i 6
5	xxii 7.
24, 7.	x 19 xiv 24.
26, 5 8 12	xviii 25
6.	xxiii 2
30, 1—4	xiv. 4.
31, 20.	ii 6
32, 1	Intr. 15. 1 1.
5.	ii 6
34, 3	vi 2.
9.	xxiii 20.
35, 18.	xviii. 25.
36, 5	viii. 2.
8.	xvii 19.
9.	xiv. 5.
38, 11.	xiii. 9
13 14.	xiii 15.
41, 9	xiii 6.
45, 6	xv. 28 xxi 2.
7	xxi 2.
10	vii. 12.
46, 10.	Intr 13. 1 5.
47, 5	xiv. 24.
50, 3	xv. 21
21	xv 1
51, 7	iii. 1
52, 10.	i 4.
55, 21	xiii. 9
59, 6	xiii 9
66, 10—12	xxiii. 17.
68, 5	vii 10
17 18	xiv 24, 25
26	xviii 25.
69, 21.	xiii 29
72, 5.	vii 3 xii. 10
6	xii 9 xv. 1, 10
17.	xiii. 19
74, 12.	xiii 28
13	iii. 11. xiii 36.
77, 19	xiii 9
80, 17.	xii 7
82, 6	Intr 6 xi. 4.
85 11	xiv. 11.
87, 4	ii. 9
88, 1 4—8	xiii. 34 xii. 1, 8
89, 29 &c	vii. 2 x 4. xii. 23.
93, 2	xiv. 27
96, 11.	iii. 1.
102, 26—28	xv 3, 28
103, 20	xxiii 14
104, 2	xv 1.
15	ix 9. xxii 9.

305

Z

INDEX OF TEXTS.

104, 24 25.	ix. 11, 15, 16.
105, 15	xxi 1.
109, 1—3.	xiii 9
25.	xiii. 17, 30.
110, 1.	iv 14. x 9 xiv 28.
3.	vii 2. xi. 5
4	x 14
114, 3.	xii. 15
115, 17.	xviii 14
116, 12.	xxii 5.
118, 22	x 3.
24.	xiii 24.
119, 91	viii 5
103.	ix 13.
126, 5	iv 27
132, 6	xii 20
11.	xii 23.
17	x 15
139, 8.	viii 2
12	Intr. 15
21.	xvi. 10
143, 10.	xvi. 28. xvii 5
144, 5.	xii 7
147, 14.	xviii 27.
148, 4	xi. 11.
5.	xi 16, 23.
12.	xii 34
149, 1.	xviii 25.
150, 6.	vi 5

PROVERBS

4, 25	ii 2
5, 3.	iv 2.
15	xvi 11.
6, 6	ix. 13
27.	ii 1
17, 6	v 2 viii. 6
20, 6.	v 2.
30, 21 22	vi 26.

ECCLESIASTES.

3, 2.	xx 4
7, 29.	ii. 1
9, 7, 8.	xxii 8.
10, 4	ii. 3.
11, 9. 10. } 12, 1—6. }	xv 20

CANTICLES.

1, 4.	iii. 2
2, 10—12	xix 9, 10
3, 1—4	xiv. 11—13.
11	xiii 17.
4, 1 2	iii 16.
12	xiv 5
14	xiv 11
15	xiv 5

5, 1	xiii 32 xiv 11.
3.	iii. 7 xv. 25. xx 2.
12.	xiii. 9
6, 3	xiii 31.
10.	xiv 5
8, 5.	iii. 16.

ISAIAH

1, 6	xii 7.
8	xvi 18.
16	i. 1
18	xv 21.
19	iv 19
26 27.	xviii 34
2, 2	xxi. 7
3	xviii 34.
3, 9 10	xiii. 12
14.	xii. 12 xiii 12
4, 4	iii. 16.
5, 1—6	xiii 29
6, 1	xiv 27 xvi. 16.
2	xxiii 6.
7, 9	v. 4
10 14	xi 14 xii 1, 2, 21, 22.
8, 18	i 6 xiv 30
9, 5—7.	xii 24.
11, 2	xiv 30 xvii 5.
6.	xvii 10.
10	xii 23
19, 1	x 10
25, 6 7	xxi 7
8	xii 15 xix. 10
26, 19	iv 31. xviii 15.
27, 11	xiv 14
28, 15	xix 9
16	x. 3 xiii. 25.
30, 10.	xiv 14
34, 4	xv 3.
35, 4 5 6.	xii. 12 xvii 21
38, 1. 3.	ii 15.
40, 3	iii 1 xviii. 34
42, 1.	xvi. 30.
45, 7	vi 27 ix. 7.
14.	xi 16.
16. 17	vi 1
47, 13.	iv. 18.
48, 16.	xvi 30
49, 1 2	x 12.
13 18	xviii 34, 35.
50, 6	xiii. 13
51, 1	xiii 35. xiv 3
52, 5.	xxiii 12
53, 1.	xiii 1, 13, 19.
4 8. 9	xiii 34.
7.	x 3.
8.	xi 5
9	xiii 3 xiv. 3
12	xii 20
55, 1 &c.	xviii 34.
57, 1 2	xiv 3 xv 3.
4	xiii 15

INDEX OF TEXTS.

59, 21.	xvi. 30.
60, 1. 8	xviii 34
61, 1	xvi 30 xxi 1.
10	iii 2 xxii 8.
62, 11.	x 12
63, 1.	xiii 27.
11.	xiv. 20
16	vii 10.
64, 1	ix 1
8.	vii 8.
65, 2	xiii 27, 28
15. 16.	x 16 xviii 35.
20.	xviii 34.
66, 1.	vi 8.
8.	xviii 34.
18. 19.	xii 8.

JEREMIAH.

1, 5.	xii. 25.
2, 21.	ii 1 iv 19.
27.	vii 12.
4, 4.	v. 6
8, 4	ii 5
11, 19.	xiii 19
12, 16.	xiii 15.
32, 19	viii 1.
38, 6	xiii. 12

LAMENTATIONS

| 3, 53. | xiii 35. |
| 4, 20. | xiii 7 xvii. 34. |

EZEKIEL.

1, 6 &c	ix. 3.
2, 1	ix 1.
11, 5 24	xvi 14, 30
18, 20	ii 1
31.	i 1.
28, 12—17.	ii 4
36, 25.	iii 16 xvi. 30.
38, 1.	xviii. 1, 15

DANIEL.

2, 34. 44.	xii 18. xv 28.
4, 6	xvi 31.
31.	ii 18
34	viii 5.
6, 23	v 4
7, 9—14	xv 1, 21, 24, 27.
17 &c.	xv 13, 15, 16.
8, 17	ix 1
9, 25, &c.	xii. 19.

10, 6—19.	xii. 14.
12, 1	xv. 15.
2.	iv. 31. xv. 17. xviii. 15.
7	11. 12. xv 16.

HOSEA.

2, 20.	xii. 26.
4, 2	xii 6. xv. 3.
12.	xvi. 15.
6, 3.	xiv. 14.
9, 12.	xii 26
10, 6.	xiii 14.
13, 14.	xiv. 17.

JOEL.

| 2, 28. | xvi 29 xvii 19 |
| 31. | xv. 3. |

AMOS.

2, 8	xii 6
4, 13.	x 15
8, 9 10	xiii 25.
11.	xiii 1.
9, 6.	xiv. 24.

JONAH.

| 1, 1—15 | vi. 26. xiv. 17, 18. |
| 2, 3—9. | xiv 20. |

MICAH

3, 8	xvi 29.
12.	xvi 18
5, 2.	xi. 20. xii. 20.
3	xii 26.
7, 2.	xii. 6.

NAHUM.

| 2, 1 | xvii. 12 |

HABAKKUK.

| 3, 2. 3. | xii. 20. |

ZEPHANIAH.

| 3, 7—10. | xiv 6 7 |
| 14. | iii 16. |

HAGGAI

2, 5. 6.	xvi. 29
8.	viii 6

ZECHARIAH.

1, 6.	xvi 29
2, 10	xii 8
4, 10.	vi 8
9, 9—11.	xii 10, 17. xiii 34
11, 12 13.	xiii 10, 11
12, 10 12.	xiii 41 xv. 22
14, 4	xii. 11.
6 7.	xiii 24.

MALACHI

1, 10.	xviii 25
3, 1.	xii. 8
2—5.	xv. 2
4, 2.	xiii 34.

WISDOM OF SOLOMON.

6, 16	xvi. 19
7, 13	xv 18.
13, 5.	ix 2, 16

ECCLESIASTICUS

3, 21 22	vi 4 xi. 19.
4, 31	xiii 8.
34, 9 10	v. xxiii. 17.

BARUCH. (vide iv. 35.)

3, 35—37	xi. 15. xii 4
6.	i.e. Epistle of Jeremiah, v. iv. 35.

SONG OF THE THREE CHILDREN.

v 4, 6.	ii 16
27.	ii 18
32	ix 3

HISTORY OF SUSANNAH.

	xvi 31

BEL AND THE DRAGON.

33—36	xiv 25

ST. MATTHEW.

1, 1.	xi 5
20.	x. 12
23	xi 14
24.	xii 31.
2, 2.	xii 9
3, 6 7 &c.	iii. 7.
11	iii 9
16.	xvii 9.
17.	x 2. xi. 9.
4, 5	viii. 7.
11.	x. 10.
17.	iii 14.
5, 17.	iv. 33. x 18.
23 24.	xxiii. 3.
45	vi. 16
48.	vi. 8.
6, 9.	vii 7. xxiii. 11.
24.	iv. 4.
7, 6.	i 3 xvii 36.
9	v. 4.
8, 24—26.	xiv. 17.
9, 3	v. 8.
10, 20.	xvii 4.
23.	xv 16.
28.	viii 3.
29.	vii 6.
34	vi 27.
37.	vii 15.
11, 3	iii 6 v. 11. xiv 19.
15	xxi 4.
27	vii 5. x. 1, 9. xvi. 24 iv. 7. vi 6. x. 1.
28.	i 1.
12, 28—32	iv 16 xvi. 1 xvii. 11.
40.	xiv 17.
13, 13 15	iv 19. vi. 28, 29.
32.	v 11.
43.	vii 16 xi 34. xvii. 18
14, 29—32	v. 7
16, 13—17.	xi 3.
18.	xvii. 25.
19	xiv. 26
22 23.	xiii. 5
17, 2	x. 7. xiii. 13.
20.	v 11.
18, 10	vi 6 vii. 11.
12	xv 24
19.	vi. 15.
23 35.	i 6
19, 16—18 21	viii 6. xvii 30.
26.	xvii. 29.
29.	xvii 30.
20, 12—15.	xiii 31 xv. 7.
16	xv 7
18	xiii 6
21, 9	xii 23. xv 1.
19.	i 4.
31.	iii 8 x. 11
22, 11	Intr 3. iii 2.
43	xiv 28.

INDEX OF TEXTS. 309

23, 2	xii 32.	3, 11	iii 8
37.	vi. 8	22	iii 14
38.	xiii 33.	23.	vi 17
39.	xv. 1	4, 6	viii 6
24, 2	x. 11 xv 15	41.	x 15
3	xv. 4.	8, 18.	vi 28
4—15.	xv 5—9.	9, 30 &c	xii 16.
15.	iv. 15	62.	xix 8
16 21. 22.xv 16.		10, 18	ii. 4 xiii. 31 xvi 15.
24	xv 17.	19.	iii. 11.
29.	xv. 3.	11, 13.	xvii. 12
30 31	xv. 21, 22.	12, 11	xvi 21.
42. 44.	xv. 4	28	vi 16.
25, 21.	i. 2. iii 2.	49	vi 27
29.	vi. 28.	15, 4 5.	xiii 32.
30.	xv. 21, 22.	7.	i 1.
31. &c.	xv 24, 25	20.	xvi. 30.
35. 36	viii 6. xv 26	31.	i 1.
41.	vi 27 xv 26.	16, 9	i 2.
46	xviii 29.	17, 5	v 9.
26, 20. &c.	xiii 6	34.	xv. 2, 3.
27 28	xxii. 1, 7.	21, 11.	xv. 6.
47.	xiii 9	28	xviii 34.
53.	xiii. 12.	22, 48	xiii 9
62	xiii. 16.	23, 6 7 12	xiii 14.
64	xiv 29.	32—43	xiii. 30, 31.
27, 4—7. 10.	xiii. 11	46	xiii. 33
24 25	xiii 21.	24, 1 &c	xiv 11, 12, &c.
27—29	xiii 16—18, 27.	39 40.	xii 33
51	xiii 32.	49.	xvi. 9. xvii 12
52 53	xiv 16—18		
63—66.	xiii 4 xiv 5		
28, 1—7.	xiii. 22. xiv 12, 13. x. 10.	ST. JOHN.	
9.	xiv. 1, 13.		
11. 13	xiv 14, 20.	1, 1.	iii 14. xi 10. xii. 1
		3	iv 4 vi 9. xi 12, 21.
		10. 11.	xi 24 xii 8
ST MARK.		12.	vii. 13 xi. 9.
		14	xii 1, 4.
1, 1	iii 6	18	vi 5. vii. 11 ix. 1 xiv. 27.
4, 34.	vi. 29.	23.	iii 2
9, 24.	v. 9 x. 13	29	xiii 3, 19
10, 38.	iii. 10	32 33	iii 14 xvii 9
11, 14.	xiii 18.	2, 16	vii 6
15, 23.	xiii 29	3, 3 4 5	iii 4 xi. 9 xvii 11.
		8	i 2
		14 15	xiii 20
ST. LUKE.		16 18	v 10 xi 6.
		34	xvii 19.
1, 16	x. 10. xvii. 6	35 36	x 1. xi 6 xviii 30.
26.	xii. 1	4, 14	xvi 11
32.	xii. 23 xv 27	23 24	xi 6 7 xvii. 11, 34.
35. 41.	xii. 32 xvii 6	36	xviii 20
44	iii 6 xii 26.	5, 14	x 13.
2, 4 5.	xii 31.	17. 19	vii 6 xi 23
7.	xv. 1.	21—26.	xi 13
10	x. 10	22	xv 25.
14.	xii 32	24	v 10 xi 6. xviii. 30.
22	xii 32	37.	vi 7
28, &c	x. 19. xvii. 7	43	xii 2
33.	vii 9	6, 46	vi 6. vii. 11
49	vii 6.	54	xxii 4
		64	xvi 13

INDEX OF TEXTS.

7, 19	xii 33.	10, 1 &c	xvii 26.
38. 39	xvi. 11	36	x 10
8, 29	xv 30.	38	xxi. 2.
35	xv. 2 7	48	iii 3.
38.	xi 10	11, 1 &c 26.	iii 29
39 41.	vii 13, 14	15, 1—30	xvii 29
8, 44.	xv 14	19, 40.	xviii. 26.
49	vii. 5.	21, 10 11.	xiii. 22 v. xvii 28, 31.
56. 58	xi 20	26, 28.	xvii 31.
10, 9	vii. 2. x 3.		
15	iv. 7		ROMANS.
18.	xiii 6 28.		
30	xi 15	1, 3	xii 23. xiv 21.
11, 14 &c.	v 9	19 28.	iv. 19.
12, 23	xiii 6	2, 15 16.	xv. 25.
24.	xviii. 6	4, 11—23	v. 5, 6.
25.	xviii 30.	5, 10	xxiii. 5.
13, 4	xii. 1.	12 17.	xiii 2, 28.
14, 6	vii 2 x 3. xiii 2	14.	xv. 31.
9.	xi 18	17.	xiii 2.
11	xi 16	20.	xii. 15 xiii. 31.
16—26	xvi 14 xvii. 4, 11, 34	6, 2—4.	iii. 1, 12. xx 1, 6.
15, 1.	x 5 xiv. 11.	5	iii. 12. xx. 7
10	vii 5	11.	Intr. 5.
26.	xvi 4 xvii 4, 11	12	xxiii. 13.
16, 7—15.	ib	13.	xx 8.
17, 5.	vii. 10 xi. 20 xiii 6	19.	iv 19.
10	xi 23	22.	xviii. 30.
25.	vi 16	7, 16.	iv. 19.
18, 8.	vi 26	23.	xii. 15.
19, 11	viii 5.	8, 9	xvi. 4.
17.	xiii 23.	11	xvii 32
26 27.	vii 9	14 15.	vii 14. xvii. 4, 5. xxiii. 5.
30.	xiii 32	17.	iii 15.
34.	iii 10 xiii 20	18	xvi. 20.
37	xiii 41.	26.	xvi 20.
41.	xiii 32 xiv. 5.	28	Intr. 1.
20, 1	xiv 12.	29	xxi 1.
17	vii 7 xi 18	34.	xiv 29.
19	xiv 11, 12.	35	xv. 16.
22, 23	xiv 22. xvii. 12.	10, 6.	xiv. 21.
27.	xiii 39.	9	v. 10.
		11, 17 24	xx 3. 1. 4.
		33	vi 9.
	ACTS.	13, 14.	xix 10.
		14, 9.	xv. 26
1, 5.	xvii 14.	15, 19 24.	xvii 26.
7	xv 4.	21	xiii. 7
12	x 19	30	xvi 32.
19. 28.	iv. 19.	16, 18.	iv. 2.
2, 2	iii 9 xvii 13, 14.		
3 4 &c	xvii 15, 16. &c		1 CORINTHIANS.
24.	xiv 19		
37 38	iii 15	1, 9	Intr 6 v. 1.
3, 1. 2.	xvii. 31	18 23. 24.	xii 3, 8 vi. 18
5, 1. &c.	xvi 17 xvii. 21	2, 4	xiii 8.
11	xvii 22	9	vi 9.
6, 3	xvii. 24	10 11.	iv 16. vi 6. xi 13. xvi. 23.
8, 5	xiv 7 xvii. 25	13.	xvii 1.
20	xvi 10.	3, 12 15	Intr 17 xv. 2
9, 1 &c	x 17, 18. xvii 26.	4, 15.	vii 9, 13. xi 9
32—42	xvii. 27.	6, 9 10. 11.	iii 8.

INDEX OF TEXTS. 311

6, 19.	iv. 23 xii. 26	1, 13 17	xvii 5, 35 xviii 35
7, 5	iv. 25.	19. 20.	xiv 29
8 9	iv. 26	2, 4 5.	xviii 35.
8, 6.	iv 16 x. 1, 10.	10.	ii 1.
7	iv 27	3, 5	xvii. 33
9, 22	x 5	14 15	vii 1, 5 xvii 4
10, 4	x 7 xiii 34	4, 5	Intr 7. xvi 24
11.	Intr 2 xxi 6	10	xi 10 xiv 30
11, 2	xix 8	11	xiii 29.
3	xi 14. xiii 23	22 23.	i 2
23	xxii 1	30	xvii. 37.
12, 1—4	xvi 1.	5, 11.	vi 19
8, 9	v. 11 xvi. 12 xvii. 2	25	xviii 25, 33.
28	xviii 27	26.	iii 5
14, 14	Intr 14	6, 1	vii 15.
34	Intr 14	11 14.	xxi 4
15, 1	xiv. 1·	15	Intr. 16.
3 4	xiii 34	16	v 4
5—20	xiv 21	17 18.	xvii 33
16	xviii. 17.		
25—28	x 9. xv. 29—31.		
35. 36	xviii. 17	## PHILIPPIANS	
49	xxiii 11.	1, 19.	xvii 4.
53	xviii 18	2, 7	xv. 23, 25
55	iii. 11 xiv 19	11.	vii. 5
16, 20	xxiii 3	3, 1	xviii 34
		19	xix 6
## 2 CORINTHIANS		4, 4	xviii 34
		13.	xxi. 4
1, 3	vi 1 vii. 5		
1, 22.	i 2	## COLOSSIANS.	
2, 15	xxi 4		
3, 14	xv 32	1, 15 18	xiii 23
18	xxi. 4. xxii. 9	16 17.	iv 4 xi 24
4, 3 4	vi 28, 29	20	xiii. 14, 33
5	x 17	2, 8	iv 1, 2.
7	x 15	10.	xiii 23.
5, 5	i 2	11. 12.	v 6
10	xviii 20	13 14	Intr 17
6, 7 8	xviii 27	15.	xiii 36 xx 1.
14	vi 13 v 35.	3, 1	xiv 29
16	xii 34 xxiii 11.	9.	iii 7 xx 2.
10, 14. 15	xv. 32	10	i 2
11, 14.	iv 1 v 12 xv 4.	20.	vii 15
13, 12	xviii 33.		
		## 1 THESSALONIANS	
## GALATIANS			
		4, 12	xviii 17
1, 8 9	v 12.	15 &c.	xiv 30 xv. 19, 21 xviii 29
16.	x 18	5, 21 22	vi 36.
3, 23. 24.	iv 33	23.	xxiii. 23
27.	xxi. 1		
4, 4	xii 31	## 2 THESSALONIANS.	
6	xvii. 4.		
26.	xviii 26	2, 3 &c.	xv 9
5, 22 23.	xvii. 38.	4	xv 15
6, 14. 1.	xiii 1	9	xv 14, 15.
		10 11.	xv 17.
## EPHESIANS		15	v 12
1, 3 7. 8.	xviii 35		
5	xxi. 1		

INDEX OF TEXTS.

1 TIMOTHY.

1, 4	xvii 33
13, 14.	x 18.
2, 5 6.	x 5 xiii 2.
3, 15.	xviii 25.
4, 3	iv. 27
5, 21.	v. 13.
23.	iv 27.
6, 13—15	v 13.
20.	xv. 33
23.	iv. 27.

2 TIMOTHY

1, 14.	xvii 32.
2 8	xii 23
3, 7	vide iv. 2.
4, 3. 4.	xv. 9

TITUS.

2, 11.	xv. 2.
3, 4.	xviii 35
5.	xix. 10

HEBREWS

1, 1.	xi. 1
2.	xi 24.
3	xiv. 25, 29
6.	vide xi 4
8 9.	xi 15
13	xiv 29.
2, 13.	1 6
14	iii 11. xix. 4
3, 13	xv. 32 xxiii. 15.
14.	xxi. 1.
5, 2	x. 11, 14.
5	x. 11
13. 14.	iv. 31.
6, 18	x. 14.
7, 3	xv. 32.
21 24.	x. 14
26	x 4
9, 11.	x. 16 xiii 32
19.	iii. 5.
10, 1	xvii. 29.
12.	xiv. 29
15	xvii 33.
19 20	xiii 32.
22	iii 4
29.	xvii 5.
11, 1. 6.	v. 1, 4
8 9 &c	v. 5
26 27.	x 7.
12, 2	xiv 29

15	Intr 2
12, 16	iv 24 xv 25.
21.	xii 13
13, 4.	iv 25
8.	xii 17.

ST JAMES

1, 2.	xxiii 17.
5	xiii 8
17.	vii 5.
2, 23.	v 5

1 ST PETER.

1, 11	xvii 4.
17.	vii 14
19	xix 3
2, 1	xxiii 1.
4—6	x 3
6 8	xiii 35.
22 23	xiii 3, 5.
24.	Intr. 5 xiii 33
3, 21 22	xiv 29.
5, 7.	vii 14
8.	iv 1. x 3. xix 1, 10.
14.	xxiii. 3.

2 ST PETER

1, 4.	xxii. 3
3, 13.	vide xv 3 xviii 15.

1 ST. JOHN.

1, 8	xxiii. 16.
9	Intr 6
2, 15.	vii 14
19.	vi 14.
20.	xxi. 1.
22, 23	vii 5. x 1, 14.
27.	xxi. 7.
3, 8	ii 4
10.	vii. 13.
4, 18.	xiv 13.
5, 1.	xi 7

2 ST. JOHN

11.	vi 19.

REVELATION.

5, 5.	x 3.
12, 3	xv 27

www.ingramcontent.com/pod-product-compliance
Lightning Source LLC
Chambersburg PA
CBHW071227230426
43668CB00011B/1338